VAGRANCY IN THE VICTORIAN AGE

Vagrants were everywhere in Victorian culture. They wandered through novels and newspapers, photographs, poems and periodicals, oil paintings and illustrations. They appeared in a variety of forms in a variety of places: 'Gypsies' and hawkers tramped the country, casual paupers and loafers lingered in the city, and vagabonds and beach-combers roved the colonial frontiers.

Uncovering the rich Victorian taxonomy of nineteenth-century vagrancy for the first time, this interdisciplinary study examines how assumptions about class, gender, race and environment shaped a series of distinct vagrant types. At the same time it broaches new ground by demonstrating that rural and urban conceptions of vagrancy were repurposed in colonial contexts. Representational strategies circulated globally as well as locally and were used to articulate shifting fantasies and anxieties about mobility, poverty and homelessness. These are traced through an extensive corpus of canonical, ephemeral and popular texts as well as a variety of visual forms.

ALISTAIR ROBINSON is an honorary research fellow at Birkbeck, University of London.

CAMBRIDGE STUDIES IN NINETEENTH-CENTURY LITERATURE AND CULTURE

FOUNDING EDITORS
Gillian Beer, *University of Cambridge*
Catherine Gallagher, *University of California, Berkeley*

GENERAL EDITORS
Kate Flint, *University of Southern California*
Clare Pettitt, *King's College London*

EDITORIAL BOARD
Isobel Armstrong, *Birkbeck, University of London*
Ali Behdad *University of California, Los Angeles*
Alison Chapman, *University of Victoria*
Hilary Fraser, *Birkbeck, University of London*
Josephine McDonagh, *University of Chicago*
Elizabeth Miller, *University of California, Davis*
Hillis Miller, *University of California, Irvine*
Cannon Schmitt, *University of Toronto*
Sujit Sivasundaram *University of Cambridge*
Herbert Tucker, *University of Virginia*
Mark Turner, *King's College London*

Nineteenth-century literature and culture have proved a rich field for interdisciplinary studies. Since 1994, books in this series have tracked the intersections and tensions between Victorian literature and the visual arts, politics, gender and sexuality, race, social organisation, economic life, technical innovations, scientific thought – in short, culture in its broadest sense. Many of our books are now classics in a field which since the series' inception has seen powerful engagements with Marxism, feminism, visual studies, post-colonialism, critical race studies, new historicism, new formalism, transnationalism, queer studies, human rights and liberalism, disability studies and global studies. Theoretical challenges and historiographical shifts continue to unsettle scholarship on the nineteenth century in productive ways. New work on the body and the senses, the environment and climate, race and the decolonisation of literary studies, biopolitics and materiality, the animal and the human, the local and the global, politics and form, queerness and gender identities, and intersectional theory is re-animating the field. This series aims to accommodate and promote the most interesting work being undertaken on the frontiers of nineteenth-century literary studies, connecting the field with the urgent critical questions that are being asked today. We seek to publish work from a diverse range of authors, and stand for anti-racism, anti-colonialism and against discrimination in all forms.

A complete list of titles published will be found at the end of the book.

VAGRANCY IN THE VICTORIAN AGE

Representing the Wandering Poor in Nineteenth-Century Literature and Culture

ALISTAIR ROBINSON

Birkbeck, University of London

CAMBRIDGE
UNIVERSITY PRESS

CAMBRIDGE
UNIVERSITY PRESS

Shaftesbury Road, Cambridge CB2 8EA, United Kingdom

One Liberty Plaza, 20th Floor, New York, NY 10006, USA

477 Williamstown Road, Port Melbourne, VIC 3207, Australia

314–321, 3rd Floor, Plot 3, Splendor Forum, Jasola District Centre, New Delhi – 110025, India

103 Penang Road, #05–06/07, Visioncrest Commercial, Singapore 238467

Cambridge University Press is part of Cambridge University Press & Assessment,
a department of the University of Cambridge.

We share the University's mission to contribute to society through the pursuit of
education, learning and research at the highest international levels of excellence.

www.cambridge.org
Information on this title: www.cambridge.org/9781009011242

DOI: 10.1017/9781009019392

© Cambridge University Press & Assessment 2022

First published 2022
First paperback edition 2023

A catalogue record for this publication is available from the British Library

ISBN   978-1-316-51985-1   Hardback
ISBN   978-1-009-01124-2   Paperback

For my parents,
Andrew and Alison

Contents

List of Illustrations   *page* ix
Acknowledgments   x

Introduction   1
I.1   Vagrancy Laws   12
I.2   Demographics   16

PART I: THE COUNTRY   25

1   Gypsies, Hawkers and Handicraft Tramps   27
    1.1   Picturing Itinerants in the Periodical Press   32
    1.2   George Borrow   41
    1.3   *Lavengro* and the Picturesque   45

2   Poachers   58
    2.1   The Poacher's Progress   63
    2.2   Radicalism, Poaching and *The Chimes*   70
    2.3   Kingsley, Carew and the Condition of England   73

PART II: THE CITY   89

3   Casual Paupers   91
    3.1   Metropolitan Vagrancy   93
    3.2   Casuals Rejected: Kingsley 1848 and Dickens 1856   105
    3.3   Casuals Relieved: Fildes 1869 and 1874   111

4   Loafers   130
    4.1   Solutions to the Social Problem   136
    4.2   H. G. Wells and *The Time Machine*   141

PART III: THE FRONTIER   161

5   Paupers, Vagabonds and American Indians   163
   5.1   Atlantic Crossings: Pauper Immigrants   168
   5.2   Displaced Nations: American Indians   174
   5.3   Lawless Frontiers: American Vagabonds   181

6   Beachcombers   195
   6.1   Beachcombers in Print   199
   6.2   Robert Louis Stevenson and *The Ebb-Tide*   206

Afterword: London 1902   222

Bibliography   229
Index   250

List of Illustrations

1.1 'The English Gypsies', *Penny Magazine*, 20 January 1838   *page* 34

3.1 Sir Luke Fildes, 'Houseless and Hungry' (1869)   116

3.2 Sir Luke Fildes, *Applicants for Admission to a Casual Ward* (1874)   119

6.1 Lloyd Osbourne, 'King of Manihiki with the Island Judge on Right Hand. In Front a Beachcomber' (1890)   208

7.1 Jack London, 'Men Waiting Outside Whitechapel Workhouse' (1902)   226

Acknowledgements

This book started as a PhD thesis in the English Department of University College London, and benefitted enormously from the influence of the colleagues, mentors and friends I met there. First and foremost, I would like to thank my supervisors, Matthew Beaumont and Gregory Dart, for all their insight, encouragement and intellectual generosity. I would also like to thank Juliette Atkinson, Rachele De Felice, Alex Grafen, Asha Hornsby, Eric Langley, Eva-Charlotta Mebius, Adelais Mills, John Mullan, Luke Seaber, Alison Shell, Matthew Sperling and Christopher Webb, who read chapters of this book in various stages of its production.

Beyond the confines of UCL's Malet Place, I would like to thank my PhD examiners, Josephine McDonagh and David McAllister; my MSc supervisor, Anna Vaninskaya; Peter Jones, who organised the 'Out of Place: Vagrancy and Settlement' conference in 2017; and Oskar Cox Jensen and David Hitchcock, whom I met there. David Hitchcock and Josephine McDonagh later acted as readers for this book and I owe a huge debt of gratitude to both of them: their comments were transformative. I would also like to thank the Institute of English Studies, which supported this project after my PhD with a Postdoctoral Visiting Research Fellowship, and my colleagues at the New College of the Humanities where I was teaching during its culmination.

This book would not have been possible without the British Library, Cambridge University Library, the UCL Library and all their staff. Nor would it have been possible without Cambridge University Press, which has been wonderful to work with. In particular, I would like to thank the series editors and the commissioning editor, Bethany Thomas, for all their input. A version of Chapter 6 was first published as a journal article: 'Beachcombers: Vagrancy, Empire, and Robert Louis Stevenson's *The Ebb-Tide*', *Review of English Studies*, 70.297 (2019), 930–49. I would like to thank the editor who oversaw its publication, Andrew Nash, and the anonymous readers who critiqued it.

Nick and Iain Robinson, Lesley and David Jebson, and Alison and Andrew Robinson have provided emotional, material and intellectual support over many years. Louisa Ackermann, too, has been unfailingly generous and kind, supporting me throughout this book's composition, and reading it through – twice. I am and will remain happily indebted to them all.

Introduction

In June 1822 Charles Lamb published his essay 'A Complaint of the Decay of Beggars in the Metropolis'. Witty and urbane, Lamb twits the utilitarian reformers who have confined London's beggars in prisons and workhouses and now seek to 'extirpate the last fluttering tatters of the bugbear Mendicity'. He claims that before they were incarcerated beggars performed an important social function: they were 'the standing morals, emblems, mementos, dial-mottos, the spital sermons, the books for children, the salutary checks and pauses to the high and rushing tide of greasy citizenry'. Here dehumanisation is idealisation. Like the lessons inscribed on sundials, and the 'spital sermons' preached at Easter, beggars prompt divine reflection. Also, in contrast to the hypermobile crowd, they are permanent fixtures of the city, waymarkers rooted in its physical fabric. Beggars therefore help citizens to navigate the spiritual and physical pitfalls of nineteenth-century London; they are a means of moral, historical and geographical orientation. But the beggars' existence is not just a social good, it is good in itself. 'If I were not the independent gentleman that I am', Lamb claims, 'I would chuse, out of the delicacy of the true greatness of my mind, to be a Beggar.' After all, he reasons, the beggar's rags are 'never out of the fashion'; 'the price of stock or land affecteth him not'; and 'no man goes to law with him'. The beggar 'is the only free man in the universe'.[1]

Lamb's essay is facetious, but it is also sympathetic. This sympathy is sometimes directed towards individuals, such as the crippled 'half a Hercules' and the 'old blind Tobits' ranged along 'the wall of Lincoln's Inn Garden'; but more generally, it concerns the loss of what the beggars represent – an older, more liberal, less materialistic time.[2] This is reflected in the deliberately antiquated metaphors that Lamb uses to describe the beggars' spiritual functions. Spital sermons date back to the late fourteenth century and the dial-mottos are equally venerable.[3] In an earlier essay Lamb fondly recalls the 'antique air [of] the now almost effaced

sun-dials, with their moral inscriptions' in London's Inner Temple. These
relics carry an intrinsic merit: 'if its business-use be superseded by more
elaborate inventions', Lamb observes, 'its moral uses, its beauty, might
have pleaded for its continuance. It spoke of moderate labours, of pleasures
not protracted after sun-set, of temperance, and good hours.'[4] Like the
beggars who steady the 'rushing tide' of the crowd, the dials symbolise a
less frenetic mode of life that constitutes a form of freedom. For Lamb, it
was this freedom from excessive work and excessive pleasure, from the
worldly concerns of fashions, stocks and litigation, which 'the all-sweeping
besom of societarian reformation' was slowly wearing away.[5]

Lamb's political position in 'The Decay of Beggars' is anti-utilitarian
and his chief target is London's Society for the Suppression of Mendicity.[6]
Established in 1818 by radicals and evangelicals, the Mendicity Society was
one of several philanthropic organisations founded in the early nineteenth
century that sought to halt the rapid escalation of pauperism, vagrancy and
the national poor rate.[7] This had grown from £4.3 million in 1803 to
£7.83 million in 1818.[8] The Mendicity Society was formed in the wake of
the 1816 *Report from the Select Committee on the State of Mendicity in the
Metropolis*, which found that 'gross and monstrous frauds [were] practiced
by mendicants in the capital'.[9] It therefore set out to educate the public
about the duplicitous nature of beggars and to identify and prosecute
'committed' or 'professional' vagrants – the destitute and/or itinerant
people for whom begging was a lifeline, a strategy for survival. The society
was successful. In its first annual report the Honorary Secretary W. H.
Bodkin remarked that it had 'certainly succeeded in convincing a great
portion of the public of the impolicy of indiscriminate almsgiving [and] in
punishing many daring imposters' – a total of 385 in 1818.[10] In the
following years between 1819 and 1822, when Lamb's essay was published, the Society successfully instigated a further 1,263 prosecutions.[11]

It was the austere attitude of the fiscally minded Mendicity Society that
Lamb was writing against. By idealising beggars – by recasting the so-called
impostors as emblems of morality, and interpreting their poverty as a
superlative freedom – he was trying to overturn the dogmatic and worldly
outlook of evangelical reformers. In doing so he reasserted the value of
beggars. Where the Mendicity Society warned the public to 'let investigation always precede relief', and approached them as subjects harbouring a
single truth, Lamb regarded them as emblems, books and mottos with
multiple interpretations and rich rewards for readers.[12] This characterisation consciously echoes William Wordsworth's portrayal of the indigent in
his poem 'The Old Cumberland Beggar' (1800).[13] Here Wordsworth also

entertains an anti-utilitarian agenda. He deploys the same image of the 'besom of societarian reformation', condemning statesmen 'who have a broom still ready in your hands / To rid the world of nuisances'. Moreover, he represents the vagrant as a prompt for virtue and a symbol to be studied: 'While thus he creeps / From door to door, the Villagers in him / Behold a record which together binds / Past deeds and offices of charity / Else unremembered'.[14]

Lamb's beggars and Wordsworth's vagrant perform the same social functions and belong to the same tradition of representation: what Celeste Langan calls 'Romantic vagrancy'. In her influential work, *Romantic Vagrancy: Wordsworth and the Simulation of Freedom* (1995), Langan defines this concept as 'a certain idealization of the vagrant: a reduction and an abstraction. The vagrant's mobility and expressivity are abstracted from their determining social conditions.'[15] This critique is useful for understanding the portrayal of poverty in Lamb's essay. Hunger, fatigue, unemployment, addiction, exposure – these do not trouble his beggars. However, the essay also qualifies what might be at stake in the process of idealisation that Langan describes because it demonstrates that 'abstraction' does not necessarily entail the loss of meaning implied by 'reduction'. Indeed, with his emphasis on how beggars might be read and re-read, Lamb was trying to combat a process of reduction in which beggars, and the freedoms that they represented, were redefined and delimited. The binaries that the Mendicity Society relied on – 'the infirm and the able bodied, the industrious and the idle, the deserving and the vicious' – and the categories that they later used to taxonomise London's beggars – casual beggars, Irish and Scotch beggars, black and foreign beggars, beggars with country settlements, and beggars with London settlements – all tended to contract what and how the indigent could mean.[16]

The impulse of the Mendicity Society to identify the indigent and expose their motives is typical of later approaches towards vagrancy. Victorian attitudes were likewise characterised by a materialist approach to poverty and were concerned with diagnosing, defining and controlling the vagrant body. Where Romantic vagrancy abstracted, Victorian vagrancy concretised. This is evident in the lexicon of vagrancy which expanded in the nineteenth century to include 'loafers', 'mouchers', 'casuals', 'beachcombers', 'toe-rags', 'spike-rangers', 'pikers' and 'sun-downers', among others. Some of these coinages, such as 'piker' and 'toe-rag', were colourful synonyms for 'vagrant', and chiefly used in a derogatory sense; but most had more precise meanings and identified specific vagrant types that occupied certain topographies. The 'beach-comber', 'wedded to the Pacific', was imagined in Oceania; the 'loafer' was considered 'an urban type in the main . . . who haunts the streets year in year out'; and the 'moucher' was a hedgerow tramp, picking up a living from poaching, begging and foraging.[17] To a greater or lesser extent, these terms circulated in official, literary, legal and popular discourses, and together with familiar categories, such as 'Gypsy' and 'vagabond', shaped public conceptions of vagrancy by providing a taxonomy through which vagrants could be mapped imaginatively and geographically.

The desire to categorise vagrant bodies, however, was not a new phenom-enon: it was part of a tradition stretching back to the early modern period. In the sixteenth century a 'literature of rogues' emerged which presented readers with a highly stratified and specialised underworld in which vagrants were split into numerous criminal orders. Thomas Harman's catalogue of rogues, *A Caveat or Warning for Common Cursetors* (1566), was one of the first texts purporting to detail vagrant life and is a fine example of this tradition: it includes a list of 200 vagabond types.[18] This genre was supplemented by Robert Greene's and Thomas Dekker's cony-catching pamphlets at the turn of the seventeenth century, and later by the 'rogue ballad'. Printed as broad-sides and accompanied by woodcuts, these were performed in public and private across the social spectrum, and portrayed an array of vagrant stereo-types that ranged from the uncanny beggar woman to the jovial tinker.[19] Later, in the eighteenth-century, pictorial representations of hawkers and street-sellers – itinerant traders who were readily identified as vagrants – became popular. Like the pamphlets and ballads, these pictures, known as 'cries', produced a series of readily identifiable types.[20]

These genres entertained the same assumption expressed by writers in the Victorian period, that despite their many guises, each vagrant ulti-mately possessed a stable, classifiable identity. This belief was underpinned by a moral framework that partitioned the poor into two separate classes, the deserving and the undeserving. The former were the virtuous poor who were impoverished through no fault of their own and were the deserving recipients of compassion and charity. The latter were feckless, idle, lawless and deceptive. They were seen as able-bodied imposters who should be denied alms and punished. Leaving little room for nuance, this binary structured responses to homelessness and transiency from the late medieval period onwards, and articulated a deep distrust of the poor. Summarising the historical attitudes of Western societies towards the itinerant and the destitute, Tim Cresswell observes that 'The drifter, the shiftless, the refugee and the asylum seeker have been inscribed with immoral intent.'[21]

Suspicions of immorality were often accompanied by fears of political dissonance. Between 1560 and 1640, vagrants were identified as a potential source of rebellion. During this period, England's armies were predominantly formed by poor young men who returned from war with few skills and prospects. Unemployed and habituated to travel, these veterans took to tramping and were perceived as an enemy army in embryo.[22] Later, during the interregnum, a different mobile class came under suspicion. The early Quakers were associated with spiritual and social anarchism and were accused of being a seditious force within the country. Although Quakers were often people of means, their practice of itinerant preaching meant that they could be classed as wanderers and charged as vagrants. They were therefore frequently punished under the vagrancy laws by magistrates who saw them as a threat to social and religious stability.[23] After the Restoration, other itinerant groups came under scrutiny. James II's government issued a proclamation in 1686 against unlicensed hawkers for allegedly peddling seditious and atheistic books; and similarly, in the eighteenth century, strolling balladeers were arrested in London for singing Jacobite and anti-Hanoverian songs.[24] This connection between mobility and disorder persisted in the nineteenth century. Thomas Carlyle, writing in the aftermath of the Continental revolutions of 1848, described vagrants as 'captainless soldiers', the 'destroyers of every Government that *cannot* put them under captains, and send them upon enterprises'. The threat that Carlyle identified in these 'able-bodied Lackalls' was echoed by many of his contemporaries, and the links that they perceived between vagrancy and insurrection are examined in several of this book's chapters.[25]

When the Victorians represented the wandering poor, they deployed a range of strategies and biases inherited from previous periods. However, new epistemologies and ways of knowing also impacted the portrayal of vagrants. This was particularly true of racial theories. Among these, one of the most influential was the theory of extinction, the idea that all 'savage' peoples would eventually vanish from the earth. Like all racist discourses, extinction theory was based upon prejudice rather than fact, and as a result it was an inchoate and shifting structure of interpretation rather than a rigorous set of principles. Extinction might be actuated through war, or through disease, or through acculturation with European civilisation; but one of the more popular beliefs was that the inherited traits of the savage would eventually lead to self-extermination. This prognosis of autogenocide was conferred on many of the non-European cultures that the British encountered between the early 1800s and the Second World War.[26] In addition, it was also applied to nomads and vagrants in the Victorian period. Gypsies and indigenous Americans were perceived as self-destroying from the early nineteenth century: identified as racial others in the cultural imagination, they were readily counted among the primitives who would extinguish themselves. 'Anglo-Saxon' vagrants joined these groups towards the end of the century. By the 1880s it was generally believed that white vagrants in distant lands, like the beachcombers in the Pacific, were also destined for extinction: having 'gone native', and regressed into savagery, they would inevitably perish alongside the indigenes.

The elision between the vagrant and the savage is unsurprising. Attributes that Victorian commentators identified as primitive, such as lawlessness, laziness and promiscuity, had long been ascribed to the vagrant poor in England. As Linda Woodbridge remarks in her analysis of early modern representations of vagrancy, 'The respectable projected onto vagrants qualities they disowned in themselves – social mobility, linguistic innovation, sexual misconduct, sedition, idleness.'[27] Some of these ancient stereotypes were repackaged as essential and inherited traits in racial readings of the vagrant poor. Moreover, in these interpretations, the vagrant's mobility could also become a sign of savagery, as Henry Mayhew's introduction to *London Labour and the London Poor* (1861–2) reveals. Heavily influenced by James Cowles Prichard's ethnographic study, *Natural History of Man* (1843), Mayhew wrote that 'there are – socially, morally, and perhaps even physically considered – but two distinct and broadly marked races, viz., the wanderers and the settlers – the vagabond and the citizen – the nomadic and the civilized tribes'. For Mayhew itinerancy was an indelible mark of savagery that belonged not only to the unruly 'habitual vagrant – half-beggar, half-thief', but also to a broad class of 'street-folk', 'the street-sellers – the street-performers – the cab-men – the coachmen – the watermen – the sailors'.[28] The testimonies of these people in *London Labour and the London Poor* contradicted this argument, often describing fixed homes and settled communities, and Mayhew's own analysis of metropolitan poverty was often at variance with racial theory.[29] Nonetheless, despite his lack of ethnographic rigour, Mayhew's equation of mobility and barbarism illustrates how easily vagrants might be 'scientifically' translated into savages.

The racialisation of vagrants was part of a much broader cultural programme in which the poor were interpreted in racial terms by journalists, scientists, novelists and politicians, among others. From the mid-nineteenth century social commentators began to explain the physical and social impacts of poverty in terms of heredity: precarious employment, poor hygiene, criminal actions, physical frailty and prostitution were increasingly (although not exclusively) imagined as biologically determined.[30] The racial construction of the poor as a separate and inherently dysfunctional segment of humanity reflected contemporary understandings of race. As Kenan Malik argues, for much of the Victorian period 'race was a description of social distinctions, not colour differences', and as such scientific racism was used to justify the social and material inequalities that existed in both Britain and the Empire.[31] It was used to naturalise the rule of capitalists over labourers at home, and the rule of white colonists over black and indigenous populations abroad.[32]

This is evident in the theory of degeneration. Like extinction theory, the theory of degeneration was not a coherent set of beliefs; it was an interpretive framework that was subject to change and reinvention. During the last decades of the Victorian period it was deeply influenced by social Darwinists, who applied the theory of evolution by natural selection to human societies. They argued that while the 'primitive' peoples of the Empire embodied a degraded form of the ideal white race, the vitality of that same race was being threatened by the rapid reproduction of the urban poor in Britain. This belief rested on the self-satisfied notion that Britain's civilisation was so advanced that it had neutralised the process of natural selection and nullified Darwin's formula of the 'survival of the fittest'. In turn, this allowed the mentally, physically and morally 'unfit' to propagate without the hindrances that would have prohibited them from reproducing in a state of nature.[33] Imagined as 'racially distinct and as causing the degeneration of the [Anglo-Saxon] race as a whole', it was feared that this unfit class – which included the vagrant and unemployed – would eventually overwhelm the rest of society, causing Britain and its Empire to crumble from within.[34] 'Savages in Australia or North America might become extinct', Patrick Brantlinger wryly observes, 'But savage costermongers and paupers within the gates of civilization threatened to overrun it.'[35]

Fears about degeneration sparked a series of interventionist schemes between 1880 and 1910. Coming from both liberals on the left and social imperialists on the right, many of these programmes advocated the creation of labour colonies that would ultimately eradicate the vagrant population. Although not all of the authors subscribed to racial explanations of poverty, social Darwinism was a prominent theme.[36] In 'The Cult of Infirmity' (1899), the imperialist and eugenicist Arnold White warned that 'Our species is being propagated and continued increasingly from under-sized, street-bred people.' His solution was a 'process of sterilizing unfitness and levelling up the national stamina', the first phase of which was the imprisonment of vagrants:

> Consider the army of 26,000 tramps who infest the high roads of England, rob and rape when they dare, and use the casual wards as hotels. Extirpate them by immuring them for life, not because they are wicked, but because their stock is corrupt. Until we are content to see the idle perish, if they choose to perish, little change for the better in the health of the people can be looked for. If public opinion demands the maintenance of the idle poor, maintain them; but immure them.[37]

Although this is a particularly toxic proposal, White was not alone. By the turn of the twentieth century many public intellectuals in Britain, including H. G. Wells, argued that incarcerating and/or sterilising the vagrant poor would bring moral and biological benefits to the nation. The same was also true in the United States. In the late nineteenth and early twentieth centuries 'Tramps frequently came up as examples of people who might be subjected to sterilization or segregation.'[38]

The use of racial theories to define the vagrant body had a significant impact on their representation. The discourses of extinction, degeneration, eugenics and social Darwinism turned the vagrant from a curio of the street into a specimen – a sample whose behaviours could be generalised and stand in for those of a species. Gypsies, beachcombers, loafers and other vagrant types moved in specific ways, belonged to distinct topographies, and embodied different kinds of anxiety, threat and fascination. That said, the texts discussed below, most of them written for newspapers, periodicals or the popular market, rarely evince a thorough understanding of racial theory. As John Marriott warns while discussing the racialisation of the poor by Victorian journalists, 'acknowledgement of the influence of racial and social theories has to be tempered by the recognition that they were adapted and implemented in ways that lacked rigour, coherence and consistency.'[39] Moreover, although the definition of the vagrant poor was a preoccupation of the Victorians, it was also an ancient enterprise that carried the moral trappings of its medieval and early modern past. As a result, while the attitudes of some Victorian commentators were shaped by new racist discourses, others continued to be influenced by the framework of the deserving and the undeserving poor and by stereotypes that characterised the vagrant as idle, promiscuous, seditious and deceptive. These ideas continued to impact the representation of vagrants, and while sometimes they were intermixed with new scientific narratives, often they were not.

The structure of this book reflects the Victorians' taxonomic approach to vagrancy. It is divided into three topographical parts on the country, the city and the frontier, each of which contains two chapters that discuss the representation of one or more vagrant type. Part I, 'The Country', opens with 'Gypsies, Hawkers and Handicraft Tramps', a chapter that examines how aesthetic and cultural assumptions about the Gypsy 'race' impacted their portrayal between 1830 and 1860, and how this compared with other itinerants imagined in the same rural spaces. The second chapter focuses on the vagrant poacher and argues that this figure became politically loaded in both radical and conservative literature during the 1840s. Part II, 'The City', begins with a chapter on the reality and representation of the 'casual pauper' in the second half of the nineteenth century. Otherwise known as 'spike-rangers', casual paupers stayed in the casual or tramp ward of the workhouse and became emblematic of the difficulties involved in differentiating between the deserving and the undeserving poor. Chapter 4 focuses on the loafer in the 1880s and 1890s and the ways in which theories of degeneration, social Darwinism and eugenics influenced this vagrant's representation. Both of these chapters on urban vagrants also examine the strong associations between vagrancy and insurrection discussed earlier. Part III moves further afield, analysing vagrancy on the frontier. Chapter 5 addresses three vagrant types that were depicted by British writers travelling in antebellum America: the pauper immigrant fresh from Europe, the American Indian whose vagrancy was a sign of imminent extinction, and the vagabond who lived in the 'anarchic', outer territories of the Union. The final chapter examines the beachcombers of the Pacific Islands. These vagrant figures became particularly conspicuous in British print culture during the fin de siècle and served an important function in understanding and critiquing Britain's imperial actions in the Pacific.

The book's tripartite structure brings into contact two regions that are familiar in vagrancy studies – the country and the city – and a less well-documented sphere, the frontier. This last part examines how discourses about vagrancy could circulate globally as well as locally, and responds to David Hitchcock's recent observation that 'a larger, transatlantic, history of vagrancy remains to be told.... The history of vagrancy can and should be concretely linked to the wider history of empire.'[40] In the process, it identifies the frontier as a particularly fertile region in the British cultural imagination. Conceptualised as an ungoverned and peripheral space on the edge of civilisation, it was readily populated with vagabonds, a class that was strongly associated with lawlessness. Many of the territories that I discuss in North America and the Pacific Islands were not part of the British Empire in the nineteenth century. As a result, although these frontier spaces were being colonised through the process of white settlement, and the seizure of land and resources that this often entailed, I have used 'frontier' as opposed to 'colony' to avoid confusion.

I have also used 'frontier' in preference to 'contact zone'. This last term is favoured by Mary Louise Pratt because it prioritises 'the interactive, improvisational dimensions of colonial encounters', whereas 'frontier' 'is grounded within a European expansionist perspective'.[41] The bias that Pratt draws attention to is important, illuminating the fact that frontiers are artificial and ideologically informed spaces. Nonetheless, in a study concerned with representation it is practical to maintain the expansionist perspective of the primary sources, especially given that the vagrants' environment was integral to their depiction. In the same vein, I have used the terms 'Gypsy' and 'American Indian'. These are contested terms among Romanies and indigenous Americans, respectively, and it is important to acknowledge that while some identify with them, others see them as alien labels forced upon them. They have been used in this study because they are the terms used in the primary sources. This book is chiefly concerned with the representation of vagrants and therefore preserves the nomenclature through which they were articulated and imagined. That said, in the case of indigenous Americans, I have used the names of specific nations where possible. In this, too, I follow the practice of Victorian commentators, some of whom were attentive to sociocultural differences.

The sources used in this study include literature, visual art and a large corpus of ephemeral texts. The chapters begin with a detailed cultural history of the vagrant type(s) under discussion which informs an analysis of their portrayal in popular culture and the periodical and newspaper press as well as canonical works. These works include George Borrow's *Lavengro* (1851) in Chapter 1; Charles Dickens's *The Chimes* (1844) and Charles Kingsley's *Yeast* (1848) in Chapter 2; H. G. Wells's *The Time Machine* (1895) in Chapter 4; and Robert Louis Stevenson's *The Ebb-Tide* (1894) in Chapter 6. Chapters 3 and 5 are more wide-ranging and survey the work of several major figures, including Dickens and Kingsley, Frances Trollope and Harriet Martineau, and the painter Luke Fildes. Analysing ephemeral and canonical texts alongside each other capitalises upon the different strengths that reside in these materials. Although canonical authors are valuable because their works often complicate and critique prevailing assumptions, an exclusive focus on these writers would misrepresent how vagrants were perceived: '"great" figures are often unrepresentative (or are only partly so) of the intellectual currents of any given historical epoch', Duncan Bell observes.[42] Ephemeral texts, meanwhile, provide a more reliable reflection of the cultural imagination, in part because they are so plentiful, but also because they often rely upon dominant perceptions and therefore support and shape stereotypes. As Elaine Freedgood argues, although 'their endurance is brief and their assigned value negligible ... the cultural work these [ephemeral] texts perform is neither brief nor negligible'.[43] As this overview indicates, this book has a historicist bent. Biopolitical and other Foucauldian readings are brought to bear in Chapters 3 and 4 and help decode how configurations of power were used to discipline and regulate the vagrant body in the nineteenth century. However, these theories struggle to faithfully account for the agency of actual vagrants and the shifting, sometimes contradictory ways in which they were depicted. They therefore do not play a large role in the scheme of the study.

Vagrancy in the Victorian Age contributes to a growing body of work on the literary and cultural representation of vagrancy in Britain. This includes Linda Woodbridge's *Vagrancy, Homelessness, and English Renaissance Literature* (2001), Tim Hitchcock's *Down and Out in Eighteenth-Century London* (2004), David Hitchcock's *Vagrancy in English Culture and Society, 1650–1750* (2016), Deborah Epstein Nord's *Gypsies and the British Imagination, 1807–1930* (2006) and Sarah Houghton-Walker's *Representations of the Gypsy in the Romantic Period* (2014). To some extent all of these works are interested in 'the discrepancy between the historical record, on the one hand, and contemporary representations of vagrancy, on the other', as Woodbridge puts it.[44] This has been a preoccupation of vagrancy scholars since A. L. Beier's seminal study *Masterless Men: The Vagrancy Problem in England, 1560–1640* (1985) in which he censored some historians for their 'exclusive reliance upon literary sources'. Although this study is likewise indebted to Beier's injunction that 'to be understood properly vagrants must be seen in their historical context', it is not chiefly concerned with the gap between fact and fiction.[45] Instead it seeks to elucidate the active part that printed texts played in the production of the 'vagrant', a category that is obviously social, legal and economic but also – and importantly – culturally imagined. By assessing canonical texts alongside a large and hitherto unexplored corpus of periodical and popular literature I demonstrate that Victorian print culture generated several sophisticated versions of the vagrant body that occupied important places within the social, political and geopolitical imagination.

The subtitle of this study defines the vagrant as 'the wandering poor', and in doing so remains true to the etymological root of 'vagrant', the

Latin verb *vagārī*, which means 'to wander'.[46] Meanwhile, the assertion that vagrants are 'poor', that is, impoverished compared with their contemporaries, reflects the fact that vagrancy typically entails precarity, poverty and homelessness. This definition is loose and to some extent needs to be because vagrancy was a highly protean condition. Although representations of vagrants often sought to circumscribe their identities, in practice vagrants were amorphous and hard to define legally and demographically. As Lorie Charlesworth reminds us, 'the term vagrant has a technical meaning; a person convicted of a vagrancy offence'; but as I discuss in the next section, this criminal category did not provide the concise definition that might be expected.[47] Instead the 1824 Vagrancy Act, which proved 'one of the most flexible, useful and criminal-making statutes of the century', demonstrates just how porous the vagrant state could be.[48] This is also true of the statistics, discussed in the final section of this introduction, that sought to capture the demography of the vagrant population. These similarly demonstrate the unaccountability of itinerants and confirm M. A. Crowther's observation that 'vagrants were not amenable to counting or classification'.[49]

I.1 Vagrancy Laws

The 1824 Vagrancy Act, 'An Act for the Punishment of Idle and Disorderly Persons, and Rogues and Vagabonds, in That Part of Great Britain called England', is an important piece of legislation for this study. Introduced to simplify the vagrancy laws, the act was the principle legal mechanism by which vagrants were identified and convicted throughout the Victorian period and beyond.[50] Maintaining the three vagrant classes inaugurated under a previous act of 1740, the statute describes the behaviours and occupations that could qualify people as 'idle and disorderly', 'a rogue and a vagabond' and 'an incorrigible rogue'.[51] The most minor offenders were idle and disorderly: they were beggars, unlicensed pedlars and so-called common prostitutes, a term that chiefly referred to women soliciting men in public.[52] Rogues and vagabonds comprised a larger and more distinctly criminal and/or fraudulent class. They could be fortune tellers, people armed 'with intent to commit any felonious act', mendicants who exposed wounds in order to solicit alms, or husbands who abandoned their wives and children, leaving their support to the rate payer. However, in addition to these impostors and ruffians, this category also included a more general class of 'rogues and vagabonds': 'Every person wandering abroad and lodging in any barn or outhouse, or in any deserted or unoccupied building, or in the open air, or under a tent, or in any cart or waggon, not having any visible means of subsistence, and not giving a good account of himself or herself.' Meanwhile, anyone who had previously been convicted as a rogue and a vagabond, who resisted arrest under the act, or who broke out of prison after their conviction as a rogue and a vagabond was deemed an incorrigible rogue.[53]

The extraordinary breadth of the act is a testament to the uncertain identity of the vagrant and the hostility of the legislature to unknown and unchecked itinerants. The expansive definitions of the three categories sought to encompass the wandering poor in all their many forms and, as a result, turned anyone impoverished and on foot into a potential criminal. The act's capacity to criminalise was further enhanced by its administration. The magistrates of England and Wales enforced the legislation, and it proved pliable in their hands. A rogue and a vagabond could be convicted based on their own confession, or on the evidence of 'one or more credible witness', and sentenced for up to three months' hard labour. The idle and disorderly, meanwhile, could be committed for only up to one month's hard labour, but might be 'convicted before him' – the magistrate – 'by his own view'.[54] In other words, whether someone was a vagrant or not was a summary and subjective decision. The fact that magistrates needed no legal knowledge to qualify for their posts amplified the idiosyncratic climate of the courtroom: although a paid and professional magistracy was in operation in London's police courts from 1792, and in areas with a population exceeding 25,000 from 1863, many vagrants were still tried before amateurs.[55] In *The Pickwick Papers* (1836–7), Dickens was not so far from the truth when he portrayed magistrate Nupkins conferring with his clerk before convicting Sam Weller as 'a vagabond on his own statement'.[56] Unpaid magistrates relied heavily on the legal knowledge of their subordinates, and there can be no doubt that the farce of *Pickwick* sometimes turned into tragedy.[57]

Far from defining the 'vagrant' as a legal category, the law as it was written and practised demonstrated how porous the term could be. This permeability was silently acknowledged and manipulated by the legislature throughout the nineteenth century, as the vagrancy laws were used to criminalise various other undesirables. The Vagrancy Act of 1822, a prototype of the 1824 legislation, added indecent exposure to the list of 'vagrant' crimes and classified common prostitutes as idle and disorderly persons for the first time. During the rest of the century, the act was further expanded to include the following offences: displaying obscene prints in shop windows (1838), refusing to perform tasks set in the workhouse (1842), giving false information to obtain Poor Law relief (1848), gambling for money in public spaces (1867–72), and living off 'immoral earnings' (1898).[58] In addition, the act was used to punish behaviours that were not explicitly written into it. Examining the attitudes of Victorian officials to male homosexuality and prostitution, H. G. Cocks notes that vagrancy laws 'were undoubtedly used against male street-walkers, professional or otherwise'.[59] In 1848 two men were prosecuted under the Vagrancy Act for indecent exposure after a policeman watched them have sex. The defendants had rented a parlour for privacy, but were allegedly exposed to 'public' view because another room overlooked it.[60]

The breadth and vagueness of the vagrancy legislation caused conster-nation among commentators in the 1820s. Those both for and against the new legislation were concerned that it lacked definition. The anonymous 'A Barrister' wrote in his pamphlet *The Vagrant Act* (1824) that although he was generally in favour of a measure that sought to control 'the vagrant spirit [that] prevails among the lower orders', he was nonetheless con-cerned by its ambiguities. He noted that some of the clauses needed to 'be more definitely worded' and that others were 'somewhat too general'.[61] Meanwhile, those against the acts identified a latent tyranny in their vagueness. R. B. Comyn in his 'Remarks of the Increased Power and Jurisdiction of Justices of the Peace' (1823) argued that the 1822 act gave magistrates too much room for interpretation: 'I speak not of those parts of this act where the offence is *defined*', he clarified, 'but I complain of its want of definition.'[62] This critique was also made by the *London Magazine*, the publication in which Lamb's 'The Decay of Beggars' first appeared. In an article entitled 'The Vagrant Act' (1825), it noted that 'the powers vested in the magistrates by the act for the punishment of idle and disorderly persons (5 Geo. 4. C. 83.) are extensive indeed'. Moreover, despite these wide-ranging powers, magistrates 'continually venture with-out the pale in search of outlying offences': 'there is scarcely a common every-day occurrence of life that may not be construed to be an act of vagrancy', it concluded.[63]

Historians and cultural critics, too, have frequently remarked on the 'catch all' nature of the legislation. Matthew Beaumont, David Jones, Robert Humphreys and Michal Shapira, among others, have all commented on its flexibility and the licence that it granted to officials.[64] However, the stress that is often rightly placed on the breadth of the acts mitigates against our sense of their coherence. Although interpreting begging, wandering, sleeping-out, prostitution, indecent exposure and displaying obscene prints as vagrancy seems like a clumsy bricolage, in fact these activities were closely associated in the nineteenth-century imagination. This is evident in subsequent legislation that likewise bracketed these behaviours together. In the 1839 Metropolitan Police Act it is significant that begging and prostitution were criminalised in the same sub-clause and that the sale of obscene texts, images and songs was addressed in the next.[65] Their structural relation suggests correlation. Similarly, in the 1847 Town Police Clauses Act, prostitution, loitering, indecent exposure and the sale of obscene materials were all prohibited within the same clause.[66]

What these offenses have in common, and the reason why they were legislated against en masse, is that they threatened to destabilise public space. As M. J. D. Roberts notes, the vagrancy legislation was an attempt to regulate the behaviour of the poorer classes and to ensure that the impoverished would not clutter or disorder the streets.[67] The legislation regarding obscenity, whether it was included in the vagrancy acts or elsewhere, was often similarly used to control 'decent', middle-class bodies. When the 1822 Vagrancy Act was passed it caused a public outcry because those being convicted for indecent exposure were not typical vagrants; they were employed, settled and 'respectable'. Although the objectionable clause was delimited in 1824 so that only those exposing themselves 'with intent to insult any female' were liable for prosecution, it was nonetheless the middle classes that continued to be charged with this offence.[68] Meanwhile, the display of obscene prints in shop windows, which were ostensibly private property, became a concern because of the disruptive effect that they might have on citizens moving through public space. As Lynda Nead remarks, 'The significance of the display of obscene publications is that it focuses on the problem of "seeing".... the *display* of visual commodities enables their *consumption*, merely by movement through the space of the street. Display and visibility in this context enact the ultimate promiscuity; to pass by, may be to see and to become affected by.'[69]

There are also other reasons why prostitution, indecency and obscenity were closely associated with vagrancy. As I shall discuss in the next section, prostitution was an expedient for vagrants and one of the numerous strategies that they used to survive. Vagrants were also associated with the sale and distribution of obscene material. As Deana Heath observes, 'the trade in "obscene" ephemera was itinerant in nature, conducted throughout the country by networks of often foreign hawkers such as Lascars and Chinese'.[70] Meanwhile, the clauses in the 1839 Metropolitan Police and 1847 Town Police Clauses Acts that prohibited anyone to 'sing any profane, indecent, or obscene song or ballad' were, at least in part, directed against vagrants.[71] In 'English Ballad-Singers' (1822), an antiquarian piece on ballad singing from the days of the medieval minstrels to the late eighteenth century, the *New Monthly Magazine* remarked that 'the Gipsies furnished a number of female ballad-singers' and that the balladeers would travel in a 'circuit' and sing at prominent fairs. The obscene nature of some of these performances might be inferred from their sobriquets: 'Outroaring Dick', for example, could refer to both the subject of his ballads as well as the manner in which they were delivered.[72] The affiliation between obscene ballads and vagrancy is also mentioned in Charles Heath's autobiography *The Arab of the City* (1850). Here he recalls how he and his companions 'for years led a vagrant's life' and 'used to sing many obscene songs, which were the composition of the gang, and which, for profaneness and obscenity, must bear no comparison'.[73]

I.2   Demographics

At the beginning of the nineteenth century there was a surge in the vagrant population. This was caused by acute historical factors: in 1815 an economic slump coincided with the demobilisation of soldiers after Waterloo, which together caused levels of unemployment, pauperism and vagrancy to rise.[74] However, it was also because of more permanent changes to the structure of Britain's economy. During the 1810s the expansion of the free market led to a 'dramatic increase in cyclical unemployment, vagrancy and street crime', as Gregory Dart remarks.[75] Combined with the new transport technologies that emerged later in the century, such as steamships and railways, the insecurity of the job market led to an increase in mobility throughout the nineteenth century. Urbanisation and emigration became national trends: by the 1850s more than half the country's population lived in towns and cities, and between 1821 and 1915, 10 million people left Great Britain for extra-European territories.[76] Rich and poor participated in these mass movements, and the very poorest, often forced to travel on foot, became liable to charges of vagrancy: as Langan notes, 'walking [became] not only the cure offered by liberalism, but also the disease produced by it'.[77] Spikes in the vagrant population were registered during periods of hardship and unemployment when people were most incentivised to move in search of social and economic opportunities. These occurred in the 1840s, the 1860s, the early 1880s and the mid-1890s.[78]

Although these fluctuations in the vagrant population can be mapped, its exact size remains unknown. This is because the statistics collected to record it were either partial or imprecise. The number of vagrants who lodged in workhouses was counted on 1 January and 1 July each year from

1848 onwards. Although they were probably fairly accurate, these figures accounted for only a fragment of the vagrant population at two points during the height of winter and summer. As Crowther argues, these head counts 'could not show how many had slept in barns, haystacks, doorways, brickyards and railway arches, nor those who had found refuge with a charitable organization'.[79] Since 1841 the national census had tried to account for this dark figure by recording all those who slept outside or in outbuildings.[80] However, as the report for the 1871 census noted, the figures for vagrants and Gypsies 'were so imperfectly returned that no benefit could accrue from the publication of their statements'.[81] The reason for this is that vagrants did not live at known addresses and were always on the move. The uncertainty surrounding the official statistics should make us wary of claims made by contemporaries. Assertions like those of the health reformer J. H. Stallard, who wrote in 'Paupers and Pauperism' (1869) that there were 50,000–60,000 tramps in England, should be treated as rhetorically rather than quantitatively valuable.[82]

Caveats should also be applied when considering other demographic factors, particularly the gendered nature of vagrancy. Nineteenth-century vagrancy was primarily a male phenomenon. Whereas in the seventeenth and eighteenth centuries women formed at least half of the vagrant population, female vagrancy became increasingly rare as the nineteenth century progressed.[83] David Jones notes that whereas at mid-century women comprised between a sixth and a quarter of vagrants, by the beginning of the twentieth century they accounted for only a tenth.[84] There are plausible reasons for this shift. Female vagrancy in the seventeenth and eighteenth centuries was often a corollary of war; they were wandering either in search of impressed or enlisted husbands or because they had been widowed.[85] For most of the nineteenth century, Britain avoided the major European conflicts that recurred throughout the preceding centuries and also remained untouched by the serious civil conflicts that affected many countries on the Continent. It was therefore a period of relative stability in which one of the major causes of female vagrancy was absent. Gendered responses to dearth also increased the likelihood that vagrants would be male: as a rule, men tramped for work, whereas women entered the workhouse. Throughout the Victorian period, women aged between sixteen and forty were far more likely to become indoor paupers than men in the same age bracket, and were often accompanied by children.[86] This suggests that women were inclined to remain in their place of settlement, the parish where they had a right to Poor Law relief, because of their domestic ties and the difficulty of travelling with offspring.

However, although it seems clear that most Victorian vagrants were male, it is also true that men were more likely to be categorised and recorded as vagrants. Female vagrants were liable to be classed as prostitutes. Although the majority of prostitutes were indigenous to the areas in which they lived and worked, and were therefore part of the settled community, female itinerants were nonetheless strongly associated with the sex trade. In part, this was because prostitution was one of the many survival strategies that vagrants utilised; indeed, it was a resort for many poor people, whether they were on the move or not. As Judith Walkowitz explains, most prostitutes were engaged in casual prostitution, and relied upon it to supplement their incomes only during times of economic distress.[87] However, vagrant women were also widely believed to be sexually available. This was part of an enduring legacy.[88] Since Harman's *Caveat* promiscuity had been touted as one of their defining characteristics. According to Harman, a 'doxy', or single female vagabond, was 'common and indifferent for any that will use her', while her married equivalent, the 'autem morte', was proverbially 'as chaste as a cowe' (i.e., promiscuous).[89] These assumptions of licentiousness are also evident in the nomenclature of vagrancy. A 'harlot' denoted 'a vagabond, beggar, rogue' when the word was coined in the thirteenth century; it signified 'an unchaste woman; a prostitute; a strumpet' only from the fifteenth century onwards.[90] Similarly, the fourteenth-century word 'troll', meaning to 'walk about or to and fro', is the etymological root of the sixteenth-century 'trull', 'a female prostitute'.[91] And while a 'tramp' has referred to 'one who travels from place to place on foot' since the late seventeenth century, it has identified 'a sexually promiscuous woman' from the early twentieth century.[92] In the nineteenth century, many commentators treated female vagrants as de facto prostitutes: W. D. Boase, for example, a Poor Law official writing in 1848, noted that, 'of the female English tramps little can be said, but that they are in great part prostitutes of the lowest class'.[93]

The construction of female vagrants as prostitutes would have made their experience of vagrancy radically different to that of their male counterparts. For much of the Victorian period, they were less likely to be apprehended for vagrancy. Although common prostitution was punishable under the 1824 act, prostitutes could be arrested only if they were 'behaving in a riotous or indecent manner'.[94] As the Vice Chancellor of Oxford noted in the mid-1820s, this meant that there would be relatively few arrests if constables followed the letter of the law. Moreover, even if prostitutes were carousing in the street, it was no guarantee that the police would interfere. The poet and diarist A. J. Munby, writing in June 1859, recorded 'Hogarthian' scenes in London's Haymarket: 'several halfdrunken [*sic*] prostitutes', one of whom was 'reeling', and another 'showing her legs above the knee' were observed by a passive 'peeler' (a police officer) 'with dead calm face'.[95] This account of official forbearance reflects a broader truth – that the police tolerated prostitution as an inevitable aspect of urban life, unless they were forced by public opinion to supress it. That said, from 1864 when the first Contagious Diseases Act was passed, through to 1886 when the legislation was repealed, prostitutes in some garrison towns or ports were liable to be imprisoned in lock hospitals if they were found to be suffering from venereal disease. After 1869, the measures were enforced in eighteen districts, and the women could be detained for up to nine months.[96] Female vagrants in the nineteenth century, then, were exposed to a different set of dangers to male tramps, and the assumption that they were sexually available may have clouded how they were categorised. The prostitute would have been one of many parts that the vagrant performed; however, for contemporaries, that role may have been definitive, and assigned without substantial evidence. We should therefore be cautious when handling nineteenth-century statistics, and other forms of representation, that tend to depict vagrancy as a male experience.

Notes

[1] Charles Lamb, 'A Complaint of the Decay of Beggars in the Metropolis', *London Magazine*, June 1822, pp. 532–6 (pp. 532–3).

2 Ibid., pp. 533, 535.

3 Henry Thomas, *The Ancient Remains, Antiquities, and Recent Improvements, of the City of London*, 2 vols (London: Sears, 1830), I, pp. 171–4.

4 Charles Lamb, 'The Old Benchers of the Inner Temple', *London Magazine*, September 1821, pp. 279–84 (p. 279).

5 Lamb, 'The Decay of Beggars', p. 532.

6 Gregory Dart, *Metropolitan Art and Literature, 1810–1840: Cockney Adventures* (Cambridge: Cambridge University Press, 2012), p. 153.

7 Lionel Rose, *'Rogues and Vagabonds': Vagrant Underworld in Britain, 1815–1985* (London: Routledge, 1988), pp. 17–18.

8 Jonathan Parry, *The Rise and Fall of Liberal Government in Victorian Britain* (New Haven, CT: Yale University Press, 1993), p. 33.

9 Quoted by James Harriman-Smith, 'Representing the Poor: Charles Lamb and the *Vagabondiana*', *Studies in Romanticism*, 54.4 (2015), 551–83 (p. 553).

10 W. H. Bodkin, *The First Report of the Society Established in London for the Suppression of Mendicity* (London: J. W. Whitely, 1819), pp. 26–7.

11 W. H. Bodkin, *The Fourth Report of the Society for the Suppression of Mendicity Established in London* (London: F. Warr, 1822), p. 7.

12 Bodkin, *The First Report*, p. 13.

13 See Dart, *Metropolitan Art and Literature*, pp. 153–4; Simon P. Hull, *Charles Lamb, Elia and the London Magazine: Metropolitan Muse* (London: Pickering & Chatto, 2010), pp. 143–4.

14 William Wordsworth, 'The Old Cumberland Beggar', *The Major Works*, ed. Stephen Gill (Oxford: Oxford University Press, 2011), pp. 49–54 (ll. 69–70, 79–83).

15 Celeste Langan, *Romantic Vagrancy: Wordsworth and the Simulation of Freedom* (Cambridge: Cambridge University Press, 1995; repr. 2006), p. 17.

16 Bodkin, *The First Report*, p. 13; Bodkin, *The Fourth Report*, p. 8.

17 Herman Melville, *Omoo: A Narrative of Adventures in the South Seas*, ed. Mary K. Bercaw Edwards (London: Penguin, 2007), p. 89; William Harbutt Dawson, *The Vagrancy Problem: The Case for Measures of Restraint for Tramps, Loafers, and Unemployables, with a Study of Continental Detention Colonies and Labour Houses* (London: P. S. King, 1910), pp. 2–3.

18 A. L. Beier, *Masterless Men: The Vagrancy Problem in England, 1560–1640* (London: Methuen, 1985), pp. 7–8.

19 David Hitchcock, *Vagrancy in English Culture and Society, 1650–1750* (London: Bloomsbury, 2016; repr. 2018), pp. 55–89.

20 Tim Hitchcock, *Down and Out in Eighteenth-Century London* (London: Hambledon and London, 2004), pp. 218–23.

21 Tim Cresswell, *On the Move: Mobility in the Modern Western World* (Abingdon: Routledge, 2006), p. 26.

22 Beier, *Masterless Men*, pp. 93–5.

23 David Hitchcock, '"He Is the Vagabond That Hath No Habitation in the Lord": The Representation of Quakerism as Vagrancy in Interregnum England, c. 1650–1660', *Cultural and Social History*, 15.1 (2018), 21–37 (pp. 22–3).

24 Hitchcock, *Vagrancy in English Culture and Society*, p. 29; Hitchcock, *Down and Out in Eighteenth-Century London*, p. 67.

25 Thomas Carlyle, 'The Present Time', in *Carlyle's Latter-Day Pamphlets*, ed. M. K. Goldberg and J. P. Seigel (Ottawa: Canadian Federation for the Humanities, 1983), pp. 3–60 (pp. 46, 49). Original emphasis.

26 Patrick Brantlinger, *Dark Vanishings: Discourse on the Extinction of Primitive Races, 1800–1930* (Ithaca, NY: Cornell University Press, 2003), pp. 1–6; Steven Conn, *History's Shadow: Native Americans and Historical Consciousness in the Nineteenth Century* (Chicago: University of Chicago Press, 2004), pp. 30–1.

27 Linda Woodbridge, *Vagrancy, Homelessness, and English Renaissance Literature* (Chicago: University of Illinois Press, 2001), p. 16.

28 Henry Mayhew, *London Labour and the London Poor: A Cyclopaedia of the Condition and Earnings of Those That Will Work, Those That Cannot Work, and Those That Will Not Work*, 4 vols (London: Frank Cass, 1967), I, pp. 1–2.

29 John Marriott, *The Other Empire: Metropolis, India and Progress in the Colonial Imagination* (Manchester: Manchester University Press, 2003), pp. 114–20.

30 Patrick Brantlinger, *Taming Cannibals: Race and the Victorians* (Ithaca, NY: Cornell University Press, 2011), pp. 111–35; Marriott, *The Other Empire*, pp. 101–29, 160–86.

31 Kenan Malik, *The Meaning of Race: Race, History and Culture in Western Society* (Basingstoke: Macmillan, 1996), p. 91.

32 Ibid., pp. 91–100.

33 Ibid., pp. 90–1, 109–13; Marriott, *The Other Empire*, pp. 160–81.

34 Malik, *The Meaning of Race*, p. 110.

35 Brantlinger, *Taming Cannibals*, p. 128.

36 Marriott, *The Other Empire*, pp. 171–81; Gareth Stedman Jones, *Outcast London: A Study in the Relationship between Classes in Victorian Society* (Oxford: Oxford University Press, 1971; repr. London: Verso, 2013), pp. 303–14.

37 Arnold White, 'The Cult of Infirmity', *National Review*, October 1899, pp. 236–45 (pp. 238, 243–4).

38 Tim Cresswell, *The Tramp in America* (London: Reaktion Books, 2001), p. 121.

39 Marriott, *The Other Empire*, p. 111.

40 Hitchcock, *Vagrancy in English Culture and Society*, pp. 152–3.

41 Mary Louise Pratt, *Imperial Eyes: Travel Writing and Transculturation* (London: Routledge, 1992), pp. 6–7.

42 Duncan Bell, *The Idea of Greater Britain: Empire and the Future of World Order, 1860–1900* (Princeton, NJ: Princeton University Press, 2007), p. 22.

43 Elaine Freedgood, *Victorian Writing about Risk: Imagining a Safe England in a Dangerous World* (Cambridge: Cambridge University Press, 2000), p. 3.

44 Woodbridge, *Vagrancy*, p. 2.

45 Beier, *Masterless Men*, pp. xix–xxi.

46 'Vagrant, n. and adj.', *OED Online* (accessed 8 August 2018).

47 Lorie Charlesworth, *Welfare's Forgotten Past: A Socio-Legal History of the Poor Law* (Abingdon: Routledge-Cavendish, 2009), p. 169.

48 David Jones, *Crime, Protest, Community and Police in Nineteenth-Century Britain* (London: Routledge & Kegan Paul, 1982), pp. 206–7.

49 M. A. Crowther, 'The Tramp', in *Myths of the English*, ed. Roy Porter (Cambridge: Polity Press, 1992), pp. 91–113 (p. 98).

50 Charlesworth, *Welfare's Forgotten Past*, p. 173; Robert Humphreys, *No Fixed Abode: A History of Responses to the Roofless and the Rootless in Britain* (London: Macmillan Press, 1999), p. 81.

51 Audrey Eccles, *Vagrancy in Law and Practice under the Old Poor Law* (Farnham: Ashgate, 2012), p. 10.

52 Judith R. Walkowitz, *Prostitution and Victorian Society: Women, Class, and the State* (Cambridge: Cambridge University Press, 1980; repr. 1982), p. 14.

53 5 Geo. 4, C. 83.

54 Ibid.

55 A. W. Ager, *Crime and Poverty in 19th Century England: The Economy of Makeshifts* (London: Bloomsbury, 2014), p. 92; M. J. D. Roberts, 'Public and Private in Early Nineteenth-Century London: The Vagrant Act of 1822 and Its Enforcement', *Social History*, 13.3 (1988), 273–94 (pp. 282–3).

56 Charles Dickens, *The Posthumous Papers of the Pickwick Club*, introduction by Peter Washington (London: Everyman, 1998), p. 340.

57 Ager, *Crime and Poverty*, p. 92.

58 Eccles, *Vagrancy in Law and Practice*, pp. 20–2; Jones, *Crime, Protest, Community and Police*, pp. 198–9.

59 H. G. Cocks, *Nameless Offences: Homosexual Desire in the Nineteenth Century* (London: I. B. Tauris, 2003), p. 56.

60 Michal Shapira, 'Indecently Exposed: The Male Body and Vagrancy in Metropolitan London before the *Fin de Siècle*', *Gender & History*, 30.1 (2018), 52–69 (pp. 62–3).

61 [Anon.] A Barrister, *The Vagrant Act, In Relation to the Liberty of the Subject*, 2nd ed. (London: John Murray, 1824), pp. 5, 25, 32–3.

62 Quoted by John Adolphus, *Observations on the Vagrant Act, and Some Other Statutes, and on the Power and Duties of Justices of the Peace* (London: John Major, 1824), p. 33.

63 'The Vagrant Act', *London Magazine*, January 1825, pp. 7–15 (pp. 7, 14).

64 Matthew Beaumont, *Nightwalking: A Nocturnal History of London, Chaucer to Dickens* (London: Verso, 2015), p. 246; Jones, *Crime, Protest, Community and Police*, pp. 206–7; Humphreys, *No Fixed Abode*, pp. 30, 76; Shapira, 'Indecently Exposed', p. 55.

65 Clause 58, sub-clauses 11 and 12. 2 & 3 Vict. C. 47.

66 Clause 28. 10 & 11 Vict. C. 89.

67 Roberts, 'Public and Private', pp. 276–81, 292–3.

68 5 Geo. 4, C. 83; see Roberts, 'Public and Private'; Shapira, 'Indecently Exposed', pp. 56–8.

69 Lynda Nead, *Victorian Babylon: People, Streets and Images in Nineteenth-Century London* (New Haven, CT: Yale University Press, 2000), p. 183.

70 Deana Heath, *Purifying Empire: Obscenity and the Politics of Moral Regulation in Britain, India and Australia* (Cambridge: Cambridge University Press, 2010; repr. 2013), p. 58.

71 2 & 3 Vict. C. 47.

72 'English Ballad-Singers', *New Monthly Magazine*, January 1822, pp. 212–17 (pp. 213–14). Tim Hitchcock discusses the bawdy nature of ballads sung in eighteenth-century London in Hitchcock, *Down and Out in Eighteenth-Century London*, pp. 65–7.

73 Charles Heath, 'The Arab of the City, Being the Autobiography of a London Thief', *The Ragged School Union Magazine*, February 1850, pp. 33–7 (p. 34); Charles Heath, 'The Arab of the City, Being the Autobiography of a London Thief', *The Ragged School Union Magazine*, November 1850, pp. 273–80 (p. 273).

74 John E. Archer, *Social Unrest and Popular Protest in England, 1780–1840* (Cambridge: Cambridge University Press, 2000), pp. 9–12.

75 Dart, *Metropolitan Art and Literature*, p. 152.

76 Robert Woods, *The Population of Britain in the Nineteenth Century* (Cambridge: Cambridge University Press, 1995), pp. 11, 21–2.

77 Langan, *Romantic Vagrancy*, p. 35.

78 Jones, *Crime, Protest, Community and Police*, pp. 181–2.

79 M. A. Crowther, *The Workhouse System, 1834–1929: The History of an English Social Institution* (Athens: University of Georgia Press, 1982), p. 248.

80 David Mayall, *Gypsy-Travellers in Nineteenth Century Society* (Cambridge: Cambridge University Press, 1988), pp. 23–5.

81 Quoted by Mayall, *Gypsy-Travellers*, p. 26.

82 J. H. Stallard, 'Paupers and Pauperism', *Gentleman's Magazine*, July 1869, pp. 177–89 (p. 184).

83 Hitchcock, *Vagrancy in English Culture and Society*, pp. 11–12; Hitchcock, *Down and Out in Eighteenth-Century London*, p. 209.

84 Jones, *Crime, Protest, Community and Police*, p. 183.

85 Hitchcock, *Vagrancy in English Culture and Society*, pp. 11, 140–3; Eccles, *Vagrancy in Law and Practice*, p. 207.

86 Crowther, *The Workhouse System*, pp. 233–4.

87 Walkowitz, *Prostitution and Victorian Society*, pp. 13–31.

88 Female vagrants in the seventeenth and eighteenth centuries were also assumed to be sexually available. See Hitchcock, *Vagrancy in English Culture and Society*, pp. 123–47; Hitchcock, *Down and Out in Eighteenth-Century London*, pp. 28, 93.

89 Thomas Harman, *A Caveat or Warning for Common Cursetors, Vulgarly Called Vagabonds, Set fourth by Thomas Harman Esq. for the Utility and Profit of His Natural Country* (London: R. Triphook, 1814), p. 56.

90 'Harlot, n. 1 and n. 5.c', *OED Online* (accessed 8 August 2018).

91 'Troll, v. 1', *OED Online* (accessed 26 March 2019); 'trull, n. 1', *OED Online* (accessed 26 March 2019).

92 'Tramp, n. 4.a and 4.b', *OED Online* (accessed 8 August 2018).

93 Quoted by Ager, *Crime and Poverty*, p. 86.

94 5 Geo. 4, C. 83; Ager, *Crime and Poverty*, p. 83.

95 A. J. Munby, *Munby, Man of Two Worlds: The Life and Diaries of Arthur J. Munby, 1828–1910*, ed. Derek Hudson ([London]: John Murray, 1972), p. 35.

96 Walkowitz, *Prostitution and Victorian Society*, pp. 69–89.

PART I

The Country

CHAPTER I

Gypsies, Hawkers and Handicraft Tramps

On 16 June 1860 readers of *All the Year Round* received another instalment from Charles Dickens's itinerant alter ego 'The Uncommercial Traveller', 'a town traveller and a country traveller ... always on the road'.[1] Written in a confidential style, the article is a seasonal paper providing 'notes of the Tramps whom I perceived on all the summer roads in all directions'. These notes are worked up into a catalogue of vagabonds that details the habits of 'idle tramps', such as the 'slinking tramp' and the 'savage tramp'. It also describes the picturesque lives of their more industrious counterparts: 'the many tramps who go from one oasis of town or village to another, to sell a stock in trade'; 'the tramps with carts or caravans – the Gipsy-tramp, the Show-tramp, the Cheap Jack'; and 'the tramp handicraft men', who are 'all over England, in this Midsummer time'.[2] Of this class the Uncommercial Traveller asks: 'Where does the lark sing, the corn grow, the mill turn, the river run, and they are not among the lights and shadows, tinkering, chair-mending, umbrella-mending, clock-mending, knife-grinding?'[3] The answer to this question, however, is less straightforward than Dickens's rhetoric allows. By 1860 tramping artisans were becoming a rarity on the roads, as were a number of other itinerant types. Pedlars and packmen, who carried 'a stock in trade', were increasingly uncommon.[4] Likewise, the 'tramps with carts or caravans', the Gypsies who hawked horses and fortunes, and the Cheap Jacks who sold supplies from yellow waggons were encountered less frequently.

In the early nineteenth century itinerants had a variety of occupations and performed a vital economic role. Travelling between remote villages on familiar, premeditated and often circular routes, they provided goods and services that were otherwise unavailable. As Dickens observes, these included the repair of household objects, such as kettles, clocks and chairs, which were expensive to replace in an age before mass manufacture. Moreover, they also sold fancy goods, implements and other occasional items that could not be bought from local retailers.[5] As G. E. Mingay relates, in the early nineteenth century there was a shortage of village shops and 'household necessities were bought from travelling packmen'.[6] But itinerants did more than sell and maintain material goods; they also provided entertainment. Gypsy musicians were essential to the success of village festivities and were hired to perform at public and private parties: 'Yetholm, and the Scottish Gipsies' (1851), an article in *Sharpe's London Magazine*, informs us that 'the favourite fiddler or piper of the district was often to be found in the gipsy village'.[7] Meanwhile, the Cheap Jacks were known as much for their bawdy patter as they were for driving a bargain. 'Cheap Jack possesses a vein of coarse humour', records *Chambers's Edinburgh Journal*, 'which makes all the wondering folk below think him an amazingly funny fellow.'[8]

The success of the itinerants' trade relied on the isolation of settled communities. Poor roads restricted the movement of people and goods and turned villages into ready markets for the industrious traveller. During the eighteenth century, however, the nation's infrastructure began to improve. From the 1770s through to the 1810s canals were dug to enable the low-cost conveyance of heavy goods, and from mid-century the landowning classes began to invest in road improvements and bridge-building enterprises that increased the speed and comfort of travel.[9] Between 1750 and 1811 the journey time from London to Bristol was reduced from forty to twelve hours.[10] These improvements began to draw remote settlements into a countrywide transport network and to break open the small markets that had once been the preserve of the Gypsy and the packman. That said, although new roads and innovations, like macadamisation, increased the speed at which people, objects and news could travel, the mail and stagecoach service was not a national system enjoyed by all. Not only did it fail to reach far-flung regions of the United Kingdom, but the expense of travelling by coach prohibited the poorer classes from enjoying its benefits.[11] As a consequence, itinerants were able to resist the encroachments made upon their social and economic functions. This opposition, however, collapsed with the advent of the railway.

The speed at which the railroad expanded is astonishing. Radiating out from Britain's major cities, 6,000 miles of track were laid between 1830 and 1850. A swift and inexpensive form of transport, the railways brought low-cost wares from cities to villages, and likewise enabled rural labourers to travel to municipal centres.[12] The markets traditionally served by itinerants were exposed to competition. The influx of cheap goods threatened both the hawking and service industries practised by tramps. The articles they sold were often more expensive than the manufactured alternative, and the availability and relative affordability of these new products decreased the demand for tinkers, knife-grinders, chair-menders and others.[13] Meanwhile, the villagers who formed the itinerants' customer base could seek out a better bargain on their own behalf because they could travel more freely. This also decreased the demand for itinerant entertainers. Whereas previously the country fair had been the villagers' chief resort for business and pleasure, the railways ensured that the local town now took its place; vagrant fiddlers and acrobats performed to an ever-dwindling audience as the fairs fell into decline.[14] The overall consequence of this, as David Mayall notes, was that Gypsies and other travellers eventually became 'an anachronistic and unwanted vestige of a past stage of economic development'.[15]

Altering economic conditions were not the only factor that impinged on itinerants: legal changes also made it increasingly difficult to maintain a life on the roads. The late eighteenth and early nineteenth century witnessed the second great era of enclosure in which landholders appropriated six million acres through nearly 4,000 Enclosure Acts.[16] As Raymond Williams observes, it is important to note that two different types of land were affected by this legislation: arable fields and uncultivated wastes. Fields formed two-thirds of the land acquired, and produced the victims that we might typically associate with enclosure – agricultural labourers who were turfed out of their cottages and stripped of their traditional grazing and foraging rites. The enclosure of wastes, meanwhile, affected a very different sort of occupant. Here, as Williams notes, it was the 'marginal independence, of cottagers, squatters, [and] isolated settlers' that was supressed.[17] Among these were vagrants who relied on the wastes in a number of ways: such wild land provided wood for fuel, food in the form of game, and workable materials, like osiers, which were used to make baskets and chair bottoms. The enclosure of land, whether waste or otherwise, also reduced the number of places where travellers could pitch their tents. The broad roadside verges, or 'slangs', were incorporated into agricultural estates, as were many of the green lanes that served as camp-sites.[18] As a result, some itinerants were forced to abandon their traditional beats. Certainly, the poet John Clare, lamenting the decline of the local Gypsy population, blamed it on the fact that 'the inclosure has left nothing but narrow lanes w[h]ere they are ill provided with a lodging'.[19]

The Enclosure Acts were one of several legislative challenges to itinerant existence. The 1824 Vagrancy Act, as I discussed in the Introduction, criminalised the unsettled poor: anyone sleeping 'in the open air, or under a tent, or in any cart or waggon, not having any visible means of subsistence' was liable to be punished as a rogue and a vagabond.[20] This legislation was supplemented by the 1835 Highways Act, which made anyone encamped 'upon any part of any highway' liable to a fine of forty shillings. In particular it targeted itinerant traders, specifying that 'any hawker, higgler, [or] gipsy' would be prosecuted; the 'higglers' enter this list because, aside from their legitimate trade in dairy and poultry, they were also strongly associated with the poached game trade (see Chapter 2).[21] Magistrates and police officers took full advantage of these laws. Although the rural police had a reputation for incompetence in the early nineteenth century, they were particularly zealous in their apprehension of vagrants.[22] This enthusiasm survived the reforms to county policing that took place between 1839 and 1856. During this period, amateur constables were replaced by professional police officers whose more efficient methods of surveillance and prosecution ensured that rural vagrants were increasingly subject to official interference.[23] One response to this was to migrate to cities. Here vagrants were less exposed and could take advantage of the economic opportunities provided by industrialisation and urbanisation. Gypsies began to settle in suburbs and to replace their hawking trade with wholesale manufacture, selling pegs and skewers directly to shops, while packmen in the drapery line stopped trading on their own accounts and became the representatives of urban tailors, outfitters and haberdasheries.[24]

The withdrawal of itinerants from rural areas must be seen within broader patterns of migration. Despite an overall growth in the national population, the rural population remained static throughout the nineteenth century, and after 1850 there was a general movement away from the countryside.[25] Between 1821 and 1841, the industrial cities of Manchester, Sheffield, Leeds and Birmingham grew by more than 40 per cent, while London, the globe's largest city in the nineteenth century, experienced unprecedented growth: between 1809 and 1900 its population expanded from 960,000 to 6.58 million.[26] Meanwhile, emigration to extra-European territories became a feature of ordinary life during the Victorian period. In 1832 the annual number of emigrants exceeded 100,000 for the first time, and by 1850 this figure had doubled.[27] These emigrants were drawn from the itinerant as well as the settled community, and America – known as the '"true Canaan" for all travellers' – was their favoured destination, offering new opportunities and a chance to escape police harassment.[28] The nineteenth-century Gypsiologist Charles Leland, writing about the Gypsy enclaves in the United States, recorded that 'it is astonishing how many Romanys come out of [England] over here'.[29]

However, despite these migratory trends, we should not imagine that itinerants vanished from the countryside altogether; tramps and Gypsies performed seasonal agricultural work throughout the nineteenth century, travelling with the ripening harvest. What did change was the tenor of vagrant life. Whereas early in the century itinerants had been a welcome and essential part of rural existence, now they were relics of a bygone order whose fate was to be either reviled or romanticised. It is little wonder, then, that many sought their fortunes elsewhere. In Parts II and III of this study I examine the ways in which the redistribution of vagrants impacted their cultural representation. This chapter, meanwhile, examines how rural vagrants were portrayed during a pivotal period of transition between 1830 and 1860.

Although the socioeconomic pressures detailed above affected several groups of rural itinerants, the impact of these changes was not represented in a uniform manner. To some extent this was because various trades reacted and adapted to circumstances differently; but primarily it was because legacies of representation influenced how the 'decline' of separate vagrant groups was figured. In particular, Gypsies were acutely racialised and inflexibly depicted in terms of the picturesque, whereas other vagrant types were not. During the nineteenth century, Gypsies were a popular literary subject and the most frequently portrayed group of rural itinerants. The recent critical studies by Deborah Epstein Nord and Sarah Houghton-Walker, which examine the characterisation of the Victorian and Romantic-era Gypsy respectively, attest to this.[30] The exclusive focus of these studies is justified by the status of Gypsies as an ethnic group and the sheer abundance of Gypsy representations; however, it also occludes important factors. Gypsies were interwoven within an itinerant economy and shared camping grounds, resources and relatives with other groups. Indeed, for contemporaries, it was not easy to identify 'genuine' Gypsies from 'gorgios', or non-Gypsies, who were engaged in similar trades.[31] This chapter examines the representation of Gypsies alongside the other itinerant types with which they lived in order to unravel the ways in which they were racially constructed and aesthetically conditioned, and also to explain why they were more susceptible to this treatment than other vagrant types. In the next section, I analyse the portrayal of rural itinerants in the periodical press: here the breadth of material produced by diverse authors for a multiplicity of publications acts as a cultural barometer and allows us to appreciate how these figures were generally perceived. I then examine the role of the Gypsy and itinerant in the works of the travel writer and Gypsiologist George Borrow, whose portrayal of vagrants both exemplifies and critiques the dominant trends of representation.

1.1   Picturing Itinerants in the Periodical Press

Writers in the early Victorian period were aware that the complexion of rural vagrancy was altering. Contemporary articles in the periodical press were swift to identify that social, legal and technological changes were causing the erosion of certain itinerant trades. Charles Knight's *Penny Magazine*, a mass-market periodical containing instructive articles for the working classes, published two items on this issue.[32] 'The Tinkers of Scotland' (1836) informed readers that Scottish tinkers, 'a race closely similar to the gipsies of England', had been severely affected by 'the change in the circumstances of social life', which had 'lessened, if not destroyed, the value of their services'.[33] This diagnosis was reiterated two years later in a lengthy cover article entitled 'The English Gypsies' (1838). With an air of relief, the article anticipated that in another generation 'one may travel from Dover to Duncansby Head, and neither see nor hear of a gypsy encampment' thanks to the 'numerous inclosures of waste lands, and the diffusion of the conveniences of cities in the country'.[34] Meanwhile, the *Leisure Hour*, the periodical wing of the Religious Tract Society, noted that 'recreative vagabonds' – strolling players, acrobats and clowns – were likewise becoming 'only matters of history'.[35] This was a happy consequence of 'the extension of railways' which had blighted the rural wakes and festivals, the markets that these vagrants relied on.[36] However, although periodicals acknowledged that itinerants of several stamps were disappearing due to the same historical factors, the ways in which these different wanderers were represented differed considerably.

Vagrancy was a micro-industry in the periodical press. Throughout the Victorian period taxonomic articles appeared that examined single or occasionally multiple species of tramp. Whether they claimed to be fact or fiction, these pieces were typically a blend of myths, laws, official reports and personal recollections: in 'The Lame Pedlar, a Story' (1838), for example, the author attests to the facticity of the tale, claiming that 'in Scotland, among the lower classes, the *lame* ... often take to this [hawking] trade'.[37] However, rural itinerants were broadly split into Gypsies, who formed a mainstay of this print economy, and all other vagrant traders: as the *Leisure Hour* notes at the beginning of 'Life among the Vagabonds' (1858): 'Independent of the gipsy race, of whom we are not going to treat in the present paper, there are in this country a numerous class, or rather a variety of classes, who ... must be ranked under the denomination of vagabonds'.[38] This sweeping division has its origins in the late eighteenth century. Although early modern Gypsies were subject to discrete laws, including several sixteenth-century acts that banished them from England and threatened them with execution, in practice they were perceived as 'vagabonds', and therefore constituted 'a shadowy group in the Elizabethan period', as A. L. Beier remarks.[39] Indeed, it seems likely that in Thomas Harman's catalogue of rogues, *A Caveat or Warning for Common Cursetors* (1566), the otherwise unmentioned Gypsies are elided with 'Dronken Tinkars' and 'Prigger[s] of Prauncers' (horse thieves), two occupations with which they were readily associated.[40] In the Romantic era such conflations became impossible. As Houghton-Walker argues, the Gypsies underwent a radical transformation in this period, and were reconfigured as a distinct and separate race of people.[41]

One of the primary reasons for this was Heinrich Grellmann's influential *Dissertation on the Gipsies* (1783). Having established a philological link between the Romani dialects used by Continental Gypsies and Sanskrit, Grellmann argued that Gypsies were a race descended from the 'Pariahs' or 'Suders', the lowest Hindustani caste. Furthermore, he believed that having fled Hindustan, this race had continued 'pure' and unaltered: 'they have remained, to the present time, what they were at their first arrival in Europe', he claimed.[42] This thesis inaugurated the racial construction of the Gypsies and had an enormous impact on how they were represented in Britain.[43] Available in an English translation four years after its publication, Grellmann's *Dissertation* was widely accepted by the country's leading Gypsy experts, who were primarily evangelical dissenters concerned with converting travellers to Christianity. In *A Historical Survey of the Customs, Habits and Present State of the Gypsies* (1816), the Northampton Quaker John Hoyland claimed that the Gypsies were a unified race: whether English or Continental they shared a 'mutual descent from the Suder caste'.[44] Fifteen years later, the Wesleyan James Crabb likewise relied on Grellmann in his *The Gipsies' Advocate* (1831). Here he stated that the Gypsies were 'a distinct race of people in every possible way' and of 'Hindoo origin'.[45] Opinions such as these were widely disseminated in the Victorian period and portrayed as indisputable facts.

In *Gypsies and the British Imagination* (2006) Nord argues that despite Hoyland's promotion of Grellmann's thesis, 'those who wrote about the Gypsies seemed unwilling to relinquish the belief that their origin was ultimately still mysterious'.[46] This claim, however, is certainly not applicable to the journalists writing for the periodical press. In 'The English Gypsies', the *Penny Magazine* asserted that Grellmann's *Dissertation* was the 'first satisfactory account of the gypsies', and that it 'establish[ed] the fact of the Indian origin of the gypsies' (Figure 1.1); in 'The Gipsies'

THE PENNY MAGAZINE

OF THE

Society for the Diffusion of Useful Knowledge.

372.]   PUBLISHED EVERY SATURDAY.   [JANUARY 20, 1838.

THE ENGLISH GYPSIES

[The Fortune-Teller.—Sir Joshua Reynolds.]

THE traveller who, with poetic fancies respecting the American Indians, first sees one wrapped up in his blanket in a log-hut tavern, can scarcely be more disappointed and mortified than the writer when he first saw a gypsy encampment. Acquainted with the established fact that the English gypsies are a portion of that Asiatic family which first visited Europe about four centuries ago, and familiar with their appearance from some of the numerous descriptions that our poets and novelists have given of them, he had fancied that there would be at least picturesque wildness in the aspect of a genuine gypsy encampment. There was this drawback to the appearance of the encampment alluded to—it was neither on a "furze-clad common," nor on the skirts of a wood, but on the sides of a narrow lane, which could scarcely be termed "bosky." The tents looked like dog-kennels, the men had a scowling aspect, the women seemed weather-beaten and miserable. They had, however, all the usual and well-known gypsy peculiarities. Their asses cropped the scanty herbage;

> " a kettle
> Slung between two poles, upon a stick
> Transverse,"

was suspended over a fire; and from amongst the group there stepped out a young girl, whose slender and not unhandsome figure, brilliant dark-eye, and

> " tawny skin,
> The vellum of the pedigree they claim,"

proclaimed her at once one of that tribe, of whom Bishop Heber said, when he met with a similar encampment in India, that they are "a race that no man can mistake, meet them where he may."

The gypsies are indeed a singular phenomenon in our history. They have been moving over the surface of our continually advancing civilization for upwards of three centuries, and still they retain their Eastern habits. Acts

Figure 1.1   'The English Gypsies', *Penny Magazine*, 20 January 1838. Author's collection

(1841) the *London Saturday Journal* noted that 'the commonly received opinion now is, that they belonged to one of the lowest castes of India'; and in 'Gatherings about Gipsies' (1848) *Reynolds's Miscellany* recorded that 'it is now, we believe, pretty generally agreed, that they came originally from Hindostan'.[47] This consensus regarding the Gypsies' origin cemented the notion that Gypsies formed a separate race, and encouraged commentators to interpret their diminishing numbers in rural England as evidence of primitiveness and inferiority. As we shall see in other chapters, the depiction of vagrants as primitive became common later in the Victorian period and often featured in narratives predicting their extinction. In the case of Gypsies, this narrative was coded in aesthetic as well as genetic terms.

In the third part of William Howitt's survey *The Rural Life of England* (1838) he addresses the 'Picturesque and Moral Features of the Country', the first section of which is entitled 'Gipsies'. As if justifying this choice, he begins by placing the Gypsies in their artistic context, declaring that 'the picture of the Rural Life of England must be woefully defective which should omit those singular and most picturesque squatters on heaths and in lanes, the Gipsies'. These, he goes on to say, have been the concern of 'all our best poets and essayists', and have thus become 'an essential portion of our poetry and literature'. Although Howitt then parrots Grellmann's 'theory that they are a Hindu tribe', and like many of his peers, comments on their dwindling numbers, what he highlights here is their literary associations with the picturesque, an aesthetic form closely allied to the pastoral that glories in the rugged, irregular and uncultivated beauty of nature.[48] Throughout the Romantic and Victorian periods Gypsies were considered native to this kind of wild landscape: as Matthew Beaumont remarks, 'the picturesque ... integrated gypsies and vagrants, but not ordinary labourers, as colourful, more or less exotic elements'.[49] In the periodical press, the familiarity and longevity of this trope was used to convey the declining state of contemporary Gypsies by contrasting their picturesque past with their squalid and prosaic present.

'The Norwood Gypsies', penned by the anonymous J.P.P.C., appeared in the *Literary Lounger* in February 1826. Striving for the same urbanity that characterised the articles in successful contemporaries, such as the *London Magazine* and the *New Monthly Magazine*, and mimicking their broadly liberal tone, this item rails against 'an improving age' that would banish the delights of rural life, such as 'wakes, fairs, and festivals', and set up 'Bible societies, mechanic's institutions, and savings banks' in their place.[50] The eviction of the Gypsies from Norwood, a famous encampment on the outskirts of southeast London, is another unwanted symptom of this modern mentality. Known in the mid-eighteenth century as the residence of Margaret Finch, the celebrated 'Queen of the Gypsies', and patronised by the Prince and Princess of Wales at that time, this enclave had become the target of a series of legislative and judicial attacks by the start of the nineteenth century.[51] Police launched raids in 1797, 1802 and 1803, and imprisoned Gypsies for various offences, including vagrancy; in 1808 the Norwood common was enclosed and the Gypsies forced into the woods of Dulwich College; and in 1815 the Gypsies were subjected to further raids and arrests, having defied the enclosure and returned to their original pitch.[52] Such harassment inevitably encouraged Gypsies to move elsewhere, although it was not until 1830 that the area ceased to be visited entirely. By the time J.P.P.C. was writing, the population, independence and aesthetic appeal of the Norwood Gypsies had dwindled; this was the cause of lament.

Reminiscing about the Norwood Gypsies as they were in the eighteenth century, J.P.P.C. remarks that 'they were a truly pastoral people, a sort of Scythian Nomades – their castle was the forest, their bower the greenwood-tree'. Compared with the barbarians of the classical world, the Scythians, the Gypsies are depicted as a vital, picturesque, primitive nation who know 'no law but the law of Nature'.[53] They form a stark contrast with their nineteenth-century descendants:

> I am told that a few disconsolate creatures still hover, like unquiet spirits, about the scenes of their former greatness; but these are no more to be compared to the parent horde, than is that attenuated bag of skin and bone, the 'Living Skeleton' to be put in competition with the flesh and blood carcase of 'Barclay and Perkins's drayman.'[54]

Here the Norwood Gypsies are presented as almost already extinct. Relegated to the world of hearsay by the author, whose 'I am told' abstracts the Gypsies from the world of verified facts, and described in ethereal terms as 'like unquiet spirits', the expiration of the Gypsies is presented as ongoing and inexorable; they already occupy the mysterious, rumour-filled spaces that belong to mythic tribes. This narrative of extinction is enhanced by the comparison between the Gypsies of the nineteenth century and 'that attenuated bag of skin and bone, the "Living Skeleton"'. Here the image of atrophy embodies the process of extinction, and the enervation and decay that attend it. While the eighteenth-century Gypsies are compared to a 'Barclay and Perkins's drayman', a byword for vigour, the contemporary Gypsy resembles a penny-gaff sideshow.[55]

This also suggests that the appeal of the enfeebled Norwood Gypsies is no longer picturesque, but grotesque; they are no longer remarkable for the wild way they live but, like the 'Living Skeleton', for the macabre way in which they remain alive. The impending extinction of the Gypsies is therefore marked by a physical and aesthetic deterioration.

This pathology was also deployed by journalists in the Victorian period. In 'The Gipsies', the *London Saturday Journal* observed that English Gypsies

> are still to be found, though in diminishing numbers, wandering here and there, and pitching their camps in rural places; and still there is to be seen in rural scenes ... 'the kettle slung', as Cowper calls it, 'on two sticks transverse'. But an increasing population, and a vigilant police, keep them subdued and dejected – the gipsies of England will probably soon waste away and disappear.

The article retains a commitment to the picturesque vision of poets like Thomas Cowper when describing the Victorian Gypsies; but it only evokes this pastoral legacy in order to signal the collapse of their existence. It is significant that while the article identifies police interference as an infringement upon itinerant life, the disappearance of the Gypsies is nonetheless couched in terms of racial atrophy. Like the diminished population at Norwood likened to a 'Living Skeleton', these Gypsies will 'soon waste away' as if afflicted by a disease. This connection between extinction and racial exhaustion is reiterated later in the article when the author states that 'in Great Britain [Gypsies] have greatly diminished, and those who still remain are but the dregs of the race'.[56] Here the language of waste signals the Gypsies' impending extinction, but is also used to imply that their picturesque wildness, their central place within 'rural scenes', has been compromised.

In 'The English Gypsies' the *Penny Magazine* adopted a comparable narrative of decline. Relating a visit to a Gypsy encampment, the author complains:

> The traveller who, with poetic fancies respecting the American Indians, first sees one wrapped up in his blanket in a log-hut tavern, can scarcely be more disappointed and mortified than the writer when he first saw a gypsy encampment ... familiar with their appearance from some of the numerous descriptions that our poets and novelists have given of them, he had fancied that there would be at least picturesque wildness in the aspect of a genuine gypsy encampment. There was this drawback to the appearance of the encampment alluded to – it was neither on a 'furze-clad common', nor on the skirts of a wood, but on the sides of a narrow lane, which could scarcely be termed 'bosky'. The tents looked like dog-kennels, the men had a scowling aspect, the women seemed weather-beaten and miserable.[57]

Here picturesque expectations garnered from a literary tradition break
down beneath the weight of reality as the pastoral encampment turns
out to be a makeshift slum. Mocking a slightly tired poetic discourse, the
article contrasts the illusive luxuriance of the 'furze-clad common' and
'bosky' wood with matter-of-fact reportage: the 'weather-beaten' Gypsies
with their tents 'like dog-kennels' are described in plain, prosaic language.
This aesthetically disappointing scene later becomes associated with racial
decline, making us question how 'genuine' this Gypsy encampment really
is. Strongly recalling the tents 'like dog-kennels', the author informs us
that Gypsies on the Scottish border 'intermarried' with 'sturdy and idle
vagrants' and produced 'a race of mongrels'; and similarly, that 'London is
more frequented by mongrel and degenerate gypsies, and by mere imposters, than by those who still retain the lineaments of the tribe'.[58] This
account of 'interbreeding' chimes with contemporary theories of extinction
which claimed that miscegenation led to the autogenocide of savages. As
Patrick Brantlinger observes while discussing the dominance of this idea in
nineteenth-century accounts of indigenous Americans, 'Racial as opposed
to cultural identity depends on a fantasy of purity, of unmixed blood....
Miscegenation from such a racist perspective can only be tragic.'[59] 'The
English Gypsies' duplicates this perspective. Tellingly compared to
American Indians at the start of the passage, the Gypsies have muddied
their bloodlines through the error of miscegenation and undermined their
aesthetic appeal in the process.

'The Gipsies' and 'The English Gypsies' highlight that in the wake of
Grellmann, whose opinion they promote, concerns about the decline of
the Gypsies began to emerge. The narratives that recorded this deteriora-
tion were underwritten by the assumption that they formed a separate race.
Although it emerged in the Romantic period, this idea was significantly
developed by the Victorians: the 'racialized commentary' about Gypsies,
David Cressy remarks, was 'mostly a Victorian invention'.[60] Within this
discourse, miscegenation threatened to undermine the integrity of the
Gypsy race. In 'Gipsies' (1848) *Sharpe's London Magazine* celebrated
'The gipsy of the pure unadulterated breed', but warned that 'the gipsy
ranks ... have ever been swelled by the idle and dissolute' which has led to
the creation of 'the gipsy of the half-breed'. These Gypsies belong to a
'degenerate age' and are as separate from the 'pure sybilline race' as the
'mere wandering vagrant'.[61] Not all commentators subscribed to this
notion, but whether they believed it or not, it was generally accepted that
the extinction of the Gypsies was imminent. This was repeatedly articulated in terms of aesthetic degeneration. As we have seen, the picturesque

tradition haunted the Gypsies' 'degraded' state; it was the first point of reference for journalists and served as a touchstone for authenticity. It is this that made their depiction in the Victorian period distinct from that of other rural itinerants who pursued similar lives on the road.

Those who wrote about 'vagabonds' tended to treat their subjects more leniently than those writing about Gypsies. Hawkers and tramping artisans were portrayed generously, and were often incorporated into wistful visions of the past where they belonged to a pre-railway era of ease, amusement and contemplation. As the narrator of George Eliot's *Adam Bede* (1859) laments, 'leisure is gone – gone where the spinning-wheels are gone, and the pack-horses, and the slow waggons, and the pedlars who brought bargains to the door on sunny afternoons': all of these have been overturned by 'the great work of the steam-engine'.[62] Meanwhile, in 'Larry Lee the Pedlar' (1857), Edric Hewson's murder-mystery set 'more than a century ago', Lee is associated as much with convivial entertainment as he is with the 'treasures in his pack': he 'could sing a capital song', was 'abounding in jest and anecdote', and 'acted as a kind of human newsletter, conveying by word of mouth, the gossip and scandal of the day'.[63] This combination of performer and dealer is also brought vividly to life in *Doctor Marigold's Prescriptions* (1865), a bestselling Christmas number of *All the Year Round*.[64] Mimicking the 'Cheap Jack style', Dickens's framing narrative captures all the flair of the pedlars' patter as Marigold rushes through his helter-skelter history.[65] Such celebratory depictions were by no means ubiquitous. 'Life among the Vagabonds', for example, condemns the Cheap Jack 'who bawls and lies' and cheats villagers of their hard-earned wages. Nonetheless, itinerant traders generally remained free from such censure.

There are several possible reasons for this. The most obvious is that itinerant traders were not racially constructed. They originated from within and belonged to the settled population, albeit only peripherally, and therefore were not subject to the same powerful othering as Gypsies. In addition, although vagrants en masse were considered idle in this period, the travelling salesman or handicraft tramp could be perceived as industrious, whereas Gypsies, despite the fact that they engaged in the same occupations, were predominantly associated with the criminal trade of fortune telling. Finally, artisans and pedlars were not bound by the same literary legacy that hampered the narratives of Victorian Gypsies. Intensely imagined as a pastoral and nomadic people, contemporaries struggled to picture an alternative fate to extinction in an era where enclosures, railways and police legislation were causing a visible reduction in the rural population of Gypsies. As Nord observes, 'Even though London and its environs attracted the bulk of the Gypsy population, at least during the nineteenth century, Gypsies most often were cast in literary texts as pastoral figures, allied with an aesthetic of picturesque.'[66] Meanwhile, as we have already seen, those who were acknowledged to be in and around London were not considered 'genuine'. This conforms to a broader pattern of cultural misinterpretation identified by the social anthropologist Judith Okely. Discussing the ways in which Gypsiologists have been instrumental in producing toxic assumptions about Gypsies, she observes that in their work 'any cultural similarity between Gypsy and Gorgio is explained away and denigrated as "contamination"'.[67] This is the logic of Victorian journalists who, seeing Gypsies participate in a nationwide trend of urbanisation, interpreted this as a sign of corruption. Other itinerants, however, did not suffer from such a constipated tradition of representation.

Contemporaries recognised that as itinerant trades became less practicable in the country, pedlars migrated to cities. *Chambers's Edinburgh Journal*, a rival of the *Penny Magazine* and a competitor for the same working-class readership, portrayed 'The Umbrella Pedler' (1851) as a thoroughly metropolitan type.[68] This one-time rustic, whom Dickens clubs together with the chair-mender and knife-grinder, does good business in foul weather at the pleasure gardens of Vauxhall and Cremone, where he sells his stock to the 'thousands of callow Cockneys' caught out in the rain. 'The trade in second-hand umbrellas', we are told, 'is one which is very industriously pursued in every part of the metropolis' and chiefly consists of hawking. In addition, like the Gypsies who sold pegs and skewers wholesale, these handicraftsmen are also engaged to larger retailers for whom they repair umbrellas at a rate of 'two shillings per dozen'.[69] Free from aesthetic expectations, *Chambers's* presents the umbrella-mender as a resourceful and adaptable figure who belongs very much to the mid-century cityscape.

A similar example of the urbanised itinerant is the book-hawker, or 'literary packman', as the *Leisure Hour* calls him. Reminiscing about the early nineteenth century in a manner similar to Eliot, the author of 'Literary "Packmen"' (1860) observes:

> The profession of the pedlar, or travelling packman, has dwindled down to comparative insignificance since the days when pack-horses were an institution in this country. We have made most marvellous changes since then – from a plodding jade of a horse . . . at the rate of twenty miles a day, to a train of twenty or thirty baggage vans, each loaded with its six or seven tons, and following the great iron horse at the rate of twenty or thirty miles an hour.[70]

This introduction of the railway has caused the demise of the 'literary packman', who up until the 1820s pursued a 'profitable trade in book-hawking' in hamlets, villages and small market towns that had no other source of literature. Now, however, the trade has become defunct, and 'the most characteristic literary hawker of the present day is the trash packman of London'. The shift from the 'literary packman' of the early nineteenth century to the 'trash packman' of 1860 might suggest a narrative of decline akin to that of the Gypsies. This is certainly the case in terms of the literary quality of his goods: whereas the 'literary packman' traded in the 'English Classics', the 'trash packman' deals in 'cheap serial literature'. However, to prevent misunderstanding, the article assures us that 'nothing derogatory is signified by the word "trash"' and that it is only a trade term. Indeed, the image we are given of the trash packman is one of lively industry; he is depicted as 'unwearied and punctual ... pelting along on his route, laden with the ponderous reams' that he sells wholesale to retailers of sweets, trinkets and tobacco.[71]

Itinerant pedlars and hawkers enjoyed a more hopeful prognosis than their Gypsy counterparts. This was because they were more ambiguous, less susceptible to racial construction and, as a consequence, had a less proscribed future. In addition, the literary burden of pedlars was much lighter. Admittedly, the travel writer Robert Heron claimed that hawkers possessed 'habits of reflection and of sublime contemplation', and this in turn influenced William Wordsworth's construction of the 'venerable Armytage', the philosophic pedlar who tells the tale of 'The Ruined Cottage' (1814).[72] Such a representation, however, never became a main-stay of English literature; pedlars were never monotonously depicted as fulfilling this sagacious role. Meanwhile, authors generally presented Gypsies either as picturesque or as having been picturesque. George Borrow, however, was an exception to this rule, which makes his work worthy of attention. As we shall see, although Borrow engaged with the picturesque presentation of both Gypsies and other itinerants, the texts that he produced subverted, manipulated and confounded this aesthetic schema.

1.2 George Borrow

George Borrow was a writer, missionary and philologist and is credited with being Britain's first Gypsiologist.[73] His two-volume study *The Zincali: An Account of the Gypsies of Spain* (1841) established Borrow's expertise and reveals that he was receptive to the popular theories pioneered by Grellmann. Here he acknowledges that philological studies of the Romani dialects found in Germany, Hungary and England have led to 'the establishment of the fact, that the Gypsies of those countries are the descendants of a tribe of Hindus'. In addition, like his contemporaries writing for the periodical press, he was also convinced that the English Gypsies were destined for extinction: 'the English Gypsies at the present day are far from being a numerous race', he wrote; 'it is probable that, ere the conclusion of the present century, they will have entirely disappeared'.[74] Borrow's writings, then, were influenced by, and contributed to, many of the beliefs that shaped the representation of Gypsies in the early Victorian period. However, they were also informed by a detailed knowledge of the itinerant economy and the ways in which Gypsies and 'vagabonds' coexisted on the roads. I argue that this nuanced Borrow's depictions of vagrant life in ways that have been overlooked by his critics.

Although he often capitalised on his reputation as an authority on Gypsies, Borrow was a keen observer of itinerants in general. In *Romano Lavo-Lil: Word-Book of the Romany* (1874) he included an account of his 1866 visit to Kirk Yetholm, a famous Gypsy village in Scotland. In this formal version of his venture he claims that he went 'hunting after Gypsies whom I could not find'.[75] However, as his expeditionary notebook makes clear, while his purpose may have been to track down Gypsies, his interest extended to all vagrants. On 18 July he recorded that he was overtaken by a 'man who had a pack on his back – [a] scotch pedlar'; on 21 July he noted a pair of balladeers, a 'vagabond and girl, regular tramps, singing before the door' of a hotel; and on 2 August a 'vagrant weaver'.[76] These splinters of observation, which remain unexplored within the notebook, speak of an instinctive urge to record such figures. It is also significant that Borrow reflexively noted their occupations. As he revealed in his travelogue *Wild Wales* (1862), the itinerant economy was of particular interest to him. While recalling his 1854 tour of the principality, Borrow makes repeated reference to the displacement of the Gypsies by Irish tramps. Prompted by some scorch marks on the roadside, the signs of a recent encampment, Borrow's Welsh guide, John Jones, informs him that 'the Gwyddelod [Irish] made their appearance in these parts about twenty years ago, and since then the Gipsiaid [Gypsies] have been rarely seen'. These Irish migrants have taken over not only the Gypsies' campsites, but also their traditional occupations: 'the men tinker a little, sir', Jones explains, and 'the women tell fortunes'. This is confirmed by Bosvile, a Gypsy that Borrow meets on the road to Birmingham, retreating from the 'woild Irish': 'the fellows underwork me at tinkering, and the women outscream my wife at telling fortunes', he laments, 'what can a poor little Roman family do but flee away before them?'[77]

One reason why Borrow was at pains to detail this economic shift was because his interest in itinerants was at once artistic and occupational. Borrow depicted rural vagrancy as a picturesque mode of life, but he also sporadically took part in the itinerant economy, and this gave him a singular insight into functional forms of vagrancy. Although he was deliberately evasive about much of his life, especially the so-called veiled years between 1824 and 1833, it is nonetheless easy to surmise that during his twenties and thirties he spent some time tramping, pursuing various jobs on the road. This is most clearly evinced in the texts I discuss below, his picaresque autobiographies *Lavengro* (1851) and *The Romany Rye* (1857), where he gives a detailed account of his life as a tinker and horse trader during the late 1820s. But his itinerant experience is a theme that emerges in his other works as well. In *The Zincali* his recollections of Gypsy encounters are bound up with a vagrant past: for example, he notes that in Italy he met a band of Hungarian Gypsies while resting 'at nightfall by the side of a kiln', a snug refuge from the 'piercingly cold' air.[78] Later, in his travelogue *The Bible in Spain* (1843), he depicted a more prosperous itinerant existence. Between 1835 and 1840 Borrow was engaged by the British and Foreign Bible Society to print and distribute a Spanish New Testament on the Iberian Peninsula. In the process, he became something of a hawker as he travelled from village to village, selling copies of the Testament to the Spanish peasantry. When he returned to the major cities, where he kept his stocks, he employed locals to peddle these books on his behalf: in Lisbon, for example, he hired 'colporteurs' – or literary pack-men – 'to hawk the books about the streets'.[79]

While *The Zincali* established Borrow as a Gypsy-fancier, *The Bible in Spain* made him a household name. In its first year alone it sold nearly 20,000 copies, underwent numerous reprints, and went on to become the first book in John Murray III's Colonial and Home Library, a collection of popular works published in cheap editions. Borrow's next book, *Lavengro*, did not fare so well. Slow to sell, it took John Murray eighteen years to rid himself of the 3,000 copies that formed the first edition.[80] Although *Lavengro* and its sequel *The Romany Rye* went on to become popular texts in the early twentieth century, they divided critics and proved unappetising to the book-buying public. One reason for this was the intensely pictorial and fragmentary nature of the work: as Ann M. Ridler argues, 'it needed ... Cubism in painting and Modernism in literature to begin to habituate some of the public to the idea of a multivalent, multi-faceted portrait image' of the kind Borrow produced.[81] A review of *Lavengro* published in the *Athenaeum* speaks to this, complaining that the 'long-talked of biography' (it had been prematurely advertised in 1848 and 1849) could 'scarcely be called a book at all: – being more like a portfolio of sketches'.[82] Other critics, however, welcomed this pictorialism. In an otherwise condemnatory review, *Fraser's Magazine* complimented Borrow on his 'vivid' and 'picturesque' style, while the *New Monthly Magazine* compared him to Michelangelo and Raphael, and praised the manner in which 'every sketch is lightly touched, and with a master's hand'.[83] This formal aspect of *Lavengro* and *The Romany Rye*, their sketch-like quality, also governed their later critical reception.

The picturesque vignettes that form the autobiographies have been consistently interpreted as signs of Borrow's nostalgia. Ian Duncan argues that Borrow's England is 'pre-modern, pre-industrial, unreformed and unenclosed'; Monika Mazurek likewise notes that he presents 'a nostalgic image of Georgian England'; and, according to Houghton-Walker, Borrow populates this landscape with a 'nostalgic, romanticized gypsy form'.[84] Such claims do not bear up under scrutiny. Although Borrow did not chronicle the rural poverty of the 1820s in the manner of William Cobbett, his England is still far from bucolic. Of particular concern to Borrow, as we might expect, are the socioeconomic changes that threaten certain itinerant trades. In *The Romany Rye*, Borrow articulates these anxieties through his Gypsy companion Jasper Petulengro. In an anachronistic reference to the professionalisation of the rural police force, which started only in 1839, Jasper first relates how 'all the old-fashioned good-tempered constables are going to be set aside, and a paid body of men to be established, who are not to permit a tramper or vagabond on the roads of England'. And if this were not bad enough, he goes on to disclose the whisperings that he has heard about the railway, an invention that will 'set aside all the old roads, which in a little time would be ploughed up, and sowed with corn, and cause all England to be laid down with iron roads, on which people would go thundering along in vehicles, pushed forward by fire and smoke'. In this apocalyptic vision of universal enclosure, where all the 'old roads' have been turned into corn fields, the only spaces that Jasper can occupy are the dangerous 'iron roads', where he foresees 'my tent being overturned by a flying vehicle; my wife's leg injured; and all my affairs put into great confusion'.[85] Such a prediction, while comic in its naive literalism, is a symbolic rendering of a socioeconomic fact: that the railways will displace the Gypsies.

Borrow's England, then, is uneasy – pregnant with incipient change. Moreover, although the laws, technologies and enclosures that Jasper fears are yet to be implemented, they belong to a succession of similar efforts: as Borrow reminds us later in *The Romany Rye*, the downfall of the highwaymen, 'the heroes of the road', was a result of 'the inclosure of many a wild heath in the country' and the establishment 'of a well-armed mounted patrol'.[86] The difficulties that the Gypsies face are therefore the product of a concerted historical effort to exert control over the English landscape and its people. As a consequence, nineteenth-century England does not exist *before* a fundamental change, but is already in the *midst* of that change. This outlook can also be detected in Borrow's presentation of Gypsies. As Nord argues, in *Lavengro* and its sequel Borrow 'neither makes a fetish of [the Gypsies'] allegedly primitive way of life nor romanticizes their pristine associations with an older, rural Englishness'. Proof of this is his depiction of them as subject to historical forces, which distinguishes him 'from those who persisted in regarding the Gypsies as frozen in time, an indelible reminder of a forgotten age'.[87] But Borrow's awareness of the pressures that Gypsies faced is not just historical; it is also aesthetic. Although he engages with the picturesque representation of Gypsies, he does not produce a 'romanticized gypsy form', as Houghton-Walker argues. Instead, his descriptions are often the very moments when he is at his most critically aware, not only of the England he is depicting, but also of the ways in which writers interpret it. In his descriptions of Gypsies and other itinerants, Borrow repeatedly ironises the picturesque and highlights the slippage between fact and fantasy.

1.3   *Lavengro* and the Picturesque

In opening chapters of *Lavengro*, Borrow recounts his childhood growing up during the Napoleonic Wars. His father, Thomas Borrow, was a captain in the West Norfolk Militia, and his family followed 'the "route" of the regiment'.[88] In *Lavengro* it is not long before the soldiers come to Norman Cross in Huntingdonshire, where they are employed guarding a prisoner-of-war camp. While the regiment keeps watch, Borrow wanders across the 'flat and somewhat fenny' countryside, 'a district more of pasture than agriculture, and not very thickly inhabited' (24). It is within this wilderness that he meets an anonymous vagrant viper-catcher and herbalist, who 'do[es] not live in this neighbourhood in particular' but 'travel[s] about' (26). He is described as follows:

> I frequently passed a tall elderly individual, dressed in rather a quaint fashion, with a skin cap on his head and stout gaiters on his legs; on his shoulders hung a moderate sized leathern sack; he seemed fond of loitering near sunny banks, and of groping amidst furze and low scrubby bramble bushes, of which there were plenty in the neighbourhood of Norman Cross. (25)

Borrow's description of this figure is picturesque. The 'stout gaiters' point to a roaming life on fen and marshland, and the 'skin cap' – perhaps a poaching trophy – suggests wild and lawless habits. Indeed, it might even remind us of Matthew Arnold's Peran Wisa, the savage Tartar from *Sohrab and Rustum* (1853) who wears a 'skin cap, / Black, glossy, curl'd'.[89] Meanwhile, Borrow's description of his idle 'loitering' beside the 'sunny banks' speaks of a leisurely and pastoral existence that chimes with the uncultivated and sparsely populated landscape. This pastoral interpretation of the trapper intensifies when they become better acquainted, and we are given further details about his life. 'He generally carried a viper with him which he had made quite tame, and from which he had extracted the poisonous fangs; it would dance and perform tricks. He was fond of telling me anecdotes connected with his adventures with the reptile species' (27). Recalling Doctor Marigold or Larry Lee, the itinerant is associated with entertainment as much – if not more – than his trade. Instead of exploiting natural resources for monetary gain, the viper-catcher converts them into an amusing and perhaps profitless distraction. And instead of always grubbing away in the bush, he takes time to gossip; just as he 'seemed fond of loitering' he is also 'fond of telling me anecdotes'. Disporting in the wilderness, idleness is the vagrant's mode. This is certainly a figure that would belong in 'a nostalgic image of Georgian England'; however, the conversations between Borrow and the hunter undermine this picturesque image, opening up ironies within Borrow's description.

The discrepancies between Borrow's perspective and that of the viper-catcher emerge swiftly. For example, when Borrow first sees him thrust a viper into his leathern sack he describes it as 'far from empty', and yet we are more or less immediately told by the hunter that vipers 'are getting scarce, though this used to be a great neighbourhood for them' (26). Similarly, the single anecdote he relates about 'his adventures with the reptile species', which concerns an encounter with 'the king of the vipers' (27), is elicited only by Borrow's incessant questioning; far from being eager with the tale, the hunter explicitly states, 'I don't like talking about the matter' (27). Finally, it becomes apparent that although Borrow depicts him as living a life of ease, the livelihood of the viper-catcher is far from secure. Reflecting on his age and his inability to continue in his trade, the hunter informs Borrow: 'I must shortly give up this business, I am no longer the man I was, I am become timid, and when a person is timid in viper-hunting he had better leave off' (27). By the end of this episode Borrow's pastoral vision has broken down, and in its place is an image of hardship that begins to resonate with Wordsworth's description of an itinerant leech-gatherer: 'From Pond to Pond he roamed, from moor to moor, / Housing, with God's good help, by choice or chance'.[90]

Itinerant life was precarious at all times, but for herbalists or 'simplers', like the viper-catcher and leech-gatherer, this was perhaps especially true at the turn of the nineteenth century when Borrow and Wordsworth report encountering them. There is an obvious symmetry between these figures, both of whom are elderly vagrants whose grip seems to falter on a failing trade; the leech-gatherer also complains that 'Once I could meet with [leeches] on every side; / But they have dwindled long by slow decay.'[91] Although Duncan and George Hyde suggest that Borrow's trapper is patterned on the leech-gatherer, their similarities might also be rooted in a shared historical reality.[92] In 1817, a few years after Borrow's scene is set, the antiquarian John Thomas Smith chose to include William Friday in his *Vagabondiana*, a pictorial record of the vanishing beggars of London. Friday, as Smith observes, illustrates that 'the environs produce characters equally curious with those of London, particularly among that order of people called Simplers'; these rustics 'supply the city-markets with physical [i.e., medicinal] herbs' and are 'alternately snail-picker, leech-bather, and viper catcher'.[93] Neither a Londoner nor one of the 'mendicant wanderers' that Smith initially seeks to document, it is telling that Friday is included among his departing beggars, because it signals that he and his fellow simplers are likewise endangered. No doubt their chief threat came from the sprawling suburbs – London's bourgeois spread – which, as Jerry White relates, ate up the squatters' wastes that surrounded the capital in the early nineteenth century.[94] Choked with weeds and bordered by mud-banks, these would have once provided a rich supply of resources for the herbalist.

Similar environmental changes endanger the viper-catcher. It is significant that Borrow's encounter occurs in Huntingdonshire, a county whose fenland was improved and drained in the late eighteenth and early nineteenth century.[95] Although in 'The Fens of England' (1854) *Chambers's Edinburgh Journal* welcomed the drainage of such 'fenny waste', claiming that its only inhabitants are 'frogs and moorhens', in fact the livelihood of some trappers depended on these wild spaces.[96] Drainage necessarily

altered the ecosystem of the fens, destroying the conditions that allowed
many species to successfully breed. Although Borrow does not directly
address this issue, it is reasonable to assume that the viper-hunter's complaint that the snakes 'are getting scarce' is an allusion to it. However,
while the disruption of Borrow's picturesque vision allows social concerns
to bubble to the surface, he was nonetheless primarily concerned with
critiquing the manner in which itinerants were portrayed. As we have seen
in the periodicals, the authenticity of Gypsies in particular was determined
by whether they fulfilled the aesthetic expectations of gorgio commentators. Borrow challenges this practice here by highlighting the simple fact
that the picturesque is a question of perspective; it is superimposed on the
itinerant from without. This critique becomes further nuanced in *Lavengro*
when Borrow recalls his first encounter with Gypsies. In this episode the
gulf between romance and realism is fully realised as Borrow engages with,
and actively refutes, the pastoral tropes used to depict (and define)
Gypsy life.

Still residing at Norman Cross after the viper-catcher's departure,
Borrow recalls his discovery of a Gypsy camp:

> One day it happened that, being on my rambles, I entered a green lane
> which I had never seen before; at first it was rather narrow, but as
> I advanced it became considerably wider; in the middle was a drift-way
> with deep ruts, but right and left was a space carpeted with a sward of trefoil
> and clover; there was no lack of trees, chiefly ancient oaks, which, flinging
> out their arms from either side, nearly formed a canopy, and afforded a
> pleasing shelter from the rays of the sun, which was burning fiercely above.
> Suddenly a group of objects attracted my attention. Beneath the largest of
> the trees upon the grass, was a kind of low tent or booth, from the top of
> which a thin smoke was curling; beside it stood a couple of light carts,
> whilst two or three lean horses or ponies were cropping the herbage which
> was growing nigh. (30)

The scene depicted here is burdened with the kind of tired poetic clichés
that were derided in 'The English Gypsies'. The familiar location of the
'green lane', the pastoralism of the ground 'carpeted with a sward', and the
natural arbour formed 'chiefly [of] ancient oaks' would have seemed
hackneyed to contemporaries. To some readers, they perhaps felt familiar
from Mary Russell Mitford's *Our Village* (1824–32), an extremely popular
series of 122 essays, vignettes and tales of rural life: its first volume went
into fourteen editions in eleven years, while the fifth (and last) sold out on
the day of its publication.[97] In the second volume Mitford included a
sketch entitled 'The Old Gipsy'. Here the narrator, much like Borrow,

ventures down a 'seldom-trodden path' and eventually comes to 'a little green' where she finds a group of Gypsies who 'had pitched their tent under one of the oak trees': 'it was a pretty picture', she notes, 'its rich woodiness, its sunshine, its verdure, the light smoke curling from the fire'.[98] Perhaps without Mitford in mind, Borrow mirrors this encounter, which as Houghton-Walker observes, is 'structured according to traditions and clichés'.[99] The setting in the remote green lane studded with oaks, the tent under the trees, and the smoke 'curling' from the fire are all held in common.

However, here the similarities end. As the narrator of 'The Old Gipsy' looks on at the encampment, she describes it in terms of a static tableau: there is 'an old crone, in a tattered red cloak', 'a pretty black-eyed girl', a 'sun-burnt urchin', and another, 'slender lad ... basking in the sun ... in all the joy of idleness'.[100] Each figure is easily seen from outside the camp, and can be immediately identified as a stereotype that belongs to the poetic Gypsy scene. Indeed, a comparison that the narrator draws between the matriarchal crone and Walter Scott's Meg Merrilies suggests that literary depictions of Gypsies not only are accurate, but can become an able substitute for actual experience, enabling the reader to successfully negotiate real-life engagements. Borrow's encounter is far more unsettling. Instead of being able to espy the occupants from a distance, he has to 'advance[] till I was close' (30) in order to see the Gypsies, in this case a husband and wife. He is therefore within the circumference of the camp before he lays eyes on them, and once he does he is forced into a rapid retreat as they come 'rushing out upon me' (30). At a glance, he sees that the woman has 'dark and swarthy' skin 'like that of a toad' and is dressed in the unbecoming rags of 'a slight boddice' (31). Meanwhile, the man is a 'figure equally wild': 'his frame was long and lathy, but his arms were remarkably short, his neck was rather bent, he squinted slightly, and his mouth was much awry' (31). In contrast to Mitford's static frieze, Borrow presents us with a scene full of frantic motion and charged with potential violence. By drawing near the Gypsies, Borrow exposes the threat that they might pose and their appearance under closer inspection. While the traditional Gypsy garb, the 'tattered red cloak', might look pretty from afar, the ragged bodice is irredeemably seedy. Similarly, although the man is 'long and lathy', not unlike the lounging 'slender lad', his body proves a crabbed and truncated vehicle. Such Gypsies form a grotesque vision in which the wild ruggedness of the picturesque is pushed to comic and feral extremes: rags become eye-sores; olive skins turn to toad hides; and languid bodies are twisted up into something faintly ogreish.

The uncomfortable absurdity of the Gypsies is exaggerated throughout the remainder of Borrow's confrontation. At first, the Gypsy woman suggests murdering him: 'I'll drown him in the sludge in the toad-pond over the hedge' (31), she tells her misshapen partner. However, as soon as he reveals his tame snake, a gift from the viper-catcher, they begin to worship him as 'a goblin – a devilkin' (35). He swiftly disabuses them of this notion, but nonetheless, when they discover that he can read, they insist that he should go with them: 'be our God Almighty, or at any rate our clergyman', the woman wheedles, 'live in a tilted cart by yourself and say prayers to us night and morning' (35). Here it is of course ironic that a people renowned for fortune telling, and thereby playing on the credulity of others, should be so superstitious themselves. This is part of Borrow's effort to ridicule the picturesque, which would portray Gypsies as all-knowing and all-seeing: a 'pure sybilline race', in the words of *Sharpe's London Magazine*. Just as he constructs and then disrupts an idyllic version of the viper-hunter's life, so Borrow upsets the stereotypical Gypsy encampment. By portraying their violence, volatility and ugliness he attempts to dispel the Gypsy dream. In this way, Borrow is engaged in the same endeavour as Eliot in *The Mill on the Floss* (1860), a novel that contains perhaps the most famous Gypsy encounter in Victorian literature.

Clever, spirited but chronically misunderstood, Maggie Tulliver, a girl of nine, runs away to join the Gypsies on Dunlow Common. Having been 'so often told she was like a gypsy' by her mother, she naturally assumes that they will 'gladly receive her'. She even believes that they might make her their queen because of her book learning and 'superior knowledge'. However, once she reaches their shabby camp, 'a little semicircular black tent' pitched on the verge of a lane, her romantic 'picture of gypsy life' undergoes a dramatic reversal. Having had her pockets riffled, and observed the dirt and discomfort in which they live, Maggie begins to believe that 'they meant perhaps to kill her' and that the 'fierce-eyed' Gypsy patriarch is 'the devil' himself. This melodramatic reading of the Gypsies, in which the fairy tale of adoption collapses into an equally fantastical nightmare, is a product of Maggie's 'active imagination'.[101] In a bathetic conclusion, one of the Gypsies takes her home, hoping for half a crown.

Eliot's portrayal of a child's encounter with Gypsies is an exemplification of the argument made in her essay 'The Natural History of German Life' (1856): that the bourgeois mind is still 'under the influence of idyllic literature' and that as a consequence peasants – or in this case itinerants – are constantly misrepresented in artistic and literary works.[102] Maggie, although still a girl, possesses this mentality. Her 'picture of gypsy life' is a result of the same middle-class instincts that inform her resolve to teach 'the gypsies to use a washing-basin'.[103] It is even tempting to see this episode as a riposte to *Lavengro*, and to imagine that Borrow was one of the writers who Eliot deemed a pernicious influence on the public for idealising the poor.[104] After all, Maggie's belief that her literacy will prove a source of prestige, and her unfounded fear that the Gypsies mean to murder her, both belong to the reality of the boy Borrow. Whether Eliot knew *Lavengro* or not is a point of speculation, although it is a tantalising possibility given that she was familiar with his earlier work. During the three and a half years in which she researched and wrote her dramatic poem *The Spanish Gypsy* (1868), *The Zincali* became a key resource.[105] Later, she referred to it in *Middlemarch* (1871–2), describing the idiotic young Cranch as 'squinting, as if he did it with design, like the gypsies when Borrow read the New Testament to them'.[106] But to see Maggie's adventure as a realistic reworking of *Lavengro* risks misinterpreting Borrow, and misses the fact that these authors, at least to some extent, shared an aesthetic agenda.

The opening scenes of *Lavengro* establish a claim that runs throughout both of Borrow's autobiographies: that the romantic and picturesque ideal of itinerant life is essentially untrue. As he remarks in *The Romany Rye*, having recently adopted the tinkering trade: 'had I not better become in reality what I had hitherto been merely playing at – a tinker or a gypsy? But I soon saw that I was not fitted to become either in reality. It was much more agreeable to play the gypsy or the tinker than to become either in reality.'[107]

However, while Borrow contested the aesthetic standards by which his contemporaries measured the authenticity of Gypsies, he nonetheless subscribed to the same belief in extinction that was popularised in the periodical press. 'Gypsy law does not flourish at present in England', he mourned in *The Zincali*, 'nor does Gypsyism.'[108] Moreover, as in the articles published in *Sharpe's London Magazine* and the *Penny Magazine*, he believed that 'interbreeding' might actuate this destructive process. Although Borrow's Gypsies still 'rove about a distinct race' in *Lavengro* and *The Romany Rye*, there is also a 'mixed breed, called half and half', which are the product of the 'marriages and connections ... between gorgios and Romany chies'. It is the 'chies', or women, who safeguard the purity of the Gypsies and, as Borrow intimates through Jasper, also imperil it. 'Romany chies are Romany chies still, though not exactly what they were sixty years ago', observes the patriarch, 'if ever gypsyism breaks up, it will be owing to our chies.'[109] Borrow also evinces this belief in *The Zincali*. Discussing what he identifies as the second Gypsy law, 'Be faithful to *the husbands*', he comments: 'This was a very important injunction, so much so, indeed, that upon the observance of it depended the very existence of the Rommany sect, – for if the female Gypsy admitted the gorgio to the privilege of the Rom, the race of the Rommany would quickly disappear.'[110]

Racial theories of the kind that Borrow and his peers espoused about Gypsies became more pronounced within the discourse of vagrancy as the nineteenth century progressed, and began to impact the representation of several other vagrant types. Between 1830 and 1860, however, their sphere of influence was relatively limited, and in representations of rural 'vagabonds' they were absent. This is the case with the vagrant poacher, a figure who became particularly conspicuous in British print culture during the 1840s, and who is the subject of the next chapter.

Notes

1 [Charles Dickens], 'The Uncommercial Traveller', *All the Year Round*, 28 January 1860, pp. 321–6 (p. 321).

2 [Charles Dickens], 'The Uncommercial Traveller', *All the Year Round*, 16 June 1860, pp. 230–4 (pp. 230–4).

3 Ibid., p. 232.

4 G. E. Mingay, *Rural Life in Victorian England* (London: Heinemann, 1977), p. 178.

5 Ibid., pp. 176–7; David Mayall, *Gypsy-Travellers in Nineteenth Century Society* (Cambridge: Cambridge University Press, 1988), pp. 3, 46–9.

6 Mingay, *Rural Life*, p. 176.

7 Mayall, *Gypsy-Travellers*, p. 55; 'Yetholm, and the Scottish Gipsies', *Sharpe's London [Magazine]*, January 1851, pp. 321–5 (p. 322).

8 'Cheap Jack', *Chambers's [Edinburgh] Journal*, 10 October 1846, pp. 236–8 (p. 237).

9 Ruth Livesey, *Writing the Stage Coach Nation: Locality on the Move in Nineteenth-Century British Literature* (Oxford: Oxford University Press, 2016), pp. 14–15; Boyd Hilton, *A Mad, Bad, & Dangerous People?: England, 1783–1843* (Oxford: Oxford University Press, 2008), pp. 14–15, 131.

10 Hilton, *A Mad, Bad, & Dangerous People?*, p. 15.

11 Livesey, *Writing the Stage Coach Nation*, pp. 14–19.

12 Herbert L. Sussman, *Victorians and the Machine: The Literary Response to Technology* (Cambridge, MA: Harvard University Press, 1968), p. 10.

13 Mayall, *Gypsy-Travellers*, pp. 65–6.

14 Donna Landry, *The Invention of the Countryside: Hunting, Walking and Ecology in English Literature, 1671–1831* (Basingstoke: Palgrave, 2001), p. 94; Mingay, *Rural Life*, pp. 175–6.

15 Mayall, *Gypsy-Travellers*, p. 3.

16 Mingay, *Rural Life*, pp. 12–15; Raymond Williams, *The Country and the City* (London: Chatto & Windus, 1973), pp. 96–102; also see Landry, *The Invention of the Countryside*, pp. 78–9.

17 Williams, *The Country and the City*, pp. 101–2.

18 Mayall, *Gypsy-Travellers*, p. 20; Mingay, *Rural Life*, p. 15.

19 John Clare, *John Clare by Himself*, ed. Eric Robinson and David Powell (Ashington: Carcanet Press, 1996), p. 87.

20 5 Geo. 4, C. 83.

21 4 Will. 4, C. 50.

22 Mayall, *Gypsy-Travellers*, pp. 148, 153–4; George K. Behlmer, 'The Gypsy Problem in Victorian England', *Victorian Studies*, 28.2 (1985), 231–53 (pp. 235–7).

23 Mayall, *Gypsy-Travellers*, p. 155; also see Hilton, *A Mad, Bad, & Dangerous People?*, p. 607.

24 Mayall, *Gypsy-Travellers*, pp. 19, 66; Mingay, *Rural Life*, p. 177.

25 Mingay, *Rural Life*, pp. 19–21; Williams, *The Country and the City*, p. 188.

26 Jerry White, *London in the Nineteenth Century: A Human Awful Wonder of God* (London: Vintage, 2008), p. 68; Williams, *The Country and the City*, p. 152.

27 John Darwin, *The Empire Project: The Rise and Fall of the British World System, 1830–1970* (Cambridge: Cambridge University Press, 2009; repr. 2015), pp. 41–3.

28 Mayall, *Gypsy-Travellers*, p. 21. Also see David Cressy, *Gypsies: An English History* (Oxford: Oxford University Press, 2018; repr. 2020), pp. 204–7.

29 Charles Leland, *The Gypsies*, 4th ed. (Boston: Houghton, Mifflin, 1886), p. 229.

30 See Sarah Houghton-Walker, *Representations of the Gypsy in the Romantic Period* (Oxford: Oxford University Press, 2014); Deborah Epstein Nord, *Gypsies and the British Imagination, 1807–1930* (New York: Columbia University Press, 2006).

31 Mayall, *Gypsy-Travellers*, pp. 29–30; Cressy, *Gypsies*, p. 187.

32 Aileen Fyfe, *Steam-Powered Knowledge: William Chambers and the Business of Publishing, 1820–1860* (Chicago: University of Chicago Press, 2012), p. 21.

33 'The Tinkers of Scotland', *Penny Magazine*, 24 December 1836, pp. 502–3 (p. 502).

34 'The English Gypsies', *Penny Magazine*, 20 January 1838, pp. 17–19 (p. 18).

35 Christopher Kent, 'Introduction', in *British Literary Magazines: The Victorian and Edwardian Age, 1837–1913*, ed. Alvin Sullivan, 4 vols (Westport, CT: Greenwood Press, 1983–6), III, pp. xiii–xxvi (p. xv).

36 'Life among the Vagabonds', *Leisure Hour*, 16 December 1858, pp. 787–90 (p. 789).

37 'The Lame Pedlar, a Story', *Chambers's [Edinburgh] Journal*, 20 January 1838, pp. 411–12 (p. 411). Original emphasis.

38 'Life among the Vagabonds', p. 787.

39 A. L. Beier, *Masterless Men: The Vagrancy Problem in England, 1560–1640* (London: Methuen, 1985), p. 58.

40 Thomas Harman, *A Caveat or Warning for Common Cursetors, Vulgarly Called Vagabonds, Set fourth by Thomas Harman Esq. for the Utility and Profit of His Natural Country* (London: R. Triphook, 1814), pp. 25–6, 41–2.

41 Houghton-Walker, *Representations of the Gypsy*, pp. 18–20.

42 Quoted by David Mayall, *Gypsy Identities, 1500–2000: From Egipcyans and Moon-Men to the Ethnic Romany* (London: Routledge, 2004), p. 153.

43 Mayall, *Gypsy Identities*, pp. 152–3; Judith Okely, *The Traveller-Gypsies* (Cambridge: Cambridge University Press, 1983), pp. 1–13.

44 John Hoyland, *A Historical Survey of the Customs, Habits, and Present State of the Gypsies* (York, 1816), p. 154.

45 James Crabb, *The Gipsies' Advocate; or, Observations on the Origin, Character, Manner, and Habits of the English Gipsies*, 2nd ed. (London: Lindsay, 1831), pp. 10, 14.

46 Nord, *Gypsies and the British Imagination*, p. 8.

47 'The English Gypsies', p. 19; 'The Gipsies', *London Saturday Journal*, 12 June 1841, pp. 277–9 (p. 278); 'Gatherings about Gipsies', *Reynolds's Miscellany*, 17 June 1848, pp. 509–10 (p. 509).

48 William Howitt, *The Rural Life of England*, 2 vols (London: Longman, Orme, Brown, Green & Longmans, 1838), I, pp. 219–33.

49 Matthew Beaumont, *Nightwalking: A Nocturnal History of London, Chaucer to Dickens* (London: Verso, 2015), p. 240; also see Landry, *The Invention of the Countryside*, pp. 16–21; Nord, *Gypsies and the British Imagination*, pp. 5–7.

50 [Anon.] J.P.P.C., 'The Norwood Gypsies', *Literary Lounger*, February 1826, pp. 88–96 (p. 88); W. Paul Elledge, 'The New Monthly Magazine', in *British Literary Magazines: The Romantic Age, 1789–1836*, ed. Alvin Sullivan, 4 vols (Westport, CT: Greenwood Press, 1983–6), II, pp. 331–9; Helen B. Ellis, 'The London Magazine', in *British Literary Magazines: The Romantic Age, 1789–1836*, ed. Alvin Sullivan, 4 vols (Westport, CT: Greenwood Press, 1983–6), II, pp. 288–96.

51 Jerry White, *London in the Eighteenth Century: A Great and Monstrous Thing* (London: Bodley Head, 2012), p. 144.

52 Mayall, *Gypsy-Travellers*, pp. 154–5.

53 'The Norwood Gypsies', p. 90.

54 Ibid., p. 92.

55 In 'London Draymen' (1841) the *London Saturday Journal* characterised the draymen of the brewer's Barclay and Perkins as particularly powerful: 'we went over the great establishment of Barclay, Perkins, and Co.; and certainly, while we saw much to wonder at, and much to admire, we reserved some of our admiration for the draymen ... Every thing connected with this most wonderful brewery is "stupendous" – stupendous buildings, stupendous vats,

stupendous binns, stupendous stores, stupendous horses, and stupendous Draymen.' 'London Draymen', *London Saturday Journal*, 24 April 1841, pp. 193–4 (p. 194).

56 'The Gipsies', p. 278.

57 'The English Gypsies', p. 17.

58 Ibid., pp. 18–19.

59 Patrick Brantlinger, *Dark Vanishings: Discourse on the Extinction of Primitive Races, 1800–1930* (Ithaca, NY: Cornell University Press, 2003), p. 61.

60 Cressy, *Gypsies*, p. 267.

61 'Gipsies', *Sharpe's London Magazine*, July 1848, pp. 169–72 (pp. 170–1).

62 George Eliot, *Adam Bede*, ed. Margaret Reynolds (London: Penguin, 2008), p. 559.

63 Edric Hewson, 'Larry Lee the Pedlar', *Sharpe's London Magazine*, January 1857, pp. 231–8 (p. 231).

64 It sold 200,000 copies in its first few weeks. Melissa Valiska and Melisa Klimaszewski, 'Introduction', in *Doctor Marigold's Prescriptions*, ed. Melissa Valiska and Melisa Klimaszewski (London: Hesperus Press, 2007), pp. xi–xvi (p. xi).

65 Charles Dickens, *Doctor Marigold's Prescriptions*, ed. Melissa Valiska and Melisa Klimaszewski (London: Hesperus Press, 2007), p. 15.

66 Nord, *Gypsies and the British Imagination*, p. 6.

67 Okely, *The Traveller-Gypsies*, p. 10.

68 Fyfe, *Steam-Powered Knowledge*, pp. 21–4.

69 'The Umbrella Pedler', *Chambers's [Edinburgh] Journal*, 16 August 1851, pp. 102–4 (p. 102).

70 'Literary "Packmen"', *Leisure Hour*, 5 April 1860, pp. 212–14 (p. 212).

71 'Literary "Packmen"', pp. 213–14.

72 Robert Heron quoted by Celeste Langan in *Romantic Vagrancy: Wordsworth and the Simulation of Freedom* (Cambridge: Cambridge University Press, 1995; repr. 2006), p. 256. On Heron's influence on Wordsworth, see ibid., pp. 256–8.

73 Behlmer, 'The Gypsy Problem', pp. 239–43; Mayall, *Gypsy Identities*, pp. 156–62; Okely, *The Traveller-Gypsies*, pp. 7–8.

74 George Borrow, *The Zincali: An Account of the Gypsies of Spain*, 9th ed. (London: John Murray, 1901; repr. 1907), pp. 316, 32.

75 George Borrow, *Romano Lavo-Lil: Word-Book of the Romany* (London: John Murray, 1874), p. 314.

76 George Borrow, *George Borrow's Tour of Galloway and the Borders 1866*, ed. Angus Fraser (Wallingford: Lavengro Press, 2015), pp. 11, 16, 29.

77 George Borrow, *Wild Wales: Its People, Language and Scenery* (London: Collins, 1965), pp. 78, 479.

78 Borrow, *The Zincali*, p. 11.

79 George Borrow, *The Bible in Spain; or, The Journeys, Adventures, and Imprisonments of an Englishman in an Attempt to Circulate the Scriptures in the Peninsula*, ed. Ulick Ralph Burke (London: John Murray, 1905; repr. 1928), p. 16.

80 Michael Collie, *George Borrow: Eccentric* (Cambridge: Cambridge University Press, 1982), pp. 179–83, 209–10; David Williams, *A World of His Own: The Double Life of George Borrow* (Oxford: Oxford University Press, 1982), p. ix.

81 Ann M. Ridler, *George Borrow as a Linguist: Images and Contexts* (Wallingford: A. M. Ridler, 1996), p. 413; also see Monika Mazurek, 'George Borrow: The Scholar, the Gipsy, the Priest', in *Victorian Fiction beyond the Canon*, ed. Daragh Downes and Trish Ferguson (London: Palgrave Macmillan, 2016), pp. 71–86 (pp. 73–4).

82 Collie, *George Borrow*, pp. 196–7; 'Lavengro: The Scholar – The Gypsy – The Priest', *Athenaeum*, 8 Februrary 1851, pp. 159–60 (p. 159).

83 'Lavengro – "The Master of Words"', *Fraser's Magazine*, March 1851, pp. 272–83 (p. 280); 'Borrow and Lavengro', *New Monthly Magazine*, April 1851, pp. 455–61 (p. 455).

84 Ian Duncan, 'Wild England: George Borrow's Nomadology', *Victorian Studies*, 41.3 (1998), 381–403 (p. 391); Houghton-Walker, *Representations of the Gypsy*, pp. 12–13; Mazurek, 'George Borrow', p. 75.

85 George Borrow, *The Romany Rye* (London: Heron Books, 1970), pp. 38–9.

86 Ibid., pp. 145–6.

87 Nord, *Gypsies and the British Imagination*, pp. 93–5.

88 George Borrow, *Lavengro* (London: Heron Books, 1969), p. 13. Further references to *Lavengro* will be made to this edition and in the text.

89 Matthew Arnold, *Sohrab and Rustum*, in *The Poems of Matthew Arnold*, ed. Miriam Allott, 2nd ed. (London: Longman, 1979) pp. 319–55 (ll. 100–1).

90 William Wordsworth, 'Resolution and Independence', in *The Major Works*, ed. Stephen Gill (Oxford: Oxford University Press, 2011), pp. 260–4 (ll. 110–11).

91 Ibid., ll. 131–2.

92 Duncan, 'Wild England', p. 391; George Hyde, 'Borrow and the Vanity of Dogmatising: "Lavengro" as Self-Portrait', *Cambridge Quarterly*, 32.2 (2003), 161–73 (p. 164).

93 John Thomas Smith, *Vagabondiana; or, Anecdotes of Mendicant Wanderers through the Streets of London: With Portraits of the Most Remarkable, Drawn from the Life by John Thomas Smith, Keeper of the Prints in the British Museum* (London, 1817), p. 44.

94 White, *London in the Nineteenth Century*, pp. 67–77.

95 H. C. Darby, *The Draining of the Fens* (Cambridge: Cambridge University Press, 1956; repr. 1968), p. 242.

96 'The Fens of England', *Chambers's [Edinburgh] Journal*, 18 November 1854, pp. 321–4 (pp. 321–2).

97 Kevin A. Morrison, 'Foregrounding Nationalism: Mary Russell Mitford's *Our Village* and the Effects of Publication Context', *European Romantic Review*, 19.3 (2008), 275–87 (p. 276).

98 Mary Russell Mitford, 'The Old Gipsy', in *Our Village: Sketches of Rural Character and Scenery*, 2 vols (London: George Bell, 1876), I, pp. 436–44 (p. 438).

99 Houghton-Walker, *Representations of the Gypsy*, pp. 41–4.
100 Mitford, 'The Old Gipsy', p. 438.
101 George Eliot, *The Mill on the Floss*, ed. A. S. Byatt (London: Penguin, 2003), pp. 112–20.
102 George Eliot, 'The Natural History of German Life', in *Selected Essays, Poems and Other Writings*, ed. A. S. Byatt (London: Penguin, 1990), pp. 107–39 (p. 109).
103 Eliot, *The Mill on the Floss*, p. 116.
104 Eliot, 'The Natural History of German Life', pp. 110–11.
105 Nord, *Gypsies and the British Imagination*, p. 121; Rosemary Ashton, *George Eliot: A Life* (London: Hamish Hamilton, 1996), p. 292.
106 George Eliot, *Middlemarch: A Study of Provincial Life*, ed. Rosemary Ashton (London: Penguin, 1994; repr. 2003), p. 305. On the origin of this reference, see Ann M. Ridler, 'George Eliot and George Borrow – A Note on Middlemarch', *George Eliot – George Henry Lewes Newsletter*, 5 (1984), 3–4.
107 Borrow, *The Romany Rye*, p. 83.
108 Borrow, *The Zincali*, p. 27.
109 Borrow, *The Romany Rye*, pp. 58, 68, 79.
110 Borrow, *The Zincali*, pp. 27–8. Original emphasis.

CHAPTER 2

Poachers

Mary Russell Mitford's 'The Old Gipsy' first appeared in the *Monthly Magazine*, a periodical that specialised in short fiction.[1] It was one of two stories published in January and February 1826, both of which dealt with the same Gypsy encampment. Where the first number related the antics of a sly 'old crone', its sequel – 'The Young Gipsy' – turned to the matriarch's granddaughter – 'pretty black-eyed' Fanny. Full of sororal concern for her younger brother, Fanny is eager to 'have a house over him in the cold winter nights' and sets about finding employment for him in the village. She eventually places him with the upright Thomas Lamb, 'my lord's head gamekeeper', who is responsible for protecting the pheasants, hares and partridges that live on his master's estate. However, these official duties are neglected after he falls in love with Fanny and begins to overlook the nightly predations of her other brother, Dick, who ransacks his coveys. This sign of the keeper's infatuation becomes the cause of gentle mirth at the end of the tale when Lamb petitions the magistrate for 'a summons for some poachers': 'how can you expect', quips the gleeful magistrate, 'to keep your pheasants, when that gipsy boy with his finders [dogs] has pitched his tent just in the midst of your best coppices?'[2]

The figure of the poaching Gypsy would have been familiar to Mitford's readers. During the eighteenth century Gypsies had become strongly associated with poaching, so much so that being caught in their company could lead to accusations of night poaching, a crime punishable by transportation.[3] Such assumptions were maintained in the nineteenth century. Writing in the mid-Victorian period, the journalist and naturalist Richard Jefferies recorded the cat-and-dog life led by Gypsies and gamekeepers. In *The Gamekeeper at Home* (1878), a collection of essays detailing the delicate ecosystem of the preserves, and the woodcraft needed to sustain them, he captures the frustrations that keepers experienced while trying to patrol their estates:

> The gipsies, who travel the road in caravans, give him endless trouble; they are adepts at poaching, and each van is usually accompanied by a couple of

dogs. The movements of these people are so irregular that it is impossible to be always ready for them.. . . . Under pretence of cutting skewer-wood, often called dog-wood, which they split and sharpen for the butchers, they wander across the open downs where it grows, camping in wild, unfrequented places, and finding plenty of opportunities for poaching.[4]

Of course, Gypsies were not the only ones who found such opportunities. Poaching was practised extensively among settled and itinerant populations because hunting was the exclusive privilege of the landowning elite. Under the 1671 Game Act only those with a property worth £100 per year, or those who held a ninety-nine-year lease property worth £150 per year, had the right to kill game. This statute, which remained in force until the 1831 Game Law Bill, excluded all but 0.5 per cent of the population from the sport. After 1831 the property qualification was replaced by a game certificate, priced at a relatively moderate £3 13s. 6d.; this was intended to enable more (middle-class) sportsmen to enjoy the legitimate chase. However, it was largely ineffective because the certificate holder could hunt only with the landowners' consent. Jealous of their woods and warrens, landlords acted as a bulwark to the democratising aims of the act, denying even their tenant farmers permission to kill the game that fed on their crops.[5] Moreover, the landowners' power over game intensified as the nineteenth century progressed. Throughout the century there was a general tendency towards the consolidation of land and the creation of larger farms. This meant that by 1873, when the rural population was ten million, 50 per cent of the land was owned by 7,000 people.[6] Such inequality in land ownership, and therefore access to game, sustained the widespread poaching that was endemic in nineteenth-century England. As the union leader Joseph Arch wrote, recalling Warwickshire in the 1830s, 'it was hardly an exaggeration to say that every other man you met was a poacher'.[7]

'Poaching was a national pastime', as Donna Landry observes, but the reasons for it varied.[8] Some poached for pleasure: poaching, after all, is hunting by another name. Others were politically motivated. James Hawker was a lifelong poacher from the 1840s onwards: he recorded, 'I have poached more for Revenge than Gain. Because the [game preserving] Class poached upon my liberty when I was not able to defend myself.'[9] The historian Harry Hopkins remarks that 'bred-in-the-bone, do-it-yourself radicals', like Hawker, formed a particularly resilient poaching class.[10] The majority, however, poached as a cure for hunger and to supplement inadequate diets. A spike in the number of poaching convictions often accompanied national food shortages, and, more generally, game provided an important source of protein for working people, the majority of whom could not afford farmed meat until it became readily available in the mid-1880s.[11] In a similar vein, poaching could also provide an additional revenue stream. There had long been a thriving trade in poached game that continued throughout the nineteenth century, even after the sale of game was made legal in 1831. Centred on London's Newgate and Leadenhall Street, this black market had once been exclusively served by itinerants. 'Higglers', hedge-side pedlars who nominally traded in poultry and dairy, bought game in the country to hawk in the city, and Gypsies were always 'suspected of being recipients of poached game'.[12] Like the other itinerant trades discussed in Chapter 1, this monopoly was broken by the advent of the stagecoach and the railways, whose employees acquired a significant share in the business. Nonetheless, while the coachman was eventually replaced by the engine driver, higglers continued to participate in this illicit economy.[13]

The association between poachers and these vagrants preoccupied law-makers. Higglers were prohibited from purchasing the £2 licence required to deal legally in game by the 1831 bill, and they were one of the itinerant groups specifically targeted by the 1835 Highways Act.[14] Officials sought to legislate vagrant receivers out of business. But the connection between the vagrant and the poacher was not simply transactional. At a fundamental level, these two figures were perceived as cognate, something which has already been suggested by the enduring link made between Gypsies and poachers. When trying to identify poachers, authorities often suspected migrants, including harvesters and itinerant handicraft men, such as mole-catchers.[15] Moreover, once they had caught them, poachers were conflated with vagrants within the legal system. Both were subject to summary justice, and the majority of poaching cases would have been addressed in the magistrates' court, a space in which the distinctions between the poacher, vagrant, trespasser and mendicant could all begin to blur. As Timothy Shakesheff notes, if a poaching offence could not be proved, then suspects were often convicted for trespassing instead.[16] Given the catch-all nature of the vagrancy laws, it seems likely that these were also used to force successful prosecutions. Meanwhile, even if a poacher was referred to the assizes court for a more serious offence, like night poaching, the vagrant could still emerge as their legal double. Those convicted under the 1800 Night Poaching Act could be punished under the pre-1824 vagrancy laws as incorrigible rogues, the sentence for which was two years' hard labour or transportation; the 1828 Night Poaching Act, which remained in force until the end of the century, also carried these penalties.[17]

The legal kinship between the vagrant and the poacher was not without justification; professional poachers possessed many vagrant qualities. To a greater or lesser extent, those who poached regularly were on the move. Local preserves had a limited amount of game and might be guarded by armed keepers entrusted with the power of arrest. As a consequence, poachers would travel great distances to secure a larger or safer haul. In 1828, for example, John Smith and William Morris, two Herefordshire labourers, were discovered poaching twenty-three miles from their homes.[18] In the pre-railway era this was a considerable distance; internal migrants, resettling elsewhere in the country, typically travelled less than thirty miles.[19] Moreover, it is unlikely that two labourers would have journeyed by stagecoach, a relatively expensive mode of transport. They would probably have tramped.

Poachers were also sometimes compelled to take to the road. Although Hawker claims that he sometimes became vagrant by choice, giving up his factory job in Leicester to 'Have a Ramble', he also notes that a fine levied for poaching, or an outstanding warrant for his arrest, sometimes forced him to flee: 'often it was Game what Drove me from my Home', he admits.[20] Jefferies also records a vagrant type among the 'three kinds of poachers' that he catalogues in *The Gamekeeper at Home*; the so-called mouchers who 'loiter along the roads and hedges picking up whatever they can lay hands on'.[21] Although he quickly dismisses them here, he gives a more detailed and sympathetic account of these outcast figures in his collection of essays, *The Amateur Poacher* (1879). Here he describes the moucher as a homeless figure who lingers on roadsides and on the outskirts of suburbs. He 'sleeps on the heaps of disused tan' by the river, or else 'sleeps in some shed or under a straw-rick.' If the weather gets too severe, then the constable arrests him, but only for his own good: 'in sheer pity he is committed every now and then to prison for vagabondage – not for punishment, but in order to save him from himself'.[22] Confined under the vagrancy laws, sleeping in the open and relying on his woodcraft to filch what he can, the moucher is a type we will meet again in a literary context.

The literary poacher, whether vagrant or otherwise, has been neglected by critics. While historians like Hopkins, David Jones and Harvey Osborne have asserted the prevalence and importance of poaching in the nineteenth century, discussions regarding the representation of poachers has been limited to a few chance observations. Landry, for example, observes that 'the literary poacher of the nineteenth century was more romantic' than its eighteenth-century predecessors, while Shakesheff argues that the Victorian poacher was portrayed as an idle drunkard.[23]

Both of these views have their place, but they oversimplify a complex and deeply contested figure. As Hawker's testimony reveals, poaching in the nineteenth century could be a deliberately political act. This had historical precedent: in her survey of hunting from 1066 to the twenty-first century, Emma Griffin records that poachers in the early modern period decapitated and disembowelled deer as acts of protest; that during the English Civil War (1642–51), deer were again slaughtered in defiance of the king; and that in the early eighteenth century, deer were once more targeted by political dissidents in Windsor Forest.[24] These were poached and mutilated in an atmosphere of 'Robin Hoodery', as Hopkins notes.[25] By the nineteenth century, then, poaching was politically charged and aligned with radicalism. What made poachers even more threatening was the fact that they were committing a 'social crime': an illegal act that was deemed a crime by the state but not by the local community where it was performed.[26] As a consequence, the perpetrators of these offences accrued popular support and protection from their neighbours. This heightened what was at stake when condemning poachers in print, or else turned them into sympathetic figures that could be exploited by radical authors. It is within this context that this chapter will explore the relationship between poaching and vagrancy in early Victorian literature.

Although the majority of nineteenth-century poachers were not vagrant, a significant number of literary poachers are. In this chapter I argue that the reasons for this were political. Writers of pro-establishment morality tales, like Hannah More and John Nicholson, emphasised the immorality of poaching and its potential to become a 'gateway' crime to capital offences. In these texts vagrancy becomes a sign of the poacher's dissipation and social alienation. Meanwhile, radical writers co-opted the poacher for their own ends. Authors such as Charles Dickens and Charles Kingsley used the vagrant poacher to condemn permissive laws, which included the vagrancy and game laws, and to highlight social inequalities. Often deploying the techniques of melodrama in which the oppressed and impoverished are pitted against the powerful and malign, these texts depict vagrant poachers as the victims of unjust magistrates, the representatives of an arbitrary legal system.

In both pro-establishment and radical texts, poachers were always represented as male. This is unsurprising given that poaching was considered a 'male crime' and that officials therefore tended to treat poaching offences committed by women as singular and inexplicable events. This clouds the fact that women were active in the poaching industry, particularly in the transportation and snaring of game.[27] In his autobiography,

I Walked by Night (1935), the notorious poacher Frederick Rolfe recalled that his first (unnamed) wife accompanied him on his midnight expeditions during the 1880s. 'Many and many a night she came out with me, for she was no hindrance to the game.... Many a hare have she carried under her coat for me, and many a Phesant.'[28] The activity of such female poachers, however, went unrecognised in literary texts. Instead, women were portrayed exclusively as passive wives or widows and as the victims of either the poacher's vice or the law's iniquity. They also sometimes suffered the poacher's fate and became vagrant outcasts, a condition that was freighted for them with physical, moral and sexual danger.

2.1 The Poacher's Progress

Hannah More's pamphlet *Black Giles, the Poacher* (1796) is an important antecedent to the anti-poaching morality tales of the nineteenth century. It is one of the 114 texts that form the *Cheap Repository* (1795–8), a collection of songs, allegories and tales that were organised and edited by More for the moral improvement of the poor. Modelled on popular literary forms like the broadside ballad and the chap-book, and priced within the means of working families (between ½ and 1½d. per instalment), the *Cheap Repository* sought to instruct, entertain and uphold the values of the Church and the Crown. As More's biographer Charles Howard Ford comments, one of the *Cheap Repository*'s aims was to counter 'the critiques of monarchy and aristocracy by radical reformers'.[29]

Published in two parts in 1796, *Black Giles* was part of this general programme, but the tale was also a response to an annual issue. Poaching crimes occurred year on year, but they tended to be concentrated between October and March. In part, this was because winter was a period when employment opportunities were scarce and household expenditure on food, fuel and clothing increased. Labourers therefore poached for the pot and to earn an extra income.[30] In addition, it was also because game was in season during these months. As Osborne has convincingly argued, it was *natural* rather than *economic* rhythms that primarily determined the pattern of offending.[31] Such a predictable cycle no doubt influenced the publication of *Black Giles* in November and December, a time when poaching would have been conspicuous among working communities, many of which shielded their poachers from inquisitive officials. But More's morality tale also engages with an immediate concern – the surge in violent affrays between armed poaching gangs and gamekeepers that occurred during the 1790s. A period of bad harvests and economic hardships, the Napoleonic era saw an intensification in the number of raids made on the nation's game preserves.[32] Given the recent revolution in France and the ensuing Reign of Terror, such blatant defiance of the land-owning elite seemed like a possible prelude to revolution.[33] As a staunch advocate of the established order, More was eager to discourage this opposition.[34]

The titular poacher in *Black Giles* is a social outlaw. This is signalled at the beginning of the first instalment when the reader is introduced to Giles and his 'vagrant family', squatting in a 'mud cottage, with broken windows' on a moorland 'common'. The children earn a living by begging at the wayside while Tawney Rachel, his wife, travels 'about the country telling fortunes'. Here we see the connection between Gypsies and poaching again. Although Rachel is never explicitly identified as a Gypsy, her occupation and her epithet evoke long-standing stereotypes about the business and complexion of female Gypsies.[35] The family's vagrant status places them physically and socially outside the village community and is an attribute that allows More to construct Giles as an indiscriminate predator. His theft of the poor Widow Brown's apple crop, which she relies on as a safeguard from poverty, is the main evidence of this.[36] Far from being the harmless perpetrator of a 'social crime', this poacher is a criminal outsider who targets the vulnerable.

More clearly articulates this view through the righteous parson-magistrate, Mr Wilson. Described as 'not only a pious clergyman, but an upright justice', Wilson condemns poaching on moral grounds, and in doing so upholds the rights of the landed elite. In the midst of sentencing the poacher Jack Weston, an 'honest fellow' who has gone astray, he reiterates the narrator's earlier claim that 'there is hardly any petty mischief that is not connected with the life of a poacher'. Preaching from the bench, he warns Weston that 'poaching is a regular apprenticeship to bolder crimes. He whom I may commit as a boy to sit in the stocks for killing a partridge, may be likely to end at the gallows for killing a man.'[37] Wilson supports the national hierarchy and the paternalistic ethos that orders it. As a parson and a magistrate, and therefore a representative of church and state, he embodies the two institutions that claimed to guard and guide the populace. This is further demonstrated by his attempts to reclaim Giles's son, Dick. Throughout the narrative, Wilson, the spiritual father, wrestles for Dick's obedience with Giles, the boy's biological father, and in the end proves victorious when Dick publicly confesses that he helped his father to rob Widow Brown. This display of repentance is a vindication of the parson and his politics. Meanwhile, Giles is radically depoliticised.

'Black' is a significant epithet in the history of poaching. In the early 1720s a gang of poachers with blackened faces began to mutilate the deer in Waltham Chase and Farnham Park at a time when Sir Jonathan Trelawny, the Bishop of Winchester, was trying to replenish the herds. Their motives were political: the extensive forests that deer require occupied valuable land that could be used to feed and enrich ordinary labourers. The bishop's attempt to breed deer, most of which had been killed during the English Civil War, was therefore seen as an act of impoverishment. The gang became known as the 'Waltham Blacks', and other groups, such as the 'Berkshire Blacks', followed their example.[38] The result was the passage of the infamous 1723 Black Act, named after them, which wrote over 200 capital offences into law: the first of these was to be armed and near game with a blackened face.[39] This act was still in force when More was writing, and the political significance of being a blackened poacher must have lingered on. Even in the late nineteenth century there was a notorious poaching gang called the 'Isleham Blacks' who operated in East Anglia.[40] However, when More describes Giles as 'Black' she obscures the epithet's political significance by using it as an emblem of depravity.

As we might expect, More's morality tale ends in just deserts. Giles crushes himself beneath the loose rubble of a wall while attempting to steal a net that lies on top of it. When Wilson arrives, Giles is mortally wounded and confesses his crimes. However, as the stern narrator informs us, 'people cannot repent when they will', and his salvation is far from assured. In the meantime, Wilson has reclaimed Dick. At the end of the story there is every hope that he will 'leave off his vagabond life', as the parson-magistrate suggests, and become a member of the settled community.[41]

Several elements of More's tale became the stock-in-trade of the nineteenth-century 'poacher's progress', an overlooked version of the morality tale that charts the moral, physical and material decline of the poacher and terminates in a judicial sentence or death. These texts similarly portray poaching in ethical rather than political terms, and in doing so emphasise the principal message of *Black Giles*: that 'poaching is a regular apprenticeship to bolder crimes'. Vagrancy is also a central theme in these texts. As in *Black Giles*, it is a sign of the poacher's outcast status, but it also signals a key moment of dislocation when the poacher ceases to be part of settled society. Unlike More's text, the poacher's progress typically begins by representing the poacher as part of a community, and narrates his estrangement from it. In addition, it tends to be written as much to entertain as to instruct. Perhaps as a consequence, while these texts depict the corrupt poacher, they do not offer a moral pattern in the form of a Mr Wilson.

John Nicholson's narrative poem *The Poacher: A Tale from Real Life* was another timely response to widespread concerns about poaching. Published in 1825 along with his most famous poem, *Airedale in Ancient Times*, it appeared during an agricultural depression that lasted from 1822 until the Swing Riots of 1830.[42] Like most periods of economic hardship, it was accompanied by a surge in poaching activity and a spate of debates about it. Parliament discussed the ethics of mantraps and spring-guns, which had been widely deployed to protect the preserves (they were banned in 1827).[43] Meanwhile, the poaching ballad underwent a revival, and songs such as 'Van Diemen's Land' (c. 1828) enjoyed a wide circulation.[44] These broadsides offered a romantic vision of poaching. As James Hepburn notes, in more than fifty ballads composed on this theme during the nineteenth century, all of them were 'preoccupied with the melodrama or daring of the activity'.[45] The opening lines of 'Van Diemen's Land' provide an instance of this: 'Come all you gallant poachers, that ramble void of care, / That walk out on a moonlight night with your dogs and gun and snare.'[46] It is tempting to see Nicholson's poem, written in the mock-epic form, as a riposte to such heroics.

From the first lines of *The Poacher* it is clear that it will contain little in the way of gallantry. Shunning that traditional opening feature of epic, the invocation of the muse, the speaker declares:

> This subject wants no Muse the breast t'inspire,
> Deep learning, – nor the Apollonian lyre;
> Fine tropes and figures here can nought avail,
> 'Tis but a plain and simple rustic tale, –
> A tale of poachers, partridge, grouse, and hares,
> Gamekeepers' acts, their dangers and their fears;
> And who the persons that are most too blame,
> Or those who buy, or those who steal the game.

The speaker then embarks on the history of the 'Prince of Poachers', a man whose name – Ignotus, meaning 'unknown' – ironises his elevated status. Ignotus begins his career killing rabbits, and when 'his parents chide him not ... but praise his skill', goes on to hunt partridges and pheasants. It is not long before the amateur becomes a professional and, recalling Shakesheff's observation, a drunkard as well. Like the ballads, *The Poacher* also contains scenes of conflict between poachers and game-keepers, their 'superior foes'; but any valiant action on the part of 'strong Ignotus' is undermined by his neglected wife and children, whose poverty provides a tragic backdrop to the poem. As he wades further into sinful courses, his wife dies from starvation, and Ignotus becomes a vagrant roaming through Yorkshire:

> Loos'd from his wife, with whom he jarring liv'd,
> His children bread thro' charity receiv'd.
> One night he spent where lies fam'd Robin Hood,
> The next where Harewood's ancient castle stood;
> The beauteous vale of Wharf he wander'd o'er, –
> Expecting wealth, but still was always poor.

The distances that Ignotus travels here are significant; Kirklees Park, which claims the grave of Robin Hood, is some twenty miles from Harewood's castle. Ignotus's extensive wandering, and his abandonment of his children, signal that he has reached the nadir of his dissipation. His vagrancy marks his divorce from all familial, social and geographic ties. For Nicholson it is the last stage of the poacher's progress before death sweeps him away. Drunk one winter night while carrying his 'pilfer'd load', he steps onto some river-ice and falls into the water.[47] Sadly, Nicholson met a similar fate. An alcoholic in his fifties, he took a drunken tumble into the River Aire, and soon died from exposure.[48]

Nicholson was a staunch royalist and was writing for patronage. After the publication of *Airedale in Ancient Times*, he tried to earn his living by peddling pamphlets of his poems to the squires and gentlemen of Yorkshire.[49] With this customer base in mind, it is no surprise that he condemned the 'rustic plunderers, who sport by night, / And fearlessly invade another's right'.[50] Indeed, this is the audience that the poacher's progress tends to address. While More tried to warn labourers away from the evils of poaching, later narratives are not driven by the same moral impetus. This can be seen in Edmund Phipps's 'The Poacher's Progress' (1841). Like Nicholson's poem, the narrative relates the moral decline of a poacher. Addis, a Herefordshire labourer, falls into poaching by slow degrees and gives up 'honest industry for idleness and debauchery'; the theme of drunkenness recurs. Having become a 'determined poacher', he then becomes a thief and is imprisoned for stealing some chickens. While he serves his sentence, his wife dies and his children are taken in by 'some humane ladies'. After his release, Addis is ostracised by his village and forced to become a vagrant. 'He was driven to the most wretched expedients, and would then be absent for months from his native village, dark whisperings being current that at those times he was associated with gangs of gipsies and others, committing depredations through the country at large.' Once more, vagrancy is a staging post on the road to dissolution, serving as a sign of moral laxity. In the end, Addis reaches his lowest depths when he is arrested and sentenced to death for murdering a gamekeeper. Phipps concludes with a moral exhortation addressed to the 'Peasants of England': 'avoid poaching as ye value your temporal and eternal happiness'.[51] However, given that this warning was printed in the *New Monthly Magazine*, an expensive periodical then priced at 3s. 6d., it was unlikely to carry much reformative power.[52]

'The Poacher' (1841), written by the anonymous N.W. as a two-part serial for the *New Sporting Magazine*, is also addressed to a wealthy readership. Although it uses the same structure as the narratives by Nicholson and Phipps, 'The Poacher' is less dour, and both instalments revel in Tom Scott's skill as he dodges the gentry in both the field and the courtroom. The first number recounts a trial in which Tom, a seasoned hedge-lawyer, 'pull[s] out a little dirty book, which turned out to be the new [game] act', in order to overturn the magistrates' conviction; and the second recalls a poaching affray in which a friend of the narrator finds himself locked in combat with the redoubtable Tom.[53] However, having celebrated Tom's fighting spirit in the second number, the narrative nonetheless ends on a condemnatory note as the humorous anecdotes give way to a truncated poacher's progress. Confined to the final page, the narrator informs us that Tom absconded from his village and 'went a gipsying' before being arrested for theft, and sentenced to transportation for life. Like the other progress narratives, then, 'The Poacher' eventually emphasises that poaching leads to more serious crimes. As the narrator observes in the final paragraph, 'there is no question that poaching leads to theft, and that he who goes out by night to fill his pockets with game, will fill them with other things if that fails'.[54] Nonetheless, although 'The Poacher' concludes with this familiar moral, it is still delayed and subordinated to the reader's enjoyment. This indicates that the nineteenth-century poacher was not just a cautionary figure, but could also be attractive, exciting and, as Landry notes, romantic.

It is significant that N.W.'s 'The Poacher' and Phipps's 'The Poacher's Progress' appeared in 1841, the start of the so-called Hungry Forties. This was a decade in which poaching and the game laws re-emerged as an issue of contention. In 1839 John Bright and Richard Cobden established the Anti-Corn Law League, a radical political faction that sought the abolition of the corn laws, which prohibited the importation of foreign grain and therefore kept the price of bread artificially high. The game laws were another of their targets for reform. They argued that by laying out land in preservations, and not allowing tenants to kill the game that damaged their crops, the land-owning elite were actively reducing the stock of wheat that could be turned into bread, which further inflated its price.[55] More generally, the suitability of the 1831 Game Law Bill was also being questioned at this time. Although the bill was designed to reduce the number of poaching offences, in fact they were rapidly rising. Between 1831 and 1844 the annual number of successful prosecutions had doubled, reaching 4,500.[56] Pamela Horn puts this growth into perspective: she notes that during 1843 at least a quarter of the summary convictions made by the magistrates of Bedfordshire, Berkshire, Buckinghamshire, Herefordshire, Oxfordshire, Rutland and Wiltshire were executed under the game laws.[57] But it was not just that the conviction rate was rising. There were also fears about the mounting violence of the affrays between heavily armed poachers and keepers: forty-one gamekeepers were murdered between 1833 and 1843.[58] It is therefore not surprising that the poacher's progress should have re-emerged as a narrative tradition or that an abridged version of Nicholson's poem was printed in the *Mirror of Literature* in January 1845.[59]

That said, despite the violence and criminality that some writers attached to poachers, they were nonetheless ambivalent figures. Remembering 'the dark days of protection', Hawker gives a vivid sense of what the 1840s were like for labouring communities:

> The mid-1840s were wretched times. Sheep Stealing, Highway Robbery and Burglary were common. It was not Safe to go out after Dark. If a Man stole a Sheep he Had 14 years Transportation. If hunger made a man go into the woods to get a pheasant, he too would get fourteen years. Two men in Oadby Had 14 years – Jack Baurn, Bill Devonport – for attempting to take Pheasants in Tugley Wood, in 1847, so this is No Dream.[60]

The indignation evident in Hawker's account of Baurn and Devonport was felt by many writers during this period. Charles Dickens, Charlton Carew and Charles Kingsley all shared Hawker's sympathy for the poacher. Far from being a villainous renegade, the poacher, in their eyes, was a victim of the legislature. The laws that provoked particular contempt were those that seemed to punish poverty – the New Poor Law, the game laws and the vagrancy laws. During the 1840s, the poacher became a symbol of their injustice, and his vagrancy took on a new set of meanings. Instead of signalling his immorality and the selfish rejection of his duties, it began to be interpreted as a symptom of society's failings, and the inefficacy of the laws that governed it.

2.2   Radicalism, Poaching and *The Chimes*

During October 1844 a steady stream of letters issued from the Peschiere, a sixteenth-century palazzo in Genoa where Dickens was at work on *The Chimes* (1844). Principally addressed to John Forster, his friend and literary agent, these capture the violent energy with which he wrote. Possessed by a 'fierce writing humour', he would take up his pen early in the morning and 'blaze away, wrathful and red-hot' until three o'clock in the afternoon. The immediacy with which Dickens described the writing process reflected an urgent need to see his story published. In part, no doubt, this was for commercial reasons: Dickens was writing a Christmas Book, and was hoping for significant sales come December. But another reason was that *The Chimes* – as the title implies – was timely in itself. Dickens emphasised this in his letters. Writing on 8 October, he declared, 'it has a grip upon the very throat of the time', and a fortnight later, now in a more reflective mood, he claimed, 'I think it well-timed and a good thought.'[61] He was not wrong. It is the assertive and radical stance that Dickens took on several contemporary issues that made *The Chimes* such a rich text.

To some extent, Dickens was always a radical. Although his commitment vacillated, and he was never allied to any political party, he was nonetheless a firm advocate of 'root-and-branch reform', as Sally Ledger has observed.[62] *The Chimes* is the fullest expression of this belief. Since Robert Peel's re-election in 1841, several anti-Tory squibs and satires had escaped from his pen, finding homes in the liberal pages of the *Examiner* and the *Morning Chronicle*.[63] By October 1844 Dickens was the proponent of a number of radical beliefs, and these have been fruitfully explored by critics. Josephine McDonagh reveals the relationship between Meg's act of near-infanticide, the faeries that swarm throughout the story's illustrations, and Dickens's hostility towards Malthusianism, one of the key tenets of the New Poor Law. In doing so she firmly roots *The Chimes* in a tradition of anti–New Poor Law writing.[64] Ledger similarly discusses *The Chimes* as part of this tradition, noting that it rejects the precepts of political economy upon which the New Poor Law was based. In addition, she argues that it likewise refuses the New Poor Law's predecessor and ready alternative – paternalism. *The Chimes* is therefore a truly incendiary text that is both anti-Tory and anti–New Poor Law.[65] Michael Sheldon also places *The Chimes* within an anti-Tory context, claiming that it expresses Dickens's 'free trade radicalism' and his anti–Corn Law principles.[66] Together, these readings support Michael Slater's verdict that

The Chimes was 'the most overtly Radical fiction he ever wrote'.[67] However, despite the fact that this has become a dominant interpretation, Dickens's most radical symbol – Will Fern, the vagrant poacher – has generally passed without remark. Through Will, Dickens launches an acerbic attack on the permissive laws that persecuted poverty, and the paternalistic logic that underwrote them.

Will is a foil for Sir Joseph Bowley, MP, the self-styled 'Poor Man's Friend and Father'.[68] Possibly based on the Duke of Buckingham and Chandos, Sir Joseph is a caricature of paternalists and protectionists, as his early victimisation of Will reveals.[69] Their antagonistic relationship is established in the Second Quarter when Trotty Veck, the wizened porter-protagonist, is ushered into Sir Joseph's library bearing a letter from Alderman Cute. Requesting advice, Cute informs Sir Joseph that Will has tramped up to London from Dorset to 'look for employment' and was 'found at night asleep in a shed'; the constables arrested him, and he is due to appear before the justice-alderman in the morning. In his swift reply Sir Joseph states that Will has a 'turbulent and rebellious spirit' and that 'his committal for some short term as a Vagabond, would be a service to society.'[70] This underscores the irony of Sir Joseph's claim to be the 'Poor Man's Friend', a critique made more piquant by the fact that he is Will's Dorset landlord. In addition, this moment also introduces the permissive laws as one of the political targets of the text. In this first encounter between labourer and gentleman, Dickens makes it clear that such laws – in this case the 1824 Vagrancy Act – can be easily misused by petty tyrants such as Bowley, who can condemn from afar without even facing the accused. Dickens makes this point even more forcibly in the next Quarter.

Having left Sir Joseph's mansion bearing the Alderman's instructions, Trotty literally bumps into Will. He is 'jaded and foot-sore' and bubbling with radical sentiments. Setting himself firmly against the humbug pater-nalism of 'gentlefolks', he deplores the way they 'search and search, and pry and pry' into the lives of the poor, but do nothing to relieve their poverty. His tirade ends on a dejected note with a foreboding image of the class divide: 'I only want to live like one of the Almighty's creatures', he tells Trotty, 'I can't, I don't; and so there's a pit dug between me, and them that can and do.' This discontent re-emerges during Trotty's New Year's vision when Will confronts Sir Joseph at a birthday gala held at Bowley Hall. No longer the 'sun-browned, sinewy, country-looking man' that Trotty met in the street, Will is 'old, and grey, and bent' and has 'just come from jail'. 'Beyond all hurt or harm', and back on the estate where he 'lived many a year', he makes a bold address, challenging the gathered gentlefolks with the iniquities of their permissive laws:

> 'Now, gentlemen', said Will Fern, holding out his hands, and flushing for an instant in his haggard face, 'see how your laws are made to trap and hunt us when we're brought to this. I tries to live elsewhere. And I'm a vagabond. To jail with him! I comes back here. I goes a-nutting in your woods, and breaks – who don't? – a limber branch or two. To jail with him! One of your keepers sees me in the broad day, near my own patch of garden, with a gun. To jail with him! I has a nat'ral angry word with that man, when I'm free again. To jail with him! I cuts a stick. To jail with him! I eats a rotten apple or a turnip. To jail with him! It's twenty mile away; and coming back I begs a trifle on the road. To jail with him! At last, the constable, the keeper – anybody – finds me anywhere, a-doing anything. To jail with him, for he's a vagrant, and a jail-bird known; and jail's the only home he's got.'[71]

In this melodramatic set piece, the labourer is depicted as the innocent victim of a malignant legal system. As we shall see, the Manichean opposition between good and evil upon which melodrama relies became a favoured technique among radical writers.[72] However, whereas they often juxtaposed the persecuted poacher and his dependents against a wicked landlord, Dickens is careful to highlight that the problem is systemic, not individual. Although Bowley is Will's ideological antagonist, and has been identified by Sheldon as the story's 'central villain', it is nonetheless 'your *laws* [that] are made to trap and hunt us'.[73] Here the metaphor recalls the privileged blood sports of the elite, but it refuses to identify any upper-class individual as specifically at fault. Meanwhile, Will's register of offences carves out and re-orientates a criminal trajectory with which we are already familiar: the poacher's progress.

Will is not the vagrant poacher of the morality tale. For a start, his vagrant state precedes his reliance on poaching. His use of the legal term 'vagabond' at the beginning of his catalogue, the same term that Sir Joseph uses in his instructions to Alderman Cute, suggests that the reader was a witness to the start of Will's criminal career. Convictions for trespassing, poaching and vagrancy then seem to follow indiscriminately as Will becomes a target for officials and assumes the miserable condition of Jefferies's moucher, living off whatever he can forage among fields and hedgerows. Nonetheless, there is a logic to Will's progress through the courts. He does not graduate to 'bolder crimes', but consistently remains a petty offender. In fact, in an inversion of the traditional poacher's progress, Will's crimes become pettier and pettier, until he cannot be found 'anywhere, a-doing anything' without being prosecuted. This succession of offences highlights the injustice of the permissive laws and the bias inherent in the magisterial system; however, it is still significant that a succession of smaller crimes, like a series of bolder ones, ultimately leads to the committal of a felony – arson.

In the Fourth Quarter, still in the midst of Trotty's vision, Fern steals up to Meg Veck's garret and confesses to her that 'there'll be a Fire to-night':

> There'll be Fires this winter-time, to light the dark nights, East, West, North, and South. When you see the distant sky red, they'll be blazing. When you see the distant sky red, think of me no more; or if you do, remember what a Hell was lighted up inside of me, and think you see its Flames reflected in the clouds.[74]

Fern's narrative arc, then, ultimately fulfils More's precept. However, it is significant that it concludes with incendiarism. Unlike the murders or thefts committed by Addis and Scott, arson was a common act of protest. From the end of the Swing Riots until the 1860s it was the most popular form of agricultural dissent.[75] Will's felony is therefore not a sign of moral debasement but a symbol of political vengeance. The apocalyptic, all-encompassing fire burning 'East, West, North, and South', an image of revolution that ironises the 'service to society' Sir Joseph performed when he ordered Will's imprisonment, would also have had an immediacy for contemporary readers: 1844 was the second worst year for incendiarism in the nineteenth century.[76] Through Will the vagrant poacher, Dickens suggests that the fires of that year are a prelude to an even more destructive wave of political dissent led by those who suffer most from society's iniquitous laws. In other words, if the legal system that punishes poverty is not reformed, then revolution is inevitable.[77]

2.3 Kingsley, Carew and the Condition of England

Revolution never came, although the rift between labourers and land-owners, workers and capitalists, continued to grow throughout the 1840s. This period typically evokes factory disputes and Chartist demon-strations, scenes that have been memorialised in Condition-of-England novels like Elizabeth Gaskell's *Mary Barton* (1848) and *North and South* (1854). The industrial tenor of the workers' discontent, however, has been emphasised by historians and critics who have generally overlooked agri-cultural protests, including the acts of incendiarism and poaching that were endemic throughout the decade.[78] These acts of resistance against landowners caused radical and conservative MPs considerable anxiety. During 1845–6 John Bright led a parliamentary inquiry into the game laws as part of his broader crusade against protectionism. However, although the select committee concluded that starvation wages and a fear of the workhouse were the primary causes of poaching, these findings had little impact. The surprise repeal of the corn laws in 1846 by the Tory Prime Minister Robert Peel took the impetus out of further investigation, and the introduction of the 1848 Hares Act was the only perceptible difference it made; this allowed tenants to kill hares without a game licence, although they still needed their landlord's permission.[79] Meanwhile, the government, concerned by the violence of poaching affrays, began to compile lists of serious poaching infractions in 1843–4, and continued this work in 1848–9.[80] Poaching also remained a preoccupation of radical writers during these years. In two neglected Condition-of-England novels, Charlton Carew's *The Poacher's Wife: A Story of the Times* (1847) and Charles Kingsley's *Yeast: A Problem* (1848), the poacher is used once more to critique permissive laws and the landlords' monopoly on game.

The reception of Carew's *The Poacher's Wife* was polarised. Like *The Chimes*, which had been lauded by the Chartist *Northern Star* and condemned by the ultra-Tory *John Bull*, the reviews were divided along party lines.[81] Right-wing reviewers were overwhelmingly unimpressed. The conservative *Spectator* dismissed it as belonging to 'the humanity and clap-trap school', a view that was echoed a month later in an article in the *Critic*, where the novel was pronounced a 'ludicrous failure', an example of 'the worst school of namby-pamby'.[82] Meanwhile, left-leaning journalists gave it an enthusiastic welcome. The review in *Lloyd's Weekly* praised the 'powerfully told' novel because it 'display[ed] vividly the horrors that arise from the present system [of game laws]', and the reviewer for the *Mirror of Literature* prophesised that it 'will last when more ephemeral publications are forgotten, because it illustrates a great social question'.[83] Undoubtedly, one of the most contentious elements of the novel was its portrayal of the aristocracy and the squirearchy, who are represented by Lord Plaistic and Sir Ralph Oldham: the *Spectator*, for example, resented Carew's 'attacks upon the aristocracy and country gentlemen', while *Lloyd's Weekly* noted that sadly they were 'true specimens of the hard-hearted class of landlords'.[84] It is these that furnish *The Poacher's Wife* with villains and instigate the persecution of the poacher, Gilbert Locksley, and Dinah, his wife.

The Poacher's Wife is ghosted by a poacher's progress in which Locksley is framed for a series of crimes that escalate in severity and force him to assume a vagrant existence. At the beginning of the novel he is one of Sir Ralph's tenant farmers who, having been denied permission to shoot game, is forced to watch the squire's hares and pheasants 'destroy his labour and eat his crops'. With a wife and baby to support, and reduced to the point of starvation, he joins a gang of drunken poachers, and executes a moon-light raid on one of Sir Ralph's coveys. However, having secured the game, Locksley's renegade companions abandon him and ambush the squire's carriage. Although he is innocent of the crime, Locksley is arrested for highway robbery and sent to prison by Sir Ralph. He escapes only to be framed for the murder of Snipe, Sir Ralph's gamekeeper, and is forced to flee from the constables. In the final chapters of volume one he is depicted as a 'care-worn fugitive', and does not appear again until the end of the novel.[85]

The fugitive quality of Locksley's vagrancy is significant. Strongly reminiscent of the final phase of Will Fern's saga, in which he cannot be 'anywhere, a-doing anything' without being harassed by gamekeepers or the police, it conditions his movement. Anxious, almost wild, the fugitive is reactionary as he flies from his pursuers. He is therefore like a hunted animal, a fitting symbol for the poacher who occupies the uncomfortable middle ground between predator and prey. Will Fern characterises himself as a form of quarry when he describes the permissive laws as tools to 'trap and hunt us'; and likewise Locksley, while being chased by constables, is described as a 'cunning fox', another metaphor that evokes a hunting culture.[86] Such imagery reinforces the vagrant poachers' vulnerability. Moreover, it inscribes their movement with a haphazard quality. Although they are not aimless, because they practise purposeful evasion, their route (or rout) shifts with the conditions of the chase. This helter-skelter movement is very different to that which belongs to the vagrant poachers of the morality tale tradition. Black Giles, Addis and Tom Scott are all associated with Gypsies, and are therefore allied to the premeditated movement of itinerants that I outlined in Chapter 1. Such movement is articulated by More and others as a methodical pursuit: their vagrant poachers exist on the other side of the predator–prey equation.

Locksley is not the only character to become a vagrant. Dinah, too, becomes homeless when Sir Ralph evicts her after her husband's flight. Friendless and aimless, she is described as 'a woman who is driven from house and home, wandering about the country' and, later, as 'wandering into the world without the prospect of relief, either bodily or mental'.[87]

Deprivation, however, is not the only danger that Dinah faces as a woman on the road. As Charlotte Mathieson observes, 'women's travel in general was often represented in terms of disreputability and sexual threat' because a woman's respectability was predicated on her place within the home.[88] Women travelling abroad could be perceived as transgressive, and this was especially true of vagrant women, who, unlike many other female travellers, were completely untethered from the domestic hearth. This is the realisation that Hetty Sorrell comes to in George Eliot's *Adam Bede* (1859). Discovered sleeping in a 'hovel of furze near a sheepfold' by a smock-frocked labourer, the pregnant and unmarried outcast becomes the subject of a cross-examination. 'What do you do gettin' out o' the highroad?' the labourer asks, 'Why dooant you keep where there's finger poasses an' folks to ax the way on?' Alarmed by the 'gruff old man' and his inquisition, she tries to tip him sixpence, ostensibly as a reward for giving her directions, but also as an assertion of her respectable rank. 'You'd better take care on't', he replies, 'else you'll get it stool from yer, if you go trapesin' about the fields like a mad woman a-that-way.'[89]

The rejection of Hetty's gift confirms her ambivalent position; but it also reveals her lucky escape. Dinah is not so fortunate. Having spent a night in a barn she, too, is discovered by a labourer. However, before letting her pass he demands payment for her lodging. 'What's the coin you pay in, I should like to know?' he asks; 'I'll have a kiss afore you go; that's flat.' He seizes her 'round the waist' but, forestalled by the early arrival of the farmer, steals her money instead of the kiss and forces her into the road. The brutality of this scene is underwritten by the labourer's assumption that Dinah is a prostitute who has already 'been up to some nice pranks' in the night. This emerges through a series of euphemisms. His lewd question about 'the coin you pay in' and subsequent demand for a kiss elicits the relationship between the prostitute and their client and the interchangeability of money and sex that it relies on. The same economy is also evoked when he surprises her in the barn and immediately pronounces her 'a neat bit of goods', a metaphor that commodifies her body and insinuates that it is for sale.[90]

The elision between the prostitute and the vagrant woman was common in Victorian culture (see the Introduction), and as a result the female vagrant was often imagined in terms of her potential promiscuity and sexual availability. Even if she was not a prostitute, her sexual (mis)conduct could still steer her characterisation. Hetty's status as a fallen woman, for example, eclipses her vagrant condition: her 'objectless wandering' is first and foremost a symbol of her sexual transgression.[91] Meanwhile, Carew emphasises Dinah's vulnerability by portraying her fall from respectability (always coded in sexual terms) as imminent. Although she retains her virtue and is successfully reabsorbed into bourgeois society at the end of the novel, she first has to escape the predatory labourer, and then has to avoid the taint of a house 'damnatory to any woman', a London brothel where she is lured by the false promise of seeing Locksley.[92] Carew's portrayal of the poacher's wife after her separation from her husband and her home conforms to gender stereotypes. Beset by physical and moral dangers, and repeatedly characterised as 'bewildered' while on the road, she proves herself to be delicate and dependent. These traits enhance her vulnerability outside the domestic sphere and confirm her femininity. After all, as Lynda Nead reminds us, fragility was a hallmark of middle-class womanhood during the Victorian period.[93]

Carew's formulaic treatment of Dinah differs from his deeply ambivalent depiction of poachers. Although the narrator castigates permissive laws that persecute poverty, Carew nonetheless iterates More's notion that poaching is 'the first step in the long road of crime' and that the poacher inevitably 'finishes a career of wretchedness' at 'the gallows'. Moreover, although Locksley might be one of 'the wretched victims of those power-begotten edicts', the game laws, Carew's portrayal of other poachers is far less sympathetic. The gang that Locksley joins is made up of desperadoes who are not only poachers but also highwaymen and housebreakers. Later, he also depicts a poacher turned arsonist, Jackson, whose incendiarism is condemned as a wanton act of personal vengeance. As Jackson explains to his accomplice: 'If they *will* make me a jail-bird, they must stand the consequence.... As well be called a rick-burner as a poacher, and have revenge into the bargain – ah, revenge as shall make the rich man quake, and pay for his game law with his corn and his hay.' Although Jackson emphasises that arson is a form of reprisal, Carew nonetheless goes on to explicitly denounce it as a selfish undertaking committed in the 'blind spirit of revenge'.[94] In doing so he depoliticises what Dickens recognised as a meaningful form of protest. Although Carew ostensibly lobbies for the reform of permissive laws through the persecution of Locksley and Dinah, the poacher is not always a victim in *The Poacher's Wife*, but a complex and often undesirable figure. This is also evident in Kingsley's novel *Yeast*.

Kingsley was a clergyman, a novelist and a radical. Although his biographer Brenda Colloms identifies him as a radical Tory, in the summer of 1848 he declared himself a Chartist.[95] He then became the assistant editor of the weekly periodical *Politics for the People*, the short-lived organ of Christian Socialism (it lasted only seventeen issues).[96] However, despite his radical sentiments, Kingsley was conflicted about poaching and the game laws. Towards the end of his life he remarked in a collection of essays, *Prose Idylls* (1873), that he had always lived in 'poaching counties, and on the edges of one forest after another'.[97] When he moved to Eversley in 1842, the same parish in which he would eventually be buried, he was settling in such a place. Located in Hampshire and comprised of two hamlets on the borders of Windsor Forest, the ancient haunt of the Waltham Blacks, Kingsley's congregation was formed of farming and labouring families.[98] Consequently, there was more than one poacher in his weekly audience, and these figures inspired a number of sermons, at least one of which was preached in 1848.[99] If this was anything like 'The Value of Law', published six years later in his second series of *Sermons on National Subjects* (1854), then he warned his parishioners to 'avoid poaching, even once in a way' because 'the beginning of sin is like the letting out of water; no one can tell where it will stop'.[100] However, while he admonished poachers from the pulpit, his attitude changed when writing for the periodical press. This is evident in *Yeast*, which was first serialised in *Fraser's Magazine* between July and December 1848.

Established in 1830, *Fraser's* was published by James Fraser, financed by Hugh Fraser, and edited by William Maginn, a once prolific writer for *Blackwood's Edinburgh Magazine*. The venture was Maginn's idea: he wanted to provide himself with a periodical outlet for his radical Tory sentiments that no longer meshed with the more staid conservatism of *Blackwood's*.[101] From the beginning, then, *Fraser's* was calculated to appeal to Tories and, with a sale price of half a crown, competed with the likes of *Blackwood's* and the *New Monthly Magazine* for a middle- and upper-class readership. Its initial circulation is difficult to estimate; after its first year it boasted 8,700 subscribers, but this seems unlikely given that Fraser declared that it was a money loss as late as 1834.[102] A few years later, *The American Almanac* (1839) estimated that *Fraser's* monthly 'circulation [was] little short of 1,500' during 1838, which would place it respectably on par with periodicals like the *Gentleman's Magazine* and Frederick Marryat's *Metropolitan Magazine*.[103] In 1847 it passed into the hands of John William Parker, whose son, John Parker, had attended King's College London with Kingsley.[104] He was made the new editor of *Fraser's* and determined to abandon Maginn's rollicking style; however, although he wanted to change the tone of the magazine, he still sought to maintain its country-house readership.[105] Kingsley's novel then, in which squires are satirised and poachers justified, was never calculated to please either the readers or his friend and editor. Throughout the autumn instalments, Parker received an increasing number of complaints, and asked Kingsley to terminate the novel early.[106]

The September number of *Yeast* featured an affray between 'a large gang of poachers, who had come down from London', and a posse of gamekeepers and villagers led by Lancelot, Kingsley's gentleman protagonist. Like the gang in *The Poacher's Wife*, these men are thorough criminals: 'when they had swept the county pretty clean of game', we are told, 'they would just finish off the season by a stray highway-robbery or two'. However, although Kingsley condemns these urban poachers, he is sympathetic towards their rural counterparts, the labourers who kill a hare or pheasant to feed their families. This sentiment is voiced by Tregarva, a local gamekeeper and spiritual sage who guides Lancelot throughout the novel: 'I have no mercy on these Londoners. If it was these poor, half-starved labourers, that snare the same hares that have been eating up their garden-stuff all the week, I can't touch them, sir, and that's the truth.'[107] Through Tregarva, Kingsley dichotomises the poacher, presenting him as either an outright criminal or a victim of the landowners' greed.

This opposition was reinforced in the novel's next instalment in which Lavington, a caricature of the bluff and gouty squire, discovers one of Tregarva's 'filthy, rascally, Radical ballads'.[108] Presented as the lament of 'a poacher's widow', the ballad is an apostrophe addressed to the local landlord. Bemoaning the loss of her husband, she condemns the squire who 'made him a poacher . . . when you'd give neither work nor meat', and blames him for his death: 'There's blood on the game you sell, squire, / And there's blood on the game you eat!' By the end of the poem it is clear that the squire, an advocate of 'the gaol and the workhouse', is also responsible for the break-up of the family and the vagrant status of the now-outcast widow. In the penultimate stanza the widow rises from her spot in 'the gloomy fir-woods', where she has been weeping, and 'wearily over the rough flints / Went wandering into the night'.[109] Here the 'wandering' condition of the poacher's wife is reminiscent of Dinah's fate, while the fact that she is going 'into the night' suggests that she, too, is directionless, disorientated and at risk of going astray. This melodramatic narrative further polarises the presentation of poachers in *Yeast*, emphasising the ignorance and cruelty of squires and confirming the rural poachers' victimhood. This flattens the complexity of poachers and poaching, smothering it with melancholy sentiment. Kingsley, a rural parson whose parishioners included real poachers, perhaps realised this and sought to redress it in his extensive revisions.

Following the success of his second Condition-of-England novel, *Alton Locke* (1850), Kingsley persuaded Parker to publish *Yeast* in book form in 1851. In the intervening years he had made several alterations to the foreshortened serial, the most significant of which was the insertion of a new chapter before the poaching affray. In this episode Kingsley introduces the character of Crawy, a poacher only briefly referred to in *Fraser's Magazine*, who is arrested by Lancelot and Tregarva while setting night lines to catch Squire Lavington's fish. He is a much more ambiguous figure than either the metropolitan poacher or the victimised labourer. A moucher living off hedgerows, he is a 'scarecrow of rags and bones' with 'such a visage as only worn-out poachers, or tramping drovers, or London chiffoniers [scavengers] carry'. An impoverished vagrant figure, he spends his time, like Will Fern, in and out of gaol for petty offences. As he confesses to Tregarva while begging to be released: "taint a month now as I'm out o' prizzum along o' they fir-toppings ... I should like to ha' a spell o' fresh air, like, afore I goes in again.'[110] Arrested for the common crime of wood theft, having stolen the 'fir-toppings' pruned for fuel, and resigned to another term in prison, Crawy lives a dogged life between the constable and the gamekeeper.[111] Moreover, again like Will Fern (or Gilbert Locksley), there is something fugitive about his existence. Watching him from afar, Lancelot remembers that 'time was when he had looked on a poacher as a Pariah "hostem humani generis" [enemy of mankind] – and only deplored that the law forbid him to shoot them down, like cats and otters'.[112] Here Lancelot's simile, drawn from contemporary hunting culture, makes Crawy's position as an outlaw explicit; cats and otters, along with stoats, crows, hawks, buzzards, rats, owls, magpies and foxes, could be legally killed by anybody, anywhere and without a licence because they were classified as 'vermin'.[113]

Crawy possesses many of the traits that mark Fern and Locksley out as victims of an iniquitous system. Poaching and prison, we are told, are his only alternatives to starvation. Within the 'limited labour-field' of southern England he cannot get fieldwork, and 'the rights of property' ensure that he cannot farm because the wastes 'belong to poor old Lavington' and are preserved for the growth of 'game and timber'. However, although Kingsley portrays the vagrant poacher as a victim of social inequalities, he also emphasises that his present misery is a punishment for past sins. As Tregarva tells Lancelot, Crawy began his poaching career as a boy 'miching away in church-time'.[114] Here 'miching' locates Crawy at a junction between poaching and vagrancy. As Linda Woodbridge remarks, the term belongs within 'the discourse of vagrancy', denoting 'not only a simple truant but specifically one who pretends to poverty'.[115] Meanwhile, Jefferies notes that there is 'a resemblance between the present provincial word "mouching" and Shakespeare's "mitcher"', a reference to *1 Henry IV* (1598), in which Falstaff asks if Prince Hal shall 'prove a micher and eat blackberries'.[116] This alignment of the vagrant and the poacher in the micher is augmented by Thomas Hood's digressive sketch, 'The Friend in Need' (1841). Here we are informed that 'when a young micher plays truant, it is not for a lounge about the homestead, but to roam in forbidden paths, or to visit places that are tabooed, the poacher's hut, or the gipsy's tent'.[117] Crawy's outcast condition, then, is not just dependent on systemic forces, but is also a product of personal transgressions; in the first instance, neglect of his spiritual welfare in favour of poaching and wandering. This is confirmed by the description of Crawy's 'bleared cheeks and drooping lips, and peering purblind eyes' – the sagging badges of drunkenness – and his 'perplexed, hopeless, defiant, and yet sneaking' expression.[118] Here the face of the moucher emblematises the warning that Kingsley gives would-be poachers in 'The Value of Law': 'hand in hand with poaching go lying, and deceit, and sneaking, and fear, and boasting, and swearing, and drinking, and the company of bad men and bad women'.[119] In the revised version of *Yeast*, Kingsley presents us with a far more ambivalent vagrant poacher then either Dickens or Carew. This perhaps reflects the bourgeoning conservatism that would eventually turn him into a Tory, but it is also dependent on changing attitudes towards poaching and a de-escalation of social tensions after the 1840s.

Whether it occurred in the woods or on the page, poaching was often political. In this chapter I have traced how vagrancy was incorporated into poaching narratives for didactic and political ends, especially during the 1840s. In this decade radical writers re-appropriated the poacher's progress and inscribed vagrancy with new meaning. Whereas in the morality tales it had been a symptom of the poacher's immorality, it now became a symbol of systemic injustice and the abuse of power. It would be a mistake, however, to think of these radical writers as belonging to a cohesive 'tradition'. Although Dickens, Carew and Kingsley shared similar principles and utilised the same vagrant figure in their narratives, the aims of their texts vary enormously. *The Chimes*, with its wholesale rejection of all incumbent and alternative political orders, is much more extreme than either *The Poacher's Wife* or *Yeast*, both of which are ultimately ambivalent towards poachers and display a much more tepid radicalism. Moreover, it should be recognised that the vagrant poacher was not solely used for didactic purposes during this period. In Frederick Marryat's boys' adventure, *Joseph Rushbrook; or, The Poacher* (1841), Joey lives a 'vagrant life' poaching in Dorset and is forced onto the road when his father kills a double-crossing higgler.[120] But despite its thematic similarities with the texts discussed in this chapter, the novel has no overt moral or political agenda. As the reviewer for the *New Monthly Magazine* remarked: 'We hope also it will not enter [the reader's] head to look for a moral in the poacher's story, for when he remarks that extraordinary good fortune attends nearly all those who least deserve it, he may be reduced by such examples to exclaim, "Evil, be thou my good!" and follow a mode of life likely to end in misery and disgrace.'[121]

Notes

1 Kenneth Curry, 'The Monthly Magazine', in *British Literary Magazines: The Romantic Age, 1789–1836*, ed. Alvin Sillivan, 4 vols (Westport, CT: Greenwood Press, 1983–86), II, pp. 314–19. Signed under 'M', Mitford's stories appeared in the following issues: M., 'An Old Gipsy: A Village Sketch', *Monthly Magazine*, January 1826, pp. 13–17; and M., 'The Young Gipsy: A Village Sketch', *Monthly Magazine*, February 1826, pp. 129–34.

2 Mary Russell Mitford, 'The Young Gipsy', in *Our Village: Sketches of Rural Character and Scenery*, 2 vols (London: George Bell, 1876), I, pp. 449–58 (pp. 453–4, 457).

3 Donna Landry, *The Invention of the Countryside: Hunting, Walking and Ecology in English Literature, 1671–1831* (Basingstoke: Palgrave, 2001), p. 82. Also see Sarah Houghton-Walker, *Representations of the Gypsy in the Romantic Period* (Oxford: Oxford University Press, 2014), p. 24.

4 Richard Jefferies, *The Gamekeeper at Home: Sketches of Natural History and Rural Life*, in *The Gamekeeper at Home/The Amateur Poacher*, ed. Richard Fitter (Oxford: Oxford University Press 1948; repr. 1978), pp. 1–168 (p. 135).

5 Emma Griffin, *Blood Sport: Hunting in Britain since 1066* (New Haven, CT: Yale University Press, 2007; repr. 2008), pp. 110–11, 153–4; Harry Hopkins, *The Long Affray: The Poaching Wars in Britain* (London: Secker & Warburg, 1985; repr. Faber and Faber, 2008), pp. 62–4, 197–9.

6 Raymond Williams, *The Country and the City* (London: Chatto & Windus, 1973), pp. 185–6.

7 Joseph Arch, *The Story of His Life: Told by Himself* (London: Hutchinson, 1898; repr. Garland, 1984), p. 13.

8 Landry, *The Invention of the Countryside*, p. 73.

9 James Hawker, *A Victorian Poacher: James Hawker's Journal*, ed. Garth Christian (Oxford: Oxford University Press, 1961; repr. 1978), p. 95.

10 Hopkins, *The Long Affray*, p. 265.

11 David Jones, *Crime, Protest, Community and Police in Nineteenth-Century Britain* (London: Routledge & Kegan Paul, 1982), p. 69; Harvey Osborne

and Michael Winstanley, 'Rural and Urban Poaching in Victorian England', *Rural History*, 17.2 (2006), 187–212 (pp. 204–6).

12 Jefferies, *The Gamekeeper at Home*, p. 135. Also see Hopkins, *The Long Affray*, p. 89.

13 P. B. Munsche, *Gentlemen and Poachers: The English Game Laws, 1671–1831* (Cambridge: Cambridge University Press, 1981), pp. 59–60.

14 Hopkins, *The Long Affray*, p. 197.

15 Jones, *Crime, Protest, Community and Police*, pp. 73–4.

16 Timothy Shakesheff, *Rural Conflict, Crime and Protest: Herefordshire, 1800–1860* (Woodbridge: Boydell Press, 2003), pp. 146–8.

17 Munsche, *Gentlemen and Poachers*, pp. 25–6.

18 Shakesheff, *Rural Conflict*, p. 150.

19 Josephine McDonagh, 'Urban Migration and Mobility', in *Charles Dickens in Context*, ed. Sally Ledger and Holly Furneaux (Cambridge: Cambridge University Press, 2011), pp. 268–75 (p. 271).

20 Hawker, *A Victorian Poacher*, pp. 16, 19.

21 Jefferies, *The Gamekeeper at Home*, p. 112.

22 Richard Jefferies, *The Amateur Poacher*, in *The Gamekeeper at Home/The Amateur Poacher*, ed. Richard Fitter (Oxford: Oxford University Press 1948; repr. 1978), pp. 169–352 (pp. 270–2).

23 Landry, *The Invention of the Countryside*, p. 85; Shakesheff, *Rural Conflict*, pp. 153–4.

24 Griffin, *Blood Sport*, pp. 74–5, 100.

25 Hopkins, *The Long Affray*, p. 66.

26 John E. Archer, *Social Unrest and Popular Protest in England, 1780–1840* (Cambridge: Cambridge University Press, 2000), p. 14; also see Shakesheff, *Rural Conflict*, pp. 156–60.

27 Harvey Osborne, '"Unwomanly Practices": Poaching Crime, Gender and the Female Offender in Nineteenth-Century Britain', *Rural History*, 27.2 (2016), 149–68.

28 [Frederick Rolfe], *I Walked by Night: Being the Life & History of the King of the Norfolk Poachers, Written by Himself*, ed. Lilias Rider Haggard (Woodbridge: Boydell Press, 1974), pp. 49–50.

29 Charles Howard Ford, *Hannah More: A Critical Biography* (New York: Peter Lang, 1996), pp. 127–9.

30 Shakesheff, *Rural Conflict*, pp. 151–3.

31 Harvey Osborne, 'The Seasonality of Nineteenth-Century Poaching', *Agricultural History Review*, 48.1 (2000), 27–41 (pp. 27–8).

32 Landry, *The Invention of the Countryside*, p. 6.

33 Hopkins, *The Long Affray*, pp. 76–9, 163–4.

34 Ford, *Hannah More*, p. 129.

35 David Cressy, *Gypsies: An English History* (Oxford: Oxford University Press, 2018; repr. 2020), pp. 54, 193–4, 233–4.

36 Hannah More, *Black Giles, the Poacher: With Some Account of a Family Who Had Rather Live by Their Wits than Their Work* (London: C. J. G. & F. Rivington, 1830), pp. 6, 3, 8–9.

37 More, *Black Giles*, pp. 9–11.

38 Hopkins, *The Long Affray*, pp. 65–7.

39 E. P. Thompson, *Whigs and Hunters: The Origin of the Black Act* (London: Allen Lane, 1975), pp. 21–4.

40 Jones, *Crime, Protest, Community and Police*, pp. 80, 84.

41 More, *Black Giles*, pp. 24, 19.

42 Archer, *Social Unrest and Popular Protest*, pp. 15–20.

43 Griffin, *Blood Sport*, p. 153; Hopkins, *The Long Affray*, pp. 25, 171–5.

44 Roy Palmer notes that 'Van Diemen's Land' attained huge popularity in the early 1830s when it was being printed in Edinburgh and Glasgow in Scotland, and Preston, Manchester, Birmingham and London in England. It was circulated orally until at least the 1970s. Roy Palmer, 'Birmingham Broadsides and Oral Traditions', in *Street Ballads in Nineteenth-Century Britain, Ireland, and North America*, ed. David Atkinson and Steve Roud (Farnham: Ashgate, 2014), pp. 37–58 (pp. 55–8).

45 James Hepburn, *A Book of Scattered Leaves: Poetry and Poverty in Broadside Ballads in Nineteenth-Century England: Study and Anthology*, 2 vols (Lewisburg, PA: Bucknell University Press, 2000–1), II, p. 337.

46 Roy Palmer, *The Painful Plough: A Portrait of the Agricultural Labourer in the Nineteenth Century from Folk Songs and Ballads and Contemporary Accounts* (Cambridge: Cambridge University Press, 1973), p. 35 (ll. 1–2).

47 John Nicholson, *The Poacher: A Tale from Real Life*, in *Airedale in Ancient Times* (London, 1825), pp. 63–92 (pp. 63, 65, 80, 89–90).

48 James Ogden, 'Nicholson, John (1790–1843)', in *Oxford Dictionary of National Biography*, www.oxforddnb.com (accessed 15 February 2018).

49 Ibid.

50 Nicholson, *The Poacher*, p. 89.

51 [Edmund Phipps], 'The Poacher's Progress', *New Monthly Magazine*, April 1841, pp. 487–97 (pp. 493, 497).

52 See [Advertisements], *Examiner*, 25 December 1841, pp. 630–2 (p. 632).

53 [Anon.] N.W., 'The Poacher', *New Sporting Magazine*, February 1841, pp. 127–30 (p. 128).

54 [Anon.] N.W., 'The Poacher', *New Sporting Magazine*, April 1841, pp. 257–62 (p. 262).

55 Hopkins, *The Long Affray*, pp. 210–12; Jones, *Crime, Protest, Community and Police*, pp. 62–4.

56 Hopkins, *The Long Affray*, p. 208.

57 Pamela Horn, *Life and Labour in Rural England, 1760–1850* (Basingstoke: Macmillan, 1987), p. 141. Jones notes that this is also true of Suffolk; see *Crime, Protest, Community and Police*, p. 62.

58 Griffin, *Blood Sport*, p. 157.

59 See, 'The Poacher: A Tale from Real Life', *Mirror of Literature*, 18 January 1845, pp. 56–8.

60 Hawker, *A Victorian Poacher*, pp. 2, 95.

61 Charles Dickens, *The Pilgrim Edition of the Letters of Charles Dickens*, ed. Madeline House, Graham Storey and Kathleen Tillotson, 12 vols (Oxford: Oxford University Press, 1965–2002), IV, pp. 200–1, 206.

62 Sally Ledger, *Dickens and the Popular Radical Imagination* (Cambridge: Cambridge University Press, 2007), p. 6.

63 Michael Sheldon gives an overview of these publications. See Michael Sheldon, '*The Chimes* and the Anti–Corn Law League', *Victorian Studies*, 25.3 (1982), 328–53 (pp. 330–7).

64 Josephine McDonagh, *Child Murder and British Culture, 1720–1900* (Cambridge: Cambridge University Press, 2003), pp. 118–22.

65 Ledger, *Dickens and the Popular Radical Imagination*, pp. 124–32.

66 Sheldon, '*The Chimes* and the Anti–Corn Law League', p. 330.

67 Michael Slater, *Charles Dickens* (New Haven, CT: Yale University Press, 2009), p. 229.

68 Charles Dickens, *The Chimes: A Goblin Story; or, Some Bells That Rang an Old Year Out and a New One In*, in *Christmas Books*, intro. Eleanor Farjeon (Oxford: Oxford University Press, 1954; repr. 1997), pp. 77–154 (p. 106).

69 Sheldon, '*The Chimes* and the Anti–Corn Law League', pp. 339–41.

70 Dickens, *The Chimes*, pp. 106–8.

71 Ibid., pp. 110–12, 131–3.

72 There is a long history of melodrama being used in popular radical culture, a tradition that Ledger argues *The Chimes* is part of. See Ledger, *Dickens and the Popular Radical Imagination*, pp. 6–7, 38, 117–32.

73 Sheldon, '*The Chimes* and the Anti–Corn Law League', p. 338.

74 Dickens, *The Chimes*, pp. 147–8.

75 Archer, *Social Unrest and Popular Protest*, p. 21.

76 In total 245 arsonists were convicted, but the number of fires lit was at least 1,000 according to Jones. Jones, *Crime, Protest, Community and Police*, pp. 33–5. Also see Archer, *Social Unrest and Popular Protest*, pp. 21, 27; and Hopkins, *The Long Affray*, pp. 193–4.

77 Slater notes that both Carlyle and Dickens thought that if society did not reform, then it would be consumed by a destructive revolution. See Michael Slater, 'Carlyle and Jerrold into Dickens: A Study of *The Chimes*', *Nineteenth-Century Fiction*, 24.4 (1970), 506–26 (pp. 507–8).

78 Archer, *Social Unrest and Popular Protest*, p. 27; Jones, *Crime, Protest, Community and Police*, pp. 54–67, 82.

79 Hopkins, *The Long Affray*, pp. 217–26, 232.

80 Jones, *Crime, Protest, Community and Police*, p. 64.

81 Slater, *Charles Dickens*, pp. 231–2.

82 'Cleveland – The Poacher's Wife', *Spectator*, 13 March 1847, pp. 256–7 (p. 257); 'The Poacher's Wife: A Story of the Times', *Critic*, 3 April 1847, p. 265.

83 'The Poacher's Wife', *Lloyd's Weekly*, 25 April 1847, p. 8; 'The Poacher's Wife', *Mirror of Literature*, 1 March 1847, pp. 206–10 (p. 210).

84 'Cleveland – The Poacher's Wife', p. 257; 'The Poacher's Wife', *Lloyd's Weekly*, p. 8.

85 Charlton Carew, *The Poacher's Wife: A Story of the Times*, 2 vols (London: Charles Ollier, 1847), I, pp. 69, 191.

86 Ibid., I, p. 187.

87 Ibid., I, p. 239; Carew, *The Poacher's Wife*, II, p. 16.

88 Charlotte Mathieson, '"A Still Ecstasy of Freedom and Enjoyment": Walking the City in Charlotte Brontë's *Villette*', *Journal of Victorian Culture*, 22.4 (2017), 521–35 (p. 526); also see Lynda Nead, *Myths of Sexuality: Representations of Women in Victorian Britain* (Oxford: Blackwell, 1988; repr. 1990), pp. 12–47.

89 George Eliot, *Adam Bede*, ed. Margaret Reynolds (London: Penguin, 2008), pp. 420–2.

90 Carew, *The Poacher's Wife*, II, pp. 29–31.

91 Eliot, *Adam Bede*, p. 423.

92 Carew, *The Poacher's Wife*, II, p. 271.

93 Nead, *Myths of Sexuality*, pp. 28–9.

94 Carew, *The Poacher's Wife*, I, pp. 85–7; Carew, *The Poacher's Wife*, II, pp. 55–6. Original emphasis.

95 Brenda Colloms, *Charles Kingsley: The Lion of Eversley* (London: Constable, 1975), p. 19; Thomas Hughes, 'Prefatory Memoire', in *Alton Locke, Tailor and Poet: An Autobiography* (London: Macmillan, 1885), pp. ix–lxi (p. xix).

96 Susan Chitty, *The Beast and the Monk: A Life of Charles Kingsley* (London: Hodder and Stoughton, 1974), pp. 109–10.

97 Charles Kingsley, *Prose Idylls: New and Old*, 2nd ed. (London: Macmillan, 1874), p. 245.

98 Chitty, *The Beast and the Monk*, p. 67.

99 Charles Kingsley, *Charles Kingsley: His Letters and Memories of His Life*, 3rd ed., ed. Frances Kingsley, 2 vols (London: Henry S. King, 1877), I, p. 154.

100 Charles Kingsley, 'The Value of Law', in *Sermons on National Subjects* (London: Richard Griffin, 1854), pp. 32–44 (p. 42).

101 Rebecca Edwards Newman, '"Prosecuting the Onus Criminus": Early Criticism of the Novel in *Fraser's Magazine*', *Victorian Periodicals Review*, 35.4 (2002), 401–19 (pp. 402–3).

102 Patrick Leary, '*Fraser's Magazine* and the Literary Life, 1830–1847', *Victorian Periodicals Review*, 27.2 (1994), 105–26 (p. 107).

103 *The American Almanac and Repository of Useful Knowledge, for the Year 1838* (Boston: Charles Bowen, [1839]), p. 95.

104 Chitty, *The Beast and the Monk*, p. 104.

105 Leary, '*Fraser's Magazine* and the Literary Life', p. 120.

106 Colloms, *Charles Kingsley*, pp. 108–9.

107 Charles Kingsley, 'Yeast; or, The Thoughts, Sayings, and Doings of Lancelot Smith, Gentleman', *Fraser's Magazine*, September 1848, pp. 284–300 (pp. 296–7).

108 Charles Kingsley, 'Yeast No. IV', *Fraser's Magazine*, October 1848, pp. 447–60 (p. 457).

109 Ibid., p. 458.

110 Charles Kingsley, *Yeast: A Problem* (London: John W. Parker, 1851), pp. 142–4.

111 Archer, *Social Unrest and Popular Protest*, pp. 13–15.

112 Kingsley, *Yeast*, p. 145.

113 Hopkins, *The Long Affray*, pp. 42–4.

114 Kingsley, *Yeast*, pp. 146, 149.

115 Linda Woodbridge, *Vagrancy, Homelessness, and English Renaissance Literature* (Chicago: University of Illinois Press, 2001), p. 35.

116 Jefferies, *The Gamekeeper at Home*, p. 112; William Shakespeare, *King Henry IV, Part 1*, ed. David Scott Kastan (London: Arden, 2002; repr. 2004), II.4.397–8.

117 Thomas Hood, 'The Friend in Need', *New Monthly Magazine*, March 1841, pp. 389–99 (p. 397).

118 Kingsley, *Yeast*, p. 142.

119 Kingsley, 'The Value of Law', p. 43.

120 Frederick Marryat, *Joseph Rushbrook; or, The Poacher*, 3 vols (London: Longman, Orme, Brown, Green, 1841), I, p. 34.

121 'Joseph Rushbrook', *New Monthly Magazine*, August 1841, pp. 561–3 (p. 563).

PART II

The City

CHAPTER 3

Casual Paupers

In *London Labour and the London Poor* (1861–2), his stupendous 'cyclopaedia of the industry, the want, and the vice of the great Metropolis', Henry Mayhew recorded that there was an annual influx of vagrants into London.[1] 'They come up to London in the winter', he wrote, 'not to look for any regular work or employment, but because they know that they can have a nightly shelter, and bread night and morning for nothing, during that season.'[2] Although couched in the discourse of the 'deserving' and the 'undeserving' poor, this observation made at mid-century remained true throughout the rest of the Victorian period.[3] Writing in 1899 the journalist and one-time tramp T. W. Wilkinson noted that there was 'a general exodus from the road in the autumn': Gypsies moved to winter lodgings when the leaves began to fall, 'leaving their moveable homes dirty and tenantless', while the 'rank and file of the army – the unmitigated roadsters' followed them 'after all chance of obtaining work in the fields [was] gone'.[4] These vagrants arrived when the municipal refuges opened in November. There they would join the local homeless population, the native beggars of the town whose numbers would swell in winter as unemployed labourers and their dependents were forced onto the streets. The vitality of many trades was determined by the weather, and bricklayers, carpenters, painters and dockworkers could be frozen out of work for weeks at a time, while sailors were sometimes weather-bound throughout the coldest months.[5] The vagrant population of 'The City' was diverse.

Mayhew suggested that when vagrants retreated from the country during winter it was because 'If they remained in the provinces at that period of the year they would be forced to have recourse to the unions, and as they can only stay one night in each place they would be obliged to travel from ten to fifteen miles per day, to which in the winter they have a strong objection.'[6] This was not without justification. Journeys such as these were perilous. Without reliable food and shelter, exposure and starvation would have been imminent threats. Even if they managed to tramp from one workhouse to the next without being stranded by illness or the elements, then there was still no surety they would be received. In 'Told by a Tramp' (1866), a letter written to *All the Year Round*, an anonymous informant claimed that rural workhouses refused to admit wayfarers into their 'casual' or 'vagrant' wards if another union's workhouse was within reach. He recorded that one time, having 'got to a place named Orsett', in Essex, the relieving officer ordered him to 'get on to Billericay, which was nine miles further'.[7] Understandably, then, tactics were used to avoid the open road in winter. One of these was 'retiring into the workhouse', as Wilkinson remarked.[8] Any destitute person with a settlement could admit themselves into their parish's workhouse, and leave again at will. Another strategy was to secure a gaol sentence. David Jones has identified a seasonal pattern to the petty crimes committed in the casual wards. The colder months witnessed an escalation in the number of workhouse offences, such as window breaking and vandalism, because the reliable shelter afforded by the prison was preferable to the single night's lodging provided in the casual ward.[9]

By far the most common policy, however, was to move to a town or city. As Mayhew cynically observed, the municipal charities attracted vagrants; but there were other advantages as well. When harvest work was unavailable, the city offered alternative sources of casual or short-term employment that unskilled and semi-skilled vagrants could perform. Although the winter might put bricklayers and dockers out of a job, it provided work for woodchoppers, gas-stokers, lightermen and sweeps. Iron and steel works also took on more labour during the winter.[10] Moreover, towns and cities had an assortment of accommodation that could be used flexibly according to the means and wants of the indigent. As well as night refuges run by philanthropists, and casual wards managed by Poor Law Guardians, there were also a range of common lodging-houses-that varied in terms of price, comfort and cleanliness. These features were shared to a greater or lesser extent by all towns and cities. That said, Part II of this study focuses almost exclusively on London. Whereas Part I ranged from Yorkshire in the northeast to Devonshire in the southwest, in this section I have focused on one locality. London had the most workhouses, the greatest expenditure of charity, and the largest casual workforce of any city in Britain. As a result, it also had the largest vagrant population: as the American journalist Daniel Kirwan remarked in his metropolitan travelogue, *Palace and Hovel; or, Phases of London Life* (1870), 'there is not such a city in the world as London for vagrancy and vagabondism'.[11]

In this chapter, I first explore the resources available to vagrants in the metropolis, the strictures imposed upon them by the law and the treatment they received in the casual wards. These, I argue, conditioned the way in which vagrants walked, and produced a particular type of 'metropolitan vagrancy'. Characterised by vibration and oscillation, and bound by the circumference of the city, this was a seasonal phenomenon generally restricted to the winter months when vagrants resorted to the capital for work, relief and refuge. This was a constrained form of movement that was contoured by the resources that the vagrant poor were able to access and the mounting restrictions that were placed on them by Poor Law officials, who increasingly tried to curtail the vagrants' mobility through practices of observation, identification and detention. In the second part of the chapter I examine an understudied depiction of urban homelessness that was, in part, a product of these attempts at control: the queue outside the casual ward. An image common to novels, articles, paintings and illustrations, the queue of tramps or 'casual paupers' was an ambiguous emblem that expressed many of the concerns that were evoked by the anonymous and often impassive vagrant. It articulated anxieties about the difficult distinction between the deserving and undeserving poor, and the indiscriminate charity that this gave rise to. In addition, it also conveyed fears about the illiberality of the Poor Law and the potentially revolutionary response that this might provoke from the vagrant crowd.

3.1 Metropolitan Vagrancy

It is impossible to determine the actual number of vagrants in nineteenth-century London. Like the national statistics that I discussed in the Introduction, those produced for the capital were equally inaccurate. These figures, while providing a general indication of the vagrant population, are therefore most useful as a barometer of public feeling. In 1851 the journalist George Augustus Sala, a colleague and friend of Charles Dickens, recorded that out of three million Londoners, 70,000 were commonly thought to be homeless.[12] A decade later in 1861, the *London City Press* concluded that in addition to the 'immense number of delocalized outcasts' who occasionally relied on public and parochial relief when unemployed, there were '12,000 to 15,000 wandering vagabonds in the metropolis'. These habitual tramps, it suggested, accounted for 5 per cent of the total vagrant population, which hovered between 240,000 and 300,000.[13] Such enormous figures also featured in James Greenwood's

survey of vice, *The Seven Curses of London* (1869). Here he claimed that the
capital harboured an 'immense army of juvenile vagrants' numbering
100,000.[14] Meanwhile, Kirwan estimated that there were 'thousands of
casuals who receive lodgings in the work-houses' and a further '15,000
vagrants who do not frequent the work-houses' at all.[15] Taken singly, these
accounts do not tell us much, but as a body they present the capital as the
enduring home of the homeless poor, a large and unnerving citizenry.

The extent of vagrancy in London was reflected by the number of its
charities. As Jerry White has noted, philanthropy became prevalent in the
nineteenth-century metropolis: out of 911 charities active at the century's
end, only 169 predated 1800.[16] Moreover, compared with the nation as a
whole, 'the charities of London in extent, variety, and amount, [were]
perfectly stupendous', as the reformer J. H. Stallard remarked. Writing in
1868, he recorded that out of £3.8 million given to charities each year,
£2.7 million was distributed in the capital, and that £2.1 million of this
was spent on 'the relief of bodily wants, [such] as food, dwelling, clothes':
these were the necessities that vagrants lacked, and as a result they went to
London.[17] In *Ragged London in 1861* (1861) the journalist John
Hollingshead recorded that during the previous winter the 'soup-kitchens,
ragged-schools, asylums, refuges, and all the varied machinery of British
charity, [had] been strained to the utmost'.[18] In truth these outlets of relief
always had an eager and extensive clientele. In 1856 Sala visited Playhouse
Yard, Cripplegate. In a lead article in *Household Words* entitled 'Houseless
and Hungry', he reported that 'the average number of destitute persons
admitted nightly is five hundred and fifty', but that 'as many as six
hundred have been accommodated'.[19] Meanwhile, in her pamphlet *Our
Homeless Poor* (1860), the reformer Ellen Barlie claimed that during
1859 the Field Lane Refuge had sheltered 12,000 people, and helped
1,200 into employment.[20] These were two of the largest asylums in the
1860s; others included Boar's Head Yard, South London Refuge, Newport
Market Refuge and Dudley Stuart's Refuge. Later in the century, the
Salvation Army also founded refuges, first at Limehouse in 1888, and then
in Clerkenwell, Westminster and Whitechapel, all of which had been
opened by 1891.[21]

The accommodation provided by refuges was deliberately austere.
Throughout the Victorian period philanthropists were concerned that
the public's generosity would demoralise the poor by encouraging them
to rely on charity. Conditions in the refuges, where a vagrant could
typically stay for a week, were therefore spartan, as Sala's account testifies:
'We ascended a wooden staircase, and came into a range of long, lofty,

barn-like rooms, divided into sections by wooden pillars.... Ranged on either side were long rows of bedplaces, trough-like, grave-like, each holding one sleeper.'[22] This description of the dormitories at Playhouse Yard, where the inmates slept on straw mattresses and under leather covers, could also be applied to those at Field Lane, where Barlie describes identical conditions.[23] Both reporters welcomed these circumstances, assuring their readers that the wards provided no attractions for the idle vagabond. For the vagrant poor, however, these refuges were sometimes far less satisfactory. In 1866 'A Real Casual' wrote a series of letters to the journalist and civil servant J. C. Parkinson, who published them in *Temple Bar: A London Magazine for Town and Country Readers*. 'A Real Casual' complained that in Field Lane the inmates slept on 'bare boards without straw or anything' and that 'the whole place had a strong smell of tramps'; while the South London Refuge, which slept up to 150 men, was 'much worse than the casual wards', the most unpopular form of accommodation readily available to vagrants.[24]

In 1900 London was seventeen miles across and contained twenty-eight casual wards. Ominously known as 'the spike' by its habitués, the casual ward was the official mechanism of Poor Law relief for vagrants. Here they could spend a night in the workhouse in exchange for a morning's labour, but the conditions within were unpleasant. As the workhouse historian Simon Fowler notes, 'The worst-treated people in the workhouse were undoubtedly the vagrants or "casuals" ... while conditions improved in the rest of the workhouse, in the casual wards they remained largely unchanged during the 90 years of the New Poor Law.'[25] As we shall see throughout this chapter, this is not entirely true: circumstances did change – they became more severe. For the houseless poor, however, London's grid of casual wards formed an important if unforgiving safety net; they were a barrier between the vagrant and dire privation. Moreover, although applicants were not allowed to apply for relief at any given casual ward more than once a month, the large number of both tramps and workhouses within the metropolis meant that vagrants could nonetheless subsist off the Poor Law authorities for long periods of time. Indeed, Wilkinson informs us that the term 'spike-ranger' was used to describe those tramps who managed to rely exclusively on the casual wards. These vagrants, hardened to rough weather and workhouse conditions, were predominantly male.[26]

Although female casuals were significant in literary and visual depictions of the wards, women rarely used them. In 1845 only 15 per cent of the casual paupers registered in workhouses were female, and by 1906 this figure had dropped to just 9 per cent.[27] As we saw in the Introduction, women were more likely than men to enter the workhouse as permanent inmates, and this is certainly one factor that accounts for this low number. However, other elements may also have played a part. There were fewer beds available for female casuals. According to the *Report on the Departmental Committee on Vagrancy* (1906), the metropolitan casual wards supplied 568 beds for women compared with 1,248 beds for men.[28] Women were also, perhaps, more adept at earning money by hawking, begging and prostitution; if accompanied by children, women were likely to be successful beggars, while the assumption that female vagrants were sexually available (see the Introduction) may have made procuring custom easier for them than their male counterparts.[29] Certainly John Rutherford, the author of *Indoor Paupers: By One of Them* (1885), believed that it was easy for women to escape the hardships of the casual ward. Speaking of his own experiences within the workhouse system, he declared that 'women given to haunting casual wards are, without exception, the most shiftless and stupid of their sex; for there are a hundred methods of avoiding these places open to women which are denied to men'.[30] He does not elaborate what these methods are. Nonetheless, the truth of his statement is borne out by reports that London's common lodging-houses sheltered a more even number of men and women. Although the statistics for such places are sparse compared with those of the casual wards, it seems significant that when Kirwan visited one, he recorded that 'among the sixty persons present, there were at least twenty-five women, composed of female tramps, prostitutes, and peddlers of different kinds of commodities'.[31]

The common lodging-house offered a more desirable form of accommodation than the workhouse or the refuge. Otherwise known as the 'rope shop', because as Sam Weller tells Mr Pickwick, 'the beds are made of slips of coarse sacking' pulled over 'two ropes', lodging-houses gave freedom to the tramp.[32] Although the accommodation might not be much better, they provided an escape from the rules and requirements of the wards and refuges. The most frequent objection to the refuges was their evangelical atmosphere. In the 1890s Josiah Flynt, a social investigator who became a tramp incognito, visited the Salvation Army shelter in Whitechapel where a weary inmate complained that the Salvationists 'want us to sing's loud's ef we'd just got out of bed' after a day walking the streets.[33] Such zealotry was also a grievance of 'A Real Casual'. Field Lane Refuge, he asserted, was 'governed by religious fanatics', while the preachers at the South London Refuge 'would cram you full of religion and allow you to starve'.[34]

Meanwhile, in the casual wards conditions were worse: tramps would have their clothes and possessions confiscated and had to perform a work task in the morning. Typically, this was oakum picking or stone breaking, a job that required practice and skill: as 'A Real Casual' relates, when he was 'set to break two bushels' of granite in St Giles Workhouse his palms quickly became 'sore and blistered'.[35] Moreover, the casual paupers were subject to intimidation by the workhouse porters. When Flynt was questioned by the porter at Poplar Workhouse, '[he] was so frightened that [he] would have told him anything he wanted'.[36] And Mary Higgs, another incognito investigator, reported that she felt sexually threatened. In her study *Glimpses into the Abyss* (1906), she wrote, 'I had never realised before that a lady's dress, or even that of a respectable working-woman, was a *protection*. The bold, free look of a man at a destitute woman must be felt to be realised.'[37]

The common lodging-house, then, was a welcome alternative to philanthropic or parochial relief, but it cost money. The lodging-house nomenclature suggests that the standard price for a bed might be as low as 2d. When a policeman catches Alton out at night in Charles Kingsley's *Alton Locke* (1850), he advises him to go to 'a twopenny-rope shop'.[38] Similarly, in Dickens's last and uncompleted novel, *The Mystery of Edwin Drood* (1870), the lodging-house in the cathedral city of Cloisterham, a 'crazy wooden house . . . all warped and distorted', is called the Travellers' Twopenny.[39] In London, however, the price of a single bed was typically 4d. (8d. for a double). This would grant access to one of the capital's numerous lodging-houses, which numbered 1,241 in 1875.[40] Customers would get a bed in a dormitory, occasionally separated by gender, and would have access to a kitchen where they could cook and socialise. The conditions within, however, were notoriously unhygienic. Writing in 1842, the reformer and civil servant Edwin Chadwick argued that only police inspection could halt 'the continued impartation, if not the generation, of epidemic disease by the vagrant population who frequent' lodging-houses.[41] However, although his caution was heeded, and they were placed under police supervision from 1851, they continued to be hotbeds of dirt and disease.[42] Higgs's extensive investigation into lodging-house life contains numerous anecdotes about their uncleanliness: to spend a night in a four-penny bed was to be 'investigated by an uncertain number of "insect pests"', she assures us.[43]

The prevalence of the rope shop attracted the vagrant to London as much as the casual ward, the refuge and the soup kitchen; but the vagrant poor could not always afford to stay in these lodgings. As Raphael Samuel suggests, 'there was a good deal of interchange between the lodging-houses, on the one hand, where accommodation had to be paid for, and the casual wards and refuges, on the other, where it was free'.[44] This interchange largely depended on the availability of casual labour and the ability of the vagrant to perform it. Casual labour was made up of short engagements, was often unskilled and was almost always seasonal. As Gareth Stedman Jones argues in *Outcast London* (1971), metropolitan industries relied upon a large reservoir of labour that could be drawn upon during periods of peak production, and left to stagnate throughout the rest of the year: 'almost every major trade in London', he explains, 'attracted a surplus of underemployed workers who could be said to live on casual earnings'. By 1891 this workforce included 400,000 people, a tenth of the population of London, but in addition to this there were also thousands of vagrants who were also willing to take on occasional work.[45]

While defining the importance and the scope of London's casual labour market, Stedman Jones draws a distinction between the casual pauper and the casual worker: 'vagrants were quite distinct from ordinary casual labourers, both in their habits and their economic attitudes', he states. Nonetheless, there is an unavoidable slippage between these two figures. As he goes on to admit, for both contemporaries and historians 'it is difficult to draw a precise line of demarcation between the two groups'.[46] This is hardly surprising. Both classes relied on the same systems of relief; they were both dependent on seasonal fluctuations in trade; and they both lived in the same over-crowded areas of the city. Moreover, although the more prosperous casual labourers were relatively static, nested within communities where shopkeepers would give them easy credit and where they had beneficial relationships with local foremen, at the bottom end of the scale there was greater mobility and a regular exchange of occupations between vagrants and casual labourers. While vagrants struggled alongside labourers for early morning work at the docks or on building sites, the poorest labourers took up itinerant occupations, including scavenging and hawking.[47] These economies of makeshift could involve travelling long distances within the city and had a distinctly vagrant complexion: as Mayhew reports, 'it usually takes the bone-picker from seven to nine hours to go over his rounds, during which time he travels from 20 to 30 miles'. Earning 8d. would be an 'excellent day's work' for the scavenger, enough for food and a single bed in a lodging-house. Those who were elderly or very young, however, only earned 2d. or 3d.[48] Such days might end in the refuge, the casual ward or out on the street.

The permeability of the labour market, and the insecurity of jobs, often escaped contemporary commentators. With their desire to taxonomise, Victorians would depict a stratified social order in which everyone had a permanent place. In *In the Slums* (1884), an account of his missionary work in St Giles, the Anglican priest D. Rice-Jones described his parishioners as

> Costermongers, bricklayers' labourers, scavengers, dealers in rags and bones, sandwich-men, chimney-sweeps, odd men from Covent Garden market, scene-shifters and hangers-on of the theatre, artisans who are always out of work, women and girls who earn a poor living in all sorts of ways, and a migratory people without visible means of living.[49]

Here Rice-Jones obscures the fact that the 'migratory people without visible means of living' belong to the same class as those who have identifiable occupations, and appear to be fixed within his parish. In fact, all of these classes were mobile and interchangeable. Some may well have confined themselves to St Giles all the year round, but others would be seasonal visitors coming for the winter, and would have moved from parish to parish. This movement through London was shaped by the resources and opportunities afforded by the city, and resulted in what I call 'metropolitan vagrancy'. As noted above, this movement was typified by vibration and oscillation, occurred mainly during the winter and was guided and to some extent controlled by the city's legislature and its structures of relief.

In her account of London's modernisation, Lynda Nead identifies circulation as the major concern of the Victorian urban planner. Metropolitan improvements sought to create 'purposeful movement: of water, air, traffic, people and commodities'; this can be seen in the construction of London's railways, roads, suburbs and sewers, all of which served to decongest the city in various ways. Movement, it seemed, was the key to countering the problems caused by urbanisation. But not all movement was good. As Nead argues, 'the urban ideal was not irrational velocity or indiscriminate mobility, but ordered circulation through networks of streets, pipes and tunnels'.[50] Vagrancy, which was perceived as another consequence of urbanisation, was therefore a disruptive force within the city. Erratic and aimless, it needed to be controlled, and throughout the Victorian period legislation was used to curtail it. Just as sewers were built to channel waste, the substance with which the vagrant 'residuum' was often compared, so laws were passed and casual wards established in order to funnel the very poorest through the city. These attempts to circumscribe the 'irrational' movement of outcasts should be seen as part of the same programme of modernisation that caused slums to be cleared and the Underground to be built. It is also through them that the origins and the quality of metropolitan vagrancy can be described.

The 1824 Vagrancy Act had already ensured that sleeping out in the open was a crime; but Robert Peel's 1829 Metropolitan Police Act assigned the apprehension of the homeless perpetrators as one of the specific duties of London's new modern police force. Under the act, a police officer, or 'peeler', as they were known, was empowered to arrest 'all persons whom he shall find between sunset and the hour of eight in the forenoon lying in any highway, yard, or other place, or loitering therein, and not giving a satisfactory account of themselves'.[51] In theory, this meant that the vagrant could not sleep in the street but had to keep moving all night: it is on the basis of this legislation that Jo, the luckless crossing sweeper in Dickens's *Bleak House* (1852–3), is 'moved on as fur as ever I could go and couldn't be moved no furder' by Inspector Bucket and his colleagues.[52] In practice, however, there were stopping points where the police permitted vagrants to rest. The Indoor Pauper, John Rutherford, who spent a month as a London casual before he admitted himself into a workhouse, noted that although some vagrants dozed in parks during the day to refresh them-selves for a 'nightly prowl', others slept at night within the arches of London Bridge and Blackfriars Bridge and on the benches in Trafalgar Square and on the Embankment.[53] The effect of this was to ghettoise the vagrant, at least during the hours of darkness, which made them easier to locate, question and apprehend. It is no coincidence that a detective unerringly escorted Kirwan to London Bridge, where he was shown 'a perfect gypsy encampment' under the first arch.[54]

The Metropolitan Police Force, an integral part of the modernising city, was therefore engaged in promoting healthy circulation: rather than allow-ing vagrants to block the streets, they kept them on the move and channelled them in particular directions. The casual wards performed similar work. As the Fabian intellectuals Sydney and Beatrice Webb pointed out, the 1834 New Poor Law made no special provision for vagrants, and it was not until the early 1840s that the casual ward was instituted. A 'separate semi-penal establishment', the casual ward was designed to segregate immoral tramps from indoor paupers and to ensure that their work was harder and their diet poorer than the permanent inmates: in no way was wandering to be encouraged.[55] The metropolitan wards also restricted and directed movement in insidious ways. In their original form casual wards provided one night's shelter to the vagrant in return for a morning's labour. This meant that having entered the work-house the vagrant would not be released until late in the morning the following day. As Robert Humphreys notes, this precluded them from the casual job market, which recruited workers early, and typically on a daily basis.[56] Casual paupers were therefore prevented from working and earning the few pence required for a lodging-house, which was the easiest escape route from the casual-ward system. Reliance on the casual ward was further encouraged by the fact that beds were limited, and the queue for admission therefore began to form early in the afternoon. As a result, the vagrant who wanted to be sure of shelter often left one casual ward only to line up outside another a few hours later. This restricted the time in which they could find work or beg money, and this limitation was compounded by the fact that a single ward could be used only once a month, which – in theory – compelled the houseless to walk to the next available refuge. The structure of casual ward relief therefore enforced a reliance on the Poor Law and conditioned the movement of vagrants, obliging them to tramp between workhouses.

As the nineteenth century progressed, legislation ensured that the metropolitan casual wards became more coercive. In 1864 and 1865 the Metropolitan Houseless Poor Acts were introduced: ostensibly liberal measures, they required that all vagrants were admitted to the workhouse regardless of their character or place of settlement. However, as Seth Koven notes, they also aimed to clear the streets of a public nuisance; they guaranteed that there was no excuse for sleeping out, which was, of course, already a criminal offence.[57] After 1870, when the Local Government Board began to administer the Poor Law, the workhouses were increasingly used as a deterrent, and the casual ward statutes became more overtly draconian.[58] The 1871 Pauper Inmates Discharge and Regulations Act was brought before the House of Lords by John Wodehouse, first Earl of Kimberley, expressly for 'the repression, as far as was consistent with humanity, of vagrancy'.[59] It enjoyed an easy passage through the Lords and the Commons, and mandated that casuals could not be released until 11 o'clock on the morning after their admission.[60] More importantly, it decreed that all metropolitan workhouses be treated as a single institution, and established a new penalty for using a casual ward more than once in a given month: three days' confinement. Of course, for vagrants living in London this drastically restricted their chances of abiding by the law, and increased their chances of incarceration. The new act can therefore be seen as a method of slowing down the movement of vagrants by turning casual wards into holding stations that would gradually capture and release the

houseless, and thus ensure that they filtered through the metropolis at a
regular rate. This intensified the casual ward's penal atmosphere, which
was again augmented by the 1882 Casual Poor Act. Under this statute,
vagrants were now held for a minimum of two nights, and if they used the
same ward within a month, then they were held until the fourth morning
after their admission. The London workhouses were still considered one
institution. Although in 1892 a more sympathetic amendment was made
allowing vagrants to be released at 5.30 a.m. in summer and 6.30 a.m. in
winter to find work, these acts remained in force well into the twentieth
century.[61]

From a legislative standpoint, we witness the development of a hermet-
ically sealed system in which casuals are guided by police and Poor Law
officials from one holding area to the next. Their movement is limited by
the location of these sites of detention and controlled by a procedure of
capture and release. This system is reminiscent of Michel Foucault's
carceral archipelago, a network of penal and semi-penal institutions from
which there is no escape, only an endless exchange of one form of
detention for another.[62] It also invites biopolitical readings that are also
inspired by Foucault. In 'Right of Death and Power over Life' in the first
volume of *The History of Sexuality* (1976) and in his contemporary lecture
series *Society Must Be Defended* (1975–6), Foucault argues that during the
late eighteenth century a new, biopolitical form of power began to emerge.
Unlike the classical sovereign who demonstrates power by taking life,
biopolitical power tries to generate life. 'One might say that the ancient
right to take life or let live was replaced by a power to foster life or disallow
it to the point of death,' Foucault writes.[63] This shift in the art of
government is accompanied by a change of focus. Whereas the sovereign
is concerned with disciplining or destroying individuals in order to maintain its hegemony, biopower seeks to 'foster life' by regulating society at
the level of the species: its primary focus is not the body but the population. This does not mean that techniques designed to discipline individuals
fall out of use. Instead, they are supplemented by new techniques, such as
statistics and forecasts, that measure the size, mortality, fertility and
longevity of the population in order to increase its well-being through
regulation. Together the discipline of the individual and the regulation of
the mass form the twin poles of biopower.[64]

The casual-ward system was a microcosm in which both these types of
power were implemented. The series of coercive acts discussed above
turned the wards from sites of succour into instruments of discipline and
regulation. On the one hand, they monitored the vagrant population by

directing its movement and keeping it within a sphere of surveillance; on the other hand, they disciplined the vagrant body by keeping it confined and forcing it to work. These measures were introduced to safeguard the health of the population, or – in Foucault's phrase – to 'foster life' within it. The hostile conditions produced in the wards were supposed to protect the public from the physical and moral evils of vagrancy. They not only served as a deterrent for the working poor, warding them away from the alleged 'charms' of vagrant life, but also minimised the contact between the habitual tramp and the labouring classes, and thus reduced the chances of 'contamination'.

The idea that the vagrant body was a social toxin was prominent throughout the Victorian period. Chadwick warned that vagrants 'spread physical pestilence, as well as moral deprivation' in 1842; in 1866 Stallard referred to vagrancy as a 'vast disease' that threatened to demoralise the populace; and in 1899 Millicent Garrett Fawcett blamed 'the importation of small-pox' into London on 'the huge army of degraded poverty to which we give the name of tramps'.[65] The fear that vagrants were vectors for moral, social and biological disorders was eventually registered in the design of the casual wards. In 1868 a circular from the Poor Law Board instructed the Poor Law Guardians to lodge vagrants in single cells rather than in communal wards, which were depicted as 'school[s] of vagrancy and petty crime'.[66] The single cell, an architectural form imported from the prison system where it was introduced in 1839, separated the vicious from the virtuous, and the sick from the healthy, thus ensuring that neither vice nor disease could spread among the vagrants and endanger the population at large. That it was public health rather than the well-being of the individual that motivated the authorities is reflected at a procedural level. Mary Higgs (among others) reported the ubiquitous practice of 'stoving' whereby the tramps' clothes were placed in a heated oven; this process was introduced to disinfect their clothes, but it also creased and damaged them, making it more difficult for them to find employment.[67] Later, George Orwell, the most famous social investigator to infiltrate the workhouse casual ward, reported that in the 1930s the inmates had to undergo a mandatory medical examination but that 'the inspection was designed merely to detect smallpox, and took no notice of our general condition'.[68] The doctors were employed only to identify contagious diseases that placed the public at risk.

A biopolitical narrative accounts for the way in which vagrants were monitored and disciplined in order to promote the moral and physical health of the general population and allows us to conceptualise how and

why the casual wards were supposed to work. However, it would be a
mistake to think that this system of regulation was non-negotiable and
inescapable. As Deana Heath notes, Foucault's theories often 'reveal the
way that bodies are worked upon by configurations of power, but they do
little to illumine how people both respond to and deconstruct such
configurations'.[69] A strict Foucauldian reading, then, risks neglecting the
agency of the individual, and this is certainly true in the case of the casual-
ward system, which offered vagrants a degree of choice.

Although the senior civil servants who managed the Poor Law wanted
the casual wards to work in concert, this never actually happened.
Workhouses were parochial affairs at the mercy of local politics. Their
Masters and Guardians determined how vagrants were treated, and conditions were unequal in the metropolis throughout the nineteenth century.[70] As 'A Real Casual' attests, each ward had a reputation: in the mid-
1860s Marylebone Workhouse was 'a very decent place' and the casuals
were allowed to smoke in bed, 'a luxury denied at every other place in
London', whereas the ward in Holborn Workhouse was 'perfectly without
fire, and might as well be in the open air'.[71] Moreover, even though the
attitude towards casual paupers hardened at a legislative level, this did not
necessarily translate to tougher treatment by workhouse staff. In 1905 the
Departmental Committee on Vagrancy heard evidence that neither Poplar
nor Whitechapel enforced the four-day detention period mandated by the
1882 Casual Poor Act for casuals who stayed more than one night in a
metropolitan ward during the course of a month. They also heard that
these workhouses, along with those at Thavies Inn and Islington, had
refused to introduce the single-cell system.[72] This lack of consistency
meant that although vagrants did move from one workhouse to the next,
their movements were determined, to some extent, by the conditions that
they expected to meet there. They were not without volition. Vagrants
were also able to negotiate the system in other ways. 'A Real Casual' was
able to enter Lambeth at least six times during his month as a casual
because 'it [was] scarcely likely [the porter] would recognize one among
the many he takes in every night'; and Greenwood, who spent a night in
the same ward in 1866, noted that one juvenile vagrant there bragged that
he had been in the same ward for 'three successive nights'.[73]

The Porter, the Master, the Poor Law Guardian – these figures were not
omniscient, and this fact was well known. As a result, anxieties about how
the wards were being used, and whether or not the applicants were
deserving, surfaced throughout the period. These were captured in the
actions and writings of incognito social investigators, such as Greenwood,

Flynt, Higgs and Jack London, all of whom went into the casual wards 'to learn and make known the truth'.[74] They were also powerfully expressed by the numerous depictions of the casual queue. As London noted in his undercover exposé of the East End, *The People of the Abyss* (1903), this was a common sight in the Victorian metropolis. He recorded that for the workers who lived opposite Whitechapel Workhouse, 'each and every day, from one in the afternoon till six, our ragged spike line is the principal feature of the view commanded by their front doors and windows'.[75] In depictions of these waiting and often passive vagrants, writers and artists forced their audience to confront the illegibility of the city's homeless and the political, social and spiritual fears that they provoked.

3.2 Casuals Rejected: Kingsley 1848 and Dickens 1856

In 1847, the worst year of the Irish Famine (1845–9) coincided with a severe financial crisis. The famine resulted in the death and displacement of millions of people. One million died in the Irish workhouses from disease and starvation; 2.1 million emigrated to America; and tens of thousands crossed the Irish Sea to England.[76] The majority of these ended up in London's slums: Whitechapel, Leyton, Saffron Hill and West Ham all had Irish 'colonies', while the Rookery of St Giles was known as 'Little Ireland'. By 1851 there were 109,000 Irish-born Londoners living in the metropolis.[77] Meanwhile, over-speculation in grain imports and railway companies caused one of the worst economic crashes of the century, which triggered the collapse of many firms and banks, leading to the widespread loss of savings and livelihoods.[78] During this period the vagrant population was already riding high, as it had been throughout most of the 1840s, but the famine and financial crisis together caused it to surge. In 'The Pauper Hotels of England' (1848), *Bell's New Weekly Messenger* reported that between 1846 and 1847 the aggregate number of English vagrants relieved by seventy-nine unions had more than doubled, reaching 32,683. These same workhouses had also admitted 11,548 Irish casuals, an increase of 574 per cent on the previous year. As the article's title implies, *Bell's* was unsympathetic towards the wandering poor: 'the number of crafty rogues is rapidly increasing', was the conclusion it drew from the statistics.[79] This attitude became a mainstay of public opinion.

Throughout the summer of 1848, MPs called upon Charles Buller, the President of the Poor Law Board, to respond to 'the great increase of vagrant poor' throughout England. In particular, they were anxious about the number of Irish casuals claiming relief, and the influx of tramps into cities: Leeds, Manchester and Norwich had all seen a significant growth in vagrancy, 'whilst in the City of London it had increased to an enormous extent'.[80] At the root of these petitions were concerns about the poor rate and the amount that voters would have to pay. In the period of economic uncertainty that followed the financial crash, the middle and upper classes were looking to retrench, to repair losses acquired when stocks plummeted and to secure the remainder of their capital. They were therefore reluctant to pay for an apparently ever-increasing vagrant population. In August that year, Buller responded to these concerns by issuing a Minute to the Poor Law Guardians. Here he claimed that 'the system which has of late years been adopted in the relief of [the] casual poor has been the principal cause of the extension of vagrancy'. Tougher measures would be required if vagrants were to be deterred: the work task should be enforced in every union; the police should be used as Assistant Relieving Officers; and the deserving poor should be issued with official tickets detailing their character and verifying their destination. His main policy, however, was that casual paupers should no longer be given indiscriminate relief. The able-bodied and undeserving should be denied succour: 'A sound and vigilant discrimination in respect of the objects of relief, and the steady refusal of aid to all who are not ascertained to be in a state of destitution, are obviously the most effectual remedies against the continued increase of vagrancy and mendicancy.'[81] This strategy was underpinned by Buller's belief that it was 'the thief, the mendicant, and the prostitute, who crowd the vagrant wards'.[82] The press, too, adopted this conviction.

Although the upsurge in vagrancy was a theme of parliamentary debates throughout the summer, it was not until the autumn that the newspapers seized upon it. As journalists quipped throughout the period, this was a habit of the Victorian press: 'discussions in the newspapers about the homeless poor are a standing order of the day at this season', remarked one reporter in November 1863.[83] This year, however, this annual topic became imbued with bitterness. Taking Buller's lead, the press portrayed vagrants as fraudsters. In September, *Bell's* declared that the 'wicked rogues who obtain relief at the unions under false pretences ... fatten upon the means provided for honest persons'.[84] The following month the *Staffordshire Advertiser*, reporting on a meeting of the midland Guardians, opened its account with the assertion that 'there is no doubt that vast numbers of persons travel from Union-house to Union-house in the most systematic manner, and make this description of vagrancy their *profession*'. It also quoted the *Medical Times*, which diagnosed 'the pie-bald multitude' of tramps as 'chiefly composed of professional beggars, thieves, thimble-riggers, poachers, prostitutes, and scoundrels of the very worst description'.[85] A few days later the *Spectator*, recalling the link between vagrancy and disease, referred to tramps as the 'parasitical enemy' and 'human vermin'.[86] The casual wards, then, were full of undeserving imposters. However, although this assumption dovetailed with Buller's Minute, the newspapers were far more severe when it came to their treatment. While Buller refused to specify 'any additional test or punishment that shall prevent the abuse of relief', right-wing newspapers cried out for harsher penalties.[87] The *Spectator* recommended 'a special form of punishment, such as *travaux forces* [hard labour]'; *Bell's* wanted to enforce whipping, a sentence that could be served to male incorrigible rogues under the 1824 Vagrancy Act; and *Fraser's Magazine* wished to extend the applicability of this punishment 'by flogging every man or boy convicted of begging'.[88] It was within this cut-throat milieu that Kingsley serialised *Yeast*, also in *Fraser's Magazine*.

Kingsley's chief concern was the agricultural poor, and *Yeast* primarily addressed rural poverty and the sins that it engendered (see Chapter 2). However, Kingsley was never chained to Hampshire: London was only an hour and a half away by train, and as the assistant editor of *Politics for the People*, and an attendant at F. D. Maurice's weekly meeting of Christian Socialists, he made the journey frequently. During his visits to Maurice and John Parker, who was the publisher of both *Fraser's* and *Politics for the People*, it is easy to imagine that he passed the queues outside the casual wards as he travelled north from Waterloo to their rooms in Lincoln's Inn and the Strand.[89] But whether he regularly encountered these sights or not, in the November instalment of *Yeast* he included a workhouse scene that both captures and critiques the hostility then felt towards the casual poor.

Bearing a note from London for Lancelot, whose fortune has been imperilled by the collapse of his uncle's bank, the vicar of Whitford stops 'at the city of A——' in order to dissuade Luke (Lancelot's cousin) from joining the Catholic Church. After an unsuccessful interview he leaves Luke's lodgings worrying whether his own High Church principles pushed Luke from Anglicanism. As he paces through the night he steps into a gothic nightmare: 'grey clouds were rushing past the moon like terrified ghosts'; 'the wind was sweeping and howling down the lonely streets'; and the 'gaunt poplars groaned and bent, like giants cowering from the wrath of Heaven'. In this apocalyptic and supernatural cityscape the only people left are the houseless poor who have been rejected from the casual ward:

As he went on, talking wildly to himself, he passed the Union Workhouse. Opposite the gate, under the lee of a wall, some twenty men, women, and children, were huddled together on the bare ground. They had been refused lodging in the workhouse, and were going to pass the night in that situation. As he came up to them, coarse jests, and snatches of low drinking-songs, ghastly as the laughter of lost spirits in the pit, mingled with the feeble wailings of some child of shame. The vicar recollected how he had seen the same sight at the door of Kensington Workhouse, walking home one night in company with Luke Smith; and how, too, he had commented to him on that fearful sign of the times, and had somewhat unfairly drawn a contrast between 'the niggard cruelty of popular Protestantism,' and the fancied 'liberality of the middle age'.[90]

Outside the workhouse we see the vagrants whom Buller would reject from the casual ward: the idle vagabonds with their 'coarse jests' and vulgar 'drinking-songs'. Intermixed with these reprobates, however, are wailing children, their innocent dependents. Here Kingsley presents us with a critique of Buller's system and his belief in the power of the discriminating eye that belongs to everyone of 'ordinary intelligence'.[91] Not only does the composition of the crowd highlight a lack of discernment, but the vagrants' presentation seems to deny the possibility that the deserving and the undeserving can be separated. Passing the workhouse, the vicar sees only the vague forms of 'some twenty' casuals 'huddled together', and even when he draws near they do not become more visible. Likewise, although the vicar's ear picks up the noise of jests, songs, laughter and crying, all of these sounds are 'mingled' in a general cacophony. The vagrants, then, are impervious to the discriminating senses.

This resistance to differentiation leads to an irresolvable ethical conundrum. Although Kingsley condemns the severity of Poor Law relief, he also acknowledges that there is no ready alternative. His general censure of the system is articulated by the vicar's diagnosis of the casual line as a 'fearful sign of the times'. One of several references made to Thomas Carlyle during the course of the novel, this phrase directs us to his 1829 essay 'Signs of the Times'. Here Carlyle characterises the nineteenth century as 'the Mechanical Age', a period in which efficiency, profit and production govern the spiritual and material aspirations of England. One consequence of this is that 'men are grown mechanical in head and in heart, as well as in hand'.[92] For Kingsley and like-minded contemporaries, Buller's stringent Minute, designed to reduce the poor rate and the number of idle persons, was yet more evidence of this unfeeling attitude. As *The Times* opined in a contemporary article, also published in November 1848, those who 'are most competent to scrutinize a mendicant's case' – which presumably included Workhouse Masters and Poor Law Guardians – 'are so convinced of extensive imposture that they pass by and become hardened against everything that begs'.[93] However, the alternative to this, which Kingsley identifies as indiscriminate almsgiving, is equally abhorrent. In a parody of the 'liberality of the middle age', the vicar, finding he has 'no silver', gives away 'some fifteen or twenty sovereigns' to the casuals. Such haphazard acts of charity were severely censured in this period: in 'Beggars and Almsgivers' (1849), for example, an article published in the *New Monthly Magazine*, they are castigated as 'the seeds of demoralisation, debauchery, and crime'.[94] Kingsley likewise condemns the vicar's actions. His recklessness is signalled by the 'whining and flattery, wrangling and ribaldry' of the vagrants, postures that confirm their greed and moral degradation. Meanwhile, the fact that the vicar 'hurried off', 'not daring to wait and see the use to which his money would be put', captures the shame he feels at his improvidence.

Kingsley uses the image of the casual line to address a problem of the modern metropolis, the 'deformation' or depersonalisation of the gift. In human societies the act of charity has historically been made between known participants. In the modern city, however, such exchanges often take place between strangers: urbanisation breeds alienation. One consequence of this anonymity, which is of course exaggerated in the case of the mobile vagrant, is that benefactors cannot be sure of whom they are giving to, and whether the charity that they are dispensing is appropriate. As a result, within Victorian London, 'the gift relationship [was] replaced by a promiscuous compound of indiscriminate almsgiving and careless Poor Law relief', as Stedman Jones explains.[95] Kingsley, setting his casual scene in the city of A——, but likening it to one outside Kensington Workhouse, implies that these metropolitan conditions are also in evidence elsewhere. The inadequacy of Poor Law relief, on the one hand, and the complexities of personal philanthropy, on the other, coalesced in the figure of the outcast casual. Unknown and strongly associated with vice and crime, their often-pitiable physical condition evoked the inner conflict between liberality and reticence that accompanied charity in the streets. This was an abiding concern throughout the Victorian period and can be seen in Dickens's 'A Nightly Scene in London' (1856), an article which is also set on a November night, 'very dark, very muddy, and raining hard'.[96]

While walking with a friend Dickens 'accidently strayed into Whitechapel' on 5 November 1855. There he was arrested by the sight of five vagrants 'crouched against the wall of the Workhouse':

They were motionless, and had no resemblance to the human form. Five great beehives, covered with rags – five dead bodies taken out of graves, tied neck and heels, and covered with rags – would have looked like those five bundles upon which the rain rained down in the public street.

'What is this!' said my companion. 'What *is* this!'

'Some miserable people shut out of the Casual Ward, I think,' said I.

We had stopped before the five ragged mounds, and were quite rooted to the spot by their appearance. Five awful Sphinxes by the wayside, crying to every passer-by, 'Stop and guess! What is to be the end of a state of society that leaves us here!'[97]

Faced with five featureless, genderless heaps, Dickens gropes for an apt simile to explain the static forms. The vagrants, however, resist interpretation. Veering between agrarian 'beehives' and profane corpses, each attempt that Dickens makes to be figurative collapses and becomes a reassertion of the vagrants' literal condition: they are 'covered with rags'. This is an obvious symbol of poverty that nonetheless baffles Dickens and acts as a bulwark to further analysis. Their illegibility is also registered by Dickens's companion. His repeated query, 'what is this!', a question that slurs into an exclamation, speaks of a panic induced by alienation as much as it does of humanitarian outrage. The uncertainty that these immobile and anonymous figures create is elaborated throughout the article.

Having been granted an interview by the Master of Whitechapel Workhouse, Dickens questions him about the characters and histories of the outcasts: 'they are not shelterless because they are thieves for instance. – You don't know them to be thieves?' he asks. His concern is philanthropic; he wants to know whether it would be responsible to 'give them a trifle'. All he can glean from the Master, however, is that they are 'women, I suppose' and that the workhouse has rejected them because the casual ward is full. Other than that, the local authorities 'don't know anything about them'. This anonymous condition is maintained even when Dickens interviews them himself. Walled behind an impassive mien, a product of their poverty, they are 'all dull and languid' and receive his questions and his money with equal indifference: 'no one cared to look at me; no one thanked me', Dickens remarks. This unworldly detachment is translated into a supernatural quality at the end of the article when Dickens watches them shuffle out of sight. They 'melted away into the night in the strangest manner I ever saw'.[98] We are left with a profound sense of their inscrutability.

In this article Dickens models responsible charity. Placed within the same philanthropic framework outlined by Kingsley, Dickens tries to negotiate between two extremes: the indifference of the Poor Law and indiscriminate giving. He questions the Workhouse Master, he questions the vagrant poor, and (unlike the vicar of Whitford) he goes to a public house to 'get change for a sovereign' when he finds himself 'without silver': in the context of an anonymous stranger gold would be too great a gift.[99] In addition, he refuses to prejudge the casuals as deserving or undeserving based upon their appearance, gender and situation. Female vagrancy, as we have seen, was strongly associated with sexual deviancy, and acute poverty of the kind that Dickens portrays was commonly regarded as part of the prostitute's destiny. As Nead observes while discussing their representation in mid-Victorian visual culture: 'The entire narrative of the downward progress could be expressed in the dress and appearance of the prostitute – the gaudy, showy dress of the streetwalker signified that she had started her descent, whilst the faded rags of the outcast showed that she was very close to death.'[100] Dickens's bedraggled quintet, 'gaunt with want' and 'covered with rags', is in this final stage; but despite this correspondence, he refuses to rely on popular stereotypes, and in doing so pursues the ideal of treating each charitable case on its own individual merits.[101]

Nonetheless, despite these measures the vagrants are still unknown, and Dickens's charity is ultimately still impartial. Moreover, neither Dickens's questions nor his shillings provide a satisfactory response to the riddle of the 'awful Sphinxes': 'what is to be the end of a state of society that leaves us here!' Although the sphinx is a pervasive symbol in the history of art and literature, and is saturated with significance, it seems likely that this is a reference to Carlyle, who poses and answers a similar question in *Past and Present* (1843). Discussing a Chartist demonstration, another passive assemblage of the 'hungry' and the 'desperate' who 'came all out into the streets, and – stood there', Carlyle says that although they were dumb, 'they put their huge inarticulate question, "What do you mean to do with us?"' This, Carlyle intones, 'is the first practical form of *our* Sphinx-riddle. England will answer it; or, on the whole, England will perish.'[102] The five vagrants outside the workhouse, then, gesture towards the revolutionary potential of the outcast and the indigent. This capacity is, of course, emphasised by the fact that Dickens encounters them on the fifth of November, a day well remembered for gunpowder, treason and plot.

3.3 Casuals Relieved: Fildes 1869 and 1874

The passage of the 1865 Metropolitan Houseless Poor Act met with a mixed response. Its promise to provide food and shelter to every vagrant who applied to the casual ward, no matter their character or past conduct, was welcomed by the liberal press: the *Daily News* announced that the new act would 'be thoroughly satisfactory to all real well-wishers of the homeless poor', and the *Illustrated Times*, while acknowledging that some casuals were 'not altogether saints', nonetheless asserted that this was 'no reason why they should be left to starve'.[103] The Poor Law Guardians, however, were dissatisfied with the new measure on two counts. First, the act revoked the power of workhouse officials to reject the undeserving poor; second, they believed that expanding the provision made for casual paupers would lead to an increase in vagrancy. The Bermondsey Guardian Mr Mars was convinced that it would 'increase vagrancy one hundred fold' and 'make nothing but a nation of vagabondism', while Mr Tubbs, a Marylebone Workhouse official, claimed that England seemed to be 'reverting to the times of Queen Elizabeth, when vagrants roamed about with impunity'.[104] The attitude of Tubbs and Mars was shared by many of their colleagues, and as a consequence the act was unevenly enforced. Reporting in late October 1865, the *Illustrated Times* discovered that 142 casuals had been rejected from the Bermondsey Workhouse during the course of a week, and 'left to find refuge in other parishes or to pass the night in the streets'.[105] Such defiance meant that by January 1866 'an impression had gone abroad that the Houseless Poor Act had broken down and was a failure', as the Metropolitan Inspector of the Poor Law Board acknowledged.[106] It was at this fraught moment that Frederick Greenwood, editor of the *Pall Mall Gazette* (*PMG*), instigated an undercover exposé of life in a metropolitan casual ward: 'A Night in a Workhouse' (1866).

Greenwood's investigation was opportunistic. As the Guardians baulked against the Houseless Poor Act, a severe winter closed over London, placing its homeless at risk of exposure.[107] Meanwhile, the *PMG*, an evening newspaper for West End gentlemen, had begun to flounder and needed a boost in sales. Greenwood therefore decided to commission his brother, James Greenwood, to report on the topical issue of the casual poor, much as Dickens had done in 'A Nightly Scene in London'. The difference would be that James would dress himself as a 'sly ruffianly figure' and enter the ward himself. Choosing Lambeth Workhouse as his destination, James set out in January 1866 to test whether the Guardians were obeying the Houseless Poor Act. However, he also had an ulterior motive: to uncover the truth about the casual poor. As he explains in the first number of his three-part series, he aimed 'to learn by actual experience how casual paupers are lodged and fed, and what the "casual" is like, and what the porter who admits him, and the master who rules over him; and how the night passes with the outcasts whom we have all seen crowding about workhouse doors on cold and rainy nights'.[108] Here Greenwood promises to surmount the anonymity of the vagrant, emblematised by the familiar sight of the casual line, the outcasts 'crowding about workhouse doors'. What he discovered was that the ward – a frigid shed with a floor 'encrusted with filth' and one wall missing – was populated by a 'ruffian majority' who were 'at liberty to do just as they liked'; they swore, smoked, sang and bullied the 'peaceable decent men' who formed the 'industrious few'.[109]

The influence of 'A Night in a Workhouse' should not be under-estimated. It directly impacted the *PMG*'s sales, earning it anywhere between 1,500 and 9,000 new subscribers (sources vary), and thus saved the paper from bankruptcy.[110] Moreover, it sparked a series of copycat investigations commissioned by the metropolitan press: in the following days and weeks, the *Observer*, *The Times*, the *Telegraph*, the *Daily News*, the *Saturday Review* and the *Morning Star* all sent their reporters on midnight excursions to the casual wards of London.[111] These homages to 'A Night in a Workhouse' helped to establish its legacy. James Greenwood enjoyed enduring fame as 'The Amateur Casual', the pseudo-nym he adopted in the aftermath of the investigation: twenty years on, references to 'The Amateur Casual' could still go unglossed in the news-paper and periodical press, while undercover exposés, like C. W. Craven's 1887 'A Night in the Workhouse', capitalised on Greenwood's success and celebrity. As Luke Seaber has recently argued, 'A Night in a Workhouse' inaugurated a 'half-century Golden Age of Greenwoodian incognito social investigation' in which a number of other 'amateurs' infiltrated casual wards across the country for both the copy and the thrill.[112] For this study, however, the most important consequence of the Greenwoods' investigation was the way that it altered perceptions of the casual poor.

Having revealed the deplorable condition of both the casual ward and its inmates, Greenwood signs off his report: 'the moral of all this I leave to you'.[113] A few chose to interpret it as a confirmation that the Poor Law was uncharitable. In 'A Night in the Casual Ward of the Work-House, in Rhyme' (1866), the anonymous M.A. versified Greenwood's narrative, and took on his invitation: the penultimate stanza, boldly entitled 'MORAL', reads: 'John Bull will now most plainly see / The want of Christian charity; / Or e'en of that philanthropy / That ought to rule the Workhouse!'[114] Many more, however, latched onto the depraved nature of Greenwood's casuals, complaining that the Houseless Poor Act, and the inadequate organisation of the casual wards, had led to the indiscriminate admission and interaction of the deserving and the undeserving, and that this would lead to the demoralisation of the innocent. Those who adopted this position took their cue from Frederick. On 16 January, the day following the final instalment, the editor placed the following conundrum before his enlarged readership:

> Take thirty or forty tramps of the worst kind, make them herd together in an empty shed naked and miserable throughout the whole of a long winter's night, and what can you expect except to produce a sort of chapel of ease to the Cities of the Plain for the hideous enjoyment of those who are already bad, and the utter corruption of those who are obliged to hear what they cannot prevent?[115]

This account of how vicious 'tramps of the worst kind' are allowed to mingle in an indiscriminate 'herd' with the innocent, who are in turn corrupted by what they are 'obliged to hear', became the standard narrative of the casual ward. In 'The Houseless Poor in Stepney' (1866), *The Times* disclosed that female casuals are 'pigged' together, 'the fever-smitten London tramp with the healthy girl from the country, and the clean wayfarer with the parasite-covered denizen of the street'. Moreover, as in The Amateur Casual's account, 'the quiet and helpless, the young and the old, are left to the mercy of the ruffians'.[116] Similarly, in 'The Lambeth Guardians and the Casual Poor' (1866), the *Daily News* revealed that when they visited the Lambeth Workhouse they discovered that the vagrants were still 'clustered together for the sake of animal heat' and that 'the weak and feeble were at the complete mercy of the strong and ruffianly'.[117] And in *The Female Casual and Her Lodging* (1866), J. H. Stallard argued that the Houseless Poor Act had resulted in 'an indiscriminate herding together of the hardiest and most impudent vagrants in the Metropolis' and that the deplorable organisation of the workhouses had turned the casual ward into 'a school of vagrancy and petty crime'.[118]

We should, however, be wary of this narrative. In the summer of 1866 Stallard orchestrated an incognito investigation into female casual wards, having been persuaded by Greenwood's notion that disguise could uncover the character of the vagrant poor, a class whose 'confidence is not easily obtained by strangers'. But the testimony of the anonymous 'pauper widow' whom he sent into the wards contradicts his claim that casuals are fierce vagabonds: she tentatively declares that they are 'not altogether bad'.[119] Likewise, Rutherford, who describes 'A Night in a Workhouse' as a 'clever and highly coloured sketch', reports that 'strange tales have been told of the recklessness and ruffianism of the wretches who haunt casual wards. So far as I could see, there is little foundation for them'.[120]

Nonetheless, the potency of the Greenwoods' narrative exposes a cultural anxiety. No matter their political allegiance, commentators were universally concerned by the indiscriminate nature of relief and the kind of casuals that were being allowed into London's workhouses. At the root of this was a fear that the 'herding' of casuals would engross the vagrant population by enabling the old stagers to entrap innocents in a life of vagabondage; this suspicion appeared all but confirmed as the number of vagrants began to escalate between 1866 and 1869.[121] Within this context the significance of the casual queue altered: it no longer represented the problem of whom to relieve because everyone (in theory) would be received. Instead, it marked the threat of contamination and demoralisation, and this raised what was at stake when it came to differentiating the habitual tramp and the honest wayfarer. Only by identifying, monitoring and controlling the professional vagrant could the innocent be protected.

Luke Fildes's illustration 'Houseless and Hungry' (1869) (Figure 3.1) both broached and assuaged concerns about discrimination. Appearing on 4 December 1869 in the first issue of the *Graphic*, a magazine that targeted the same upper- and middle-class market as the *PMG*, Fildes's engraving portrays a line of casuals queuing outside a police station waiting to claim their tickets for admission to the ward.[122] With a shallow foreground, the illustration brings the casuals close, which allows the audience to inspect the vagrants and enforces a sense of intimacy; these qualities are enhanced by 'the journal's portable character', as the art historian Caroline Arscott notes, and the fact that the picture took up a full page.[123] Viewers are consequently placed in an empowered position similar to that of the police officer, whose erect stance and hawk-like visage suggest that he is a minute and careful observer as he stares down the casual line. Like him, they are discriminating spectators who watch the crowd without being watched; apart from a sinewy youth, lowering at the audience beneath the brim of his cap, nearly all the casuals are turned away. This association between policeman and viewer is intensified by the text accompanying the picture. A catalogue of the vagrants arrayed before us, it reveals that the old man on the far left 'has only been in London three days, and purposes to leave in the morning'; that the next two men 'are vagabonds'; that the central figure with 'the quasi-respectable air' is an alcoholic and a radical; and that the 'mechanic' holding his child 'has been ill' and is now looking for work. Just like the policeman, who will tell you that the vagabond in the slouched hat is a 'well-known beggar' and that the drunkard 'is a character', the audience becomes privy to information that enables them to identify imposters.[124] The text and image together, then, are a comforting

Figure 3.1   Sir Luke Fildes, 'Houseless and Hungry' (1869). Private collection/Bridgeman Images

combination: as Arscott remarks, they allow the viewer to 'enact the procedure assigned to the police' of surveying and interpreting the casual poor.[125]

Nonetheless, both the article and illustration also point to the anxieties evoked by the casual line. What Fildes portrays is the model of vagrant relief. The police officer is being used as an Assistant Relieving Officer for the casual ward, a policy that was recommended in Buller's August Minute and which became common practice after Greenwood's investigation.[126] Moreover, it is clear that the officer is an able monitor and that he can control the vagrant ruffians, all of whom are subdued in his presence. Despite this, there is still a sense that the system is ineffective. The itemised description of the casuals concludes with a confirmation that the Houseless Poor Act is in force: 'all these people, with many others, received tickets, and were admitted into the casual ward of one of our great workhouses'. This assurance, however, is tainted by the fact that while some of the casuals will 'carry out their professed intention of seeking work', the rest will 'spend another idle, shiftless day in the streets or parks, and . . . present themselves next night at another metropolitan police office, to be examined and certificated, and subsequently bathed, sheltered, and fed'.[127] In other words, they are spike-rangers, preying on the poor rates. The picture also has qualities that might have made contemporaries uneasy.

Entitled 'Houseless and Hungry', like Sala's compassionate article on the Asylum for the Houseless Poor, the illustration might be calculated, as Andrea Korda argues, 'to evoke sympathy, even indiscriminate sympathy'.[128] The two family groups, one clustered near the drunk, the other walking in the foreground, are especially pitiable. In this last case, the virtue of the single, ragged woman is secured by the presence of her children. If depicted alone, or just with her babe, this figure would have been identified by contemporaries as a prostitute or fallen woman, and therefore deserving of her outcast state; however, apart from new-borns, the evidence of transgression, children were generally omitted from visual depictions of 'sexually deviant' women on the streets. Indeed, it was popularly believed that prostitutes were rendered sterile by their 'unnatural' occupation.[129] Mayhew, recalling his visit to the female inmates of Tothill Fields Prison in 1856, remarked that those with infants in the nursery ward were of a 'superior caste to those seen in the other wards': 'the very fact of their being mothers is sufficient to prove that these prisoners do not belong to the class of "public women," since it is a wondrous ordination of Benevolence that such creatures as are absolutely shameless and affectionless should be childless as well'.[130] The female vagrant, then, flanked by her anxious children, would have been a safe object of pity for the audience.

But this is not true of all the casuals. Many are ambiguous, even sinister. As Arscott notes, when viewing the vagrants without the guiding text, we are confronted with 'a rank of rigid expressions' that baffle moral judgements.[131] Like Dickens's 'five bundles of rags', many of them are immobile and impassive, their intentions and histories a disconcerting blank. Meanwhile, the youth standing on the right is menacing as he glares at the viewer: although his bare feet indicate his wretched want, his expression is full of wrathful accusation. For audiences coming to the first issue of the *Graphic*, the pitiable, illegible and disturbing aspects of Fildes's illustration would have been particularly piquant: assuming that they read the pages consecutively, they would first be confronted with the illustration, and only once they had studied it, and turned the page, would they encounter the explanatory text.

Fildes's illustration was met with approbation. According to his son and biographer, L. V. Fildes, it prompted Dickens to appoint him as illustrator for *Edwin Drood*, which proved a pivotal commission in his career.[132] The power of the picture lay in the fact that, although it was ultimately reassuring, it expressed a popular concern that the houseless poor might really be unknown, despite the involvement of the police. These fears were exacerbated by the growth of the vagrant population. By the end of the 1860s it was thought to have risen from 30,000 at the beginning of the decade to around 80,000.[133] Contemporaries were alarmed, and many agreed with Stallard that vagrancy was 'reaching gigantic proportions and need[ed] immediate attention'.[134] Stallard himself advocated the need for surveillance: in a lecture in 1870 made to the Chalmers Association in Edinburgh, he declared that 'it is only by continuous observation, and not always then, that malingering is exposed'; and in his pamphlet *Pauperism, Charity, & Poor Laws* (1869) he proposed that each vagrant should be registered and photographed in order to 'trace the habits of the individual and prove the act of vagrancy'.[135] These convictions were shared by influential groups, including the Charity Organisation Society. They used 'technologies of information collection, surveillance, and investigation' to ensure that applicants for relief were genuine and to prove acts of vagrancy, mendicancy and fraud.[136] Throughout the 1870s its mission to halt the demoralisation of the poor by withdrawing relief and putting an end to their reliance on charity enjoyed a groundswell of popular support.[137] It was within this atmosphere of animosity that Fildes reappraised 'Houseless and Hungry' and reconfigured it in *Applicants for Admission to a Casual Ward* (1874) (Figure 3.2).

Figure 3.2   Sir Luke Fildes, *Applicants for Admission to a Casual Ward* (1874). Royal Holloway, University of London

Applicants for Admission was one of four oil paintings submitted to the Royal Academy Exhibition between 1873 and 1875 that were based on illustrations drawn for the *Graphic*. All four, which alongside Fildes's work included *Leaving Home* (1873) and *Deserted* (1874) by Frank Holl, and Hubert Herkomer's *Last Muster* (1875), are examples of what has since been called social realism, a form in which investigation and documentation are blended with artistry. This approach is exemplified by Fildes's habit of employing the vagrants he 'discovered in his nightly wanderings round the London streets' as models.[138] Art historians have noted that when Fildes reworked 'Houseless and Hungry' he made several significant changes. The use of oils, of course, allowed him to introduce colour to the casual line: what was the 'mechanic's' family (now sporting two extra children) is picked out in yellows, pinks and turquoise-greens; the woman in the foreground, her child at her side, is highlighted with touches of red; and a cripple on the far right, a new addition to the scene, adds a streak of scarlet with his soldier's coat. These gleams of colour, worked into an otherwise murky canvas, indicate the moral worth of these applicants and highlight the most distressing groups. Fildes also altered the composition of his panorama, introducing more women and children to the painting. He replaced one of the sturdy vagabonds, for example, with a mother and her daughter; like the mechanic's children and the child in the foreground, she, too, is picked out in virtuous green. These additions help to make the casuals more pitiable as a whole, and draw thoughts of the 'deserving' poor to the forefront of the viewer's mind. The most striking alteration, however, is the narrativisation of the picture.[139]

Narrative, or genre paintings, were popular in the Victorian period. These were paintings that invited 'reading', and shared several features with the Victorian novel, including serialisation and a reliance on physiognomy.[140] The appeal of these pictures was that they encouraged audiences to piece together the narrative of the painting's subjects by examining the details of their faces, frames, postures and clothes. In the case of city scenes, such as John Ritchie's *A Summer Day in Hyde Park* (1858) or William Powell Frith's *Derby Day* (1856–8), the canvas was crowded with 'serried rows or self-contained clumps of figures, each with its own story to tell', as Alan Robinson explains.[141] In *Applicants for Admission*, Fildes turned 'Houseless and Hungry' into a narrative painting by reworking the rigid physiognomies of the applicants into faces that might be more easily interpreted.[142] More than that, he invited close visual reading by painting his panorama on an eight-foot canvas. Like the casuals on the page of the *Graphic* that were pressed up close, the sheer size of those in the painting forces us to look at them, and allows us to examine them in detail. *Applicants*, however, is not as straightforward as the cityscapes by Ritchie and Frith. As Arscott comments, it 'equivocates between the anecdotal and the illegible', and in this way it both solicits and frustrates our attempts to read it.[143]

Faced with the gallery of casuals, many seem easy to interpret. Most of the deserving poor have legible postures and faces that speak of their need or their virtue. Within the family group the father is tender with his child, while the boy's gaunt and pallid face attests to their hunger. Similarly, the woman walking away is looking down towards her baby in a manner that suggests compassion, while her little girl, peaky round the cheeks and leaning in towards her mother, testifies to their want and isolation. Another figure easily interpreted is the applicant talking to the police officer. Like a vision of the boy grown up, he is also pale and haggard, his hands knotted together in a skeletal gesture that exposes several tendons. And if the message was not clear that this man is starving, Fildes includes a stringy dog at his feet attacking a scrap of bone: as Sala wrote to Fildes in a congratulatory note, his only reservation was 'that *dog* of yours, gnawing a bone: he is not wanted: You have written up "Hunger" plainly enough on your canvas.'[144] But some of the other casuals are not so easy to read. The men talking to the soldier, whose face is turned away, are shrouded in shadow, while the old man in the doorway of the police station is an enigma: his face is just a blur. These figures have unreadable motives, histories and affections, and none of them is clearly undeserving. This is not, however, where the legibility of *Applicants for Admission* ends, because one of the main features of this painting, which has hitherto been ignored, is its clear critique of the casual-ward system.

Critics past and present have focused on the casuals. When *Applicants for Admission* appeared in the Royal Academy Exhibition it received a mixed response from reviewers, but these were primarily focused on the file of wayfarers and whether they were a fit subject for art. Some, like the *Saturday Review*, determined that they were 'too revolting for an art which should seek to please, refine, and elevate', while others, like the *Athenaeum*, declared them a success, saying that 'there is not a figure that is not genuine in design or faithful and true in sentiment'.[145] Later critics, including Korda, Arscott and Robinson, have noted that we are meant to pity the casuals.[146] What has been overlooked is that we are also meant to criticise the police officer. The officer is another figure that Fildes altered. Whereas in 'Houseless and Hungry' he was a stock-still observer detached from the crowd, he is now grouped with the starving casual, his portly figure and ruddy face contrasting sharply with the vagrant. Indeed, as he leans back to peer at the relief ticket, the brim of his helmet drawn over his eyes, he mirrors the slumped drunk in the centre of the painting, the only casual we are encouraged to condemn. He, too, has a rubicund face, indicating his alcoholism, while his broad paunch identifies him as a successful scrounger who has mooched off charities and the poor rate. Moreover, his belly, like that of the police officer, is juxtaposed with the empty guts of the man to his right, who cringes into his innards like the starving vagrant. The parallels between these two groups, I suggest, prompts us to condemn the police officer and the casual-ward system. The official's likeness to earlier, satirical representations of beadles may have helped elicit this response from Fildes's first audience. As Sally Ledger observes, images of 'the bloated, overfed figure of the parish beadle, who contrasts ironically with the starving poor whom he disciplines', circulated throughout the 1830s and 1840s.[147]

The muster of blank and unreadable casual paupers presented in 'Houseless and Hungry' raised anxieties about discrimination, but soothed these by providing a textual guide that aligned the reader with the observant and knowing official. In *Applicants for Admission* Fildes reworked his illustration for opposite ends. Through his presentation of the police officer he raised uncomfortable questions, not about the character of the casuals, many of whom were made more legible through the process of narrativisation, but about the nature of the administration. It is no longer only the casuals whom we are supposed to critically assess, but also the police, the casual ward and the Poor Law Board (now called the Local Government Board). Meanwhile, the relationship between text and image has been reversed. Whereas in 'Houseless and Hungry' the text was a source of comfort and clarification, in *Applicants for Admission* its presence is disconcerting, complicating the easy legibility of the virtuous poor. In the 1874 Royal Academy Catalogue the following quotation was partnered with the painting:

> Dumb, wet, silent horrors! Sphinxes set up against the dead wall, *and none likely to be at the pains of solving them until the general overthrow*.
> Charles Dickens, extract from a letter in the third volume of Forster's *Life of Dickens*.[148]

Without knowing 'A Nightly Scene in London', or having read the as-yet-unpublished volume of John Forster's *Life of Dickens* (1872–4), Fildes selected this extract from a letter Forster showed him in which Dickens described the workhouse scene in Whitechapel.[149] His choice of quotation solidified his connection with the famous author, but it also did more than that. It emphasised that the casuals, no matter how wretched and pathetic they looked, might harbour an insurrection. In the context of the catalogue, the soldier and his companions in particular may have been granted a conspiratorial, even mutinous air. This revolutionary potential of the metropolitan vagrant is also a theme in the next chapter.

Notes

1 Henry Mayhew, *London Labour and the London Poor: A Cyclopaedia of the Condition and Earnings of Those That Will Work, Those That Cannot Work, and Those That Will Not Work*, 4 vols (London: Frank Cass, 1967), I, p. iii.

2 Ibid., II, p. 138.

3 It had been true since at least the sixteenth century when vagrants likewise took advantage of the shelter and relief offered by towns and cities during the winter. See A. L. Beier, *Masterless Men: The Vagrancy Problem in England, 1560–1640* (London: Methuen, 1985), pp. 76–8.

4 T. W. Wilkinson, 'Vagrants in Winter', *Good Words*, December 1899, pp. 31–6 (pp. 31–3). Also see Jerry White, *London in the Nineteenth Century: A Human Awful Wonder of God* (London: Vintage, 2008), p. 116.

5 Gareth Stedman Jones, *Outcast London: A Study in the Relationship between Classes in Victorian Society* (Oxford: Oxford University Press, 1971; repr. London: Verso, 2013), pp. 36–7, 44; Raphael Samuel, 'Comers and Goers', in *The Victorian City: Images and Realities*, ed. H. J. Dyos and Michael Wolff, 2 vols (London: Routledge & Kegan Paul, 1973), I, pp. 123–60 (pp. 142–3, 146).

6 Mayhew, *London Labour and the London Poor*, II, p. 138.

7 'Told by a Tramp', *All the Year Round*, 28 April 1866, pp. 371–4 (p. 372).

8 Wilkinson, 'Vagrants in Winter', p. 34. Also see Simon Fowler, *Workhouse: The People, the Place, the Life behind Doors* (Richmond: National Archives, 2007), pp. 21–3.

9 David Jones, *Crime, Protest, Community and Police in Nineteenth-Century Britain* (London: Routledge & Kegan Paul, 1982), pp. 201–2.

10 Stedman Jones, *Outcast London*, pp. 35–6; Samuel, 'Comers and Goers', p. 148.

11 Daniel Joseph Kirwan, *Palace and Hovel; or, Phases of London Life*, ed. A. Allan (London: Abelard-Schuman, 1963), p. 64.

12 [George Augustus Sala], 'The Key of the Street', *Household Words*, 6 September 1851, pp. 565–72 (p. 565).

13 'The Casual Poor', *London City Press*, 9 November 1861, p. 4.

14 James Greenwood, *The Seven Curses of London*, ed. Jeffrey Richards (Oxford: Basil Blackwell, 1981), p. 3.

15 Kirwan, *Palace and Hovel*, p. 65.

16 White, *London in the Nineteenth Century*, p. 422.

17 J. H. Stallard, *Pauperism, Charity, & Poor Laws: Being an Inquiry into the Present State of the Poorer Classes in the Metropolis, the Resources and Effects of Charity, and the Influence of the Poor-Law System of Relief: With Suggestions for an Improved Administration* (London: Longmans, Green, Reader, and Dyer, 1868), pp. 15–16.

18 John Hollingshead, *Ragged London in 1861*, ed. Anthony S. Wohl (London: J. M. Dent, 1986), p. 6; Stedman Jones, *Outcast London*, pp. 45–6.

19 [George Augustus Sala], 'Houseless and Hungry', *Household Words*, 23 February 1856, pp. 121–6 (p. 125).

20 Ellen Barlie, *Our Homeless Poor: and What We Can Do to Help Them* (London: James Nisbet, 1860), p. 22.

21 Robert Sandall, *The History of the Salvation Army*, 7 vols (London: Thomas Nelson and Sons, 1947–86), III, p. 105.

22 [Sala], 'Houseless and Hungry', p. 124.

23 Barlie, *Our Homeless Poor*, pp. 13–14.

24 'A Real Casual on Refuges: With Introduction and Notes by J. C. Parkinson', *Temple Bar*, April 1866, pp. 32–44 (pp. 34–7).

25 Fowler, *Workhouse*, p. 182.

26 Wilkinson, 'Vagrants in Winter', p. 31.

27 Fowler, *Workhouse*, p. 189.

28 *Report on the Departmental Committee on Vagrancy*, 3 vols (London: Wyman & Sons, 1906), I, pp. 29–30.

29 Tim Hitchcock notes that begging with children was a common strategy for female beggars in eighteenth-century London. Tim Hitchcock, *Down and Out in Eighteenth-Century London* (London: Hambledon and London, 2004), pp. 117–19.

30 [John Rutherford], *Indoor Paupers: By One of Them* (London: Chatto & Windus, 1885), p. 102.

31 Kirwan, *Palace and Hovel*, pp. 202–3.

32 Charles Dickens, *The Posthumous Papers of the Pickwick Club*, intro. Peter Washington (London: Everyman, 1998), p. 210.

33 Josiah Flynt, *Tramping with Tramps: Studies and Sketches of Vagabond Life* (New York: Century Co., 1899), p. 259.

34 'A Real Casual on Refuges', pp. 37–8.

35 'A Real Casual on Casual Wards: With an Introduction and Notes by J. C. Parkinson', *Temple Bar*, March 1866, pp. 497–517 (p. 512); Fowler, *Workhouse*, p. 196.

36 Flynt, *Tramping with Tramps*, p. 261.

37 Mary Higgs, *Glimpses into the Abyss* (London: P. S. King, 1906), p. 94. Original emphasis.

38 Charles Kingsley, *Alton Locke, Tailor and Poet: An Autobiography* (London: Macmillan, 1885), p. 60.

39 Charles Dickens, *The Mystery of Edwin Drood*, ed. Matthew Pearl (London: Vintage, 2009), p. 47.

40 White, *London in the Nineteenth Century*, pp. 324–5, 331.

41 Edwin Chadwick, *Report on the Sanitary Condition of the Labouring Population of Great Britain*, ed. David Gadstone (London: Routledge/Thoemmes, 1997), p. 356.

42 White, *London in the Nineteenth Century*, p. 331.

43 Higgs, *Glimpses into the Abyss*, p. 242.

44 Samuel, 'Comers and Goers', p. 128.

45 Stedman Jones, *Outcast London*, pp. 52–66.

46 Ibid., p. 88.

47 Ibid., pp. 61, 81–8, 172–3.

48 Mayhew, *London Labour and the London Poor*, II, p. 139.

49 D. Rice-Jones, *In the Slums: Pages from the Note-Book of a London Diocesan Home Missionary* (London: James Nisbet, 1884), p. 2.

50 Lynda Nead, *Victorian Babylon: People, Streets and Images in Nineteenth-Century London* (New Haven, CT: Yale University Press, 2000), pp. 9, 13.

51 10 Geo. 4, C. 44.

52 Charles Dickens, *Bleak House*, ed. Nicola Bradbury (London: Penguin, 1996; repr. 2003), p. 731.

53 [Rutherford], *Indoor Paupers*, pp. 2–4.

54 Kirwan, *Palace and Hovel*, p. 65.

55 Sidney Webb and Beatrice Webb, *English Poor Law Policy* (London: Longmans, 1910), pp. 33–6.

56 Robert Humphreys, *No Fixed Abode: A History of Responses to the Roofless and the Rootless in Britain* (London: Macmillan Press, 1999), p. 101.

57 Seth Koven, *Slumming: Sexual and Social Politics in Victorian London* (Princeton, NJ: Princeton University Press, 2004), pp. 33–4.

58 Roy Porter, *London: A Social History* (1994; repr. London: Penguin, 2000), pp. 300–1.

59 John Wodehouse quoted by Hugh Owen, 'Introduction', in *The Pauper Inmates Discharge and Regulations Act, 1871: With Introduction and Notes by Hugh Owen*, ed. Hugh Owen (London: Knight & Co., 1871), pp. 5–22 (p. 12).

60 See ibid., p. 5.

61 Humphreys, *No Fixed Abode*, pp. 99–107; Stedman Jones, *Outcast London*, pp. 272–3.

62 Michel Foucault, *Discipline and Punish: The Birth of the Prison*, trans. Alan Sheridan (London: Penguin, 1977), pp. 293–308.

63 Michel Foucault, 'Right of Death and Power over Life', *Biopolitics: A Reader*, ed. Timothy Campbell and Adam Sitze (Durham, NC: Duke University Press, 2013), pp. 41–60 (p. 43).

64 Foucault, 'Right of Death and Power over Life', pp. 44, 48; Michel Foucault, '"Society Must Be Defended," Lecture at the *Collège de France*, March 17, 1976', in *Biopolitics: A Reader*, ed. Timothy Campbell and Adam Sitze (Durham, NC: Duke University Press, 2013), pp. 61–81 (pp. 63–4, 67).

65 Chadwick, *Report on the Sanitary Condition of the Labouring Population of Great Britain*, p. 357; J. H. Stallard, *The Female Casual and Her Lodging: With a Complete Scheme for the Regulation of Workhouse Infirmaries* (London:

Saunders, Otley, 1866), p. 69; Millicent Garrett Fawcett, 'The Vaccination Act of 1898', *Contemporary Review*, March 1899, pp. 328–42 (p. 337).

66 Stallard, *The Female Casual and Her Lodging*, p. 66.

67 Higgs, *Glimpses into the Abyss*, p. 274. Also see Fowler, *Workhouse*, p. 194.

68 George Orwell, *Down and Out in Paris and London* (London: Penguin, 2001), p. 157.

69 Deana Heath, *Purifying Empire: Obscenity and the Politics of Moral Regulation in Britain, India and Australia* (Cambridge: Cambridge University Press, 2010; repr. 2013), p. 210.

70 Fowler, *Workhouse*, pp. 12–13.

71 'A Real Casual on Casual Wards', pp. 508, 514.

72 *Report on the Departmental Committee on Vagrancy*, II, pp. 118–20.

73 'A Real Casual on Casual Wards', p. 504; Greenwood, *Seven Curses of London*, p. 155.

74 [James Greenwood], 'A Night in a Workhouse', *Pall Mall Gazette*, 12 January 1866, pp. 9–10 (p. 10).

75 Jack London, *The People of the Abyss*, 2nd ed. (London: Hesperus Press, 2013), p. 71.

76 Gordon Bigelow, *Fiction, Famine, and the Rise of Economics in Victorian Britain and Ireland* (Cambridge: Cambridge University Press, 2003), p. 81; Jude Piesse, *British Settler Emigration in Print, 1832–1877* (Oxford: Oxford University Press, 2016), pp. 7–8.

77 White, *London in the Nineteenth Century*, pp. 132–4.

78 Bigelow, *Fiction*, p. 81.

79 'The Pauper Hotels of England', *Bell's New Weekly Messenger*, 24 September 1848, p. 4.

80 'Vagrancy', *Evening Mail*, 12 June 1848, p. 1; 'The Increase in Vagrancy', *Morning Chronicle*, 9 August 1848, p. 2.

81 Charles Buller, 'Official Enforcement of the Distinction between Vagrancy and Destitution', *Spectator*, 4 November 1848, pp. 1059–60.

82 Ibid., p. 1060.

83 'The Homeless Poor', *Saturday Review*, 21 November 1863, pp. 664–5 (p. 665). Nearly forty years later T. W. Wilkinson remarked that 'that hardy annual, the increase of vagrancy, crops up for discussion in the newspapers about October or November'. See Wilkinson, 'Vagrants in Winter', p. 32.

84 'The Pauper Hotels of England', p. 4.

85 'The Vagrancy Question: Important Meeting of Union Clerks and Guardians at Stoke-on-Trent', *Staffordshire Advertiser*, 28 October 1848, p. 8. Original emphasis.

86 'Improved Treatment of the Poor', *Spectator*, 4 November 1848, p. 1062.

87 Buller, 'Official Enforcement', p. 1059.

88 'The Pauper Hotels of England', p. 4; 'Improved Treatment of the Poor', p. 1062; 'The Plague of Beggars', *Fraser's Magazine*, April 1848, pp. 395–402 (p. 402). On the vagrancy laws, see Lorie Charlesworth, *Welfare's Forgotten*

Past: A Socio-Legal History of the Poor Law (Abingdon: Routledge-Cavendish, 2009), p. 171.

89 Susan Chitty, *The Beast and the Monk: A Life of Charles Kingsley* (London: Hodder and Stoughton, 1974), pp. 110–11; Thomas Hughes, 'Prefatory Memoire', in *Alton Locke, Tailor and Poet: An Autobiography* (London: Macmillan, 1885), pp. ix–lxi (p. xi).

90 Charles Kingsley, 'Yeast No. V', *Fraser's Magazine*, November 1848, pp. 530–47 (pp. 533–4).

91 Buller, 'Official Enforcement', p. 1060.

92 Thomas Carlyle, 'Signs of the Times', in *Thomas Carlyle: Selected Writings*, ed. Alan Shelston (Harmondsworth: Penguin, 1971), pp. 59–85 (pp. 64, 67).

93 *The Times*, 7 November 1848, p. 5.

94 'Beggars and Almsgivers', *New Monthly Magazine,* March 1849, pp. 301–6 (p. 301).

95 Stedman Jones, *Outcast London*, p. 252.

96 Charles Dickens, 'A Nightly Scene in London', *Household Words*, 26 January 1856, pp. 25–7 (p. 25).

97 Ibid., p. 25.

98 Ibid., pp. 25–6.

99 Ibid., p. 26.

100 Lynda Nead, *Myths of Sexuality: Representations of Women in Victorian Britain* (Oxford: Blackwell, 1988; repr. 1990), p. 175.

101 Dickens, 'A Nightly Scene in London', p. 26.

102 Thomas Carlyle, *Past and Present*, ed. Chris R. Vanden Bossche (Berkeley: University of California Press, 2005), pp. 18–20. Original emphasis.

103 'Marylebone Workhouse and the Casual Poor', *Daily News*, 25 October 1865, p. 4; 'Poor-Law Guardians in Rebellion', *Illustrated Times*, 28 October 1865, p. 262.

104 'The Houseless Poor', *South London Press,* 21 October 1865, p. 5; 'Marylebone Workhouse and the Casual Poor', p. 4.

105 'Poor-Law Guardians in Rebellion', p. 262.

106 'The Houseless Poor Act', *Morning Post,* 1 January 1866, p. 3.

107 Koven, *Slumming*, p. 33.

108 [Greenwood], 'A Night in a Workhouse', 12 January 1866, pp. 9–10.

109 Ibid., p. 10; [James Greenwood], 'A Night in a Workhouse', *Pall Mall Gazette*, 13 January 1866, p. 10; [James Greenwood], 'A Night in a Workhouse', *Pall Mall Gazette*, 15 January 1866, pp. 9–10 (p. 10).

110 J. W. Robertson Scott, *The Story of the 'Pall Mall Gazette'* (London: Oxford University Press, 1950), p. 169; B. I. Diamond, J. O. Baylen and J. P. Baylen, 'James Greenwood's London: A Precursor of Charles Booth', *Victorian Periodicals Review*, 17.1–2 (1984), 34–43 (p. 39).

111 Koven, *Slumming*, p. 49.

112 Luke Seaber, *Incognito Social Investigation in British Literature: Certainties in Degradation* (Cham: Palgrave Macmillan, 2017), p. 46.

113 [Greenwood], 'A Night in a Workhouse', 15 January 1866, p. 10.

114 [Anon.] M.A., 'A Night in the Casual Ward of the Work-House, in Rhyme: Dedicated to the Million', in *Vicarious Vagrants: Incognito Social Explorers and the Homeless in England, 1860–1910*, ed. Mark Freeman and Gillian Nelson (Lambertville, NJ: True Bill Press, 2008), pp. 76–80 (p. 80).

115 'Casual Wards', *Pall Mall Gazette*, 16 January 1866, pp. 1–2 (p. 1).

116 'The Houseless Poor in Stepney', *The Times*, 27 January 1866, p. 12.

117 'The Lambeth Guardians and the Casual Poor', *Daily News*, 26 January 1866, p. 8.

118 Stallard, *The Female Casual and Her Lodging*, pp. 5, 66.

119 Ibid., pp. 2, 4, 58.

120 [Rutherford], *Indoor Paupers*, p. 10.

121 Jones, *Crime, Protest, Community and Police*, pp. 181–2.

122 For a thorough account of the *Graphic*, see Andrea Korda, *Printing and Painting the News in Victorian London: 'The Graphic' and Social Realism, 1869–1891* (Farnham: Ashgate, 2015), pp. 49–56.

123 Caroline Arscott, 'From Graphic to Academic', in *Art and the Academy in the Nineteenth Century*, ed. Raphael Cardoso Denis and Colin Trodd (Manchester: Manchester University Press, 2000), pp. 102–16 (p. 110).

124 'Houseless and Hungry', *Graphic*, 4 December 1869, pp. 9–10 (p. 10).

125 Arscott, 'From Graphic to Academic', p. 109.

126 Koven, *Slumming*, p. 49.

127 'Houseless and Hungry', p. 10.

128 Korda, *Printing and Painting*, p. 60.

129 Nead, *Myths of Sexuality*, p. 100.

130 Henry Mayhew and John Binny, *The Criminal Prisons of London and Scenes of Prison Life* (London: Griffin, Bohn, 1862), p. 475.

131 Arscott, 'From Graphic to Academic', p. 110.

132 L. V. Fildes, *Luke Fildes, R.A.: A Victorian Painter* (London: Michael Joseph, 1968), pp. 13–14.

133 Jeffrey Richards, 'Introduction', in *The Seven Curses of London*, ed. Jeffrey Richards (Oxford: Basil Blackwell, 1981), pp. v–xxi (p. xi).

134 Stallard, *Pauperism, Charity, & Poor Laws*, p. 33.

135 Ibid., p. 34; J. H. Stallard, 'The Scottish Poor Law, Examined in Its Relation to Vagrancy', in *Pauperism and the Poor Laws: The Lectures Delivered in Edinburgh under the Auspices of the Chalmers Association in 1869–70 with Kindred Papers*, ed. Thomas Ivory (Edinburgh: Seton & Mackenzie, 1870), pp. 1–22 (p. 21).

136 Koven, *Slumming*, p. 98.

137 Stedman Jones, *Outcast London*, pp. 271–80.

138 Arscott, 'From Graphic to Academic', p. 104; Fildes, *Luke Fildes*, p. 25; Korda, *Printing and Painting*, pp. 1–7.

139 Arscott, 'From Graphic to Academic', pp. 113–15; Korda, *Printing and Painting*, pp. 120–1.

140 Alan Robinson, *Imagining London, 1770–1900* (Basingstoke: Palgrave Macmillan, 2004), p. 127; Julia Thomas, *Victorian Narrative Painting* (London: Tate Gallery, 2000), pp. 12–15.

141 Robinson, *Imagining London*, p. 137.

142 Arscott, 'From Graphic to Academic', pp. 113–15.

143 Ibid., p. 114.

144 Quoted by Fildes, *Luke Fildes*, p. 27. Original emphasis.

145 'The Royal Academy', *Saturday Review*, 2 May 1874, pp. 561–2 (p. 562); 'The Royal Academy', *Athenaeum*, 2 May 1874, pp. 599–602 (p. 602).

146 Arscott, 'From Graphic to Academic', pp. 113–15; Korda, *Printing and Painting*, pp. 120–1; Robinson, *Imagining London*, p. 151.

147 Sally Ledger, *Dickens and the Popular Radical Imagination* (Cambridge: Cambridge University Press, 2007), p. 82.

148 Quoted by Arscott, 'From Graphic to Academic', p. 111. Added emphasis.

149 Fildes describes how he came by the quotation in an interview with the *Magazine of Art*. See W. W. Fenn, 'Our Living Artists', *Magazine of Art*, January 1880, pp. 49–52. For the letter, see Charles Dickens, *The Pilgrim Edition of the Letters of Charles Dickens*, ed. Madeline House, Graham Storey and Kathleen Tillotson, 12 vols (Oxford: Oxford University Press, 1965–2002), VII, p. 742.

CHAPTER 4

Loafers

The term 'loafer' refers to 'one who spends his time in idleness', according to the *OED*.[1] However, it also signifies a species of vagrancy, a fact that is borne out in its derivation. Although its etymology is obscure, the *OED* speculates that loafer comes from the German *landläufer*, which can be translated as 'land-loper': 'one who runs up and down the land; a vaga-bond'.[2] The American Gypsyologist Charles Leland also noted this con-nection in *The English Gypsies and Their Language* (1873), but in addition he specified that the verb 'to loaf' originally meant 'to steal':

> When the term first began to be popular in 1834 or 1835, I can distinctly remember that it meant to *pilfer*. Such, at least, is my earliest recollection, and of hearing school boys ask one another in jest, of their acquisitions or gifts, 'Where did you loaf that from?' A petty pilferer was a loafer, but in a very short time all of the tribe of loungers in the sun, and disreputable pickers up of unconsidered trifles, now known as bummers, were called loafers.[3]

Loafers, then, are vagrants, idlers and petty criminals. Moreover, as Leland suggests, by aligning them with 'bummers', they do not belong specifically to the metropolis. In *A Dictionary of Slang, Jargon & Cant* (1889) Leland records that 'bummer' is an American expression of 'Pennsylvania origin' meaning 'a slow, lazy fellow ... a loafer'.[4] Whereas the casual pauper was almost invariably placed within the British city, the loafer was a more mobile figure within the collective imagination. In 'Vagrants and Vagrancy' (1888), for example, the *London Quarterly Review* noted that 'in India the loafer is only too well known'.[5] This is attested to by Flora Annie Steel's 'In the Permanent Way' (1898), a short story set in British India in which the dissipated protagonist, Nathaniel Craddock, is described as 'a loafer in many a bazaar and *serai* [caravanserai]'; similarly, in Rudyard Kipling's novel *Kim* (1901), Kim's father, who stayed in India after his regiment returned to Britain, 'fell to drinking and loafing'.[6] More generally, an article, 'On Loafers' (1890), recorded that gentlemen who fail to secure success in Britain are often sent abroad by relatives: 'loafers of this class are shovelled off in heaps to the colonies', the author playfully explains.[7] We shall meet some of these in Chapter 6, beached in the Pacific Islands.

However, although loafers had a presence in the United States and the British Empire, they were also prominent in the metropolis. In 'Homeless at Night' (1892), an article published in the *English Illustrated Magazine*, the journalist Leonard Noble states that 'the loafing class' comprises 'the largest class of [homeless] men' in London.[8] Likewise, in 'The Abodes of the Homeless' (1899), the Anglican clergyman and founder of Toynbee Hall, Samuel Barnett, records that loafers, 'because they are idle', are one of the city's three vagrant types; the other two are 'single men who have either refused or thrown off familial obligations', and those who 'can do no regular work'.[9] These categories, along with the city's criminals, formed what was popularly known as the 'residuum', a term coined in 1867 by the radical politician John Bright to refer to the ineffectual, underemployed and sometimes malevolent community that lingered below the working class.[10] Although loafers were consistently depicted as a single, typically male element within this group, the distinctions between its several members often blurred. In Barnett's division of the homeless, for example, the difference between the indifferent loafer and the man who ignores his obligations is unclear, as is the material difference between the loafer who won't work and the unemployed labourer who can't. In Francis Peek's 'The Workless, the Thriftless, and the Worthless' (1888), an article that similarly sought to categorise the unemployed, we are told that the lowest of the three classes, the 'Worthless', is 'for the most part composed of vagrants and mendicants', but that it is also 'practically one' with 'the absolutely criminal': 'the two classes melt into one another'.[11]

The loafers' undefined boundaries frustrated late Victorian commentators. Their habit of seeping into both the criminal class below and the out-of-work labourers above made them disconcertingly anonymous. It is, however, this capacity of the loafer to absorb and express the varied and sometimes conflicting traits of the unemployed that makes 'loafer' a useful term. In this chapter I use it to signify members of the residuum, the mobile and recalcitrant underclass that lurked in the city's slums and whose presence in the metropolis became an enduring concern in the late nineteenth century. This anxiety was incited by the publication of Andrew Mearns's *The Bitter Cry of Outcast London* (1883). Only a 'little pamphlet', it turned the 'smouldering question' about housing the poor into a 'brightly burning one', bringing the horrors of overcrowded slum-life to light.[12] 'Incest is common', testified Mearns, 'and no form of vice and sensuality causes surprise or attracts attention.' Ruthless in its pursuit of sordid poverty, this account sparked several imitations, including George Sims's *Horrible London* (1883).[13] Together, these led to a radical reshaping of how the urban poor were imagined. As Judith Walkowitz explains, in the wake of Mearns and Sims, 'The presence of the "residuum" immensely expanded as a generalized problem: instead of a small number of idle and casual poor living in a few pockets of poverty, the chronically poor residuum now appeared to be a substantial portion of the population.'[14] This was the rediscovery of the poor: the acknowledgement that London did not conceal one or two slums, but harboured what came to be known in the early 1880s as 'slumdom', a maze of courts and alleys through which the residuum prowled.[15] Anxieties about this class continued to mount in the last decades of the nineteenth century as a severe economic depression and a wave of ill-advised slum clearances dislocated thousands of workers from their jobs and homes. This caused a growth in the residuum that prompted middle-class commentators to reimagine the loafer as a serious social and political threat, a fact that is reflected in the unprecedented use of the term during the 1880s and 1890s.[16]

London's slums were strategically eliminated throughout the nineteenth century, often under the guise of necessary infrastructure projects, like the construction of streets or railways. In the last quarter of the century, however, slum clearance became an object in itself. The consequence was a series of mass evictions: between 1876 and 1900, 39,000 people were expelled from their homes, nearly half of whom were made homeless between 1878 and 1881. Although there were plans to rehouse the evicted tenants in more sanitary accommodation, these rarely provided a satisfactory alternative. Often built after demolition had taken place, they not only charged higher rents, but also imposed codes of conduct that were alien to the urban poor. As a result, those evicted sought shelter in the remaining slums, which became increasingly overcrowded. By the 1880s this situation had become severe: congested tenements created deplorable living conditions and kept the residuum circulating through the metropolis.[17] The housing of the urban poor, and the loafers among them, was precarious because many of them did not have a steady or reliable income, and their lodgings were held on the most tenuous terms. Rooms and beds were rented by the week or night, and competition among prospective tenants meant that slum landlords could afford to evict tardy residents. As Sims explained in his pamphlet *How the Poor Live* (1883), if a lodger 'does not get enough during the day to pay his rent, out he goes into the street with his wife and children, and enter another family forthwith'.[18] Slum clearances therefore forced the very poor to move from one impermanent residence to the next.

Often this involved exchanging one lodging-house for another. As Sims recorded, and as I discussed in the previous chapter, the clientele of these lodging-houses were often vagrant:

> Some of them are tramps and hawkers, but most of them are professional loafers, picking up in any way that presents itself the price of a night's lodging. They are a shifting population, and rarely remain in one house long. Some of them only get a night in now and then as a luxury, and look upon it as a Grand Hotel episode. They sleep habitually in the open, on the staircases, or in the casual ward.[19]

This wandering community, which had been enlarged by the housing crisis, became further engrossed during the depression of 1884–7, one of the worst of the nineteenth century.[20] Where previous economic downturns had been relatively trade-specific, with this slump went a whole gamut of industries and their workers.[21] As the most dispensable and economically vulnerable class, many casual labourers found themselves without a job or home. The result was an engorged and menacing homeless population in which the 'deserving' unemployed mingled indiscriminately with 'undeserving' loafers – it was the problem of the casual queue writ large. The crisis came in 1887 in the exceptionally hot summer of Queen Victoria's jubilee, when hundreds of houseless men, women and children decamped from the slums and moved into Trafalgar Square. According to the liberal politician and journalist Bennet Burleigh, these people were unemployed labourers and artisans who were tramping about the city in a desperate search for work; they were 'not all vagabonds, from choice, but leading a nomadic life within the confines of the metropolis'.[22] Other commentators, however, were less sympathetic.

As summer edged into autumn the vagrant camp remained, and began to pose a serious threat to social order, at least according to the mainstream press. In part, this was because the '300 tramps and vagrants in Trafalgar Square', who remained in the open throughout a chill October, represented the fearful desperation that had arisen from the depression.[23] But it was also because these vagrants were identified as the main participants in the socialist and anarchist rallies that gathered throughout October and November that year. In 'Five Nights in the Streets of London' (1887), the *Pall Mall Gazette*'s undercover correspondent interviewed several tramps, one of whom informed him that 'if it was a severe winter, like the last was,

there would be "ructions" in London'.[24] This indication of disruptive
intent was confirmed a month later in an editorial in the *Gazette*, which
informed readers that the demonstrators, then gathering several times a week
in Trafalgar Square, were mostly 'professional vagrants'.[25] The police also
made this connection between the political disturbance and London's
loafers. In a bid to reclaim Trafalgar Square, by now an epicentre of
homelessness and radicalism, the Commissioner of Police, Sir Charles
Warren, tried to secure the contested territory. In late October he published
a notice ordering all philanthropists to stop distributing food to the houseless
in the Square, and warned that any person 'found wandering or sleeping in
the open air at night' would be arrested under the Vagrancy Act.[26] Less than
two weeks later went further, and banned all public meetings. This order
led to an escalation in social and political tensions, which eventually culmi-
nated on 13 November in 'Bloody Sunday', a police-induced riot in and
around the square in which 200 were injured and at least two people died.[27]
The socialist activist Eleanor Marx was present that day: 'I have never seen
anything like the brutality of the police,' she wrote.[28]

The press coverage and the events that built up to Bloody Sunday
highlight that London's loafers, its 'professional vagrants', were perceived
as a potentially revolutionary force. We should not, however, imagine that
the residuum was envisaged as a unified class with a distinct political
agenda. Although Peek described the 'Worthless' as 'a powerful weapon
in the hands of the anarchist' this was not because they were ideological
adherents, but because they were 'the idle and the vicious', and therefore
delighted in destruction.[29] Instead of a distinct class with a common cause,
the residuum was an error of urbanisation, a tangle of inefficient casual
workers, criminals and idlers who had been attracted by the opportunities
and atmosphere of the city. As the *Saturday Review* noted in 'The Slum
and the Cellar' (1883):

> London is a gigantic Cave of Adullam, which constantly draws to itself
> every one who is in need, and who not only has no work to do, but would
> not, or could not, do it if work lay ready to his hand.... Such men are the
> large class of cab-touts, all the people who hang about theatre doors, all the
> countless loafers who gather in a moment round every street spectacle and
> street accident. They and their wives and their large families will be always
> and irresistibly attracted to London, in the hope of chance earnings, charity,
> and a life of emotion and adventure.[30]

The loafers therefore comprised a disorderly class, the fate of which was
puzzled out in the 'social problem', a reformulation of the Condition-of-
England question that Charles Dickens, Elizabeth Gaskell and Charles

Kingsley tried to address in the mid-nineteenth century. Thinkers confronting the social problem wanted to make the unemployed productive and to raise the moral and social standards of the very poor. In order to do so, however, it was felt that the most hopeless members of the residuum would need to be sifted out. These people were identified by Charles Booth, the statistician and social reformer, as 'Class A'.

Class A, as Booth explains in the first volume of *Life and Labour of the People of London* (1892–1902), is 'the lowest class, which consists of some occasional labourers, street-sellers, loafers, criminals and semi-criminals'. Along with the 'homeless outcasts' that Booth also includes in this group, these people are an attendant problem of urbanisation, 'a necessary evil in every large city', and amount to about 11,000, or 1.25 per cent of the population of East London.[31] Booth's classification and statistics proved immensely influential after they were first published in 1889. The following year William Booth, the founder of the Salvation Army, published his evangelical battle cry, *In Darkest England and the Way Out* (1890), and extrapolated Charles Booth's figures in order to generate his famous 'Submerged Tenth'. He reasoned that if there were 11,000 homeless people in East London, then there were 165,000 in the United Kingdom. Similarly, if there were 100,000 starving casual labourers, whom Charles Booth designated Class B, then there were 1,550,000 in the country. If the paupers, criminals and lunatics were added to this figure, then this created a population of two million, to which a further million should be added in order to represent their dependents.[32] Three million people, 10 per cent of the United Kingdom's population, formed what one contemporary called 'the Devil's Tithe', and comprised the 'vast despairing multitude' that William Booth vowed to save.[33] What he did not mention was that Charles Booth's figure for Class A was 'a very rough estimate'; 'these people are beyond enumeration', the investigator acknowledged.[34] Like other statistics claiming to detail the number of vagrants, then, these should be approached with caution. Nonetheless, for contemporaries they gave a convincing sense of the scale of the social problem, and further clarified its class structure.

In this chapter I explore responses to Class A in nonfiction and literature, and the representations of the loafer that these generated in the fin de siècle. First I discuss the articles and book-length reports that sought to define and solve the problems of unemployment, inefficiency and vagrancy in late nineteenth-century Britain. These were underwritten by theories of degeneration and the nascent science of eugenics, ideas that ensured that the vagrant poor were increasingly characterised in scientific terms as a biological threat to society and the white 'imperial' race. The second half of this chapter examines how this anxiety was expressed in the realist slum fiction of Arthur Morrison and Margaret Harkness, and in particular how the portrayal of loafers in slum novels and social investigations shaped H. G. Wells's first dystopia, *The Time Machine* (1895). Although the influence of social investigation has long been noted, Wells's engagement with the slum novel, and what he perceived to be its failings, has hitherto been overlooked. I argue that whereas slum novelists were preoccupied with the present state of loafers, Wells investigated their capacity for future revolution. In doing so, he created the Morlocks, an enduring image of the biological and political threat that the residuum appeared to harbour.

4.1 Solutions to the Social Problem

The anonymity of the unemployed was a concern of social reformers during the late nineteenth and early twentieth century. During the unemployment crisis in the 1880s it elicited a series of 'coercive and interventionist' schemes to deal with the urban poor, as Gareth Stedman Jones has noted.[35] These were aired in authoritative studies of the social problem and in the periodical press. In particular, they found a home in the *Contemporary Review* and its rival the *Nineteenth Century*. Founded in 1866 and 1877, respectively, these belonged to a new generation of periodical review that was established from the late 1860s onwards. Unlike their journalistic peers, such as the *Review of Reviews*, they were resolute in their seriousness, excluding fiction and focusing on topical and theological issues. The *Contemporary Review* had a strong religious leaning, exchanging the dogmatic political stance adopted by the older reviews, like the Tory *Quarterly Review*, for a Christian one. The *Nineteenth Century* was also politically neutral, but had a more secular outlook. In 1887 and 1888 they published lengthy articles on the unemployed by both left-wing liberals and right-wing imperialists. In doing so they used what Laurel Brake identifies as the 'symposium format', in which one issue was scrutinised by political antagonists for the edification and excitement of the readership; in both cases this was imagined to be male and decidedly middle-class.[36] What is perhaps surprising about this highly organised debate is that there was little disagreement between the commentators: everyone agreed that the residuum was a menace that needed to be segregated and eliminated.

Writing in the *Contemporary Review* in 1888, Peek opined that the unemployment problem was one of identification: the honest out-of-work labourers, who formed 'probably not two per cent. of the destitute', were intermixed with the incapable, the inefficient and the idle. His solution was a rigorous work test of the kind that should, in theory, have been administered by the Poor Law authorities. He argued that 'the require-ment of hard work as a condition of relief will speedily separate the deserving from the vicious', thus reducing the social problem to the 'problem of dealing with the worthless, the mass of vagrants, mendicants, drunkards and hopeless loafers who infest our streets'.[37] Peek's reasoning was mirrored by his peers. In 'The Unemployed' (1887), which likewise featured in the *Contemporary Review*, Burleigh argued that 'relief works' should be established in London that would occupy the unemployed in 'repairing roads, erecting baths, wash-houses, and a better class of artisans' dwellings'. Not only would this solve the unemployment situation, but it would allow society to eradicate the loafer: 'once ensure that no deserving man or woman shall want, and the sturdy beggars and vagabonds need receive no mercy', he proclaimed.[38] Barnett made similar proposals in 'A Scheme for the Unemployed' (1888), published in the *Nineteenth Century*. He lobbied for a series of home colonies, or 'training-farms', that would equip the unemployed with agricultural skills. Like Burleigh's relief works, these farms would winkle out the undeserving: 'What loafer would endure to be sent out of London to occupy a hut apart from his family and his friends, to do dull work in the fields, to submit to continual training of mind and body, to be deprived even of the excitement of gas-light'?[39]

Sinister and exacting, these solutions to the unemployment crisis char-acterised the residuum as an unalterably idle and intractable product of the city. These assumptions were underwritten by degeneration theory which had long cited the slums as a source of physical and moral enervation.[40] However, whereas in previous decades the degeneration of the urban poor was linked with environmental poverty, by the 1880s it was increasingly identified as a hereditary defect. Although degeneration was 'a fluid category' and 'irreducible to any fixed theory', as John Marriott observes, it was now often understood in Darwinian terms.[41] Social Darwinists argued that civilisation in Britain had become so refined, humane and advanced that it had neutralised Darwin's law of evolution by natural selection and enabled the weakest members of society – the physically, mentally and morally 'unfit' – to reproduce more effectively than before. Those who would have perished quickly in a state of nature were therefore able pass on their traits to the next generation and augment the defective proportion of the population. In this vision of society, Britain harboured a fifth column of degenerate saboteurs that burdened society by their idleness and compromised the vitality of the populace by propagating faulty characteristics.[42] This threat to the health of the 'imperial race' prompted drastic solutions, many of which were inspired by Francis Galton, the founder of eugenics. Taking social Darwinism to radical and more pernicious extremes, he argued that it was humankind's duty to 'deliberately and systematically' improve the species through the selective breeding of the most 'fit' and, as a corollary, the elimination of the degenerate.[43]

For those social reformers who believed in social Darwinism and/or eugenics, the residuum had no native place bar the grave. In 'The English Workers as They Are' (1887), an article in the *Contemporary Review*, the socialist leader H. M. Hyndman wrote that the degenerate 'can but die out, leaving, it is to be hoped, no progeny as a burden on a better state of things'.[44] This was a view adopted by commentators from across the political spectrum. Writing two years earlier, again in the *Contemporary Review*, the prominent eugenicist and imperialist Arnold White likewise insisted that there 'are men from whom the grace of humanity has almost disappeared. Physically, mentally, and morally unfit, there is nothing that the nation can do for these men, except to let them die out by leaving them alone.'[45] The social benefit to be gained from the residuum's extinction was amplified by the fear that the degenerate were 'rapidly increasing'.[46] This was thought to lead to what Karl Pearson, a prominent eugenicist and disciple of Galton, described as 'race suicide', a process by which the middle classes were 'demographically engulfed by unfit lower class people'.[47] Responses to this anxiety were extreme. In the 1880s, as bourgeois London sweated out the unemployment crisis, White suggested that society should 'sterilize the vicious by refusing aid to the unthrifty and the idle'.[48] Such policies designed to control the reproduction of the degenerate later issued from White's pen during the Boer War (1899–1902), when panic flared because working-class recruits were deemed unfit to fight for the Empire.[49] 'If we are to become a healthy people', he wrote in *Empire and Efficiency* (1901), 'the permanent segregation of habitual criminals, paupers, drunkards, maniacs, and tramps must be deliberately undertaken.'[50] Meanwhile, H. G. Wells, who would later distance himself from Galton's theories, was similarly bewitched by the long-term promises of eugenics.[51] In *Anticipations* (1901), his forecast of the future, he argued that the 'People of the Abyss', those who 'are either criminal, immoral, [or] parasitic in more or less irregular ways upon the more successful classes', should be exiled, reformed or eradicated. He claimed that global supremacy in the year 2000 would belong to 'the nation that most resolutely picks over, educates, sterilizes, exports, or poisons its People of the Abyss'.[52]

These ideas remained popular throughout the Edwardian period. In *The Vagrancy Problem* (1910), the civil servant William Harbutt Dawson argued 'that society is justified ... in legislating the loafer out of existence' and provided a detailed schematic of home colonies designed to detain 'vagrants and loafers', able-bodied paupers, 'dissolute persons', 'confirmed inebriates' and 'unmarried women of inferior mental and moral capacity'. This proposal was motivated by assumptions about the congenital unfitness of these groups. Although the colonies might have a reformative function in some cases, Dawson warned that 'it is possible that the great majority [of inmates] will return again and again to detention and may even prove irremediable and entirely unfit to be restored to society. In the main, therefore, the Detaining Colonies may, in the end, prove to be largely institutions of restraint.'[53] What differentiates Dawson's schemes from those urged in the late Victorian period is that they were a re-articulation of what was by now official opinion. The 1903 Viceregal Poor Law Reform Commission for Ireland wanted four detention colonies to be built for vagrants and able-bodied paupers.[54] The 1904 Departmental Committee on Vagrancy, to which Dawson submitted evidence, recommended that 'a class of habitual vagrants should be defined by statute' and that these should 'be committed to a labour colony for a term not exceeding three years'.[55] And the 1905 Royal Commission on the Poor Law likewise argued that detention colonies should be established. Although the Commission splintered between its inauguration in 1905 and the completion of its investigation in 1909, the Majority and Minority reports it produced both favoured detention colonies.[56]

These schemes were biopolitical in nature. Not all biopolitical regimes adhere to eugenic thinking, but the biopolitical state and the eugenicists of the late Victorian and Edwardian periods share a common aim: to produce a prosperous and productive population. According to Michel Foucault, the biopolitical state tries to achieve this by exercising 'the right to make live and let die'.[57] This is also what the eugenicists proposed. As Jill Rappoport observes, the eugenics movement in Britain used several strategies in order to foster a healthy population. These included educating women about their choice of sexual partner and encouraging them to forgo personal preference and passion for the good of the nation. Only physically, mentally and morally strong partners should be selected for procreation. Techniques such as this were focused on ensuring the strength and longevity of the population by influencing the type of person being born;

they were attempts 'to make live', or perhaps more precisely, 'to make virile'. Meanwhile, the second half of Foucault's formula – 'and let die' – found expression in more notorious proposals. Eugenicists argued that charities and public-health measures interfered with natural selection, which not only kept the 'unfit' alive, but allowed them time to breed and pass their defects to the next generation. They therefore proposed that succour should be withdrawn from the needy so that the degenerate would die out before they could reproduce. In addition, as we have seen in their responses to vagrancy, they also lobbied for more direct interventions, such as confinement and sterilisation.[58]

Eugenics, as Catherine Mills argues, provides a particularly good example of how biopower operates. It identifies biological threats through technologies of regulation, including statistics and surveillance, and then seeks to eliminate those threats at the level of the individual. It therefore exercises the twin poles of biopower, regulation of the population and discipline of the individual, in order to strengthen the health of the population as a whole.[59] This population is constructed in explicitly racial terms. As Foucault remarks, racism is a powerful tool for biopolitical regimes, allowing them 'to create caesuras within the biological continuum addressed by biopower'. Such caesuras enable 'the break between what must live and what must die' to be conceptualised, and seem to ensure the prosperity of the 'superior' and implicitly white race by promising that 'the death of the bad race, of the inferior race (or the degenerate, or the abnormal) is something that will make life in general healthier: healthier and purer'.[60] In Victorian Britain the loafer lay outside this privileged sphere and, due to the influence of eugenics, was imagined as belonging to a separate race, one that should be exterminated. This constituted a decisive shift in how the homeless were imagined, but it was entirely consistent with eugenic thinking during the fin de siècle. As Angelique Richardson observes, 'Galtonian eugenics was a class-based application of evolutionary discourses; its aim was to regulate population by altering the balance of class in society. Through eugenics, class in Britain became a racial category.'[61]

By the end of the first decade of the twentieth century the biopolitical fantasy of Galton and his followers was close to realisation. Those employed to advise the state championed the cause of detention colonies, and their recommendations were taken seriously. In 1910 the Prevention of Destitution Bill was brought before parliament and debated in the House of Commons. Based on the Minority Report, the bill advocated a wholesale reform of the Poor Law administration, including the creation of detention colonies that would be overseen by a new Minister for Labour. While 'the classification, treatment, employment, and control of persons' had not been determined, the bill was clear that 'any person convicted of an offence punishable with imprisonment under the Vagrancy Act, 1824, or the Paupers Discharge and Regulations Act, 1871, may be sentenced to be detained for a term not exceeding twelve months in a reformatory detention colony'.[62] Although this is more lenient than the maximum three years proposed by the Departmental Committee, and does not incorporate contemporary calls for sterilisation, it should be remembered that under the 1824 act an idle and disorderly person could be incarcerated only for one month. Under the new bill the maximum punishment for such offenders would be increased twelvefold.

Ultimately, the bill was never passed, and this particular biopolitical experiment was aborted. Nonetheless, it is still salutary to consider Rachel Vorspan's analysis that 'had the Liberal government not been preoccupied with more pressing matters in the years before World War I, or had the war itself not reduced the vagrancy problem to insignificance, early twentieth-century England might have witnessed . . . penal labour colonies for the "undeserving"'.[63] Moreover, although the bill was rejected, it still demonstrates the influence of degeneration theory and eugenics, and how representations of vagrancy were impacted by the discourses of scientific racism. Just as extinction theory helped to position Gypsies as a separate and vanishing race, so degeneration theory articulated the loafer as racially discrete. In the ephemeral and literary texts examined in this study, these racial theories were deployed with varying degrees of emphasis, coherence and understanding. Such variation is even evident within the corpus of single writers. Although Wells was unnervingly optimistic in *Anticipations*, claiming that the People of the Abyss were 'the people of no account whatever, the classes of extinction', this was not always the case.[64] In his first book-length foray into the future, *The Time Machine*, he envisaged a much more troubling destiny for humanity, one in which degeneration had caused it to split into two races, the Eloi and the Morlocks. In the next section, I argue that the Morlocks represent the future of the residuum and that they embody both the biological nightmare identified with this underclass and its revolutionary potential as well.

4.2   H. G. Wells and *The Time Machine*

'I was born at a place called Bromley, in Kent, a suburb of the damnedest, in 1866', wrote Wells to Grant Richards, the editor of *Phil May's Annual*.

Scrawled in November 1895, the letter is a jaunty biographical sketch that
tumbles through a list of failure, illness, rejection, success and – finally –
public approbation, the glory of which is the 'fuss' being made over *The
Time Machine*.[65] Wells's buoyancy reflects a newfound financial security,
likewise bought to him by the novella, and an escape from the petty-
bourgeois struggle for respectability, which he had been engaged with for
most of his life. The Bromley of his boyhood was one in which flagging
middle-class families tried desperately to differentiate themselves from
their poorer neighbours. Like many areas that had been opened up by
the new railways, Bromley had become a victim of the uncontrolled
suburbanisation that characterised London's growth from the 1840s to
the 1870s.[66] Throughout this period jerry-built developments became
popular speculations for investors, and it was in one of these that the
Wells lived. 'Shops and dwellings of the type of my home', Wells tells
us, 'were "run up" anyhow.'[67] Unfortunately, these speculations often
proved unremunerative because the market they were meant to accommodate, the middle classes, did not exist in the required quantity.[68]
Consequently, as Wells goes on to note of Bromley, 'slum conditions
appeared almost at once in courts and muddy by-ways'.[69] This is why
Bromley was 'a suburb of the damnedest', because Wells had to live
cheek-by-jowl with 'inferior' people, people he despised but was separated
from by the narrowest margins.

Wells's proximity and early prejudice towards the 'lower classes' is
exhibited in his *An Experiment in Autobiography* (1934), in which he
recounts his days as a schoolboy at Bromley Academy. A throwback from
an earlier time, Bromley Academy was run by Thomas Morley, a fantas-
tically pompous man of the Turveydrop type who would 'carry himself
with invariable dignity and make a frequent use of the word "Sir"'; he also
made frequent use of the cane, 'books, rulers and anything else that came
handy' to discipline his charges. Despite this, and the fact that he fitted a
'Dickens-like caricature', Wells was adamant that the antiquated Academy
provided a better education than the free National School. He insisted that
although his parents could barely afford it they were right to eke out the
fees for as long as they could rather than throw him among the 'Bromley
Water Rats', as he and his peers called the National School pupils. At the
root of this was a firm belief: 'just as my mother was obliged to believe in
Hell, but hoped that no one would go there, so did I believe there was and
had to be a lower stratum, though I was disgusted to find that anyone
belonged to it'.[70] The reality of this 'lower stratum', the social hell that
haunted Wells, must have seemed to draw nearer and nearer as the family's

fortunes declined. Already living in a house-cum-crockery-shop 'run up' like a slum, the Wells family were soon hampered with unhappy debts. Awkward bills began to accumulate until those school fees that marked the slippage between Wells and the Water Rats could no longer be squeezed from the household finances. For a moment it looked like Wells would have to join the 'inferior' classes in the National School, but fortunately Morley let him stay on gratis while his parents searched for a suitable apprenticeship.[71] Despite this escape, however, Wells remained in a financially precarious position. On meeting George Gissing in 1896 he remarked that when he first read *New Grub Street* (1891) he compared himself to Edwin Reardon, who 'lived like myself as a struggling writer in Mornington Road with a wife named Amy'.[72] Mercifully, Wells avoided the fate that Reardon predicts for himself: 'The abyss.... Penury and despair and a miserable death.'[73] Nonetheless, Wells's prolonged existence on the brink of poverty, and his fear of the 'lower stratum', had a significant influence on his social and political thought, and found expression in his early fiction.

Wells became one of the many writers who brooded over the residuum during the fin de siècle. Some of these commentators lobbied for intervention in the periodical press, as we have seen, while others addressed the problem primarily through fiction. This is particularly true of the slum novelists Margaret Harkness and Arthur Morrison. The 'ordinary East End loafer type' recurs in the four slum novels that Harkness reeled off between 1887 and 1890, and became a preoccupation on and off the page.[74] In 'A Year of My Life' (1891) she recorded that she had investigated how the residuum were managed on the Continent and in the colonies because 'my principal interest is with a class below the unskilled labourers: I mean the scum of our population that haunts the slums of our great cities'.[75] For Morrison, too, the residuum was an artistic and social concern. In his most famous novel, *A Child of the Jago* (1896), he populates his East End slumscape with loafers: 'there were loafers near Mother Gapp's, loafers at the Luck Row corner – at every corner – and loafers by the "Posties", all laggard of limb and alert of eye'.[76] When the *Daily News* interviewed him following his novel's successful reception, he proposed what should be done with these ne'er-do-wells: 'I believe', he said, 'in penal settlement ... Why not confine them as lunatics are confined? Let the weed die out, and then proceed to raise the raisable.'[77] Such sentiments were also echoed by Harkness. In her article 'The Loafer: What Shall We Do with Him?' (1889), she bemoaned the fact that 'we let these drunkards and vagabonds infest our streets' and argued that 'the State should send him to a Home

Colony, where he will be kindly treated, but not allowed to do mischief by propagating'.[78] In both these schemes we encounter the solution of confinement and sterilisation later promoted by White and Wells.

The 'lower stratum' exerted a fascination over Harkness and Morrison. Despite this, the enduring threat that it seemed to pose never emerged as a dominant theme in their fiction. This was because the social and historical scope of their novels was too limited, at least according to Wells. When he reviewed Morrison's *A Child of the Jago* for the *Saturday Review* he was full of praise for what he called 'one of the most interesting novels this year has produced', but he noted that its 'design, it must be confessed, is a little narrow'. As he went on to explain:

> It is as if Mr. Morrison had determined to write of the Jago and nothing but the Jago. It is the Jago without relativity.... He sees the Jago, is profoundly impressed by the appearance of the Jago, renders its appearance with extraordinary skill. But the origin of the Jago, the place of the Jago in the general scheme of things, the trend of change in it, its probable destiny – such matters are not in his mind.[79]

The myopia with which Wells charged Morrison might also be applied to Harkness. Her novels, similarly, tend to be embedded within the late nineteenth-century slumscape and to attend to little else. Her novel *In Darkest London* (1889), for example, grinds through the slums of Whitechapel, Seven Dials and Bethnal Green, but the didactic tours conducted by her characters do not venture beyond these impoverished districts bar a brief excursion to Kent. Even here, however, it is the ubiquity of misery and degradation that Harkness emphasises: 'the serpent is more subtle than any beast of the field; he is here just as much as in the East End of London'.[80]

The relentless emphasis that Harkness placed on slum conditions can be understood as part of her commitment to social reform. Her novels were 'tracts to move the heart', and their value lay in their philanthropic power: 'I care nothing for art', she declared in an interview in 1890, 'my purpose is all.'[81] For Harkness, the novel functioned as an urgent and timely intervention that was successful only if it provoked an emotional response within the reader. Forcing readers to confront contemporary realities through a harrowing description of the late Victorian slums was one way to achieve this. Meanwhile, speculations regarding the slums' 'trend of change' and 'probable destiny' were academic indulgences. This is what Harkness suggests in her novel *A Manchester Shirtmaker* (1890) in which she introduces an anonymous 'philanthropist (or economist?) who spent his time in "making enquiries"'. From the moment he is introduced, the narrator encourages us to distrust the competence of this philanthropist. The query about whether he is a 'philanthropist (or economist?)', and the wry quotation marks that hover over 'making enquiries', stress the vagueness of his occupation and gesture towards an unproductive amateurism. This suspicion is confirmed when he enters a lodging-house and begins to lecture its attendant on 'the loafer', arguing that he belongs to a 'hereditary class of vagabonds' who should be 'enclosed in a home colony . . . where they cannot do harm by propagating'. This is the same suggestion that Harkness made in 'On Loafers' a year earlier, but whereas in the article it is framed as a pragmatic solution to a social problem, in the novel it is an ineffectual hypothesis. This is the view of the phlegmatic attendant who has 'not heard of home colonies' but asserts that 'England is a free country'. In *A Manchester Shirtmaker*, then, Harkness discredits the conjectural stance of the philanthropist who identifies loafers as the 'Problem of the Future', but cannot propose an effective or acceptable solution for dealing with them today.[82] Meanwhile, Wells favoured the prophetic approach.

When he wrote his review of *A Child of the Jago*, Wells had already addressed the blinkered design of the slum novel by writing about the residuum from the perspective of the dystopian future. As in utopia, the chief aim of dystopia is to excavate the shaping forces of the future that lie hidden in the present.[83] In *The Time Machine* Wells attempts just that: he traces the development of the idle loafers from the late nineteenth century through to 'the sunset of mankind' and reveals the dramatic impact that they will have upon social dynamics.[84] That said, it would be misleading to say that Wells portrays the vagrant loafer per se. As the Time Traveller observes towards the end of his narrative, the London of 802,701 emerged from a society that had solved the social problem: 'there had been no unemployed problem, no social question left unsolved' (73). Such a state might arise from the society that Wells would depict a few years later in his metropolitan dystopia *When the Sleeper Wakes* (1899). In this London of the twenty-second century, the Labour Company, a successor of the Salvation Army, has guaranteed 'work to starving homeless people' and ensured that they can go nowhere else for succour. As Helen informs Graham, the Victorian protagonist who has slept into the future, 'Nowadays there are no workhouses, no refuges and charities, nothing but that Company. Its offices are everywhere.... And any man, woman or child who comes to be hungry and weary and with neither home nor friend nor resort, must go to the Company in the end – or seek some way of death.'[85] However, although the nineteenth-century loafer is absent from Wells's text, the revolutionary and evolutionary threat that this degenerate vagrant represented is nonetheless portrayed. It is captured in the Morlocks, the nocturnal and cannibalistic workers of the underworld who feed on the Eloi, their one-time masters.

In his seminal study, *The Early H. G. Wells* (1961), Bernard Bergonzi argued that the Morlocks 'represent an exaggerated fear of the nineteenth century proletariat'.[86] Stemming from the Time Traveller's hypothesis that the Morlocks are descended from the nineteenth-century 'Labourer' (47), this interpretation has been widely adopted by critics, many of whom have perceived a connection not only between the Morlocks and the Victorian proletariat but between the Morlocks and the middle-class Time Traveller as well. As Dan Bivona and Roger B. Henkle argue, Wells identified the Morlocks with the Time Traveller through their shared passion for technology, hence the Morlocks 'have hidden away his time machine in hope of learning how it works'.[87] But the Morlocks' act of theft at the beginning of the Traveller's narrative speaks less of the proletarian interest in mechanics than the criminality of what Karl Marx called the lumpenproletariat: the 'ragged' or 'knavish' workers.[88] This class, which according to Marx was a 'recruiting ground for thieves and criminals of all sorts, living off the garbage of society ... vagabonds, *gens sans feu et sans aveu*', was the residuum.[89] I argue that Wells encourages us to read the Morlocks as the descendants of the lumpenproletariat. The London of the future is one in which the residuum reigns.

The correspondence between the Morlocks and the residuum is evident on a formal level. Social investigation is one of the many genres that *The Time Machine* evokes, and is alluded to from the beginning of the novella when the Traveller returns from his journey, interrupting his guests in a theatrical fashion.[90] The company has gathered for dinner at his request and started without him because he is 'unavoidably detained' (16). When he enters the dining room he appears 'dusty and dirty' (17) and distinctly travel-worn. As the narrator observes, he bore 'just such a limp as I have seen in foot-sore tramps' (17) and attacked his meal with 'the appetite of a tramp' (19). This early correspondence between the bourgeois Traveller and the shabby, seamy vagrant nods toward the middle-class practice of 'slumming'. As Seth Koven relates, this was commonplace in Victorian Britain, and at its most extreme involved an element of 'cross-class dress' that became essential to the exploits of investigators like James Greenwood and Mary Higgs (see Chapter 3).[91]

The allusions made to this practice by the unwitting and concerned narrator are made explicit by more gregarious guests, who proceed to make light of the Traveller's dishevelled aspect. The voluble Journalist asks, 'Has he been doing the Amateur Cadger?' (18) and the Editor, countering this quiz with one of his own, asks, 'Does our friend eke out his modest income with a crossing?' (18). The Journalist's reference to the 'Amateur Cadger' recalls Greenwood, 'The Amateur Casual', and his steady throng of followers who masqueraded as vagrants. A 'cadger' was originally a hawker or itinerant dealer, but in the nineteenth century the word increasingly came to denote a beggar or loafer. As Daniel Kirwan recorded in 1870, '"Cadger" is a Cockney term for people who will not work and have no habitation, but go from one place to another, roaming loosely'.[92] 'Amateur Cadger' could also refer to a more nefarious form of slumming, like that practised by Arthur Conan Doyle's 'Amateur Mendicant Society' in 'The Five Orange Pips' (1891), a story where Sherlock Holmes foils a band of middle-class imposters who fund 'a luxurious club' with the alms they elicit from the indiscriminate public.[93] The Editor also suggests this remunerative form of cadging when he asks if the Traveller sweeps a street crossing. As the American journalist Elizabeth Banks relates in 'Sweeping a Crossing' (1894), her exposé of that (almost mythically) 'remunerative profession', 'wonderful tales have been told of members of the craft who have grown wealthy with plying the broom'; if this feat was ever per-formed, she observes, then it was achieved by begging and ploys 'invented to reach the sympathies of the public'.[94] The slumming of social investi-gation, then, as well its seedier side, is a presence from the outset, and becomes only more evident when the Traveller tells his tale of the future.

Several critics have detected elements of social investigation in *The Time Machine*. Some of these have been general, as with Carlo Pagetti's specu-lation that Wells modelled his Eloi and Morlocks on the slum-savages that William Booth depicted in *In Darkest England*.[95] Most, however, have been more specific, identifying the Traveller with the investigator when he descends into the subterranean lair of the Morlocks. Indeed, this is a persona that the Traveller himself briefly adopts, interrupting his narrative to declare, 'even now, does not an East-end worker live in such artificial conditions as practically to be cut off from the natural surface of the earth?' (47). Steven McLean argues that this outburst of social zeal aligns the Traveller with contemporary reformers like Charles Booth. He also notes the similarities between the portrayal of the dark and stagnant underworld, 'stuffy and oppressive' (52) and flavoured with the 'halitus of freshly shed blood' (52), and Mearns's description of the urban poor.[96] Matthew Beaumont likewise remarks on the similarity between this episode and the scenes of urban poverty traditionally found in social investigations, arguing that Wells 'exploits the uncanny thrills enjoyed by middle-class readers' of slum explorations by 'pushing them to an unbearable extreme'.[97] To these observations can also be added the contrast between the 'heavy smell' (52) of the Morlocks' den and the soil of the Upperworld, which 'smelt sweet and clean' (54) upon the Traveller's re-emergence. This juxtaposition of stagnant corruption with healthful cleanliness is a classic trope of slum literature, a means of heightening our sense of the disorder and degeneration of the urban poor.[98]

The Time Traveller's stilted progress through the Morlocks' cavern also aligns him with the urban investigator. As he narrates how he stumbled through the dark, guided only by the light of a few safety matches, he interrupts himself again, exclaiming, 'if only I had thought of a Kodak! I could have flashed that glimpse of the Underworld in a second, and examined it at leisure' (53). The comparison here between the spluttering matches and flash photography, the latest technology to be appropriated by social explorers, is at once significant and strange.[99] The advantage of the camera that the Traveller identifies is that it would provide the *same* 'glimpse of the Underworld' as the matches, only faster. By making the comparison on these terms the Traveller implicitly claims that the light of the safety match is equivalent to the camera's flash. To the discerning reader this, of course, does not make sense: the radiance and power of a match is weaker than that of a Kodak. Nonetheless, in the Traveller's description of the Morlocks' lair he silently persists in his claim, presenting the cavern in a series of snapshots in which the match-light acts as an able substitute for the magnesium glare of the missing flash. When the Traveller enters a 'large open space' (52) in the subterranean world, his vision is both sharp in terms of immediate detail, for example, when he pinpoints the 'little table of white metal' (52) furnished with a 'red joint' (52), and, at the same time, limited by the 'utter darkness beyond the range of my light' (52). This is the vision of flash photography. As Kate Flint explains while reflecting on the photographs included in Jacob Riis's *How the Other Half Lives* (1890) and Jack London's *The People of the Abyss* (1903), the flash enabled enormous amounts of detail to be revealed, but at the same time it 'created great pools of contrastive and visually impenetrable darkness'.[100] This gaze, precise but tightly bounded, is the one that the Traveller adopts in his narrative: despite the fact that he lacks the slum explorers' equipment we are still persuaded to see the Traveller inhabiting their role. It is hard to imagine that when the Traveller goes back into the future at the end of *The Time Machine*, equipped with 'a small camera under one arm' (85), he is not going in the spirit of a social investigator.

This correspondence between the Time Traveller and the slum explorer, especially during his adventure underground, invites a corresponding identification between the Morlocks and the residuum, their subject of study. This is encouraged by the fact that Wells draws on the imagery of slum literature in order to portray the Morlocks. Like the loafers found in the works of Harkness, Morrison and others, the Morlocks are represented as nocturnal, subterranean and cannibalistic.

The Morlocks are a submerged, nocturnal breed. Dwelling in their caverns by day, these troglodytes of the future venture forth only at night. Nocturnal habits like these have long been associated with aimlessness and idleness, and have been proscribed historically not only as crimes in themselves but also as evidence of other crimes and vices.[101] This culturally ingrained bias impacted depictions of the residuum who, like the Morlocks, were portrayed as a class of basement-skulkers that hid in what Burleigh called 'slum burrows', and sallied forth only at night to carouse.[102] In his short story 'In the Heart of London' (1886) D. Rice-Jones recalls his search in St Giles for a homeless waif called Jack. One of his first ports of call is a cellar where an illicit raffle is known to be held. A nest of 'subterranean caverns', it is home to the 'lowest type that could be found or imagined in the form of man' and the heroic slum-priest, like the Time Traveller, has to battle through an 'underground London' thick with a stench that 'makes [him] feel sick and faint'.[103] Unfortunately, he is too late; night has fallen and his quarry scattered. Similarly, in Harkness's *In Darkest London* we are told that once casual labourers have sunk 'into the scum of London, and become paupers, gaol-birds and vagrants', they take up residence in lodging-houses or 'thieves' kitchens'. To enter these crypts of iniquity the intrepid explorer has to go 'down a steep flight of steps to an underground place at the end of a long passage'. These, however, are only daytime retreats: 'at night the slummers show themselves to be worse than savages. They come out of the holes they call homes, and the public-houses, to enjoy themselves in truly bestial fashion'.[104]

Such depictions of the urban poor persisted into the early twentieth century. Working-class participants of the raucous City Imperial Volunteers (CIV) demonstrations on 27 and 29 October 1901 were portrayed by the journalist and politician C. F. G. Masterman in similar terms. Held in honour of London's Imperial Volunteers, who were returning home from the Boer War, a mood of celebration deteriorated into one of dissipation. According to one paper the 'slum classes, and throngs of immoral women' flooded the streets, and by nightfall 'scenes of riot and uproar' were everywhere.[105] Not everyone blamed the urban poor for the lewd display. One eyewitness, writing to the *Outlook*, described how 'one old gentleman – I am sure he was *a real* gentleman because he wore diamond rings on his fingers – chased a crowd of girls with a gilded bladder on a stick'.[106] Masterman, however, adopted the former interpretation and depicted the 'dense black masses' of the working class as the sole perpetrators of the commotion.[107] Perhaps drawing on Wells, whom he considered a 'brilliant speculator', Masterman depicted the working classes in Morlockian terms.[108] 'Denizens of another universe', the crowd is composed of nocturnal creatures who dwell in dark, cramped conditions. Consequently, they are 'unaccustomed [to] daylight and squares and open spaces' and reveal their true natures only with the onset of night. In a scene in which the urban poor almost visibly degenerate, Masterman describes how 'as the darkness drew on they relapsed more and more into bizarre and barbaric revelry'. Eventually, like a pack of wolves, they are left 'howling under the quiet stars' while the remnants of the respectable public retire in indignation.[109]

The other defining trait of the Morlocks is cannibalism. As the Time Traveller hypothesises, having explored their cavern, 'these Eloi were mere fatted cattle, which the ant-like Morlocks preserved and preyed upon' (59). This taste for human flesh is also inherited from the East End. Reformers, slum novelists and journalists readily portrayed the residuum as cannibalistic. At times this was figurative. This is the case in Sims's *How the Poor Live*, in which he compares the slums to the 'Cannibal Islands', and in William Booth's *In Darkest England*, which opens with an in-depth analogy between the metropolitan residuum and the 'human beings dwarfed into pygmies and brutalised into cannibals' that Henry Morton Stanley claimed to have discovered in Africa.[110] But the East End cannibal was also represented in more literal terms. Although the narrator of *A Child of the Jago* mocks those who believe in 'slums packed with starving human organisms without minds and without morals, preying on each other alive', this is the very scene that Morrison describes in a subsequent chapter. During a faction fight between the Ranns and the Learys, two rival clans within the Jago, Dicky Perrott comes across his mother being savaged by Sally Green, a woman notorious for 'gnawing and worrying' her opponents. 'Sprawled on her face in the foul road lay a writhing woman ... and spread over all, clutching her prey by hair and wrist, Sally Green hung on the nape like a terrier, jaws clenched, head shaking.' In a bid to protect his mother, Dicky attacks Sally, and also turns cannibal: 'when help came', we are told, his 'sharp teeth were meeting in the shoulder-flesh'.[111] Although these attacks are ostensibly driven by anger rather than hunger, the anthropophagic motive can scarcely be escaped in a novel where food is so conspicuous by its absence.

The Jago is not the only London slum where cannibal appetites are at work. In two of Harkness's novels, *Out of Work* (1888) and *In Darkest London*, cannibalism becomes a symptom of the most degraded form of slum-life. In *Out of Work* she describes a common lodging-house in which two homeless people are kept like dogs, 'quarrell[ing] together for crusts and potatoes' thrown to them by the lodgers. One of these wretches, 'a shrivelled hag', sees a baby dying on its mother's knee. The mother's eyes are closed, silently seeping tears, and the woman takes her chance. Shuffling forward she 'drew near to touch the baby's rounded knee with a claw-like finger' and then retreats, muttering.[112] Harkness does not state what the woman's intentions are, but the implication is clear: that the meaty joint of a baby near to death looked, perhaps only for an instant, like a promising meal. In *In Darkest London*, Harkness is more explicit. Here Captain Lobe is called to a slum in Bethnal Green where he finds a Christian man who has squirrelled himself away amongst the Jewry, a pariah community during this period.[113] A former slaughterman, he confesses to Lobe that having 'to kill and kill makes a man like a cannibal' and that one day, possessed by a 'thirst' for 'human blood, human flesh' he struck down a vagrant woman and killed her.[114] In the end, we are told, he did not eat her, too horrified by what he had done.

In their descriptions of near-cannibals in the East End, Morrison and Harkness were participating in a literary trend in which anthropophagic desires were ascribed to impoverished and vagrant figures. As I have discussed elsewhere, Charles Dickens used this motif in *Great Expectations* (1860–1).[115] When Pip is surprised by the half-starved Magwitch at the beginning of the novel, the vagrant convict lingers on the boy's 'fat cheeks' while 'licking his lips': "Darn Me if I couldn't eat'em," said the man, with a threatening shake of his head, "and if I han't half a mind to't!"[116] In the case of Harkness and Morrison, the cannibal instincts of the slummers reveal their savage and degraded state. As Patrick Bantlinger notes, cannibalism in the Victorian period 'marked the low end of the evolutionary totem pole from savage to civilized'.[117] That the Morlocks submit to these instincts not only exposes the extent of their own debasement, but also reveals the degraded future that awaits the Victorian residuum, the class with which I have argued they are aligned.

Although *The Time Machine* is primarily a story concerned with biological degeneration, this contains a political narrative in which the

Morlocks' cannibalism accrues further meaning. As Beaumont has argued, the Morlocks' slaughter of the Eloi represents a form of sociopolitical degeneration in which Marx's proletarian uprising has come to fruition. This revolution was presented by Marx as already secretly seeded within the works of Victorian capitalism. Like the physical decline of the human race that was feared by contemporary commentators, the socialist revolution was a corruption that was already underway.[118] Powered by Wells's 'exclusively evolutionary understanding of history', *The Time Machine* weds society's political trajectory to that of humanity's biological degeneration.[119] In this political reading of the text the cannibalistic practice adopted by the Morlocks marks the advent of revolution: the anthropophagous act is the literal and symbolic overthrow of the bourgeoisie (or at least its remains). As Katherine Hume notes in her psychoanalytic analysis, 'Haves normally exploit, "eat," or consume Havenots in a capitalist system; that is how the image [of cannibalism] usually enters socio-economic discourse. In *The Time Machine*, however, the cannibalistic urges are instead projected onto the Havenots.'[120] The reversal of the cannibalistic image is therefore emblematic of capitalism overturned.

However, this is not the revolution that Marx predicted. Rather than the communist world that the Traveller initially believes he might have discovered, he instead unearths a society that has collapsed into anarchism. This is also signified by the act of cannibalism. Recording the final days of the First French Revolution, Thomas Carlyle pungently described how 'the Revolutionary Tribunal, after all it has devoured, has now only, as Anarchic things do, to devour itself'.[121] Wells would have been familiar with Carlyle's cannibalistic construction of revolution gone wrong: in his autobiography he recalled that he 'discovered the heady brew of Carlyle's *French Revolution*' in 1887.[122] It is also particularly fitting that a world dominated by the residuum should be anarchic: as we have seen, in the 1880s Peek and his contemporaries feared that loafers would be 'used by the anarchists to further their own ends', while for Marx, anarchy was the class ideology of the lumpenproletariat.[123]

This interpretation of the Morlocks' revolution is one of the many narratives that Wells encourages us to read through the symbolism of *The Time Machine*. The relationship between the Morlock and the anarchic vagrant is one of the associations that the White Sphinx, the dominant symbol of the novella, holds in tension. Embossed on the front cover of the first edition at Wells's suggestion, the sphinx looms large throughout the narrative: it is the first object that the Traveller contemplates when he arrives in the future; it acts as a waymarker, guiding him across the estranged landscape of London; and it is within the belly of sphinx, its 'pedestal of bronze' (35), that he eventually finds the time machine. As a symbol it is 'obdurately overdetermined', as Beaumont remarks.[124] It could gesture towards other fantastic narratives, like Jules Verne's *Le Sphinx des glaces*, as Patrick Parrinder suggests.[125] Or it could be a reference to the Decadent Movement, as Roger Luckhurst proposes when he observes that it might refer to Oscar Wilde's 1894 poem *The Sphinx*. Here the sphinx symbolises sensual decadence and decline, which would chime with Wells's depiction of the enervated Eloi.[126] Moreover, it would cohere with Wells's practice elsewhere: in *A Story of the Days to Come* (1899), another dystopia set in the same future as *When the Sleeper Wakes*, the phrase 'Sphinx of Sin' is used by the depraved millionaire Bindon to 'dignify certain unhealthy and undignified departures from sane conduct to which a misguided vanity and an ill-controlled curiosity had led him'.[127]

However, within the context of *The Time Machine*, the symbol of the sphinx also points to the social problem. As Luckhurst and Beaumont have remarked, the sphinx recalls Julian West's eager query at the beginning of Edward Bellamy's *Looking Backward: 2000–1887* (1888), a utopian text that *The Time Machine* directly responds to.[128] Having slumbered for a century, West awakes and asks, 'What solution, if any, have you found for the labour question? It was the Sphinx's riddle of the nineteenth century, and when I dropped out the Sphinx was threatening to devour society, because the answer was not forthcoming.'[129] Here the sphinx symbolises the unemployed and their capacity for destruction. By the time Bellamy and Wells were writing, these associations were well established. As I discussed in the previous chapter, in *Past and Present* (1843) Carlyle used the sphinx as an emblem for the Condition-of-England question, and to warn readers of the revolutionary consequences if it was not answered.[130] Dickens and Fildes likewise portrayed London's casuals as sphinxes in order to express their potential for insurrection, and later Harkness also participated in this tradition. In *Out of Work* she described two homeless women, begging in the street for halfpennies: 'there they sit day and night, those sphinxes. And there they will stay until *Laissez-faire* and his army lose the day, until his banners are seized by the enemy.'[131] Wells's sphinx evokes this legacy of representation. It figures as a symbol for the impoverished, vagrant and unemployed who form the residuum, and the power that they have to overthrow society and its economic order. This was imagined by some to be the political destiny of the casual and the loafer, those anonymous figures who haunted the bourgeois imagination.

Notes

1 'Loafer, n. 1', *OED Online* (accessed 8 May 2018).
2 'Loaf, v. 2', *OED Online* (accessed 8 May 2018); 'Land-loper/Land-louper, n. 1', *OED Online* (accessed 8 May 2018).
3 Charles Leland, *The English Gypsies and Their Language* (London: Trübner, 1873), p. 89. Original emphasis.
4 Albert Barrère and Charles Leland, *A Dictionary of Slang, Jargon & Cant, Embracing English, American, and Anglo-Indian Slang, Pidgin English, Tinkers' Jargon and Other Irregular Phraseology*, 2 vols ([Edinburgh]: Ballantyne Press, 1889), I, p. 200.
5 'Vagrants and Vagrancy', *London Quarterly Review*, January 1888, pp. 321–42 (p. 338).
6 Flora Annie Steel, 'In the Permanent Way', in *In the Permanent Way and Other Stories* (London: Heinemann, 1898), pp. 27–42 (p. 32); Rudyard Kipling, *Kim*, ed. Harish Trivedi (London: Penguin, 2011), p. 3.
7 'On Loafers', *Gentleman's Magazine*, April 1890, pp. 398–408 (p. 400).
8 Leonard Noble, 'Homeless at Night', *English Illustrated Magazine*, April 1892, pp. 572–6 (p. 572).
9 Samuel Barnett, 'The Abodes of the Homeless', *Cornhill Magazine*, July 1899, pp. 58–64 (p. 58).
10 Patrick Brantlinger, *Taming Cannibals: Race and the Victorians* (Ithaca, NY: Cornell University Press, 2011), p. 127.
11 Francis Peek, 'The Workless, the Thriftless, and the Worthless', *Contemporary Review*, 1 January 1888, pp. 39–52 (pp. 42–3).
12 George R. Sims, *Horrible London*, in *How the Poor Live and Horrible London* (London: Garland Publishing, 1984), pp. 111–50 (p. 113).
13 Andrew Mearns, *The Bitter Cry of Outcast London*, in *The Metropolitan Poor: Semi-Factual Accounts, 1795–1910*, ed. John Marriott and Masaie Matsumura, 6 vols (London: Pickering & Chatto, 1999), VI, pp. 80–100 (p. 87).
14 Judith R. Walkowitz, *City of Dreadful Delight: Narratives of Sexual Danger in Late Victorian London* (London: Virago Press, 1992), p. 27.
15 The *OED Online* records the first use of 'slumdom' in 1882. 'Slumdom, n.', *OED Online* (accessed 25 July 2021).
16 A keyword search in the *ProQuest British Periodicals* database reveals that from 1830, when according to the *OED* the term was coined, to 1879, the word 'loafer' was used 1,742 times, whereas between 1880 and 1899 it was used 2,942. This surge in usage is also reflected in the *British Newspaper Archive*; this database records that the term was used 13,349 times between 1830 and 1879, and 23,294 between 1880 and 1899. These searches were performed by the author on 13 June 2018.
17 Gareth Stedman Jones, *Outcast London: A Study in the Relationship between Classes in Victorian Society* (Oxford: Oxford University Press, 1971; repr. London: Verso, 2013), pp. 159–235; Jerry White, *London in the Nineteenth Century: A Human Awful Wonder of God* (London: Vintage, 2008), pp. 57–8.

18 George R. Sims, *How the Poor Live*, in *How the Poor Live and Horrible London* (London: Garland Publishing, 1984), pp. 1–110 (p. 20).

19 Ibid., pp. 17–18.

20 White, *London in the Nineteenth Century*, p. 374.

21 Stedman Jones, *Outcast London*, pp. 281–2.

22 Bennet Burleigh, 'The Unemployed', *Contemporary Review*, July 1887, pp. 771–80 (p. 772).

23 'Police Intelligence', *Standard*, 28 October 1887, p. 2.

24 'Five Nights in the Streets of London', *Pall Mall Gazette*, 9 September 1887, p. 5.

25 'Under the Black Flag', *Pall Mall Gazette*, 13 October 1887, p. 1.

26 'The Vagrants in Trafalgar Square', *Standard*, 26 October 1887, p. 2.

27 White, *London in the Nineteenth Century*, pp. 377–8.

28 Quoted by Angelique Richardson, *Love and Eugenics in the Late Nineteenth Century: Rational Reproduction and the New Woman* (Oxford: Oxford University Press, 2003), p. 20.

29 Peek, 'The Workless', pp. 43, 51.

30 'The Slum and the Cellar', *Saturday Review*, 27 October 1883, pp. 521–2 (p. 521).

31 Charles Booth, *Life and Labour of the People in London: First Series: Poverty*, revised ed., 5 vols (London: Macmillan, 1902; repr. Augustus M. Kelley, 1969), I, pp. 37–8.

32 William Booth, *In Darkest England and the Way Out* (London: International Headquarters of the Salvation Army, 1890; repr. Cambridge: Cambridge University Press, 2014), pp. 21–3.

33 Booth, *In Darkest England*, p. 23; 'London – Black and Blue', *Speaker*, 28 March 1891, pp. 365–6 (p. 366).

34 Booth, *Life and Labour*, p. 37.

35 Stedman Jones, *Outcast London*, pp. 303–4.

36 Laurel Brake, 'Periodical Formats: The Changing Review', in *Journalism and the Periodical Press in Nineteenth-Century Britain*, ed. Joanne Shattock (Cambridge: Cambridge University Press, 2017), pp. 47–65 (pp. 50, 55, 58–61, 63).

37 Peek, 'The Workless', pp. 41, 50, 53.

38 Burleigh, 'The Unemployed', pp. 775, 779.

39 William Booth and Charles Booth also advocated the creation of home colonies. However, unlike the Salvationist, who was bent on rescuing each spare soul that the residuum offered, Charles Booth foresaw that the stringent work demanded in these colonies would cause Class A to expose itself and that this could be advantageous: 'Class A, no longer confounded with "the unemployed," could be gradually harried out of existence.' Samuel Barnett, 'A Scheme for the Unemployed', *Nineteenth Century*, November 1888, pp. 753–63 (pp. 759–60); Booth, *Life and Labour*, pp. 167–9; Booth, *In Darkest England*, pp. 90–3.

40 William Greenslade, *Degeneration, Culture and the Novel, 1880–1940* (Cambridge: Cambridge University Press, 1994), p. 47.

41 John Marriott, *The Other Empire: Metropolis, India and Progress in the Colonial Imagination* (Manchester: Manchester University Press, 2003), p. 166.

42 Brantlinger, *Taming Cannibals*, pp. 127–35; Kenan Malik, *The Meaning of Race: Race, History and Culture in Western Society* (Basingstoke: Macmillan, 1996), pp. 109–11; Marriott, *The Other Empire*, pp. 166–7.

43 Francis Galton quoted by Greenslade, *Degeneration*, p. 26; also see Malik, *The Meaning of Race*, pp. 112–14; Marriott, *The Other Empire*, p. 181.

44 H. M. Hyndman, 'The English Workers as They Are', *Contemporary Review*, 1 July 1887, pp. 122–36 (p. 129).

45 Arnold White, 'The Nomad Poor of London', *Contemporary Review*, 1 January 1885, pp. 714–26 (p. 715).

46 Peek, 'The Workless', p. 50.

47 Dan Bivona and Roger B. Henkle, *The Imagination of Class: Masculinity and the Victorian Urban Poor* (Columbus: Ohio State University Press, 2006), p. 146.

48 White, 'The Nomad Poor of London', pp. 721–2.

49 Stedman Jones, *Outcast London*, pp. 330–3.

50 Arnold White, *Efficiency and Empire* (London: Methuen, 1901), p. 120.

51 John S. Partington, *Building Cosmopolis: The Political Thought of H. G. Wells* (Aldershot: Ashgate, 2003), pp. 54–7.

52 H. G. Wells, *Anticipations; or, The Reaction of Mechanical and Scientific Progress upon Human Life and Thought* (London: Chapman & Hall, 1902 [1901]), pp. 79, 212.

53 William Harbutt Dawson, *The Vagrancy Problem: The Case for Measures of Restraint for Tramps, Loafers, and Unemployables, with a Study of Continental Detention Colonies and Labour Houses* (London: P. S. King, 1910), pp. ix, 68, 76, 86.

54 Ibid., pp. 229–31.

55 *Report on the Departmental Committee on Vagrancy*, 3 vols (London: Wyman & Sons, 1906), I, pp. 59.

56 Rachel Vorspan, 'Vagrancy and the New Poor Law in Late-Victorian and Edwardian England', *English Historical Review*, 92.362 (1977), 59–81 (pp. 76–7).

57 Michel Foucault, '"Society Must Be Defended," Lecture at the *Collège de France*, March 17, 1976', in *Biopolitics: A Reader*, ed. Timothy Campbell and Adam Sitze (Durham, NC: Duke University Press, 2013), pp. 61–81 (p. 62).

58 Jill Rappoport, *Giving Women: Alliance and Exchange in Victorian Culture* (Oxford: Oxford University Press, 2012), pp. 147–51. Also see Rob Boddice, *The Science of Sympathy: Morality, Evolution, and Victorian Civilization* (Chicago: University of Illinois Press, 2016), p. 127.

59 Catherine Mills, *Biopolitics* (Abingdon: Routledge, 2018), p. 18.

60 Michel Foucault, 'Society Must Be Defended', pp. 74–5.

61 Angelique Richardson, 'The Eugenization of Love: Sarah Grand and the Morality of Genealogy', *Victorian Studies*, 42.2 (1999–2000), 227–55 (p. 235). Also see Malik, *The Meaning of Race*, p. 110.

62 *A Bill to Provide for the More Effectual Prevention of Destitution and the Better Organization of Public Assistance.*

63 Rachel Vorspan, 'Vagrancy and the New Poor Law', p. 81.

64 Wells, *Anticipations*, pp. 228–9.

65 H. G. Wells, *The Correspondence of H. G. Wells*, ed. David C. Smith, 4 vols (London: Pickering & Chatto, 1998), I, pp. 249.

66 White, *London in the Nineteenth Century*, pp. 77–9.

67 H. G. Wells, *An Experiment in Autobiography: Discoveries and Conclusions of a Very Ordinary Brain (since 1866)*, 2 vols (London: Faber and Faber, 2008), I, p. 84.

68 White, *London in the Nineteenth Century*, pp. 81, 87–8.

69 Wells, *Autobiography*, I, p. 84.

70 Ibid., I, pp. 85–6, 93–4.

71 Michael Sherborne, *H. G. Wells: Another Kind of Life* (London: Peter Owen, 2010; repr. 2012), pp. 24, 34–7.

72 Wells, *Autobiography*, II, p. 567.

73 George Gissing, *New Grub Street*, ed. John Goode (Oxford: Oxford University Press, 1993: repr. 2008), p. 198.

74 Margaret Harkness, *A City Girl*, ed. Deborah Mutch (Brighton: Victorian Secrets, 2015), p. 49.

75 [Margaret Harkness] John Law, 'A Year of My Life', *New Review*, October 1891, pp. 375–84 (p. 377).

76 Arthur Morrison, *A Child of the Jago*, ed. Peter Miles (Oxford: Oxford University Press, 2012), p. 56.

77 'The Children of the Jago: Slum-Life at Close Quarters: A Talk with Mr Arthur Morrison', in *A Child of the Jago*, ed. Peter Miles (Oxford: Oxford University Press, 2012), pp. 171–2 (p. 172).

78 [Margaret Harkness] John Law, 'The Loafer: What Shall We Do with Him?', *Labour Elector*, 21 September 1889, p. 180.

79 [H. G. Wells], 'A Slum Novel', *Saturday Review*, 28 November 1896, p. 573.

80 Margaret Harkness, *In Darkest London* (Cambridge: Black Apollo Press, 2003), p. 159.

81 'A Slum Story Writer', *Evening News and Post*, 17 April 1890, p. 2.

82 Margaret Harkness, *A Manchester Shirtmaker: A Realistic Story of Today*, intro. Trefor Thomas (Brighouse: Northern Herald, 2002), p. 70.

83 Matthew Beaumont, *Utopia Ltd.: Ideologies in Social Dreaming in England, 1870–1900* (Leiden: Brill, 2005), pp. 33–9.

84 H. G. Wells, *The Time Machine: An Invention*, ed. Roger Luckhurst (Oxford: Oxford University Press, 2017), p. 32. Future references will be made to this edition and in the main text.

85 H. G. Wells, *When the Sleeper Wakes*, ed. John Lawton (London: Everyman, 1994), p. 159.

86 Bernard Bergonzi, *The Early H. G. Wells: A Study of the Scientific Romances* (Manchester: Manchester University Press, 1961), p. 53.

87 Bivona and Henkle, *The Imagination of Class*, p. 161.

88 Nicholas Thoburn, 'Difference in Marx: The Lumpenproletariat and the Proletarian Unnamable', *Economy and Society*, 31.3 (2002), 434–60 (pp. 439–40).

89 Quoted by John Welshman, *Underclass: A History of the Excluded since 1880*, 2nd ed. (London: Bloomsbury, 2013), p. 20.

90 For a survey of the genres that Wells deploys in *The Time Machine*, see Roger Luckhurst, 'Introduction', in *The Time Machine: An Invention*, ed. Roger Luckhurst (Oxford: Oxford University Press, 2017), pp. vii–xxv (pp. xii–xviii).

91 Seth Koven, *Slumming: Sexual and Social Politics in Victorian London* (Princeton, NJ: Princeton University Press, 2004), pp. 1, 26.

92 'Cadger, n.', *OED Online* (accessed 9 February 2017); Daniel Joseph Kirwan, *Palace and Hovel; or, Phases of London Life*, ed. A. Allan (London: Abelard-Schuman, 1963), p. 70.

93 Arthur Conan Doyle, 'The Five Orange Pips', in *The Adventures of Sherlock Holmes*, ed. Richard Lancelyn Green (Oxford: Oxford University Press, 1993; repr. 2008), pp. 102–22 (p. 102).

94 Elizabeth L. Banks, 'Sweeping a Crossing', in *Campaigns of Curiosity: Journalistic Adventures of an American Girl in Late Victorian London* (Madison: University of Wisconsin Press, 2003), pp. 129–38 (pp. 130, 138).

95 Carlo Pagetti, 'Changes in the City: The Time Traveller's London and the "Baseless Fabric" of His Vision', *H. G. Wells's Perennial Time Machine: Selected Essays from the Centenary Conference '"The Time Machine": Past, Present, and Future' Imperial College, London July 26–29, 1995* (Athens: University of Georgia Press, 2001), pp. 122–34 (p. 123).

96 Steven McLean, *The Early Fiction of H. G. Wells: Fantasies of Science* (Basingstoke: Palgrave Macmillan, 2009), pp. 21–2.

97 Matthew Beaumont, *The Spectre of Utopia: Utopian and Science Fictions at the Fin de Siècle* (Bern: Peter Lang, 2012), p. 250.

98 See Kevin R. Swafford, 'Resounding the Abyss: The Politics of Narration in Jack London's *The People of the Abyss*', *Journal of Popular Culture*, 39.5 (2006), 838–60 (p. 846).

99 Kate Flint, 'Surround, Background, and the Overlooked', *Victorian Studies*, 57.3 (2015), 449–61 (pp. 457–9).

100 Ibid., p. 457.

101 Matthew Beaumont, *Nightwalking: A Nocturnal History of London, Chaucer to Dickens* (London: Verso, 2015), pp. 15, 27–8, 42.

102 Burleigh, 'The Unemployed', p. 772.

103 D. Rice-Jones, 'In the Heart of London', *English Illustrated Magazine*, December 1886, pp. 208–33 (pp. 220–3).

104 Harkness, *In Darkest London*, pp. 49, 41–2, 175.

105 'Carnival or Pandemonium', *Hampshire Advertiser*, 3 November 1900, p. 5.

106 'An Experience on C.I.V. Day', *Outlook*, 3 November 1900, p. 429. Original emphasis.

107 [C. F. G. Masterman], *From the Abyss: Of Its Inhabitants by One of Them* (London: R. Brimley Johnson, 1902), p. 2.

108 C. F. G. Masterman, 'The Social Abyss', *Contemporary Review*, 1 January 1902, pp. 23–35 (p. 34). David L. Pike has also noted the influence that Wells's Morlocks had on Masterman's depictions of the urban poor in his later work *The Condition of England* (1909). See David L. Pike, *Subterranean Cities: The World beneath Paris and London, 1800–1945* (Ithaca, NY: Cornell University Press, 2005), p. 83.

109 Masterman, *From the Abyss*, pp. 2–3.

110 Booth, *In Darkest England*, p. 9; Sims, *How the Poor Live*, p. 69.

111 Morrison, *A Child of the Jago*, pp. 28, 33.

112 Margaret Harkness, *Out of Work*, ed. John Lucas (London: Merlin Press, 1990), pp. 111–12.

113 In the 1880s and 1890s an influx of Jewish migrants generated an intense hostility towards the Jewish community. See White, *London in the Nineteenth Century*, p. 156.

114 Harkness, *In Darkest London*, p. 150.

115 See Alistair Robinson, 'Vagrant, Convict, Cannibal Chief: Abel Magwitch and the Culture of Cannibalism in *Great Expectations*', *Journal of Victorian Culture*, 22.4 (2017), 450–64.

116 Charles Dickens, *Great Expectations*, ed. Charlotte Mitchell (London: Penguin, 2003), p. 4.

117 Brantlinger, *Taming Cannibals*, p. 31.

118 Beaumont, *Spectre of Utopia*, pp. 221–52.

119 Ibid., p. 243.

120 Kathryn Hume, 'Eat or Be Eaten: H. G. Wells's *Time Machine*', *Philological Quarterly*, 69.2 (1990), 233–51 (p. 244).

121 Thomas Carlyle, *The French Revolution*, 3 vols (London: Folio Society, 1989), III, p. 283.

122 Wells, *Autobiography*, I, p. 241.

123 Peek, 'The Workless', p. 51; Thoburn, 'Difference in Marx', pp. 445, 453; Welshman, *Underclass*, p. 21.

124 Beaumont, *Spectre of Utopia*, p. 229.

125 Patrick Parrinder, *Shadows of the Future: H. G. Wells, Science Fiction and Prophecy* (Liverpool: Liverpool University Press, 1995), p. 15.

126 See Luckhurst's note in Wells, *The Time Machine*, p. 106.

127 H. G. Wells, *A Story of the Days to Come*, in *Tales of Time and Space* (London: Harper & Brothers, 1900), pp. 165–324 (p. 318).

128 Beaumont, *Spectre of Utopia*, pp. 228–32; Luckhurst, 'Introduction', pp. xv–xvi.

129 Edward Bellamy, *Looking Backward: 2000–1887*, ed. Matthew Beaumont (Oxford: Oxford University Press, 2007), p. 28.

130 Beaumont also cites Carlyle's *Past and Present* as a source for the sphinx in *The Time Machine*. See Beaumont, *Spectre of Utopia*, p. 230.

131 Harkness, *Out of Work*, p. 136.

PART III

The Frontier

CHAPTER 5

Paupers, Vagabonds and American Indians

In 1853 the American novelist Nathaniel Hawthorne travelled to England to take up his post as the US consul in Liverpool, nineteenth-century Britain's chief Atlantic port. Canadian timber and southern cotton poured off the ships from America, feeding the nation's shipbuilding and textile industries, while thousands of immigrants from Britain and Ireland passed through the city on their way to the United States.[1] It was Europe's busiest port of embarkation in the antebellum period and served, as Hawthorne put it, as 'the gateway between the Old World and the New'.[2] As a consequence, it was also the primary rendezvous for penniless Americans stranded on Britain's shores, and Hawthorne was regularly petitioned by indigent sailors seeking succour and a passage home. As he records in his essay 'Consular Experiences' (1863):

> The staircase and passageway [of the consulate] were often thronged, of a morning, with a set of beggarly and piratical-looking scoundrels (I do no wrong to our own countrymen in styling them so, for not one in twenty was a genuine American), purporting to belong to our mercantile marine, and chiefly composed of Liverpool Black-ballers and the scum of every maritime nation on earth; such being the seamen by whose assistance we then disputed the navigation of the world with England. These specimens of a most unfortunate class of people were shipwrecked crews in quest of bed, board, and clothing; invalids asking permits for the hospital; bruised and bloody wretches complaining of ill-treatment by their officers; drunkards, desperadoes, vagabonds, and cheats, perplexingly intermingled with an uncertain proportion of reasonably honest men.

Pity and contempt, suspicion and compassion intermix as Hawthorne's mood ricochets across the passage, lurching from the censorious to the sympathetic and back again. In the process, he captures the challenge of discriminating between 'honest men' and 'desperadoes' and the emotional labour involved in doing so. As he goes on to explain, the applicants that he interviewed made a 'forcible appeal to the sympathies', but at the same time he did not wish 'to make [his] Consulate a nucleus for the vagrant discontents of other lands'. With personal feelings and public duties contending with each other, Hawthorne had to strike a balance: he relieved some, refused others, and did his best to sift through the 'multitude of English rogues, dexterously counterfeiting the genuine Yankee'.[3]

Hawthorne's essay locates the consulate within Liverpool's network of charitable organisations and illustrates the resourcefulness of the city's vagrant poor. According to Hawthorne, the 'English rogues ... knew how to imitate our national traits, had been at great pains to instruct themselves as regarded American localities, and were not readily to be caught by a cross-examination'.[4] Although he portrays these claimants as brazen imposters, his account still conveys the sophisticated strategies that the poor employed to negotiate systems of relief, even ones that were ostensibly alien. The essay also exemplifies what Hidetaka Hirota identifies as 'the transnational influence of the concept of the "undeserving" poor'; Hawthorne, like the British philanthropists and workhouse officials discussed in Chapter 3, examined his applicants using the framework of the 'deserving' and the 'undeserving'.[5] This dichotomy was carried to America by the first English colonists in the seventeenth century. As Kristin O'Brassill-Kulfan notes, 'most of the relevant laws addressing indigent transiency [vagrancy] in the United States have a root in early English jurisprudence'.[6] After the thirteen colonies achieved independence, American lawmakers still sought guidance from English legislation, using early modern statutes and the 1824 Vagrancy Act to help formulate their vagrancy laws.[7] Attitudes towards poverty mirrored each other across the Atlantic.

Liverpool bore witness to these shared values in the mid-nineteenth century. Spurred by dearth and the Great Famine, 2.1 million people left Ireland between 1846 and 1855. British North America received 340,000 of these migrants; Britain between 200,000 and 300,000; and Australia and New Zealand a few thousand each. The lion's share, however, fell to the United States: 1.5 million landed on its Eastern Seaboard, and 90 per cent of these passed through Liverpool.[8] The port therefore hosted a huge number of Irish migrants during the famine years, the majority of whom were impoverished. Most had used their savings to buy a passage or had received a pre-paid ticket sent home by friends or family already settled overseas. These independent migrants were accompanied by a small group of paupers – around 121,000 – who were assisted by their landlords, the Poor Law or the Crown.[9] Others were not so lucky. Some were gulled by fraudulent currency converters or ticket-touts and were reduced to living on Liverpool's streets.[10] There they begged alongside a small number of migrants who had made the crossing only to be deported: deemed undeserving by the American authorities, they were sent back without any additional supplies of food, clothes or money, and often arrived in Liverpool in the same condition that they left the United States – destitute.[11]

American officials were wary of new arrivals entering their country, especially as the poorest could become burdens on the ratepayer. Although only Massachusetts and New York adopted deportation policies to rid themselves of indigent foreigners, destitute migrants were of national concern.[12] In the words of New Hampshire's *Portsmouth Journal*, 'The United States seem destined to be completely inundated at no distant period, with paupers imported from Europe.'[13] This fear reverberated throughout the American press, and was stoked by the large number of migrants landing in Boston, Philadelphia and New York City – the main destinations of Britain's passenger trade.[14] The United States was the most popular emigration field for the Irish before and after the famine, and for the British too. In 1832 the number of people departing Britain for extra-European territories exceeded 100,000 for the first time.[15] By 1852 this figure had climbed to 370,000, and from then on between 100,000 and 300,000 passengers set sail each year until the end of the century.[16] Two-thirds of these travelled to the United States.[17] This level of migration was intimidating, especially as the journey from Europe was often a one-way trip. Bar the fortunate few who could afford to travel by steamship, a luxury that became available from 1839, most of the passengers travelling in the antebellum period would have made the five-week crossing in the steerage compartment of a wooden sailing ship: cramped and unhygienic, the length, expense and unpleasantness of the voyage kept many people from returning.[18]

Those who left England before the American Civil War (1861–5) came from a variety of backgrounds: some were artisans, others were agriculturalists, and an increasing number were unskilled labourers.[19] Upon arrival, many travelled westward, crossing the Appalachian Mountains to reach the states of the Old Northwest – Ohio, Michigan, Illinois, Indiana and Wisconsin – where land was relatively cheap.[20] 'The Jeffersonian ideal that farmers on their own land reaped independence and virtue along with their crops was still alive and well, and it struck a responsive chord in the heart of many Britons', comments William E. Van Vugt.[21] English artisans and industrial labourers were as eager to turn their hands to the plough as farmers born-and-bred.

The Irish were typically less mobile than their English counterparts. Originating from poorer communities, they tended to arrive with fewer skills and resources, and these factors reduced their sphere of enterprise. Too poor to follow the English further afield, they often sought factory work in the northeastern states where they arrived.[22] For many of these migrants, destitution in a foreign land was a significant risk because they had exhausted their capital to finance the crossing; but whether they were Irish, English, Scottish or Welsh, no nationality was immune from poverty.

British and Irish immigration significantly increased the number of impoverished people on the Eastern Seaboard. During the 1830s, the growing Irish presence in the slums of Five Points in New York City and Fort Hill in Boston caused alarm, as did the high proportion of foreign inmates in almshouses.[23] In the Philadelphia Almshouse nearly a quarter of the nonresident paupers admitted between 1821 and 1844 were born outside the United States.[24] Predictably, tensions reached their peak in times of economic depression when newly arrived immigrants (alongside many Americans) failed to find a toehold in the labour market. In the aftermath of the Panic of 1837, a financial slump that started a decade of economic uncertainty, New York found its public and private charities overwhelmed. Between 1837 and 1838 the number of people receiving outdoor relief nearly tripled, soaring from below 30,000 to over 80,000, while the population of the municipal almshouse rose by a third, with immigrants outnumbering native-born Americans for the first time.[25] New York's mayor, Aaron Clark, was deeply alarmed. He feared that the city's generosity would turn it into 'the general rendez-voux of beggars, paupers, vagrants and mischievous persons' and banded together with the mayors of Boston, Philadelphia and Baltimore to insist that Congress deter the arrival of impoverished aliens from Europe.[26] The following year, the Select Committee appointed by Congress to investigate the issue reiterated the mayors' appeal, advising the government to stop 'the outcasts of foreign countries; paupers, vagrants, and malefactors' from being assisted across the Atlantic.[27]

The popularity of the United States among emigrants, and the hostility of US officials towards indigent Europeans, ensured that vagrancy in America became a transatlantic issue, and a recurring theme in British travel writing. This genre included travelogues in the shape of memoirs, sketches and political treatises, as well as handbooks, pamphlets and newspaper articles that provided practical advice on emigration. Although emigration literature 'tend[ed] to cluster disproportionately around the British colonies, despite the fact that America was the most common destination for real emigrants', the United States was still the focus of a growing corpus of texts that examined the habits and institutions of the new nation.[28] As the *Monthly Magazine* remarked at the beginning of its four-part series, 'Notes on America' (1832), 'Notwithstanding the great number and variety of works on American manners, politics, and statistics, with which the British public has lately been treated, in the shape of sketches, travels, and dissertations, still the subject appears to have lost none of its interest.'[29] Published between 1832 and 1865, the travelogues of Frances Trollope, Harriet Martineau, Frederick Marryat, Charles Dickens, Anthony Trollope and George Augustus Sala bear witness to this and speak to the potential profit that such works seemed to promise. Their books will be discussed alongside other travelogues and contemporary articles in the remainder of this chapter.

The following is comprised of three sections, each of which is focused on the representation of a vagrant archetype. The first examines the pauper immigrant. Hirota and O'Brassill-Kulfan have documented how this figure was met with enmity in antebellum America, prompting the implementation of various immigration and deportation policies. This section analyses how British writers responded to the treatment of European migrants, and is particularly concerned with their portrayal of the Irish, a group that was reviled on both sides of the Atlantic, but was nonetheless praised almost ubiquitously by British commentators abroad. The second focuses on the American Indian, a figure whose representation has received significant attention in recent years. Building on the work of Kate Flint, Steven Conn, Patrick Brantlinger and others, this section examines how the moral, aesthetic and scientific frameworks that were used to construct vagrants in Britain were repurposed by travel writers to analyse the indigenous peoples of North America. The final section analyses a figure that has hitherto been omitted from studies of vagrancy: the American vagabond. A precursor to the American tramp, a vagrant type that emerged with the transcontinental railroad during the 1870s, the vagabond was imagined on the colonial frontiers of antebellum America and emphasised the danger of lawlessness that attended migration.[30] Together, the three sections illustrate that the mechanisms of colonisation, including the mass movement of people, the creation of new settlements, and the displacement of indigenes, produced a range of mobile bodies. That some of these were represented as vagrants demonstrates the versatility of British conceptions of vagrancy and their ability to circulate globally as well as locally.

5.1 Atlantic Crossings: Pauper Immigrants

Frances Trollope arrived in Cincinnati, Ohio, in 1828. She was forty-eight, strapped for cash and accompanied by three of her children: Henry, Cecilia and Emily. Through the painter Auguste Hervieu, a close family friend, she met Joseph Dorfeuille, the director of the Western Museum, and was soon collaborating with him on artistic exhibits. Together they put on 'The Invisible Girl' and 'The Infernal Regions', two ambitious waxwork tableaus that incorporated mechanised models, lighting effects and sophisticated backdrops. These displays were highly successful: 'The Invisible Girl' enjoyed a popular eight-week run and 'The Infernal Regions' became a permanent instillation that lasted thirty-three years. Trollope chased this initial success by opening the Bazaar, a cultural complex that included a ballroom, exhibition gallery, saloon, coffee house and a series of stalls for the sale of fancy goods. Modelled on the Egyptian Hall in London's Piccadilly, this large and elaborate building was an easy target for unscrupulous contractors who soaked up Trollope's funds and left her in severe debt. This deepened when the Bazaar failed to entice the public, and eventually led to the seizure of her possessions by creditors.[31]

Financially embarrassed, Trollope left Ohio in 1830 and travelled through Washington, Maryland and New York before returning to England to complete her travelogue, *Domestic Manners of the Americans* (1832). Witty, acerbic and unforgiving, it was widely read on both sides of the Atlantic, making 'the Old World laugh, and the New World howl with rage'.[32] Both the British and the American editions went through four print runs by the end of the first year.[33] In her long catalogue of grievances, which included the difficulty of retaining servants, the popularity of evangelical preachers and the incessant spitting of American men, Trollope inserted the hostile reception that awaited British immigrants:

> I frequently heard vehement complaints, and constantly met the same in the newspapers, of a practice stated to be very generally adopted in Britain of sending out cargoes of parish paupers to the United States. A Baltimore paper heads some such remarks with the words
>
> 'INFAMOUS CONDUCT!'
>
> and then tells us of a cargo of aged paupers arrived from England, adding 'John Bull has squeezed the orange, and now insolently casts the skin in our faces.'[34]

Trollope noted that 'all the enquiries I could make failed to substantiate these American statements' and dismissed the report as the invention of an

Anglophobic press. As she remarked elsewhere: 'there are more direct falsehoods circulated by the American newspapers than by all the others in the world, and the one great and never-failing source of these voluminous works of imagination is England'.[35]

But there is no smoke without fire. Trollope was right to say that the American press presented a distorted view of British migration – the incomers were often less numerous and impoverished than the newspapers stated – but the British government did assist small numbers of paupers to immigrate to the United States during the 1810s, 1820s and 1830s.[36] This made the Atlantic states nervous, and it is unsurprising that Trollope found her model extract in a Baltimore newspaper. Baltimore was Maryland's largest port, and although it was not one of the primary destinations for British passengers, it still received large numbers of migrants from Europe between 1820 and 1860. According to Raymond L. Cohn, more than half of these travelled from Bremen in Germany, although a significant number also travelled from Liverpool (21.6 per cent) and the Dutch port of Rotterdam (13.8 per cent).[37] In the early 1830s this influx caused Baltimore's mayor, Jesse Hunt, to mobilise the mayors of New York and Philadelphia and to present a joint appeal to Congress to restrict the movement of indigent foreigners, just as Aaron Clark would a few years later. These efforts made no impact in 1833, but they register the concern felt among the city's citizens and officials.[38]

Meanwhile, other British commentators followed Trollope's example and dismissed the issue of European vagrancy. In *Observations on Professions, Literature, Manners, and Emigration, in the United States and Canada* (1833), the Reverend Isaac Fidler chronicled his luckless search for preferment in the Episcopal Church, a journey that took him through the states of New York and Massachusetts. Here he 'occasionally met with wanderers on the road craving charity . . . only just arrived from Europe', but he insisted that their destitution was temporary. Despite his own difficulties finding work, difficulties that wrecked his resolve and prompted a swift return to England, Fidler nonetheless portrayed the American job market as expansive and inclusive: 'Industrious people, be they ever so poor, are soon raised above the necessity of aid', he said.[39] Later, Harriet Martineau, a transatlantic celebrity whose popular *Illustrations of Political Economy* (1832–4) ensured a warm reception, made an extensive two-year tour of the United States. In her travelogue *Society in America* (1837), she recorded, 'I was told in every eastern city, that it was a common practice with parish officers in England to ship off their paupers to the United States. I took some pains to investigate the grounds of this charge, and am convinced that it is a mistake; that the accusation has arisen out of some insulated case.'[40]

Fidler and Martineau were among the first British visitors to find poverty conspicuous by its absence. In *North America* (1862), the novelist Anthony Trollope (Frances's son) described his journey through the remnants of the Union during the opening years of the Civil War. He declared, 'Men and women do not beg in the States; – they do not offend you with tattered rags; they do not complain to heaven of starvation; they do not crouch to the ground for halfpence.'[41] This observation is remarkable given the social and economic dislocation that the war caused, but it is far from original.[42] Twenty years earlier in February 1842, Charles Dickens wrote to John Forster from Boston: 'There is no man in this town, or in this State of New England, who has not a blazing fire and a meat dinner every day of his life. A flaming sword in the air would not attract so much attention as a beggar in the streets.'[43] Dickens was fresh ashore when he penned this letter, and bubbling with republican zeal; but even less charitable and more seasoned commentators did not completely gainsay his observation. Fidler noted that although 'pecuniary distress' was as acute in New York as it was in London, there was nonetheless an absence of visible begging: 'no person craves assistance who can possibly live without it', he conceded.[44] Meanwhile, Frances Trollope acknowledged that during the two years she spent in Cincinnati, 'I neither saw a beggar, nor a man of sufficient fortune to permit his ceasing his efforts to increase it.'[45] Typically, her praise has a sting in its tail.

The optimism of British visitors contrasted sharply with their American hosts. Where the former saw an abundance of opportunities, the latter were conscious of scarcity, and dreaded what one newspaper called the 'flood of foreign pauperism'.[46] This difference can be accounted for in a number of ways. In part, it rested on the myth that poverty was alien to Columbia's shores. Martineau adopted this view while dilating on the American suspicion of immigrants. She argued that poverty was feared only because it was a novelty. 'It is not much to be wondered at that gentlemen and ladies, living in Boston and New York, and seeing, for the first time in their lives, half-naked and squalid persons in the street, should ask where they come from, and fear lest they should infect others with their squalor, and wish they would keep away.'[47] Victims of a culture shock, the Americans are depicted as raw innocents confronting beggary for the 'first time' and mistaking the eyesore of deprivation for a contagious disease. In fact, scenes of poverty were far from new, especially in New York, which suffered high levels of unemployment throughout the first half of the nineteenth century. In the winter of 1816–17, 15,000 people – one-seventh of the city's population – were awarded relief, and twenty years later, the year that Martineau's *Society in America* was published, up to 40 per cent of its labour force was out of work.[48] Nonetheless, although Martineau's assumptions seem unfounded, there is still some substance to her argument. Poverty, its scale and severity, is always a matter of perspective, and Martineau, Dickens, Fidler and the Trollopes were all familiar with poverty as it presented itself in London. Although New York became the largest and fastest-growing city in the United States during the 1830s, its size paled in comparison to Britain's metropolis, the largest city on Earth. In 1840 New York's population was 313,000; London's was over two million.[49] Although both cities were undoubtedly focal points of destitution, America's first city looked small from a British standpoint. As Frederick Marryat observed in the opening pages of his *A Diary in America* (1839), 'On my first arrival I perceived little difference between the city of New York and one of our principal provincial towns.'[50]

Prior experience conditioned writers' reactions, persuading them that they saw a world almost entirely free from poverty, but so did their expectations. Martineau's argument was based on the widespread belief that settler societies abroad could remedy chronic poverty at home. It was theorised that British poverty arose from an excess of labour, which placed a strain on the economy and resulted in pauperisation. The vast and allegedly 'empty' territories of the New World were reservoirs for this surplus population, spaces into which labour might be drained, thus easing the political, social and financial pressures building within the mother country.[51] Meanwhile, the recipient country would benefit from this fresh supply of people, all of whom could be put to work. As Anthony Trollope summarised, 'Beggary does not prevail in new countries, and but few old countries have managed to exist without it.'[52] This view was adopted by British commentators, many of whom were particularly vehement about the productivity of Irish immigrants in America. Martineau observed that 'few or no canals or railroads would be in existence now, in the United States, but for the Irish labour by which they have been completed'.[53] Dickens concurred. In his travelogue, *American Notes* (1842), he asked, who but the Irish 'would dig, and delve, and drudge, and do domestic work, and make canals and roads, and execute great lines of Internal Improvement!'[54] And Fidler, speaking more generally, declared, 'The Irish are, perhaps, the most useful people in all America.'[55]

These tributes are surprising. Anti-Irish sentiments were commonplace in England and were perpetuated and naturalised by new racial theories in the Victorian era. In the first half of the nineteenth century, debates about the origin of humanity centred on the competing theories of monogenists and polygenists. Monogenists adhered to the story of Genesis, arguing that mankind could be traced to one single source – Adam and Eve. Polygenists argued that there were many points of origin and that mankind was made up of distinct races. This latter theory, which gained momentum in the early Victorian period, was used to argue that physical, moral and even economic differences were biologically inscribed. The Irish belonged to the Celtic race, which was savage, careless and ignorant, whereas the English belonged to the Anglo-Saxon race, whose 'natural' qualities happily included probity, sobriety, rationality and industry. This race science was used to uphold long-held prejudices and to justify the social and political inequalities between Britain and Ireland: the wealth of the former reflected the virtues of the Anglo-Saxon, and the poverty of the latter the feckless-ness of the Celt. A colonial history of abuse and exploitation was substituted in favour of a false but more palatable narrative.[56]

However, just because the Irish were lazy reprobates at home did not mean they were not industrious abroad.[57] New theories regarding heredity coexisted with a contradictory idea inherited from the Enlightenment that environment determined character.[58] Travelling from the overpopulated Old World to the fresh expanses of the New could catalyse a decisive change of personality: 'a strong and "healthy" character, defined by self-reliance and self-control, would be forged through a shift in environment . . . for character and context were intertwined in an intricate dialectic in Victorian political thought', Duncan Bell observes.[59] This belief underpins Anthony Trollope's remark that immigrating to the United States made the Irishman 'more of a man', and influenced other British authors as well.[60] Grace Moore and Laura Peters argue that Dickens also subscribed to environmentalist explanations of character, particularly during the early decades of his career, the 1830s and 1840s.[61] Discussing 'Seven Dials' in *Sketches by Boz* (1836), Moore notes that both the Irishman and the Englishman living in a London slum are presented as brutal drunkards, which reflects Dickens's belief that behaviour is conditioned by material circumstances. 'Rather than resorting to stock Irish stereotypes, Dickens demonstrates that the over-crowded squalor of Seven Dials would drive anyone to drunkenness and violence.'[62]

The British endorsement of the Irish is evidence that environmentalist theories were readily adopted, but they could also be easily abandoned. In *American Notes* Dickens initially eschews Irish stereotypes, noting that in Cincinnati they were 'working the hardest for their living and doing any kind of sturdy labour'; however, he later describes an 'Irish colony' where there were 'pigs, dogs, men, children, babies, pots, kettles, dung-hills, vile refuse, rank straw, and standing water, all wallowing together'.[63] Here Dickens falls back on racist tropes. As Michael de Nie observes, 'Irish ignorance supposedly led to indifference and squalor' and, as a consequence, 'they were often symbolized in the satirical press by the pig'.[64] Dickens's excessive list of animals, objects, people and excrement successfully conveys the chaotic and slovenly living conditions associated with the Irish, while the description of the people 'wallowing', the porcine verb par excellence, converts the camp into a pigsty. Any environmental explanation for this rotten poverty seems to be discounted by the English emigrants that Dickens describes in the same chapter. These travellers are 'houseless, indigent, wandering, weary with travel and hard living', and yet 'it was wonderful to see how clean the children had been kept, and how untiring in their love and self-denial all the poor parents were'.[65] Although their Atlantic crossing has resulted in vagrancy, Dickens nonetheless proffers hope by imbuing these emigrants with the Anglo-Saxon qualities of orderliness and industry, virtues that will surely lead to stability and employment.

Leon Litvack, trying to account for the inconsistent treatment of the Irish in *American Notes*, concludes that 'Dickens's ability to offer contrasting presentations in the same work points to the difficulty for scholars in pinpointing any unified attitude on the part of the novelist towards Ireland and the Irish.'[66] This is true as far as it goes. But it also strongly suggests that the environmentalist thinking identified by Moore and Peters was intermixed with long-standing cultural prejudices and competing theories of polygenesis and heredity. Dickens was certainly aware of these ideas. As Peters notes, the first chapter of *Martin Chuzzlewit* (1843–4), the novel that Dickens started soon after his return from America, opens with a detailed genealogy of the Chuzzlewit family that is 'preoccupied with issues of heredity, specifically informed by racial descent'.[67] Dickens's ambivalence about the Irish in America also places the praise of his contemporaries in perspective. At a time when anti-Irish prejudice was virulent in England, it would be naive to ascribe their chorus of acclamation solely to environmentalist beliefs. Although these may have been held by some, it seems likely that their praise was motivated by political considerations as well. A strong anti-Irish sentiment also prevailed in the United States: the Irish were imagined as innately violent, savage and profligate, and their flight from Ireland was blamed on the British government.[68] By applauding the Irish for their industrious work ethic and representing them as active labourers, British commentators masked their susceptibility to vagrancy, tacitly denied their burden on the American ratepayer and defended (to some extent) the government of Ireland.

5.2 Displaced Nations: American Indians

In his introduction to *Cast Out: Vagrancy and Homelessness in Global and Historical Perspective* (2008), Paul Ocobock writes, 'The expansion of European economic interests and overseas territories had profound implications for the uses of vagrancy laws and the indigenous peoples who would come to be known as vagabonds.' This is an important observation. However, although Ocobock is right to emphasise the malleability of legislation – the way in which 'vagrancy laws could be cut from European legal texts and pasted into colonial legislation' – legal mechanisms did not work alone.[69] Vagrancy was also constructed using moral, scientific and aesthetic discourses that were used to imagine and analyse the vagrant body. This section examines how and why American Indians were portrayed as vagrants, and how the meaning of their vagrancy shifted in British travel writing during the first half of the Victorian period. In the process, it demonstrates that some of the representational strategies used to depict and interpret itinerants in Britain were repurposed in the colonial context of the United States. This is particularly true of extermination theory and the artistic category of the picturesque, both of which were used to define American Indians and English Gypsies from the 1830s to the 1860s.

English Gypsies and indigenous Americans had been perceived as analogous figures since the early modern period. In 1621 one of the first settlers in New England remarked that the Wampanoag 'are of complexion like our English Gypsies'.[70] This association still persisted in the nineteenth century. In Walter Scott's novel *Guy Mannering* (1815), the Gypsies are described as 'living like wild Indians among European settlers'; in *Rural Rides* (1822), William Cobbett recalled an encounter with Gypsies who had 'dark skin and coal-black straight and coarse hair, very much like that of the American Indians'; and in 1873, the Gypsyologist Charles Leland noted that 'Gipsies in England are passing away as rapidly as Indians in North America.'[71] Meanwhile, on the other side of the Atlantic, 'the comparison between Gypsies and Native Americans was frequently made by travel writers'.[72] Dickens, for example, noted that the Wyandot 'were so like gipsies, that if I could have seen any of them in England, I should have concluded, as a matter of course, that they belonged to that wandering and restless people'.[73] The perceived kinship between these two groups was strong because they were subject to the same stereotypes. Although nineteenth-century Gypsies practised manufacturing in England and American Indians on the Eastern Seaboard were farmers as well as hunter-gatherers, these sedentary and 'civilised' aspects of their cultures were eclipsed by the potent idea that they were wild, exotic and nomadic.[74] These traits allowed artists and writers to incorporate them into picturesque scenes that celebrated the rugged beauties of untamed nature. This mode of representation was frequently used in the portrayal of Gypsies (see Chapter 1), and the same is also true of American Indians.

Letters and Notes on the Manners, Customs, and Conditions of the North American Indians (1841), a travelogue by the painter and ethnographer George Catlin, is replete with references to the picturesque quality of Indians.[75] Mounted on horseback, the Blackfeet are the 'wild red knights of the prairie', and 'nothing can possibly be more picturesque and thrilling than a troop or war party'. The Mandan, too, provide 'one of the most picturesque scenes to the eye': 'graceful (though uncivil)' they are 'far more wild and vivid than could ever be imagined'.[76] Catlin was born in Pennsylvania, but his portrayal of indigenous Americans had a transatlantic reach. *Letters and Notes* was finished and published while Catlin was living in London, and served as the textual accompaniment to his Indian Gallery, which was being exhibited at the Egyptian Hall, Piccadilly (the model for Trollope's Bazaar). Popular among aristocrats as well as ordinary Londoners, the exhibition contained a wide range of artefacts that Catlin had gathered on his travels, including a Crow lodge 'sufficiently large for forty men to dine under' and 'exceedingly picturesque and agreeable to the eye'.[77] It also included 500 portraits and landscapes painted by Catlin. Among these was *Picturesque Bluffs above Prairie du Chien* (1835–6), a scene populated by Indians riding canoes on the waters of the Mississippi River, and *Discovery Dance, Sacs and Foxes* (1835–7), which was described as 'A very picturesque and pleasing dance' in the exhibition catalogue.[78]

The Indian Gallery was a novelty and attracted thousands of visitors; but even as it introduced new objects and rituals to the British public, it also validated previously held beliefs. Catlin's travelogue performed similar work. Describing his response to *Notes and Letters* in December 1841, a month before he started on his American tour, Dickens declared, 'I am greatly taken with him [Catlin], and strongly interested in his descriptions. He is an honest, hearty, famous fellow; and I shake hands with him at every page.'[79] Here Dickens's metaphor suggests that he was already familiar with the book's account of Indians, and it seems likely that Catlin's picturesque characterisation was one of the features that Dickens and others would readily have accepted. After all, popular travel writers had used the same trope in the 1830s. In *Society in America*, Martineau described 'a picturesque dark group' standing beside an 'Indian lodge' on the island of Mackinaw on Lake Huron.[80] And in *Domestic Manners*, Frances Trollope incorporated Indians into a picturesque account of Canandaigua Lake, a finger lake near Niagara Falls:

> It is about eighteen miles long, but narrow enough to bring the opposite shore, clothed with rich foliage, near to the eye; the back-ground is a ridge of mountains. Perhaps the state of the atmosphere lent an unusual charm to the scene; one of those sudden thunder-storms, so rapid in approach, and so sombre in colouring, that they change the whole aspect of things in a moment, rose over the mountains, and passed across the lake while we looked upon it. Another feature in the scene gave a living, but most sad interest to it. A glaring wooden hotel, as fine as paint and porticos can make it, overhangs the lake; beside it stands a shed for cattle. To this shed, and close by the white man's mushroom palace, two Indians had crept to seek a shelter from the storm. The one was an aged man, whose venerable head in attitude and expression indicated the profoundest melancholy; the other was a youth, and in his deep-set eye there was a quiet sadness more touching still. There they stood, the native rightful lords of the fair land, looking out upon the lovely lake which yet bore the name their fathers had given it, watching the threatening storm that brooded there; a more fearful one had already burst over them.[81]

Trollope presents the lake in distinctly pictorial terms. Relying exclusively on the sense of sight, she describes it using words drawn from the vocabulary of painting: 'scene', 'back-ground', 'colouring'. These choreograph a picturesque landscape in which the mountain fringed lake is made even more austere and romantic by the onset of the storm. Against this majestic backdrop she places the two Indians. The elderly man and his young companion emphasise the aestheticised nature of the scene, forming a static tableau in which the 'attitude and expression' of each can be as easily read as if they are figures in a Victorian genre painting. In addition, like the storm brewing above them, these 'native rightful lords' contribute to our sense that Canandaigua is untamed: like Catlin's Indians in *Picturesque Bluffs above Prairie du Chien*, they exoticise and make wild the landscape. However, although the Indians enhance the picturesque quality of the scene, they also signal that it is disappearing. Forced to take refuge in a cattle shed, and shying away from the hotel that stands beside it, it is clear that they have become vagrant outsiders in their own ancestral lands. This state is confirmed by Trollope later in the text when she compares the 'cleaner and better dressed' Indians on a nearby reservation with 'those we had met wandering far from their homes'.[82] Meanwhile, their juxtaposition with the 'mushroom palace', a solid and ostentatious sign of colonisation, suggests that their displacement is part of a more extensive programme of building and settlement that will compromise the beauty of the landscape and corrupt its picturesque potential.

The Indians serve an aesthetic purpose in Trollope's passage, but they also carry a political message. Their vagrant state does not degrade them. Instead, combined with the mounting storm and their dignified melancholy, it serves as a condemnation of white settlement and the colonial mission, a mission that Trollope dissociates herself from by acting as a detached and isolated observer. Specifically, their vagrancy symbolises the displacement of Indian Nations by the US government. By 1832, the year *Domestic Manners* was published, this process was already well underway. Very few American Indians remained in the Northeast by the 1820s, and the remnants of the Iroquois and Mohicans were largely confined to reservations. Meanwhile, plans were in progress to move the southeastern Nations – the Creek, the Cherokee, the Chickasaw, the Choctaw and the Seminole – west of the Mississippi River. On 28 May 1830 President Andrew Jackson signed 'An Act to Provide for an Exchange of Lands with the Indians Residing in Any of the States or Territories, and for Their Removal West of the River Mississippi'. Although the act insisted that the Nations 'may choose to exchange the lands where they now reside', in fact they had little choice but to relinquish their homesteads in the eastern states in exchange for land in the northwest.[83] Those Indians who did not go peacefully faced significant reprisals.[84] In the case of the Cherokee this led to the Trail of Tears, their violent removal from their lands in Georgia and Alabama in the late 1830s. The estimated death toll from this forced migration varies, but it was at least 4,000 and could be as many as 10,000.[85]

Trollope was in Washington, DC, when Jackson's 'treacherous policy' was being debated, and it is this that she alludes to when she refers to the 'more fearful' storm that has 'already burst over' the Indians in the passage above.[86] The British writers who followed her bore witness to the upheaval it caused. Among these was George William Featherstonehaugh, an English immigrant and long-term resident in the United States who became a farmer, speculator and geologist in turn, and eventually served as a surveyor for the US government. This post made room for his mineralogical and literary interests, and resulted in *Excursion through the*

Slave States (1844), a chronicle of his expedition from Washington to Mexico in 1834–5. During this journey he passed through the homelands of the Creek where he found 'a nation of famous warriors degraded to the lowest pitch of drunkenness and despair'. The Creek's cession of their land east of the Mississippi had triggered a social collapse. The chiefs who were allotted land to the northwest were, according to Featherstonehaugh, ubiquitously alcoholic and heavily indebted to the white creditors who supplied them with rum and whiskey. These debts were liquidated in exchange for the land settlements, which in turn made it impossible for the Creek to settle in their new territory. As Featherstonehaugh explains, 'if any of [the chiefs] had even succeeded in retaining possession of their sections, it was evident, that under such a state of things it was impossible for isolated individuals to live amongst the white men that were now about to pour in amongst them'.

The Creek, then, were homeless. This becomes desperately apparent when Featherstonehaugh enters their former territory in Alabama:

> Everything as we advanced into the Creek country announced the total dissolution of order. Indians of all ages were wandering about listlessly, the poorest of them having taken to begging, and when we came in sight would come and importune us for money.... In other places we met young men in the flower of their age, dressed in ragged hunting-shirts and turbans, staggering along, and often falling to the ground, with empty bottles in their hands: in this wretched state of things, with the game almost entirely destroyed, it is evident that nothing will soon be left to those who have beggared themselves but to die of want, or to emigrate, a step they are so very averse to take, that in their desperation they have already committed some murders.[87]

Here vagrancy continues to highlight the abusive and unequal relationship that the Indians have with white settlers, but it has also become a symbol of their social and moral decay. They are no longer simply wanderers; they are beggars and drunkards too. This portrayal is typical of Victorian travelogues. As Kate Flint notes, 'a pattern of disappointment – squalid reality replacing the nobility that had been projected onto the idea of the Indian – was to become a very well worn commonplace in nineteenth-century travel writing'.[88] Featherstonehaugh's account subscribes to this structure: it begins with a picturesque description of the eighteenth-century brave, 'the *beau ideal* of Indian beauty' with 'dark wild eyes', and concludes with the 'wretched beings' of the present, 'most of them addicted to excessive drunkenness'.[89] Like the depictions of English Gypsies discussed in Chapter 1, the decline of the Creek is coded in aesthetic terms: Featherstonehaugh's shift away from the picturesque signals their sociocultural deterioration and their impending extinction, a fate that had been prophesised for all Indian Nations since the late eighteenth century.

The elegiac tone struck by Trollope and Featherstonehaugh was widespread in writing about American Indians. It was a transatlantic tradition practised by white British and American authors, and at its root was a belief that the Indians would soon vanish. This might happen culturally, through their absorption into colonial society, or it might happen biologically, through warfare, disease or autogenocide, but either way it seemed to be assured.[90] 'It was a conviction, rather than a prediction, and it was such a ubiquitous belief that it did not exist so much in the realm of empirical observation as in the world of unquestioned assumption', as Steven Conn remarks.[91] The narrative of autogenocide was commonly accepted and was predicated on the idea that American indigenes were irredeemably savage and that they were therefore governed by a set of innate characteristics, including violence, idleness, wildness and a lack of self-control. These traits paved the way to self-destruction. In the nineteenth century this idea was bolstered by the new brand of race science that we have already encountered. Polygenists argued that the behaviour of American Indians was determined by heredity. Among other things, this theory was used to reinforce the belief that they could not, and indeed should not, be saved from extinguishing themselves.[92]

Scientific racism served to uphold long-standing prejudices and helped justify contemporary inequalities. In this respect, indigenous Americans shared a common fate with the Irish. Although Featherstonehaugh observes that sham treaties and 'the arts of the white men' have beggared the Creek, it is nonetheless clear that their transformation has been catalysed by their 'uncivilised' ways.[93] Pervasive drunkenness, the foremost reason for the disintegration of their society, signals their hereditary lack of self-control. As Patrick Brantlinger notes, 'Whenever alcohol is emphasized as a cause of extinction, it is an instance of savagery's inability to cope with civilization; Indians learn the vices, but not the virtues, of the whites.'[94] Vagrancy, too, was a sign of immutable savagery. Instead of assimilating by settling in sedentary societies and performing wage labour, the Creek still adhere to their old hunter-gatherer lifestyle, even with 'the game almost entirely destroyed'. The inability to adapt to new circumstances was an accusation commonly levelled against Indians, albeit without justification and contrary to evidence.[95] The Cherokee, for example, adopted a government and constitution styled on that of the United States to lobby more effectively for their sovereignty in the years leading up to their displacement.[96] But in Featherstonehaugh's account the Indians' nomadism is bred in the bone, and without game or territory it declines into vagrancy.

As the narrative of autogenocide became more widely accepted, vagrancy increasingly became a sign that American Indians were unable to integrate. George Augustus Sala, who served as the *Daily Telegraph*'s Special Correspondent during the last years of the Civil War, expressed this in *My Diary in America in the Midst of War* (1865). Recalling his encounter with an American Indian on the border between Canada and the United States, he observes:

> He was, in Yankee estimation, a worn out 'cuss', shattered, unclean, and oleaginous – a creature to be 'run-out' or stamped down as though he were a 'possum or a skunk. And even here, on British soil, he was looked upon as a kind of bore and encumbrance, not, it is true, to be absolutely maltreated or violently expelled, but so prevailed upon to 'move on', and generally wiped out, as early as the proprieties of civilisation would permit of that process.[97]

Sala is merciless. There is no room for elegy in this terse account. The American Indian, deployed as a synecdoche for all American Indians, is depicted as an interloper who should be exterminated. Although Sala constructs a narrative in which American violence is contrasted with British forbearance, there is no sense that the Americans are acting immorally. Unlike Trollope and Featherstonehaugh, who condemn their treatment of the Indians, Sala presents them as merely accelerating a process that is stymied by British sensibilities, but which will eventually be achieved nonetheless.[98] The enthusiasm with which Sala welcomes the extinction of the Indians is based upon the notion that they do not contribute to 'civilised' society, a belief that he articulates through the figure of the 'oleaginous', and distinctly unpicturesque, vagrant. The blunt imperative 'move on' is the same one that English police officers used to shift vagrants off the streets. In Dickens's *Bleak House* (1852–3) the homeless boy Jo is 'moved on as fur as ever I could go and couldn't be moved no furder'.[99] Later, Sala makes this allusion to vagrancy explicit, declaring, 'I give up the Noble Savage morally. I confess him to be a shiftless and degraded vagrant, who does not wash himself.'[100] In this account, the Indian's vagrant condition becomes a symptom of idleness and immorality and, alongside his griminess, indicates his inability to acclimatise to civilised norms.

Sala's description of indigenous Americans is indicative of a more general attitude. His contemporary, Anthony Trollope, commented that the Indian Nations have 'been, or soon will be, exterminated, – polished off the face of creation, as the Americans say, – which fate must, I should say in the long run, attend all non-working people'.[101] The pitilessness of Anthony compared with his mother encapsulates a hardening of public opinion. The British had become dry-eyed within a generation. For Frances Trollope the wandering American Indians, picturesque and unjustly dispossessed, belonged to the deserving poor: they were the 'rightful lords of the fair land'. But for later commentators their vagrancy, more squalid and less idealised, signified their undeserving status: even Featherstonehaugh, a sympathetic observer, characterised the Creek as drunken idlers. These mid-Victorian texts redeployed the well-worn formula of the deserving and the undeserving poor, and in doing so illustrated its ability to travel across continents and cultures, and the manner in which it could be used to legitimise prejudice and inequity: the old moral framework worked in concert with the racial theories of polygenesis and extinction to naturalise the violence of white settlement.

5.3 Lawless Frontiers: American Vagabonds

The colonial frontier of the United States shifted westward during the antebellum period as the Indian Nations were displaced by white settlers who occupied their ancestral homelands. This violent enterprise involved the movement of thousands of people away from the East Coast settlements, where disputes about paupers waxed and waned, and into the seemingly illimitable territories of the West. As David Reynolds explains:

> During the first half of the nineteenth century America's centre of gravity lurched dramatically westward. In 1815 its border was effectively the Appalachians – the mountain chain that runs diagonally northeast to southwest some 500 miles inland from the Atlantic. Only one in seven people and four of the eighteen states were west of the mountains. By 1850, however, half America's 23 million people and half its thirty states lay beyond the Appalachians.[102]

This shift from east to west was accompanied by a smaller migration north to south. Between 1836 and 1847 the population of Texas jumped from 35,000 to just over 142,000 as planters settled with their households and slaves.[103]

For Americans, these mass movements were a continuation of a national legacy. As Tim Cresswell observes, migration and pilgrimage form the basis of many American myths, and 'mobility as a geographical phenomenon in American life is linked to a number of ideological themes, including opportunity, democracy and modernity'.[104] However, for outsiders from Europe and elsewhere, the American push towards the frontiers cemented their reputation for restlessness. Writing in 1829, the colonial reformer Edward Gibbon Wakefield complained of the 'migrating habits of the Americans', describing their 'restlessness' as 'a passion, insatiable whilst any means of indulging it remain'.[105] Three years later, the *Monthly Magazine* likewise remarked that 'there is one peculiarity of the American character which belongs equally to both [southerners and northerners]. I allude to the incessant restlessness and fondness of change of abode.'[106] *Chambers's Journal* repeated this belief in 'The United States as an Emigration Field' in 1849, noting that New England had plenty of employment opportunities thanks to 'the migratory habits of the Yankees, who wander into other districts'.[107] And in 1840, the Mexican ambassador Manuel Eduardo de Gorostiza asked, 'Who is not familiar with that race of migratory adventurers that exist in the United States, composed of the most restless, profligate and robust of its sons, who always live in the unpopulated regions'?[108]

Rootless wanderers were easily imagined in terms of vagrancy, and British writers often represented them as vagabonds or fugitives, two figures that were closely allied in the cultural imagination. The author of 'Notes on America' remarked that 'the more Southern and Western States' constitute 'a country of fever, swamps, vagabonds and squatters'.[109] Featherstonehaugh bore witness to this in Missouri. Meandering southward, he saw a tavern in St Louis 'filled with vagabond idle fellows, drinking, smoking, and swearing', and at Greenville he saw the townspeople 'roistering about at that indispensable rendezvous of every settlement, a dirty-looking store, where all the vagabonds congregate together, to discuss politics and whiskey'.[110] Arkansas, too, was associated with loose morals and dissipation. Sitting just below Missouri on the western frontier, it was denounced in 'America and Her Slave States' (1846) as 'the refuge for the thief, the swindler, and the murderer': 'the six hundred souls that fill the town of Little Rock', *Sharpe's Magazine* opined, 'are as pretty a set of rogues and vagabonds as can be found out of the Newgate [prison] of any civilized country'.[111]

In the south, Texas had a similar reputation. In the 1830s and 1840s it was a sovereign state, independent from the United Mexican States, from which it seceded in 1836, and the United States of America, which would annex it in 1845. During this period the acronym GTT – Gone to Texas – became notorious. Charles Hooton, a Grub Street hack who emigrated with naive ambitions of becoming a farmer, remarked on this in 'Texiana: Rides, Rambles, and Sketches in Texas' (1843): 'It has become almost a proverb in the United States, that, when a runaway debtor is not to be found – when a slave-stealer is totally missing, or a murderer has contrived to elude justice, – he has chalked upon his house-door, G. t. T'.[112] The fugitive complexion of Hooton's migrants is also evident in Marryat's *Narrative of the Travels and Adventures of Monsieur Violet* (1843), where Texas is represented as 'the resort of every vagabond and scoundrel who could not venture to remain in the United States'. Marryat had not ventured so far south during his own American travels, but the French explorer Lasalle, upon whose life the *Narrative* is based, assured him of the 'lawless state of the country'.[113]

In *American Notes*, Dickens also made the association between vaga-bondage and the American frontier, albeit in a slightly different vein. Preparing to leave St Louis, the western limit of his journey, he visited an 'unpretending village tavern' kept by a 'poor lady and her vagrant spouse':

> He had all his life been restless and locomotive, with an irresistible desire for change; and was still the son of his old self: for if he had nothing to keep him at home, he said (slightly jerking his hat and his thumb towards the window of the room in which the old lady sat, as we stood talking in front of the house) he would clean up his musket, and be off to Texas to-morrow morning. He was one of the very many descendants of Cain proper to this continent, who seem destined from their birth to serve as pioneers in the great human army; who gladly go on from year to year extending its outposts, and leaving home after home behind them; and die at last, utterly regardless of their graves being left thousands of miles behind, by the wandering generation who succeed.[114]

Although *American Notes* competed with Trollope's *Domestic Manners* to become 'the harshest account yet of manners and morals in the New World', Dickens's portrayal of the western character is deliberately restrained, especially when compared with the accounts of his contempo-raries.[115] The pejorative notion that Americans are the 'descendants of Cain', a son of Adam and Eve who was found guilty of murder in Genesis and condemned by God to be 'a fugitive and a vagabond in the earth', is balanced by the assertion that they are 'pioneers in the great human army', an image that swells with flattering notions of pomp, discipline and the 'progress' of civilisation.[116] Situated between roving desperadoes and hardy frontiersmen, the ambiguity that surrounds the tavern keeper and his countrymen allows Dickens to confirm the connection between vagabondry and America without 'vagabond' becoming a term of insult; indeed, it is telling that the word is suppressed in the text, only emerging through allusion. The result is a muted analysis in which the figure of the vagabond is evoked but does not disrupt the ostensibly impartial narrative.

Dickens's account is also unusual because it focuses on mobility rather than morality. Defined at the start of the passage as 'restless' and 'loco-motive', the tavern keeper's movement, and that of his compatriots, is described in some detail: they 'gladly go on from year to year extending [humanity's] outposts, and leaving home after home behind them'. Here the vagabond is depicted as moving away from *place* and into *space*. These are two distinct constructs. In *On the Move* (2006), Cresswell explains that places – such as homes, schools and cities – are 'meaningful segments of space – locations imbued with meaning and power', whereas spaces are 'countless, apparently natural, and devoid of meaning, history, and ideol-ogy'.[117] From the perspective of settler societies, the frontier fits Cresswell's definition of space. It is porous, ill-defined and always being redefined, and although it is being inducted into the annals of history through settlement, it has no recorded history to speak of. This is partic-ularly true of the American frontier. By the early nineteenth century the indigenous inhabitants of America were interpreted through the lens of natural rather than human history, and 'natural historical representations of America tended to depict the country as existing outside the flow of historical time', as Conn remarks.[118]

For Victorian commentators writing travelogues or newspaper articles, these ahistorical spaces were the natural environment of the vagabond because they were (and are) associated with freedom. As Yi-Fu Tuan observes:

> Space is a common symbol of freedom in the Western world. Space lies open; it suggests the future and invites action. On the negative side, space and freedom are a threat. A root meaning of the word 'bad' is 'open.' To be open and free is to be exposed and vulnerable. Open space has no trodden paths and signposts. It has no fixed pattern of established human meaning; it is like a blank sheet on which meaning may be imposed. Enclosed and humanized space is place. Compared to space, place is a calm center of established values.[119]

Both the threat and the freedom inherent in Tuan's account of space are accentuated by the presence of vagabonds on the frontier. Generally characterised as cheats and criminals eager to break the ethical, social and legal bonds that bridle sedentary society, vagabonds disregard the communal values that grant places their stability and security. For many commentators this resulted in the 'perfect anarchy' described by *Fraser's Magazine* in its 1848 account of the (now historic) Republic of Texas. 'The refuse from [the United States] resorted hither, fleeing from the tardy justice of their own land. Murderers, thieves, and swindlers of every hue, walked erect in open day ... and these, mixed with foreigners of the same stamp from every European country, formed the Texan nation.'[120]

American Notes echoes the widespread assumption that vagabonds were attracted to colonial frontiers; however, because the 'descendants of Cain' leave 'home after home behind them' it also nuances how the dynamics of this movement are imagined. For Dickens, home was an 'icon of morality, security and comfort', as Catherine Waters notes.[121] From the 'quiet, and neat, and orderly' house of Mr Brownlow in *Oliver Twist* (1837–9) to Wemmick's castle where the Aged P sits 'cheerful, comfortable, and well cared for' in *Great Expectations* (1860–1), he produced a steady stream of homes.[122] These are archetypal places. They are locations with obvious physical boundaries, but also with clear ethical ones: as the Cricket explains in Dickens's *The Cricket on the Hearth* (1845), home is not just 'four walls and a ceiling', but a 'quiet sanctuary' secured by the 'nightly sacrifice [of] some petty passion, selfishness, or care'.[123] Homes are also repositories for objects that serve as historical waymarkers and reinforce our sense of self. As Virginia Woolf remarked in her essay 'Street Haunting' (1927), 'We sit surrounded by objects which perpetually express the oddity of our own temperaments and enforce the memories of our own experience'.[124] The proficiency of Dickens's vagabond tavern keeper to create these places – these 'centers of felt value' – is signalled by his ironic fate.[125] Ensnared by a trap of his own construction, he would leave 'if he had nothing to keep him at home', but domestic duties and 'the old lady' have brought him to bay.

The vagabonds' capacity to create place from space in *American Notes* is part of their pioneering function, but Dickens's unusual attention to the domestic by-products of vagabondage also alerts us to questions of gender. Although the tavern keeper's wife is also on the frontier, and has therefore made the westward journey, she lacks her husband's lust for adventure and is strongly associated with domesticity. Unlike her husband, who appears eager to move on, she nostalgically remembers 'her old home' – Philadelphia – which she fondly calls 'the queen city of the world'. This contrast between husband and wife is reflected by their spatial relations: where he stands 'in front of the house', she sits within it, reflecting its rootedness through her sedentary posture. This fixed condition is accentuated by her age: unlike her husband who is 'still the son of his old self', a metaphor that suggests youthfulness and virility, she is described as an 'old lady', an 'old soul'.[126] This distinction highlights an assumption that underwrites other accounts of vagabondage – that it is the preserve of men.

This has some basis in fact. Men emigrated at a faster rate than women and were far more likely to become sojourners on the frontier, which meant that large and predominantly male communities were formed.[127] As a result, new settlements suffered from a surplus of bachelors, a circumstance that was noted by contemporaries. Hooton, marooned by poverty in the backwater port of Galveston, Texas, recorded that 'women [are] so remarkably scarce, that a maid is hardly to be met in a day's march' and that 'the widows of any mark or likelihood, are either pestered to death by loafers of all descriptions, or compelled to get married again, if only as a stroke of good policy, and in sheer self defence'.[128] Similarly, when Martineau visited Milwaukee, then part of the Michigan Territory, she reported that 'seven young women ... were the total female population' of the settlement and that its newspaper desperately 'appeal[ed] to the ladies of more thickly-settled districts ... imploring them to cast a favourable eye on Milwaukee, and its hundreds of bachelors'.[129] The disparity between men and women was also registered in the phraseology of bachelordom. As Katherine V. Snyder observes, the term 'baching it' 'arose in the context of early nineteenth-century emigration to the frontiers of British and American territories; it referred specifically to the residences and living styles of single men who were making new homes in these new worlds'.[130]

However, although women may have been scarce, they were certainly still occupying frontier regions, as Dickens, Hooton and Martineau testify. Their exclusion from depictions of vagabondage had less to do with their rarity than with gender stereotypes, and in particular their identification with the home. The pervasive Victorian belief in the 'separate spheres' naturalised the connection between women and domesticity and men, mobility and the wider world. John Ruskin, the most famous proponent of this schema, wrote that 'a man's duties are public, and a woman's private': whereas a man performs 'rough work in [the] open world', a woman's role is the 'sweet ordering [and] arrangement' of the home, 'the place of Peace'.[131] As Jude Piesse argues, this division was fundamental to mid-Victorian portrayals of successful emigration and settlement. In novels such as Edward Bulwer-Lytton's *The Caxtons* (1848–9) and George Sargent's *Frank Layton* (1854), two tales set in Australia, the rambling adventures of the male protagonists are cushioned by scenes of female domesticity.[132] In *Frank Layton*, for example, the narrator describes 'a pleasant chamber in the farm at Hunter's Creek': 'Many pretty articles of feminine adornment, and for feminine occupation of leisure hours, were there; and the rightful owners of that snug and comfortable retreat were as far as need be imagined from the rude, rough, clumsy demi-savage amazons which seem associated in some minds with the denizenship of the bush.'[133] Scenes such as this tempered the dangers that middle-class Victorians identified with emigration, such as the disturbance of English morals and social norms.[134] More generally, as Janet C. Myers remarks, domesticity was seen as 'a corrective to the licentious and unbridled mobility associated with the "strike-it-rich-quick mentality"'.[135] This was, of course, the feckless movement that characterised the American vagabond.

The centrality of women in the portrayal of 'safe' migration and settlement illuminates why they were either omitted from depictions of vagabondage or included as reluctant but faithful wives. In 'Notes on America', the author recalls an encounter with the family of an 'indolent planter' bivouacking by the roadside on their way to Alabama. Where the husband enthuses about the price of cotton, and is eager to reach the property he has purchased on the frontier, his wife complains that her husband is 'never content to remain for three years on the same farm' and reveals her longing for her old home. 'She told me that she was "raised" in Massachusetts, near the beautiful village of Deerfield, and was overjoyed to find me acquainted with that part of America. "There was nothing like it," she said, "south of the Potomac. Nothing like Deerfield meadow, with its fine old elm trees!"' The specificity of the planter's wife, her remembrance of local details, and the author's use of reported speech work in unison to convey her fondness for her birthplace. This signals her unwillingness to migrate and her femininity. Like the tavern keeper's wife, who reminisces about 'the queen city', the planter's wife has a keen appreciation for the value of home. Her femininity is also emphasised in other ways. She confides that 'her health, and that of her children, was ruined by a residence in the damp, though fertile Savanahs', a confession that not only places her in a maternal and stereotypically feminine role, but also confirms her femininity by stressing her physical delicacy.[136] As Lynda Nead argues, Victorian conceptions of middle-class womanhood were structured around notions of vulnerability, and part of this was a 'belief that respectable women were inherently weak and delicate, and were in a perpetual state of sickness'.[137] Meanwhile, the planter's indifference to his wife's plight confirms his vagabondish disposition: 'Her husband paid not the slightest attention to the complaints which she was pouring into my ear. I suppose, he would have sacrificed his whole kith and kin for a few additional pounds of cotton per acre.'[138]

North America, and colonial spaces more generally, engendered new ways of thinking about the vagrant body and contributed to the genealogy of vagrancy that this study seeks to uncover. This chapter on paupers, vagabonds and American Indians has demonstrated that assumptions about race, gender, mobility and geography coalesced to form distinct vagrant types and that these were shaped by new and existing discourses. These included the framework of the deserving and the undeserving poor, a transatlantic formula that had been producing vagrants since the early modern period, as well as aesthetic traditions and racial theories – notably polygenesis and extinction theory. These theories were supplemented by social Darwinism and eugenics in the second half of the nineteenth century, which had a dramatic impact on the representation of vagrants in Britain, as we saw in Chapter 4. Moreover, they also reinforced the widespread belief in extinction theory, which continued to influence how vagrants were imagined in the colonial sphere during the fin de siècle. This is examined in the next chapter. Moving westward, beyond the coast of California, it focuses on the beachcombers of the Pacific Islands: like the vagabonds of antebellum America, they too were portrayed as desperate renegades, living lawlessly on the frontier.

Notes

1 John Belchem, *Irish, Catholic and Scouse: The History of the Liverpool-Irish, 1800–1939* (Liverpool: Liverpool University Press, 2007), p. 2.
2 Raymond L. Cohn, *Mass Migration under Sail: European Immigration to the Antebellum United States* (Cambridge: Cambridge University Press, 2009), pp. 126–30; Nathaniel Hawthorne, 'Consular Experiences', in *Our Old Home, and English Note-Books*, 2 vols (New York: Houghton, Mifflin and Company, 1887), I, pp. 19–55 (p. 25).
3 Hawthorne, 'Consular Experiences', pp. 19–24, 47.
4 Ibid., p. 47.
5 Hidetaka Hirota, *Expelling the Poor: Atlantic Seaboard States and the Nineteenth-Century Origins of American Immigration Policy* (Oxford: Oxford University Press, 2017; repr. 2019), p. 12.
6 Kristin O'Brassill-Kulfan, *Vagrants and Vagabonds: Poverty and Mobility in the Early American Republic* (New York: New York University Press, 2019), p. 4.
7 Ibid., p. 17.
8 Belchem, *Irish, Catholic and Scouse*, p. 4; Hirota, *Expelling the Poor*, pp. 21–8.
9 Hirota, *Expelling the Poor*, pp. 36–40.
10 Belchem, *Irish, Catholic and Scouse*, p. 3.
11 Hirota, *Expelling the Poor*, pp. 156–65.
12 Ibid., pp. 1–15.

13 'Foreign Paupers', *Portsmouth Journal of Literature and Politics*, 13 December 1834, p. 2.

14 Cohn, *Mass Migration under Sail*, pp. 126–30.

15 John Darwin, *The Empire Project: The Rise and Fall of the British World System, 1830–1970* (Cambridge: Cambridge University Press, 2009; repr. 2015), p. 41.

16 Robert D. Grant, *Representations of British Emigration, Colonisation and Settlement: Imagining Empire, 1800–1860* (Basingstoke: Palgrave Macmillan, 2005), pp. 62–3.

17 Darwin, *The Empire Project*, pp. 4–5.

18 Cohn, *Mass Migration under Sail*, pp. 8–13, 223.

19 Ibid., pp. 118, 185–6.

20 Charlotte Erickson, *Leaving England: Essays on British Emigration in the Nineteenth Century* (Ithaca, NY: Cornell University Press, 1994), pp. 62–3.

21 William E. Van Vugt, *Britain to America: Mid-Nineteenth-Century Immigrants to the United States* (Chicago: University of Illinois Press, 1999), p. 11.

22 Cohn, *Mass Migration under Sail*, pp. 185–6.

23 Hirota, *Expelling the Poor*, p. 51.

24 O'Brassill-Kulfan, *Vagrants and Vagabonds*, pp. 39–40.

25 Edwin G. Burrows and Mike Wallace, *Gotham: A History of New York to 1898* (Oxford: Oxford University Press, 1999), pp. 621–4.

26 Quoted by Burrows and Wallace in ibid., p. 623.

27 Quoted by Hirota, *Expelling the Poor*, p. 57.

28 Jude Piesse, *British Settler Emigration in Print, 1832–1877* (Oxford: Oxford University Press, 2016), p. 4.

29 'Notes on America, No. I', *Monthly Magazine*, June 1832, pp. 640–6 (p. 640).

30 For an excellent study of American tramps and their representation in American culture, see Tim Cresswell, *The Tramp in America* (London: Reaktion Books, 2001).

31 Teresa Ransom, *Fanny Trollope: A Remarkable Life* (Stroud: Sutton Publishing, 1995; repr. 1996), pp. 46–61.

32 John C. Jeaffreson quoted by Ransom, *Fanny Trollope*, p. 77.

33 Ransom, *Fanny Trollope*, p. 77.

34 Frances Trollope, *Domestic Manners of the Americans*, ed. Elsie B. Michie (Oxford: Oxford University Press, 2014), pp. 121, 195.

35 Ibid., p. 195.

36 Hirota, *Expelling the Poor*, pp. 28–32, 36–9; O'Brassill-Kulfan, *Vagrants and Vagabonds*, p. 40.

37 Cohn, *Mass Migration under Sail*, pp. 126–30.

38 O'Brassill-Kulfan, *Vagrants and Vagabonds*, p. 39.

39 Isaac Fidler, *Observations on Professions, Literature, Manners, and Emigration, in the United States and Canada, Made during a Residence There in 1832* (London: Whittaker, Treacher & Co., 1833), pp. 361–2.

40 Harriet Martineau, *Society in America*, 2 vols (London: Saunders and Otley, 1837), I, p. 344.

41 Anthony Trollope, *North America*, 2 vols (London: Granville Publishing, 1986), II, p. 300.

42 Trollope might not have seen the refugees dislocated by the war. According to McPherson the homelessness that resulted from the conflict was confined to the South. Trollope travelled only through the North. James M. McPherson, *Battle Cry of Freedom: The American Civil War* (Oxford: Oxford University Press, 1988; repr. London: Penguin, 1990), p. 619.

43 Charles Dickens, *The Pilgrim Edition of the Letters of Charles Dickens*, ed. Madeline House, Graham Storey and Kathleen Tillotson, 12 vols (Oxford: Oxford University Press, 1965–2002), III, pp. 51–2.

44 Fidler, *Observations on Professions*, p. 362.

45 Trollope, *Domestic Manners of the Americans*, p. 35.

46 'Foreign Paupers', *Farmer's Gazette*, 10 April 1835, p. 3.

47 Martineau, *Society in America*, I, p. 339.

48 O'Brassill-Kulfan, *Vagrants and Vagabonds*, pp. 17–9; Burrows and Wallace, *Gotham*, p. 493.

49 Burrows and Wallace, *Gotham*, p. 576; Jerry White, *London in the Nineteenth Century: A Human Awful Wonder of God* (London: Vintage, 2008), p. 77.

50 Frederick Marryat, *A Diary in America, with Remarks on Its Institutions* (Philadelphia: Carey & Hart, 1839), p. 3.

51 Duncan Bell, *The Idea of Greater Britain: Empire and the Future of World Order, 1860–1900* (Princeton, NJ: Princeton University Press, 2007), pp. 46–7.

52 Trollope, *North America*, II, p. 299.

53 Martineau, *Society in America*, I, p. 340.

54 Charles Dickens, *American Notes for General Circulation*, ed. Patricia Ingham (London: Penguin, 2004), p. 91.

55 Fidler, *Observations on Professions*, p. 143.

56 Michael de Nie, *The Eternal Paddy: Irish Identity and the British Press, 1798–1882* (Madison: University of Wisconsin Press, 2004), pp. 5–13; Patrick Brantlinger, *Taming Cannibals: Race and the Victorians* (Ithaca, NY: Cornell University Press, 2011), pp. 136–41.

57 De Nie, *The Eternal Paddy*, p. 19.

58 See Kenan Malik, *The Meaning of Race: Race, History and Culture in Western Society* (Basingstoke: Macmillan, 1996), pp. 43–55.

59 Bell, *The Idea of Greater Britain*, p. 53.

60 Trollope, *North America*, II, p. 299.

61 Grace Moore, *Dickens and Empire: Discourses of Class, Race and Colonialism in the Works of Charles Dickens* (Aldershot: Ashgate, 2004), p. 50; Laura Peters, *Dickens and Race* (Manchester: Manchester University Press, 2013), pp. 70–4.

62 Moore, *Dickens and Empire*, p. 50.

63 Dickens, *American Notes*, pp. 181, 235.

64 De Nie, *The Eternal Paddy*, p. 17.

65 Dickens, *American Notes*, pp. 231–2.

66 Leon Litvack, 'Dickens, Ireland and the Irish: Part I', *Dickensian*, 99.2 (2003), 34–59 (p. 43).

67 Peters, *Dickens and Race*, p. 57.

68 Hirota, *Expelling the Poor*, pp. 48–51.

69 Paul Ocobock, 'Introduction: Vagrancy and Homelessness in Global and Historical Perspective', in *Cast Out: Vagrancy and Homelessness in Global and Historical Perspective*, ed. A. L. Beier and Paul Ocobock (Athens: Ohio University Press, 2008), pp. 1–34 (pp. 12, 17).

70 Quoted by David Cressy, *Gypsies: An English History* (Oxford: Oxford University Press, 2018; repr. 2020), p. 53.

71 William Cobbett, *Rural Rides* (Harmondsworth: Penguin, 1985), p. 76; Charles Leland, 'Preface', in *The English Gipsies and Their Language* (London: Trübner, 1873), pp. v–xiii (p. x); Walter Scott, *Guy Mannering*, ed. P. D. Garside (London: Penguin, 2003), p. 37.

72 Kate Flint, *The Transatlantic Indian, 1776–1930* (Princeton, NJ: Princeton University Press, 2009), p. 145.

73 Dickens, *American Notes*, p. 217.

74 On Gypsies engaged with the manufacturing trade, see David Mayall, *Gypsy-Travellers in Nineteenth Century Society* (Cambridge: Cambridge University Press, 1988), pp. 19, 66. On the lifeways of American Indians on the East Coast of the United States, see Patrick Brantlinger, *Dark Vanishings: Discourse on the Extinction of Primitive Races, 1800–1930* (Ithaca, NY: Cornell University Press, 2003), pp. 46–53.

75 Robert Woods Sayre, 'The Romantic Indian Commodified: Text and Image in George Catlin's *Letters and Notes* (1841)', in *Transatlantic Romanticism: British and American Art and Literature, 1790–1860*, ed. Andrew Hemingway and Alan Wallach (Boston: University of Massachusetts Press, 2015), pp. 259–84 (p. 267).

76 George Catlin, *Letters and Notes on the Manners, Customs, and Conditions of the North American Indians*, 2 vols (London: George Catlin, 1841), I, pp. 34, 83.

77 Ibid., I, pp. 43–4; Benita Eisler, *The Red Man's Bones: George Catlin, Artist and Showman* (New York: Norton, 2013), pp. 249–51, 256–9.

78 *A Descriptive Catalogue of Catlin's Indian Gallery: Containing Portraits, Landscapes, Costumes, &c. and Representations of the Manners and Customs of the North American Indians* (London: C. Adlard, [1840]), p. 40.

79 Dickens, *The Pilgrim Edition of the Letters of Charles Dickens*, III, p. 438.

80 Martineau, *Society in America*, I, p. 278.

81 Trollope, *Domestic Manners of the Americans*, p. 263.

82 Ibid., p. 264.

83 Indian Removal Act, 28 May 1830.

84 David Reynolds, *America, Empire of Liberty: A New History* (London: Allen Lane, 2009), pp. 138–44.

85 Fay A. Yarbrough, *Race and the Cherokee Nation: Sovereignty in the Nineteenth Century* (Philadelphia: University of Pennsylvania Press, 2008), pp. 18–9.

86 Trollope, *Domestic Manners of the Americans*, p. 146.

87 G. W. Featherstonehaugh, *Excursion through the Slave States, from Washington on the Potomac to the Frontier of Mexico; with Sketches of Popular Manners and Geological Notices* (New York: Harper & Brothers, 1844), pp. 145, 150–2.

88 Flint, *The Transatlantic Indian*, p. 31.

89 Featherstonehaugh, *Excursion through the Slave States*, pp. 146, 150.

90 Brantlinger, *Dark Vanishings*, p. 59; Flint, *The Transatlantic Indian*, pp. 5–6, 37–40.

91 Steven Conn, *History's Shadow: Native Americans and Historical Consciousness in the Nineteenth Century* (Chicago: University of Chicago Press, 2004), p. 31.

92 Brantlinger, *Dark Vanishings*, pp. 4–6, 47, 52–6; Conn, *History's Shadow*, pp. 17–19.

93 Featherstonehaugh, *Excursion through the Slave States*, p. 146.

94 Brantlinger, *Dark Vanishings*, pp. 52–3.

95 Ibid., pp. 53–4, 58; Conn, *History's Shadow*, pp. 21–31.

96 Yarbrough, *Race and the Cherokee Nation*, p. 16.

97 George Augustus Sala, *My Diary in America in the Midst of War*, 2 vols (London: Tinsley Brothers, 1865), I, p. 183.

98 Flint observes that British commentators frequently contrasted the British treatment of American Indians with that of the Americans while arguing that the United States was unfit to govern its indigenous subjects. Flint, *The Transatlantic Indian*, pp. 13–16.

99 Charles Dickens, *Bleak House*, ed. Nicola Bradbury (London: Penguin, 2003), p. 731.

100 Sala, *My Diary in America in the Midst of War*, I, p. 184.

101 Trollope, *North America*, II, p. 50.

102 Reynolds, *America*, p. 121.

103 Randolph B. Campbell, *Gone to Texas: A History of the Lone Star State* (New York: Oxford University Press, 2003), p. 159.

104 Cresswell, *The Tramp in America*, p. 20.

105 Edward Gibbon Wakefield, *A Letter from Sydney*, in *A Letter from Sydney and Other Writings on Colonisation*, ed. Ernest Rhys (London: J. M. Dent, 1929), pp. 1–106 (p. 47).

106 'Notes on America, No. III.', *Monthly Magazine*, August 1832, pp. 145–52 (p. 150).

107 'The United States as an Emigration Field', *Chambers's Edinburgh Journal*, 16 June 1849, pp. 374–6 (p. 374).

108 Quoted by Reynolds, *America*, p. 159.

109 'Notes on America, No. III.', p. 150.

110 Featherstonehaugh, *Excursion through the Slave States*, pp. 64, 81.

111 'America and Her Slave States. No. III', *Sharpe's London Magazine*, 10 January 1846, pp. 163–5 (p. 164).

112 Charles Hooton, 'Texiana: Rides, Rambles, and Sketches in Texas', *Tait's Edinburgh Magazine*, March 1843, pp. 185–92 (p. 190).

113 Frederick Marryat, *Narrative of the Travels and Adventures of Monsieur Violet, in California, Sonora, & Western Texas*, 3 vols (London: Longman, Brown, Green & Longmans, 1843), II, pp. 44, 47.

114 Dickens, *American Notes*, pp. 205–6.

115 Jerome Meckier, *Innocent Abroad: Charles Dickens's American Engagements* (Lexington: University Press of Kentucky, 1990), p. 79.

116 Genesis 4:14.

117 Tim Cresswell, *On the Move: Mobility in the Modern Western World* (Abingdon: Routledge, 2006), p. 3.

118 Conn, *History's Shadow*, p. 22. Also see William H. Truettner, 'Picturing the Murder of Jane McCrea: A Critical Moment in Transatlantic Romanticism', in *Transatlantic Romanticism: British and American Art and Literature, 1790–1860*, ed. Andrew Hemingway and Alan Wallach (Boston: University of Massachusetts Press, 2015), pp. 229–58 (pp. 236–7).

119 Yi-Fu Tuan, *Space and Place: The Perspective of Experience* (Minneapolis: University of Minnesota Press, 1977; repr. 2018), p. 54.

120 'Sketches of the Mexican War', *Fraser's Magazine*, July 1848, pp. 91–102 (p. 92).

121 Catherine Waters, 'Domesticity', in *Charles Dickens in Context*, ed. Sally Ledger and Holly Furneaux (Cambridge: Cambridge University Press, 2011), pp. 350–7 (p. 354).

122 Charles Dickens, *Great Expectations*, ed. Charlotte Mitchell (London: Penguin, 2003), p. 207; Charles Dickens, *Oliver Twist*, ed. Philip Horne (London: Penguin, 2003), p. 106.

123 Charles Dickens, *The Cricket on the Hearth: A Fairy Tale of Home*, in *Christmas Books*, intro. Eleanor Farjeon (Oxford: Oxford University Press, 1954; repr. 1997), pp. 156–234 (pp. 176, 211).

124 Virginia Woolf, 'Street Haunting: A London Adventure', in *Selected Essays* (Oxford: Oxford University Press, 2008), pp. 177–87 (p. 177).

125 Tuan, *Space and Place*, p. 4.

126 Dickens, *American Notes*, p. 206.

127 James Belich, *Replenishing the Earth: The Settler Revolution and the Rise of the Anglo-World, 1783–1939* (Oxford: Oxford University Press, 2009), pp. 29–30.

128 Charles Hooton, 'Texiana: Rides, Rambles, and Sketches in Texas', *Tait's Edinburgh Magazine*, May 1843, pp. 288–95 (p. 295).

129 Martineau, *Society in America*, I, p. 273.

130 Katherine V. Snyder, *Bachelors, Manhood, and the Novel, 1850–1925* (Cambridge: Cambridge University Press, 1999), p. 34.

131 John Ruskin, *Sesame and Lilies*, ed. Deborah Epstein Nord (New Haven, CT: Yale University Press, 2002), pp. 77, 87.

132 Piesse, *British Settler Emigration in Print*, pp. 82–95, 111.

133 [George Sargent], 'Frank Layton: An Australian Story', *Leisure Hour*, 2 March 1854, pp. 129–33 (p. 132); quoted by Piesse, *British Settler Emigration in Print*, p. 86.

134 Piesse, *British Settler Emigration in Print*, pp. 82–95.
135 Janet C. Myers, *Antipodal England: Emigration and Portable Domesticity in the Victorian Imagination* (Albany: State University of New York Press, 2009), p. 9.
136 'Notes on America, No. III.', p. 151.
137 Lynda Nead, *Myths of Sexuality: Representations of Women in Victorian Britain* (Oxford: Blackwell, 1988; repr. 1990), p. 29.
138 'Notes on America, No. III.', p. 151.

CHAPTER 6

Beachcombers

Eighty per cent of the world's islands lie in the Pacific Ocean. Of these, two account for 90 per cent of the islands' total landmass, New Guinea and New Zealand. The remaining land is divided between over 20,000 other islands that form the three subregions of the Pacific Islands: Polynesia, Melanesia and Micronesia.[1] Often separated by hundreds of miles, such spaces do not seem to invite vagrancy. On the contrary, their tightly bounded geography, as Rod Edmond observes, makes them 'natural sites of concentration'; for this reason they have been favoured as sites of detention.[2] In the nineteenth century, several Pacific islands were elected as places of imprisonment where Western fantasies of control could be fulfilled. From 1825 to 1856 Norfolk Island, situated between the northern tip of New Zealand and the eastern coast of Australia, served as a British penal colony. A byword for brutality, it was 'one of the most extreme penal environments the modern world has known'.[3] The French government put New Caledonia, one of the Melanesian archipelagos, to similar use: between 1864 and 1897 they transported 20,000 convicts there.[4] Meanwhile, in Polynesia, the Hawaiian island of Molokai hosted a leper colony from 1865. Although Hawai'i was a nominally independent kingdom until 1893, the policing of lepers (most of whom were Hawaiian) was a preoccupation of the US government; it insisted on the need for quarantine and by 1887 was enforcing segregation laws.[5]

However, although some islands became notorious as sites of containment, many more provided opportunities for escape. From the late eighteenth century vessels from Europe and North America began to cruise the Pacific in search of fur seals, whales, sandalwood and sea cucumber, or *bêche-de-mer*, a Chinese delicacy also known as trepang.[6] For sailors aboard these ships the Pacific Islands, celebrated for their perennial fruitfulness and social and sexual freedoms, were a tempting alternative to tyrannical captains and the strict rhythm of the ships' watches.[7] Although the reality was often very different, this notion proved seductive, not only for sailors

195

but also for fugitives who sought a refuge on the peripheries of Western civilisation. By the second half of the nineteenth century the Pacific Islands, or at least those that remained free from foreign government, had become renowned as safe havens for white renegades and attracted vagabonds similar to those who gravitated to the frontiers of antebellum America (see Chapter 5). As Litton Forbes records in his travelogue *Two Years in Fiji* (1875), before British annexation in 1874, '"Gone to Fiji" bore the same significance in Australia as "Gone to Texas" did in America a few years ago. The colonial newspapers were accustomed to speak of Fiji as the "modern Alsatia" and not without some reason.'[8] He goes on to note that 'the lawlessness of Fiji was its chief recommendation' to the 'runaway sailors, absconding tradesmen, and not a few convicted felons' who lived there.[9]

These deserters belonged to a vagrant class that lived in the Pacific Islands and were collectively known as 'beachcombers'. As Edward Jerningham Wakefield describes them in *Adventure in New Zealand* (1845), the beachcomber is 'idle, drunken, vagabond, and vicious in his habits' and 'wanders about without any fixed object'.[10] Originating in the South Seas, this disreputable figure was exclusively white and male – at least within the cultural imagination of nineteenth-century Britain. Although Greg Dening and Jocelyn Linnekin have used the term to refer to those Europeans, Americans and Pacific Islanders who migrated between the islands, the Victorians understood the 'beachcomber' to be a white man living on the frontier of civilisation.

Historically, beachcombers had their heyday in the medial period between the discovery of the islands and the establishment of formal white settlements.[11] This period varied between the three Pacific regions and individual island groups. Polynesia was the first region to be thoroughly explored by Europeans, and proved the most receptive to them. Melanesia and Micronesia began to have sustained contact with Westerners only after the middle of the nineteenth century, and some of their archipelagos remained notoriously hostile despite this. Known for its hospitality, Hawai'i was the first of the Polynesian island groups to attract significant European traffic, mainly whalers who stopped to re-provision on their way to hunting grounds further afield.[12] Consequently, it was also the first to accrue a population of beachcombers. These outsiders possessed skills that made them attractive to islanders: they could interpret for them when Western traders arrived; they provided technical training in carpentry, ironmongery and musket maintenance; and some were formidable warriors, in part because they were uninhibited by the indigenous taboos that checked bloodletting in local conflicts.[13] Many of them tried to acculturate by marrying islanders and allowing themselves to be tattooed, a social rite that signified a closer integration with the community (at least for the Pacific Islanders).[14]

That said, complete integration was rarely successful, and as a result, beachcombers were often on the move. In the first half of the nineteenth century groups of between thirty and fifty lived in Tahiti, Pohnpei, Fiji and Samoa, while up to 150 lived in New Zealand and Hawai'i.[15] Whether they were castaways, fugitives or adventurers, few of these beach-combers remained longer than six months before they moved to another island or took a passage home.[16] William Diapea, a beachcomber other-wise known as 'Cannibal Jack', claimed that during his fifty-year career in the Pacific he had 'touched at a great many more than 1,000 islands, and resided on nearly 100'.[17] Such movements were relatively easy. As Gillian Beer reminds us, despite their place in the Western imagination as sites of containment, islands 'are never enclosures only'; they are also markets, crossroads and, in the age of sail, 'essential and frequent stopping-off points for re-provisioning'.[18] Travel between islands was by no means limited to Europeans and Americans either. Long before white sailors began to visit the Pacific Islands its archipelagoes were linked by cultural, familial and financial networks made and sustained by strong seafaring traditions. As Epeli Hau'ofa argues, the idea that the islands are small and isolated is of European origin: 'Nineteenth-century imperialism erected boundaries that led to the contraction of Oceania, transforming a once boundless world into the Pacific Island states and territories that we know today.'[19] This Oceanic notion of the islands as interconnected, and the geographic knowledge it necessarily entailed, would have been indispens-able to beachcombers planning their next landfall.

There were many reasons why beachcombers might have wished to migrate. Unlike traders and missionaries they did not form cohesive enclaves separate from the indigenous population. Instead, they scattered themselves among native communities and depended upon local leaders for their survival. A chief could protect the beachcomber from harassment by other islanders, and could provide food, shelter, land and wives. However, they could also prove jealous lords. Considered valuable assets, beachcombers sometimes found themselves effectively imprisoned on the beach, closely watched and regulated by chiefs who feared that they would escape to another island, taking their knowledge, skills and goods with them.[20] Under such circumstances, some were prepared to exchange the idyllic-looking shore for the forecastle of a whaler or trading vessel. Here the rules were similarly strict, but there was at least a reprieve at the end of the voyage.

There were also economic reasons for moving. Although beachcombers depended on chiefs for their immediate sustenance, they were also often traders in their own right. It is no surprise that the number of beach-combers tended to spike when trading opportunities became apparent. In Fiji the beachcombing community was at its most conspicuous from 1804 to 1815 and from 1822 to 1850: these periods correspond with Fiji's short-lived sandalwood trade, which lasted from 1804 to 1816, and its more lively trade in *bêche-de-mer*, which lasted from 1822 to 1850.[21] Similarly, in the Marquesas, the first influx of beachcombers occurred between 1813 and 1821, again during a brief boom in the sandalwood trade, and the second between 1832 and 1839 when whaling vessels used the islands to resupply.[22] For the beachcombers this traffic provided a market for their island wares, which included prosaic foodstuffs as well as what Herman Melville called the 'romantic articles of commerce'. Writing in his South Seas memoir, *Omoo* (1847), he described these as 'beach-de-mer, the pearl-oyster, arrow-root, ambergris, sandal-wood, cocoa-nut oil, and edible birdsnests'.[23] In particular, beachcombers were famed for the pearls and pearl shell that they collected on the islands, as we shall see.

Beachcombers were also sometimes forced to migrate. The assumption that the Pacific Islands offered a lawless paradise meant that beachcombers and other white men could become ungovernable. Some indigenous governments, such as the government of Hawai'i, tried to use laws mod-elled on Anglo-American legislation to reset social norms and expectations. As J. Kēhaulani Kauanui explains, in the 1820s 'The threat of foreign men's violence as they demanded unlimited access to Hawaiian women commoners catalysed the earliest legal edicts regulating their sexuality', which included laws against adultery and fornication similar to those that already existed in the United States.[24] Other island communities, however, responded by expelling or executing visitors who committed untenable social infractions. In 1836, for example, the inhabitants of Kosrae and Pohnpei, two large islands in Micronesia, tried to exterminate their beach-comber populations because they had grown violent and unruly; this was a more than adequate incentive for them to move on.[25]

Rival groups of Europeans and North Americans also drove out beach-combers. Although they unwittingly formed the vanguard of Western culture in the Pacific Islands, they were almost invariably displaced by the missionaries and traders who followed them.[26] In addition, European authorities and the US government made efforts to purge the beachcomber presence on the pretext that it corrupted indigenous islanders: in 1805, for example, the governor of Port Jackson (now Sydney, Australia) expelled many of them from Tahiti, forcing them to move to more remote islands.[27] Although beachcombers criss-crossed the Pacific throughout the nineteenth century, their overall pattern of movement within the region was away from the archipelagos of Polynesia, which were the first to be colonised, and towards the more hostile regions of Micronesia and Melanesia. Meanwhile, others managed to find their way back home. James O'Connell, for example, returned to the United States where he travelled as a circus exhibit – 'The Tattooed Man' – from 1835 until his death in 1854.[28]

The focus of this chapter, however, is not on the real lives of beachcombers; instead, it examines the surge of literature about them during the 1880s and 1890s. Occurring at a time when the Pacific Islands had largely undergone what I. C. Campbell calls the 'beachcomber phase', the intermediate period between first contact and white settlement, the interest exhibited in these figures is in some ways surprising.[29] They were already, as we shall see, perceived as relics from a nearly bygone age of lawlessness and immorality, and yet they nonetheless proved fascinating for authors writing with diverse aims in a variety of genres. They are recurrent characters in travelogues, such as Forbes's *Two Years in Fiji*, where they are depicted as the remnants of a previous (dis)order. They are also the subject of several ethnographic articles that sought to entertain readers of the newspaper and periodical press with etymologies, definitions and scurrilous anecdotes about 'the jetsam and flotsam of the frontier'.[30] And by the late 1880s they were the subjects of short stories and novels, including Gilbert Bishop's *The Beachcombers* (1889) and Edward Ellis's *Lost in Samoa* (1890). As the *Daily News* informs us, these were adventure narratives written for boys that depicted plucky lads in desperate 'Fights with the vagrants of the South Seas, known by the name of "Beach Combers"'.[31] This rush of beachcomber literature, which has hitherto been unexplored, forms the context for the final part of this chapter, in which I discuss Robert Louis Stevenson's *The Ebb-Tide* (1894). Here I argue that the beachcomber, an understudied vagrant figure who captivated the imagination of Stevenson as well as many of his contemporaries, was essential to his conception and critique of empire in the Pacific.

6.1 Beachcombers in Print

Beachcombers became a feature in the British periodical and newspaper press in the late nineteenth century due to two overlapping issues: imperial

competition and expansion, on the one hand, and a desire to police the
Pacific, on the other. Between 1880 and 1900, Britain, France, Germany
and the United States partitioned the Pacific Islands so that by the end of
the century there was no island left unclaimed. Even the most politically
stable archipelagos – Hawai'i and Tonga – were territories or protectorates
of foreign powers by 1900.[32] The unification of Germany in the 1870s and
the imperial appetite it developed in the 1880s precipitated this division: as
Steven Roger Fischer notes, 'Germany's aggressive Pacific policy ... forced
rivals to chase after what they otherwise might have ignored.'[33] In the case
of Britain this 'chase' was somewhat sluggish. Although it ended up with
the largest clutch of possessions, Britain was reluctant to become involved
in the Pacific, and its actions were often reactive. Typically, they were
either responses to the territorial claims made by other powers, and
the attendant political pressure exerted by its nervous Australasian
colonies, or they were determined by the supposed and actual lawlessness
of the region.[34]

Britain's annexations of New Zealand in 1840 and Fiji in 1874 were
undertaken as last resorts, and chiefly because it was felt that the protection
of British property, and the safety of indigenous and European residents,
could not be guaranteed without the creation of legal jurisdictions.[35] Later
protectorates, like those declared over the Gilbert, Ellice and southern
Solomon Islands in the early 1890s, were directed by a slightly different set
of concerns. Unlike New Zealand and Fiji, these archipelagos had no
significant British population; however, they were targets for dubious
merchants engaged in the labour trade, or 'blackbirding', as it was known.
From the 1860s until the early twentieth century, labour recruiters transported a large number of islanders to work on European-owned planta-
tions in Australia and elsewhere in the Pacific Islands: Melanesia alone
supplied 100,000 of these workers. Traders obtained labour by violent and
duplicitous means and were suspected of being slavers in all but name.
After the failure of colonial legislation to stop abuses, the British government resolved to regulate the trade, but again could imagine doing so only
through the creation of fresh jurisdictions that would give them grounds to
interfere with trading vessels; this was a major contributing factor to later
interventions.[36]

The portrayal of beachcombers in British print culture in the 1880s was
a response to this political situation. For optimists reading about the
hitherto obscure islands now entering the Empire, they were the 'class of
men that macadamises the world' and were seen as the forerunners of
official colonial government.[37] For example, after the 1887 annexation

of the Kermadecs, a trio of islands off the coast of New Zealand, *Chambers's Journal* retold its history as a series of beachcomber exploits. The 'first reported occupiers' were 'American whalers, who ... took up their abode there, accompanied by their dark-skinned wives'; the next settlers were 'a Sydney man from Samoa, who was landed there with his Samoan wife'; the third pioneer was 'a solitary beachcomber from Tonga'; and the last 'a solitary beachcomber, who ... landed some sheep and claimed the island'.[38] These beachcombers were used to justify annexation by providing a record of Anglo-Saxon settlement that excluded any claim that the Pacific Islanders might have on the Kermadecs. Although they are represented by the 'dark-skinned wives' and the 'Samoan wife', it is significant that these women are portrayed as subservient camp-followers with little agency of their own. We have already seen this stereotype on the US frontier, where female pioneers were portrayed as helpmeets, obediently following their husbands into the wilderness (see Chapter 5). However, this trope serves an additional ideological function in the Pacific context. By characterising the Polynesians as compliant women, the article replays a racist myth in which Anglo-Saxons are superlative pioneers, and Islanders are passive, feminine and sexually available.

The beachcomber's position as imperial pathfinder, however, was far from secure. In his popular survey *The Coral Lands of the Pacific* (1880), H. Stonehewer Cooper states that 'the beachcombers would ... act as very useful pioneers'; however, he is also quick to note that 'it was on account of some of these people that a Lord High Commissioner of Western Polynesia was appointed'.[39] Here Cooper refers to the establishment of the Western Pacific High Commission in 1877. A direct response to the labour trade, it gave the governor of Fiji extra-territorial powers and a mandate to stop illegal activities committed by British subjects.[40] Far from being pioneers, Cooper suggests that beachcombers are buccaneers, a common assumption in the late nineteenth century when the two figures were often elided. In 'The Buccaneers of the Pacific' (1882) the *Western Daily Press* rails against the European traders who abuse Pacific Islanders: it denounces them as 'the modern buccaneers and "beach-combers" of the Pacific Islands'.[41] Similarly, in 'Beach-Combers' (1883), the *Standard* solemnly declares that 'when not engaged in piracy or land plundering, the buccaneers were, to all intents and purposes, of the Beach-combing order of mankind'.[42] And in 'A Nineteenth-Century Pirate' (1886), a jaunty sketch of the infamous Bully Hayes, *Chambers's* records that 'a few years ago [he] was one of the most notorious desperadoes among the numerous "beachcombers" and other questionable characters who infested the South Pacific'.[43]

Beachcombers, then, were imagined both as the pioneers of those territories now being soaked up by the Empire and as the buccaneers against whom Britain's efforts were tending. These conflicting identities were further complicated by the beachcombers' vagrant habits, which were not easily accommodated by these equally purposeful figures. In response, the writers of ethnographic articles reached for other analogous characters through which the beachcomber might be defined. The 'loafer' was used for this purpose. In 'Packet Rats and Beachcombers' (1879) the *Pall Mall Gazette* called the beachcomber 'a loafer pure and simple', while the *Standard*, acknowledging his Pacific associations, defined him as 'a "loafer", or, as the San Franciscan would say, a "bummer"'.[44] The *Standard* also drew on another comparable figure, noting that although 'the Isles of the Pacific are . . . the home of the true Beach-comber', he also resides with the American Indians as the acculturated 'squawman'.[45] Like the pioneer and the buccaneer, the loafer and the squawman are analogues that stress the beachcomber's mobility, but represent it as vagrancy. Together they emphasise that the beachcomber is 'outside of civilisation – is indeed a waif and stray not only on the ocean of life, but on the broad South Pacific', as *Chambers's* argued in 'Beachcombers' (1881).[46] This was a leading assumption that influenced contemporary commentaries about the Pacific Islands, many of which imagined beachcombers as destined for extinction with the onset of 'civilisation'.

By the last decades of the nineteenth century, extinction theory had become an unshakable 'fact'. Bolstered by social Darwinism and eugenic thinking, it was used to explain away the extermination of Africans, American Indians and Pacific Islanders. As acculturated Europeans 'gone native', like the North American squawmen, the beachcombers were considered a species of 'white savage' who would inevitably wither away along with their adopted tribes. Contemporaries suggested that this might happen in one of two ways. The first followed the popular theory that 'savage' customs, including nomadism and 'excessive' freedom or wildness, naturally led to extinction.[47] Forbes expressed this idea in his travelogue. Recounting a visit to Rotuma, an island to the north of Fiji, he recalled an encounter with Bill R——, 'the sole survivor of a bygone generation' of beachcombers: 'these lawless men, freed from every restraint and inflamed by drink, abandoned themselves to every excess, . . . and old Bill assured me that of all the seventy men who were on the island when he first landed, there was not one who escaped a violent death'.[48] Here the savagery of the beachcombers, signalled by their incontinence, is directly linked to their extermination. Frederick J. Moss, writing in his travelogue

Through Atolls and Islands in the Great South Sea (1889), espoused the same idea. Although he excuses most beachcombers, saying that 'in the old days . . . the white men [were] assuredly not so wicked as we have been led to believe', he nonetheless admits that there was a 'dangerous class' among them. 'The worst of these men', however, 'were short lived. They killed each other, died of their own debauchery, or were killed by the natives.'[49]

While some writers argued that the beachcombers' lawlessness would lead to self-extermination, others posited that bringing 'lawless' territory under colonial government would produce the same result. Cooper, an avid imperialist, noted, 'If the Anglo-Saxon race is prepared to accept the responsibility that undoubtedly belongs to it in the Southern Seas, beachcombing, as beachcombing has been understood for years, will be a thing of the past.'[50] In the same vein, he also argued that if 'a powerful controlling influence of a high order [was] established in the Pacific', then the beachcombers either would become useful workers under 'rigid discipline' or would be 'improved off the face of the earth'.[51] Meanwhile, in 'Beachcombers', *Chambers's* was less equivocal. Throughout the article beachcombers are described as survivals from a more primitive economic era who at present 'cumber the ground, and must sooner or later give way before well-organized efforts of capital': 'in great measure their doom as a class will be sealed the moment systematic trading is introduced'.[52] Commerce and civilisation were the antidotes to beachcombing. Forbes also expressed this notion, arguing that once capitalism had made survival dependent on labour in the Pacific, the beachcombers would cease to exist: 'work in some shape or other is becoming a universal necessity', he assures us, 'and soon the genus "loafer" will scarcely find a suitable habitation on the globe'.[53]

These accounts of impending extinction are familiar from earlier chapters. Together with other racial theories, ideas about extinction played an important part in the Victorian discourse of vagrancy. Gypsies, for example, were represented as a vanishing race. Popularly believed to be promiscuous, a trait that was widely ascribed to both vagrants and savages, it was imagined that miscegenation had tainted their bloodlines and guaranteed their destruction. American Indians, too, allegedly shared the same fate. Portrayed as primitives who were unable to adopt 'civilised' modes of life, it was thought that their inability to adapt to new social, cultural and geographical environments would likewise lead to their extermination. When commentators presented beachcombers as a species of savage inseparable from their environs, they were iterating old ideas in a new context. Perhaps because of the exoticism of the locale and the political importance of the ongoing imperial project, much of the emphasis was placed on the environment's effect on character. Underlying each vision of extinction was the idea that the beachcombers' existence was dependent upon a lawless environment, the original and primal landscape that Neil Rennie argues was imprinted on the Pacific's islands when they were first discovered by European explorers.[54] Once these environments had been tamed through annexation and commercial ventures, the beachcomber would disappear. This logic also governed the presentation of beachcombers in fiction.

Beachcombers tended to be portrayed as swashbuckling rogues in the South Seas adventures written for boys. Such is the case in Edward Ellis's *Lost in Samoa* (1890), a book 'full of adventure and fighting' that received scanty reviews but was praised for its 'spirited style'.[55] Given that Ellis was a famous dime novelist and the author of cowboy classics such as *Seth Jones; or, The Captives of the Frontier* (1860), it is little surprise that his three beachcombing villains – Buzz Izard, Gross Mosler and Trott Twitchell – should be desperadoes. Rigged out in hats 'as broad as the Texan sombrero' and carrying 'loaded revolvers in their hip-pockets', they belong as much to the Wild West as they do to Upolu, the Samoan island where the action is set. But despite their melodramatic role, it is immediately apparent that for Ellis the beachcombers belong to the realm of fact and that in their depiction, or at least their setting, he aims for realism. His preface to the novel is wholly concerned with the 'vagrants of the South Sea [who] are known in that section by the name of Beach Combers' and gives a thorough history of their migration through the Pacific:

> These vagrants of the South Sea have no love for law and order, and when they find an island passing under the control of a strong European Government generally hunt for one whose natives are independent. The occupation of Tahiti by the French caused a stampede of these vagabonds to Fejee, which they abandoned for Samoa when Fejee became an English possession. There are a large number of them to-day in Samoa, but if those tropical islands ever secure a stable Government they will be certain to hunt out some spot where they are under no legal restraint, and go thither.[56]

Here it is clear that Ellis's beachcombers belong as much to the encyclopaedia entry as they do to romance. Informed by a broader beachcomber literature that argued that they could not thrive in lawfully governed spaces, he places them within a colonial Alsatia. Indeed, as Joseph Farrell relates, by the early 1890s, 'Samoa had gained a reputation as the "hell hole of the Pacific", not because of the supposed violence of the native Samoans, but because of the assorted drifters and beachcombers who had made it their home and lived apart from the respectable Western residents.'[57]

Gilbert Bishop's *The Beachcombers; or, Slave Trading under the Union Jack* (1889) is another novel that carefully considers its setting. Written in the style of one of Charles Reade's 'matter-of-fact Romance[s] – that is, a fiction built on truths', Bishop sought to expose the evils of the labour trade by incorporating instances of labour abuse harvested from the newspapers.[58] Despite the *St. James's Gazette*'s conviction that the combination of court report and boys' adventure would 'create a considerable sensation', providing a story that 'Boys may delight in . . . and their fathers ponder on', *The Beachcombers* attracted little attention on publication, and the other reviews were perfunctory.[59] The beachcombers themselves are a more varied set than Ellis's. Although Bishop describes the crew of the *Polly Hawkins*, a labour trading vessel, 'as shady a lot o' beachcombers as you ever seen', in fact the beachcombers are less intimately connected with slave trading than the novel's title suggests. It opens with the disappearance of Samoan Tom, 'an old beachcomber' and harmless sot who deals in island goods, not labour. Similarly, the beachcombing Judd Gridley, whose Western patter is rumpled with comic oaths ('by the stars an' bars'), is a far cry from his 'blackbirding' compatriots.[60] Nonetheless, like Ellis's beachcombers they are all swashbuckling frontiersmen and have been placed in a lawless setting.

The Beachcombers is set in the Solomon Islands, one of the Melanesian archipelagos. Although the events of the novel take place around 1870, just after the advent 'of that newly discovered explosive they call dynamite', the Solomon Islands were presented as superlatively savage even at the time that Bishop was writing.[61] In 'The Head-Hunters of the Solomon Islands' (1890), *All the Year Round* dwelt on the islanders' 'evil reputation for man-eating' and 'their passion for head-hunting', while the politician J. F. Hogan, writing in *Chambers's* a few years later, confirmed that they are 'the most notorious cannibals in the Pacific'.[62] This reputation was maintained despite the division of the archipelago between Germany and Britain in 1884, and the protectorate that Britain declared over the southern islands in 1893.[63] In part, this was because there was no European presence there to speak of: in 1870 there were seven resident traders, and in 1890 only fourteen.[64] But it was also due to racial prejudice. As Maile Arvin has recently argued, the Pacific Islands were mapped according to race as well as geography, and this had a significant impact on how different indigenous communities were treated and represented. Polynesians were conceptualised by Europeans as 'almost white' and this naturalised colonial settlement. The argument ran that if whiteness was native to Polynesia, then so were white settlers, and if they belonged to the islands, however tangentially, then they could claim ownership over them. Conversely, the inhabitants of Melanesia were imbued with the negative traits already ascribed to many African peoples, including unalterable savagery and violence. This racist coding of Oceania ensured that Melanesian island groups like the Solomons were imagined as anarchic spaces.[65] They therefore provided the ideal backdrop for Bishop's beachcombers who want to get 'beyond the reach of the arm of the law'.[66]

Other writers of beachcomber fiction also looked to the Solomon Islands. In V. L. Cameron's 'How Jack Hawker Met His Bride' (1891), Jem Butcher, 'who had been bushranger, beachcomber, and probably pirate', and his criminal accomplice Bill Giles, who 'had been a beachcomber for some time', 'make for the Solomon Islands' after they steal Donald M'Alpine's schooner, along with his daughter and his fortune of £100,000.[67] And in Hugh Romilly's 'A Tale of the South Seas' (1891), Captain Nassau, a beachcomber-cum-trader who dwelt 'amongst the reckless Beach Combers and Mean Whites' of Fiji, 'settled to live in the Southern Solomons' rather than live in an annexed archipelago. Repeating the pattern of migration detailed by Ellis, Nassau boasts, 'For fifteen years I put up with Fiji and Fiji put up with me, and then came the British Government and the end of all good times. But I did not wait to receive the British Government. For twenty-five years I have lived in no country where the flag of any nation flies, and please God I'll do so till the end.'[68] In both these stories, as in the novels above, the writers are concerned about using a tenable location for their beachcomber characters. Even if their narratives veer off into what Robert Louis Stevenson called the 'sugar candy sham epic' of South Seas romance, they were all anxious to place their swashbucklers within realistic landscapes that could support their lawlessness.[69] It is this that makes Stevenson's choice to place his trio of beachcombers in Tahiti, the second oldest colony in the Pacific Islands, so curious.

6.2 Robert Louis Stevenson and *The Ebb-Tide*

'I should have been a beachcomber. I should have gone fifteen years ago to Samoa', Robert Louis Stevenson wrote to his publisher Edward Burlingame.[70] Dated May 1889 from Honolulu, just after his first South Seas voyage, the letter contemplates a beachcomber touched with romance. He is not the labour recruiter or the degraded desperado of

Gilbert and Ellis, but is instead like the 'gentle, soft-eyed youth from Edinburgh, now fairly on the way to become a beach-comber', that his wife Fanny encountered twelve months later on the pearl island of Penrhyn. As Fanny proclaimed, this was a 'Fortunate lad!': 'His future is assured; no more hard work, no more nipping frosts and chilly winds; he will live and die in dreamland, beloved and honoured and tenderly cared for all the summer days of his life.'[71] This is the beachcomber fantasy that encouraged hundreds of sailors to abandon ship during the nineteenth century and that both the Stevensons eventually came to realise was essentially untrue during the three Pacific voyages that they took with Lloyd Osbourne, Fanny's son.

The first of these was aboard the *Casco*, a chartered yacht that set sail from San Francisco on 28 June 1888 and cruised through Polynesian waters, visiting the Marquesas, the Paumotus islands and Tahiti, before docking in Hawai'i in January 1889. Six months later they took passage aboard the *Equator*, a trading schooner that toured the Gilbert Islands from June to December. As Roslyn Jolly notes, this voyage through Micronesia was a more challenging experience for the Stevenson party: the living conditions aboard the schooner were inferior to those on the luxury yacht; the trio had little say in where the ship weighed anchor because they were passengers rather than owners; and in the islands they visited 'law and order was far less secure than in the Polynesian islands'.[72] The last voyage they took was aboard another trading schooner, the *Janet Nicoll*, which left Sydney on 11 April 1890. Again the Stevensons were just passengers and were ignorant of the landfalls that they would make. In the end, they visited over thirty islands in five months, after which they settled in Samoa until Stevenson's death in December 1894.[73] In the months that preceded and followed the letter to Burlingame, then, the Stevensons were introduced to an enormous number of islands, their indigenous communities and the beachcombers who lived among them.

Writing aboard the *Equator* to his lifelong friend and one-time mentor Sidney Colvin, Stevenson remarked, 'The beachcomber is perhaps the most interesting character here.'[74] This was a sentiment that was shared by the whole party. Stevenson's posthumous travelogue, *In the South Seas* (1896); Fanny's diary, *The Cruise of the 'Janet Nichol'* (1914); and the photographs taken by Osbourne all enthusiastically document beachcomber life. Together they provide an invaluable resource that demonstrates the diversity of this vagrant class within the Pacific Islands. Fanny, for example, records meeting Tom Day – 'the flower of the Pacific' – who lived under an alias having 'three times deserted from men-of-war'; with

Figure 6.1   Lloyd Osbourne, 'King of Manihiki with the Island Judge on Right Hand. In
Front a Beachcomber' (1890). The City of Edinburgh Museums and Galleries:
Writers' Museum

'a strong, alert figure and the mobile face of an actor' she found him an
appealing character despite his habitual drunkenness. She also met a less
prepossessing trio of ne'er-do-wells in the form of 'an absconding produce-
merchant, a runaway marine, and a young Englishman who was wrecked',
all of whom she discovered on Manihiki. These 'three "beach-combers"'
were all well dressed' and cared for by the islanders, although they were
'under some subjection'; this inglorious position is clarified by one of
Lloyd's photographs (see Figure 6.1).[75]

As the caption reads in the first edition of *The Cruise*, the photograph
depicts: 'The King of Manihiki in the centre, with the Island Judge on his
right and Tin Jack [a trader], seated, on his left. The man squatting in the

foreground is one of the beach-combers.' In stark contrast to the 'soft-eyed' Scot destined to live in bliss, both the caption and photograph emphasise the beachcomber's humble situation. It is clear from the neat dress and self-conscious poses of the others that the photograph provided an opportunity to perform themselves and to lay claim to their social status. This is especially true of the king, who, dressed in a velveteen coat and 'a crown of red and white pandanus leaves', has assumed the trappings of royalty and a stern, regal expression to accompany them. The beachcomber, meanwhile, is conspicuously incongruous. Although he features in a portrait of island dignitaries, neither his expression nor his dress projects a definite identity. His poncho-like garment renders his stance unreadable, while his slack face, the only part of his body we can see other than his feet, refuses to fill the lacuna. Earthed before the king, and positioned below all the other participants, the beachcomber seems to have the status of a prized object rather than a specific person. The caption contributes to this by recording that he 'is one of the beach-combers' (which one does not matter); but the text also has its own agenda. The description of him 'squatting', despite the fact that he is sitting, resonates with stereotypically 'savage' postures and indicates that he has 'gone native'. At the same time, it also suggests that the beachcomber is a squatter, an unauthorised or unwanted person; this would certainly chime with one beachcomber's admission to Fanny that 'his present way of life "had an air of loafing on the natives"'.[76]

Such pitiful loafers are also noted in *In the South Seas*, where Stevenson records that the Pacific Islands are full of willing interpreters, many of whom are the 'broken white folk living on the bounty of the natives'. His most striking beachcomber, however, is the one he found 'tattooed from head to foot' sitting on the pier head of Tai o Hae, the capital of the Marquesas.[77] Strongly reminiscent of James O'Connell, 'The Tattooed Man' who belonged to the beachcombing phase, this beachcomber exerted the fascination that all anachronisms possess, and it is with him that Stevenson and Osbourne opened their novel *The Wrecker* (1892). Here the same beachcomber, the 'living curiosity of Tai-o-hae', is presented as a socially peripheral figure that belongs to a bygone period. He is perched 'at the end of a rickety pier', a structure whose placement on a boundary between land and sea marks his outsider status, even as its fragility enhances our sense of his precarity. His liminal position is further emphasised by his vivid recollections. Dangling over the water, lost in thought, we are told that 'he would hear again the drums beat for a man-eating festival'.[78] Such memories enmesh him within the pre-colonial era, because as Stevenson makes clear in his travelogue, cannibalism in the

Marquesas could now be seen only 'in the cold perspective and dry light of history'.[79] The victim of a trick in time, the beachcomber's life experience belongs not just to the past but to the distant past, and it is this as much as his tattoos that make him a curiosity.

Although *The Wrecker* – a tale of debt, smuggling, blackmail and opium – is not about beachcombers, it is fitting that it should open with one. The first of three 'South Sea Yarns' that Stevenson and Osbourne intended to write together, *The Wrecker* and its companion pieces were planned to address the 'things that I can scarce touch upon, or even not at all, in my travel book', as Stevenson explained to Colvin: these 'things' included some of the seedier beachcombers that he had encountered.[80] *The Wrecker* was the only story written in full collaboration and that did not give beachcombers a prominent part. The first half of *The Pearl Fisher*, which centres upon the exploits of 'three beachcombers', was written with Osbourne 'Up to the discovery of the champagne', but the rest was written by Stevenson alone, who compressed the tale into a novella and retitled it *The Ebb-Tide*.[81] The third novel was a 'more sentimental' yarn called *The Beachcombers*, but it was never written, and the project quickly fell from Stevenson's correspondence.[82] The planned trilogy, the travelogue, the photographs and Fanny's diary, parts of which were 'intended to be a collection of hints to help my husband's memory', reveal that beach-comber life was an imaginative preoccupation for Stevenson and Osbourne.[83] This is most evident in *The Ebb-Tide*, a novella that probes the nature and nuances of beachcombing in the late nineteenth century and engages with it on a thematic and formal level.

Where the tattooed beachcomber at the beginning of *The Wrecker* is out of place in modern Tai o Hae, the three beachcombers that we encounter in *The Ebb-Tide* in Papeete, Tahiti's capital, belong to their surroundings. Unlike their tattooed counterpart or their other contemporaries in Samoa and the Solomon Islands, there is nothing swashbuckling or adventurous about Robert Herrick, J. L. Huish or Captain John Davis. At the begin-ning of the novella they are both literally and metaphorically 'on the beach' (124), a phrase of Pacific origin that means 'destitute' or 'unemployed'.[84] Dressed in 'flimsy cotton' with 'no breakfast to mention' (124), they recall 'the occupants of an English casual ward', as one contemporary reviewer observed. This resemblance is sharpened by their residence in the disused calaboose, a place 'littered with wreckage and the traces of vagrant occu-pation' (143).[85] Although Edmond argues that these beachcombers 'could be [in] Apia, Noumea or Suva', the capitals of Samoa, New Caledonia and Fiji, respectively, it is in fact significant that they are located in Papeete, one of the oldest European settlements: it strips them of the romance that might otherwise be attached to them if they were on 'cannibal' islands or in the 'hell hole of the Pacific', and it emphasises their similarity to the pitiful vagrants of Europe, who were likewise dependent on 'open charity upon the wayside' (126).[86]

Failure and impotence are the characteristics of these beachcombers. Herrick, we are told, could not hold a job because he was 'thoroughly incompetent' (126); Davis fled to the Pacific having allowed his ship, the *Sea Ranger*, to sink during a bout of drunkenness; and Huish, 'who had been employed in every store in Papeete', had been 'discharged from each in turn' (127). In the decade following *The Ebb-Tide*'s publication, this literary type of beachcomber would become familiar to the reading public. As the travel writer John Foster Fraser recorded in 'Tramps, Hobbos, and Beachcombers' (1900), the beachcomber who lived in 'the sunny islands of the Pacific, where life was drowsy, [and] the natives complacent' was 'a thing of the past' by the end of the nineteenth century. In his place was a vagrant who shuffled 'in Eastern ports, with hope bleached out of his eyes': 'He is incompetent, and a drunkard. When he picks up a job he loses it, because it is against his nature to finish it.'[87] In Joseph Conrad's *Lord Jim* (1900), it is this degraded state that Marlow fears Jim will sink into after his disgrace aboard the *Patna*. Recalling 'the circle of his wanderings' and how 'he was known successively in Bombay, in Calcutta, in Rangoon, in Penang, in Batavia', Marlow begins to imagine that he will soon 'lose his name of an inoffensive, if aggravating, fool, and acquire that of a common loafer', 'a blear-eyed, swollen-faced, besmirched loafer, with no soles to his canvas shoes'.[88] Stevenson inaugurated this type with his beachcombing trio and their hopeless narrative of enervation and failure.

As the *Saturday Review* remarked in its article 'The Ebb-Tide' (1894), the novella's plot is remarkably disjointed: its three distinct episodes on the beach of Papeete, aboard the schooner *Farallone*, and on New Island 'seem to have been designed independently of the end in view, and tend towards no tremendous culmination'.[89] This is an observation that has been developed by critics since. Contemplating the failure of the beachcombers' criminal enterprises – which include stealing the *Farallone*'s cargo of champagne, blackmailing the wine merchant who has replaced most of it with water, and murdering Attwater, their host on New Island – Vanessa Smith remarks that 'the twists of the plot offer only a series of dead-ends'.[90] This pattern of unsuccessful schemes is essential to Stevenson's portrayal of the beachcombers as incompetent, and exists in contrast with the entrepreneurial exploits of buccaneers like Bully Hayes, who, as Davis enthusiastically recalls, 'stole vessels all the time' (148). More than that, however, it embodies on a formal level the beachcombers' vagrant movement. With each plan that collapses, the momentum of the narrative dissipates and casts it adrift, or as Philip Steer puts it, 'Stevenson's broken plots build on [a] general sense of aimless mobility'.[91] Such aimlessness is compounded by the similar material conditions that the protagonists encounter in the novella's three settings. For example, the influenza epidemic that ravages Tahiti, and the outbreaks of smallpox aboard the *Farallone* and on New Island, create a ubiquity of disease that results in there being 'little sense of spatial progression in *The Ebb-Tide*', as Oliver Buckton has argued.[92] Our sense of the beachcombers' inertia is also amplified by the universal presence of the beach.

The beach is a significant topography in Stevenson's Pacific fiction. As the title might suggest, it has a prominent place in his tale 'The Beach of Falesá' (1892), where it serves as an agora for the Pacific Islanders and resident Europeans who trade manufactured goods for copra, the dried kernel of the coconut. The beach's role as a marketplace is so ingrained that the narrator of this tale, the trader John Wiltshire, refers to the standard payment for copra as 'the price of the beach'.[93] This identification of the beach with commerce is also apparent in Stevenson's fable 'The Isle of Voices' (1893), in which the sorcerer Kalamake 'can gather dollars on the beach when he pleases' by turning seashells into coins.[94] Stevenson's beach, however, is not just a site of moneymaking. As Jenn Fuller remarks, in 'The Beach of Falesá' it is also 'the environmental equivalent of hybridity' and is depicted as a scene of cultural and genetic exchange between Pacific Islanders and Europeans.[95] Wiltshire, for example, marries and then falls in love with Uma, a Line Islander, and, at the end of the story, admits that his acculturation has settled him in the Pacific for good. 'I'm stuck here, I fancy. I don't like to leave the kids.'[96] This hybridity is also evident in Stevenson's transcription of Beach-la-Mar, the pidgin English used by Uma and Wiltshire to communicate. A product of cultural collaboration, Beach-la-Mar is depicted as the lingua franca of the Pacific and identifies the beach as a place of linguistic interchange.[97]

In Stevenson's earlier Pacific fiction the beach is fecund: a place where profit, children and meaning might be made. This is not the case in *The Ebb-Tide*. Here the beach is the visible symbol of the beachcomber's impoverished and immobile state. At the risk of paradox, Stevenson equates being beached with being adrift, two conditions that capture the impotent condition of the vagrant, while expressing his futile and purposeless movement. In the first half of the novella it is the beachcombers' literal and metaphysical existence 'on the beach' that they are trying to escape. Having been hired to sail the *Farallone* from Tahiti to Australia, Davis persuades Herrick to steal the vessel and sell its consignment in Peru, because there is only 'a beach in Sydney' (148) waiting for them. Similarly, after the cargo proves worthless, he argues that they must extort money from the wine merchant in order to avoid the beach in Peru: 'don't you think you see the three of us on the beach of Callao?' (181) he asks. Nonetheless, the beach is inescapable. We are first introduced to the trio 'seated on the beach under a *purao*-tree' (123) in Tahiti, and at the end of the narrative we leave Herrick and Davis on the 'lagoon beach' (250) of New Island. In the meantime, the *Farallone* becomes a beach of their own making when they consume its small supply of champagne and most of the food aboard. After only twelve days at sea, the *Farallone*'s promise of fruitful mobility is nullified: as Davis admits having examined the stores, 'We can't look near Samoa. I don't know as we could get to Peru' (182). At this stage in the narrative, the beachcombers are adrift aboard an empty larder, and are once more metaphorically beached. As if to enforce the inescapable nature of this position, it is at this point that they sight New Island, an atoll whose 'excellently white' (187) beach literalises their position.

New Island is a paradigmatic, almost allegorical version of the beach. The island's 'presiding genius', the 'figure-head of a ship' (190), announces it as an inescapable place of deprivation as the beachcombers enter the lagoon. Fixed 'at the pier-end, with its perpetual gesture and its leprous whiteness' (190), it is an analogue for the outcast 'curiosity of Tai-o-hae' and serves as an overtly symbolic reminder of the beachcombers' condition. Its 'leprous whiteness' indicates that the island is a place of entrapment and exile like the Hawaiian leper colony, 'the Place Dolorous – Molokai', which Stevenson visited in May 1889.[98] Meanwhile, its 'perpetual gesture' suggests that the island is a place of immobilisation, especially given that its present and eternal posture is juxtaposed with a history of mobility: before becoming salvage, 'the figure-head ... had long hovered and plunged into so many running billows' (190). Acting now as the 'ensign' for New Island, however, the figure-head prepares the way for the beachcombers' discovery that the island has been marooned in a state of inactivity by smallpox. Although it is the site of Attwater's homestead, complete with 'sheds and store-houses' (189), 'a deep-veranda'ed dwelling-house' (189), a 'dozen native huts' (190) and a chapel-like 'building with a belfry' (190), the whole estate is virtually deserted: 'the house is empty and the graveyard full' (194), explains the beachcombers' sinister host, a man whose name – Attwater – suggests that he, too, shares in the beach-combers' condition of being beached, which is also being adrift.

Upon publication, critics responded to Attwater with consternation. Writing for the *Bookman*, the anonymous Y.Y. recorded that he is 'A compound of beach-comber, fine gentleman, cynic, missionary, cove-nanting fanatic, and desperado' and concluded by saying that 'he is simply impossible'.[99] Several other reviewers agreed, noting that he was completely unrealistic.[100] Since then, critics have tried to decipher what Attwater represents. For Buckton he is the English colonist 'gone native', for Edmond he is a 'modern imperialist', for Smith he is 'the figure of the missionary' and for Farrell he is a beachcomber.[101] This last interpretation, which Edmond also finds plausible, is based on Attwater's religious fanat-icism. Farrell suggests that 'R. L. S. may have drawn on the lives and deeds of beachcombers [some of whom] ... had established pseudo-Christian cults on islands in the South Seas', while Edmond goes further, arguing that Attwater is a 'fascistic version' of John Adams, one of the beachcomb-ing mutineers of the *Bounty* who established a devout Christian colony on the Pacific island of Pitcairn.[102] Although none of these readings manages to fully encompass the deliberately abstruse Attwater, they do seem to coalesce around the figure of the beachcomber. Smith's reading of Attwater as a missionary becomes effectively incorporated into Farrell and Edmond's interpretations, while Buckton's extensive treatment of Attwater as the Englishman 'gone native' again speaks to a figure who was frequently depicted as acculturated, like the 'squatting' beachcomber in Osbourne's photograph. There are also other indications that we are invited to read Attwater as a type of beachcomber.

Introduced in a chapter entitled 'The Pearl-Fisher', the original title for the novella, Attwater's main business on the island is retrieving pearls and pearl-shell from the lagoon. Indeed, the trio's plan to either kidnap or kill him is based on Davis's surmise that he has 'pearls – a ten years' collection of them' (198). For contemporaries there was a clear correlation between pearlers and beachcombers. Cooper in his survey addresses both under the chapter heading 'Pearl Fishing and "Beachcombers"', and records that beachcombers (or 'pearl robbers') cheated islanders out of their 'finest pearls for a mere song' in the pre-colonial era.[103] Similarly, in *King o' the Beach* (1899), a boys' adventure by George Manville Fenn, the titular monarch introduces himself as 'Dan Mallam, Beach-comber ..., King o' the Pearl Islands, dealer and merchant in copra, pearl shells, and pearls'. Moreover, like Attwater, who has a 'curiosity-shop of sea-curios' garnered from 'Two wrecks at least' (201), Mallam has 'played the part of wrecker for years'.[104] This is another occupation associated with the beachcomber. As *Chambers's* notes in their etymology of the term: 'Beachcomber is a word of American coinage. Primarily, it is applied to a long wave rolling in from the ocean, and from this it has come to be applied to those whose occupation it is to pick up, as pirates or wreckers, whatever these long waves wash in to them.'[105] Attwater's island employments, like his religious practice, align him with beachcombers.

That said, Attwater is clearly not a true beachcomber; he is neither a wretched vagrant nor a buccaneer. Moreover, although like the trio he is still physically 'on the beach', he is not helpless or destitute. The beach has empowered him socially and economically by allowing him to carve out his own private fiefdom and to exploit its raw materials. This is because unlike the trio who try to escape, Attwater embraces the beach. There is a symmetry between Attwater and his chosen situation on an atoll, a geographical formation that comprises a strip of beach, raised upon a coral ring, which encloses a lagoon, or as Stevenson describes them, 'water within, water without – you have the image of a perfect atoll'.[106] The atoll, then, is also 'at-water', and neatly emblematises the paradoxical position of the beachcomber. In the end, it seems that resignation to one's place on the beach becomes the means by which one transcends a beachcombing existence. This is certainly the realisation that Davis has in *The Ebb-Tide*'s final chapter. Following his 'conversion' by Attwater, and dreading the approach of the *Trinity Hall*, Attwater's ship that has been erstwhile delayed, he confides to Herrick that he would like to permanently settle on the island: 'I'd most rather stay here upon this island. I found peace here, peace in believing. Yes, I guess this island is about good enough for John Davis' (251–2).

Through Attwater and Davis, Stevenson collapses the boundary between the migratory beachcomber and the settler. In doing so, he challenges an essential tenet of the imperial ideology that was applied to the Pacific: that incoming missionaries and traders would displace the immoral and degraded beachcombers and become a civilising force within island communities. In the meantime, the beachcombers would be driven further afield, and eventually become extinct. Stevenson replaces this process of eradication and renewal with one of transformation and continuation. In what can be seen as a reappraisal of the beachcombers' pioneering status, he suggests that beachcombing is but the larval stage out of which settlement emerges. The pitiful and wretched beachcomber is the precursor of the colonist, and the moral difference between them, assumed to be so wide, is in fact, negligible.

This construction has a precedent in 'The Beach of Falesá' where Stevenson presents beachcombers and traders as belonging to a single spectrum. Uma's stepfather, a 'beachcomber' who wandered 'all over the shop' (i.e., the Pacific Islands), eventually 'got some trade' and became a small landholder. Conversely, after Wiltshire buys out the rival trading station at Falesá, its former agents become beachcombers: we are told that 'Randall and the black, they had to tramp', and that Black Jack was 'turned out of the island'.[107] This ready transition between beachcomber and trader queries the latter's legitimacy. In addition, it contributes to the presence of the dubious 'shadow empire' that Jolly identifies in both 'The Beach of Falesá' and *The Ebb-Tide*. 'Created by traders and missionaries operating outside imperial boundaries', this other empire utilises the power structures of formal British imperialism to persuade, deceive and exploit Pacific Islanders.[108] In 'The Beach of Falesá', the community of traders represents this informal empire, and its malignancy is contained only due to the efforts of a missionary, Tarleton, who ensures that British law and commercial fair play ultimately prevail.[109]

In *The Ebb-Tide*, however, Stevenson offers no such reassurance. Attwater's joint role as both a missionary and a trader confuses the 'clear-cut ideological opposition' established between these two figures in 'The Beach of Falesá', and thus further troubles the boundary between the British Empire and its errant doppelganger.[110] This line of argument is supplemented by Attwater's manifold associations with beachcombing, which breach the simple continuum between trader and beachcomber present in 'The Beach of Falesá' and suggest that the beachcomber is an agent of empire akin to the missionary, merchant and gentleman colonist that he also represents. Through these associations the beachcomber emerges as an essential figure in Stevenson's critique of empire. By co-opting a figure that emblematised both the delinquencies of the shadow empire and the pioneering spirit claimed by its counterpart, Stevenson excavates the tortured relationship that existed between these two entities. In doing so, he offers a re-evaluation of the beachcomber. Although he steadily refuses to redeem his character, Stevenson locates the beachcomber at a vital point of slippage between these two interrelated sociopolitical structures, and destabilises the opposition between vagabonds and settlers in the process.

Notes

1 Steven Roger Fischer, *A History of the Pacific Islands*, 2nd ed. (Basingstoke: Palgrave, 2013), p. xvii.
2 Rod Edmond, *Leprosy and Empire: A Medical and Cultural History* (Cambridge: Cambridge University Press, 2006), p. 143.

3 Sean O'Toole, *The History of Australian Corrections* (Sydney: UNSW Press, 2006), pp. 36–7.
4 Fischer, *Pacific Islands*, pp. 161–2.
5 Edmond, *Leprosy and Empire*, pp. 146–7.
6 I. C. Campbell, *Worlds Apart: A History of the Pacific Islands*, revised ed. (Christchurch: Canterbury University Press, 2003), pp. 68–76; Fischer, *Pacific Islands*, pp. 97–104.
7 Rod Edmond, *Representing the South Pacific: Colonial Discourse from Cook to Gauguin* (Cambridge: Cambridge University Press, 1997), pp. 67, 73–5.
8 Litton Forbes, *Two Years in Fiji* (London: Longman, Green, 1875), p. 277.
9 Ibid., p. 278.
10 Edward Jerningham Wakefield, *Adventure in New Zealand, from 1839 to 1844; with some Account of the Beginning of the British Colonization of the Islands*, 2 vols (London: John Murray, 1845), I, pp. 338–9.
11 Campbell, *Worlds Apart*, p. 77; Caroline Ralston, *Grass Huts and Warehouses: Pacific Beach Communities of the Nineteenth Century* (Honolulu: University of Hawai'i Press, 1978; repr. St Lucia: UQ ePress, 2014), pp. 21–3, 40; Vanessa Smith, *Literary Culture and the Pacific: Nineteenth-Century Textual Encounters* (Cambridge: Cambridge University Press, 1998), p. 19.
12 Campbell, *Worlds Apart*, pp. 117, 68–71; Fischer, *Pacific Islands*, pp. 102–4, 167–9, 97–8.
13 Jocelyn Linnekin, 'New Political Orders', in *The Cambridge History of the Pacific Islanders*, ed. Donald Denoon et al. (Cambridge: Cambridge University Press, 1997), pp. 185–217 (pp. 189–90); Ralston, *Grass Huts*, pp. 21–3, 29–32.
14 Edmond, *Representing the South Pacific*, pp. 70–2.
15 Campbell, *Worlds Apart*, pp. 156–8; Ralston, *Grass Huts*, pp. 21–3.
16 Ralston, *Grass Huts*, pp. 24–5.
17 William Diapea, *Cannibal Jack: The True Autobiography of a White Man in the South Seas*, ed. James Hadfield (London: Faber & Gwyer, 1928), pp. 90–1, 6.
18 Gillian Beer, 'Island Bounds', in *Islands in History and Representation*, ed. Rod Edmond and Vanessa Smith (London: Routledge, 2003), pp. 32–42 (p. 33).
19 Epeli Hau'ofa, *We Are the Ocean: Selected Works* (Honolulu: University of Hawai'i Press, 2008), p. 34.
20 Greg Dening, *Islands and Beaches: Discourse on a Silent Land, Marquesas 1774–1880* (Honolulu: University of Hawai'i Press, 1980), pp. 135–6; Ralston, *Grass Huts*, p. 27.
21 For Fijian trades, see Campbell, *Worlds Apart*, pp. 71–6; for beachcomber populations, see Ralston, *Grass Huts*, pp. 21–23.
22 Dening, *Islands and Beaches*, p. 130.
23 Herman Melville, *Omoo: A Narrative of Adventures in the South Seas*, ed. Mary K. Bercaw Edwards (London: Penguin, 2007), p. 248.
24 J. Kēhaulani Kauanui, *Paradoxes of Hawaiian Sovereignty: Land, Sex, and the Colonial Politics of State Nationalism* (Durham, NC: Duke University Press, 2018), p. 129.

25 Campbell, *Worlds Apart*, pp. 156–8.
26 Ibid., pp. 76–77; Ralston, *Grass Huts*, p. 40.
27 Edmond, *Representing the South Pacific*, p. 63.
28 Fischer, *Pacific Islands*, p. 114; Smith, *Literary Culture and the Pacific*, pp. 46–51.
29 Campbell, *Worlds Apart*, p. 77.
30 'Beach-Combers', *Standard*, 21 December 1883, p. 2.
31 'Gift Books for the Young', *Daily News*, 11 November 1890, p. 7.
32 Campbell, *Worlds Apart*, pp. 100–6, 167.
33 Fischer, *Pacific Islands*, p. 173.
34 Campbell, *Worlds Apart*, pp. 174–80; Stuart Ward, 'Security: Defending Australia's Empire', in *Australia's Empire*, ed. Deryck M. Schreuder and Stuart Ward (Oxford: Oxford University Press, 2008), pp. 232–58 (pp. 235–40).
35 Campbell, *Worlds Apart*, pp. 167–76.
36 Ibid., pp. 131, 165; Fischer, *Pacific Islands*, p. 171.
37 'Isles of Eden', *Chambers's [Edinburgh] Journal*, 18 May 1872, pp. 315–18 (p. 316).
38 'The Kermadecs', *Chambers's [Edinburgh] Journal*, 2 April 1887, pp. 214–15.
39 H. Stonehewer Cooper, *The Coral Lands of the Pacific: Their Peoples and Their Products*, 2nd ed. (London: Richard Bentley and Son, 1882), pp. 261–2.
40 Campbell, *Worlds Apart*, pp. 174–6.
41 'The Buccaneers of the Pacific', *Western Daily Press*, 8 November 1882, p. 7.
42 'Beach-Combers', p. 2.
43 'A Nineteenth-Century Pirate', *Chambers's [Edinburgh] Journal*, 27 November 1886, pp. 762–4 (p. 762).
44 'Packet Rats and Beachcombers', *Pall Mall Gazette*, 3 July 1879, pp. 11–12 (p. 11).
45 'Beach-Combers', p. 2.
46 'Beachcombers', *Chambers's [Edinburgh] Journal*, 5 February 1881, pp. 81–3 (p. 81).
47 Patrick Brantlinger, *Dark Vanishings: Discourse on the Extinction of Primitive Races, 1800–1930* (Ithaca, NY: Cornell University Press, 2003), pp. 2–9.
48 Forbes, *Two Years in Fiji*, pp. 223–5.
49 Frederick J. Moss, *Through Atolls and Islands in the Great South Sea* (London: Sampson Low, Marston, Searle, & Rivington, 1889), pp. 60, 69.
50 Cooper, *The Coral Lands*, p. 262.
51 Ibid., p. 261.
52 'Beachcombers', pp. 83, 81.
53 Forbes, *Two Years in Fiji*, p. 224.
54 Neil Rennie, *Far-Fetched Facts: The Literature of Travel and the Idea of the South Seas* (Oxford: Clarendon Press, 1995), pp. 1–29.
55 'Books of the Season', *Lloyd's Weekly*, 2 November 1890, p. 7; 'Christmas Books', *Saturday Review*, 6 December 1890, pp. 657–9 (p. 658); also 'Gift Books for the Young', p. 7.

56 Edward Ellis, *Lost in Samoa: A Tale of Adventure in the Navigator Islands* (London: Cassell, 1890), pp. 6, 1–3.

57 Joseph Farrell, *Robert Louis Stevenson in Samoa* (London: MacLehose Press, 2017), pp. 93–4.

58 Charles Reade, 'Preface' [1868], in *Hard Cash: A Matter-of-Fact Romance* (London: Chatto & Windus, 1898), p. 3.

59 'Juvenile Literature', *St. James's Gazette*, 21 November 1889, p. 20.

60 Gilbert Bishop, *The Beachcombers; or, Slave Trading under the Union Jack* (London: Ward & Downey, 1889), pp. 95, 11, 218, 265.

61 Bishop, *The Beachcombers*, p. 288.

62 'The Head-Hunters of the Solomon Islands', *All the Year Round*, 20 September 1890, pp. 279–84 (p. 284); J. F. Hogan, 'A Secret of the Solomon Islands', *Chambers's [Edinburgh] Journal*, 23 September 1893, pp. 593–6 (p. 595).

63 Germany claimed the northern Solomon Islands in 1886. Campbell, *Worlds Apart*, p. 148.

64 Campbell, *Worlds Apart*, pp. 145–8.

65 Maile Arvin, *Possessing Polynesians: The Science of Settler Colonial Whiteness in Hawai'i and Oceania* (Durham, NC: Duke University Press, 2019), pp. 3–4, 28–9, 36–40.

66 Bishop, *The Beachcombers*, p. 18.

67 V. L. Cameron, 'How Jack Hawker Met His Bride', *Dundee Evening Telegraph*, 8 August 1891, p. 4.

68 Hugh Romilly, 'A Tale of the South Seas', *Illustrated Sporting and Dramatic News*, 14 February 1891, pp. 767–70 (p. 767).

69 Robert Louis Stevenson, *The Letters of Robert Louis Stevenson*, ed. Bradford A. Booth and Ernest Mehew, 8 vols (New Haven, CT: Yale University Press, 1995), VII, p. 161.

70 Stevenson, *Letters*, VI, p. 299.

71 Fanny Van de Grift Stevenson, *The Cruise of the 'Janet Nichol' among the South Seas: A Diary by Mrs Robert Louis Stevenson* (New York: Charles Scribner's Sons, 1914), p. 55. Although Fanny Stevenson always spelt the name of the schooner *Janet Nichol*, it was in fact spelt *Janet Nicoll*.

72 Roslyn Jolly, 'Introduction', in *The Cruise of the 'Janet Nichol' among the South Seas: A Diary by Mrs Robert Louis Stevenson*, ed. Roslyn Jolly (Sydney: UNSW Press, 2004), pp. 13–43 (p. 27).

73 Jolly, 'Introduction', pp. 24–32; Farrell, *Stevenson in Samoa*, pp. 59–64.

74 Stevenson, *Letters*, VI, p. 327.

75 Stevenson, *Cruise of the 'Janet Nichol'*, pp. 120–1, 39–40.

76 Ibid., p. 40.

77 Robert Louis Stevenson, *In the South Seas*, in *In the South Seas and Island Nights' Entertainments* (London: J. M. Dent & Sons, 1925), pp. 5–230 (pp. 10, 47).

78 Robert Louis Stevenson and Lloyd Osbourne, *The Wrecker* (London: Oxford University Press, 1950), p. 2.

79 Stevenson, *In the South Seas*, p. 70.

80 Stevenson, *Letters*, VI, p. 330.

81 Robert Louis Stevenson and Lloyd Osbourne, *The Ebb-Tide: A Trio and Quartette*, in *South Sea Tales*, ed. Roslyn Jolly (Oxford: Oxford University Press, 1996; repr. 2008), pp. 123–252 (p. 136). Future references will be made to this edition and in the text; Stevenson, *Letters*, VIII, p. 158.

82 Stevenson, *Letters*, VI, p. 330.

83 Fanny Stevenson, 'Preface', in Stevenson, *The Cruise of the 'Janet Nichol'*, pp. v–vii (p. v).

84 'Beach, n. 3.b', *OED Online* (accessed 19 October 2017).

85 'Fiction', *The Speaker*, 29 September 1894, pp. 362–3 (p. 362).

86 Edmond, *Representing the South Pacific*, p. 180.

87 John Foster Fraser, 'Vagabond Notes: Tramps, Hobbos, and Beachcombers', *Barnsley Chronicle*, 1 December 1900, p. 2.

88 Joseph Conrad, *Lord Jim: A Tale*, ed. Jacques Berthoud (Oxford: Oxford University Press, 2008), pp. 4, 142, 144, 162.

89 'The Ebb-Tide', *Saturday Review*, 22 September 1894, p. 330.

90 Smith, *Literary Culture and the Pacific*, p. 160.

91 Philip Steer, 'Romances of Uneven Development: Spatiality, Trade, and Form in Robert Louis Stevenson's Pacific Novels', *Victorian Literature and Culture*, 43 (2015), 343–56 (p. 351).

92 Oliver S. Buckton, *Cruising with Robert Louis Stevenson: Travel, Narrative, and the Colonial Body* (Athens: Ohio University Press, 2007), p. 268.

93 Robert Louis Stevenson, 'The Beach at Falesá', in Jolly, ed., *South Sea Tales*, pp. 3–71 (p. 58).

94 Robert Louis Stevenson, 'The Isle of Voices', in Jolly, ed., *South Sea Tales*, pp. 103–22 (p. 108).

95 Jenn Fuller, *Dark Paradise: Pacific Islands in the Nineteenth-Century British Imagination* (Edinburgh: Edinburgh University Press, 2016), p. 127.

96 Stevenson, 'The Beach at Falesá', p. 71.

97 As Roslyn Jolly notes in her edition of the text, Beach-la-Mar should be associated with Melanesia rather than Polynesia, but Stevenson thought of it as the lingua franca of the whole Pacific. Rosyln Jolly, 'Explanatory Notes', in Jolly, ed., *South Sea Tales*, pp. 259–89 (p. 264).

98 Stevenson, *In the South Seas*, p. 78.

99 Y.Y., 'The Ebb-Tide', *Bookman*, October 1894, pp. 19–20 (p. 20).

100 See 'Richard le Gallienne', in *Robert Louis Stevenson: The Critical Heritage*, ed. Paul Maixner (London: Routledge & Kegan Paul, 1981), pp. 455–7 (p. 456); Percy Addleshaw, 'The Ebb-Tide', *Academy*, 13 October 1894, p. 272.

101 Buckton, *Cruising with Robert Louis Stevenson*, pp. 171–9, 246; Smith, *Literary Culture and the Pacific*, p. 161; Edmond, *Representing the South Pacific*, p. 182.

102 Farrell, *Stevenson in Samoa*, p. 301; Edmond, *Representing the South Pacific*, pp. 182–4.

103 Cooper, *The Coral Lands*, p. 252.

104 George Manville Fenn, *King o' the Beach: A Tropic Tale* (London: Ernest Nister, [1899]), pp. 181, 199.

105 'Beachcombers', p. 81.

106 Stevenson, *In the South Seas*, p. 100.

107 Stevenson, 'The Beach at Falesá', pp. 30, 70.

108 Roslyn Jolly, 'Piracy, Slavery, and the Imagination of Empire in Stevenson's Pacific Fiction', *Victorian Literature and Culture*, 35 (2007), 157–73 (p. 157).

109 Ibid., pp. 161–6.

110 Ibid., pp. 165–9.

Afterword: London 1902

In August 1902 Jack London dressed himself as an 'American waif, down on his luck', and embarked on an undercover investigation of the East End. 'I wish to know how those people are living there, and why they are living there, and what they are living for. In short, I am going to live there myself', he explained in *The People of the Abyss* (1903). Inhabitation would bring revelation, London thought, and in this belief he was not alone. Although the Californian framed his adventure as a pioneering enterprise, he was one of many social explorers who participated in a tradition of cross-class dress in order to understand how the poor lived. James Greenwood, 'The Amateur Casual', inaugurated this method in 1866, and it soon spread across the Atlantic. By the mid-1890s the American-born investigators Elizabeth Banks and Josiah Flynt were also going incognito among the poor of London for journalistic and sociological purposes. What Greenwood's disciples 'discovered' was often portrayed as an exotic underworld populated by a savage species. Describing his first impression of the East End, Jack recalled that 'The streets were filled with a new and different race of people, short of stature, and of wretched or beer-sodden appearance.'[1] And later, he determined that 'the city poor folk are a nomadic breed', a statement that equated mobility and savagery, and which echoed Henry Mayhew's famous division of mankind into 'two distinct and broadly marked races': 'the wanderers and the settlers – the vagabond and the citizen – the nomadic and the civilized tribes'.[2] For Mayhew as for Jack, the metropolitan poor, 'the beggars – the prostitutes – the street-sellers – the street-performers', belonged to 'the nomadic races of England'.[3]

Jack's racial conception of the poor was also registered in his title, *The People of the Abyss*, a phrase lifted from H. G. Wells's *Anticipations* (1901).[4] In this forecast of the future Wells predicted the formation of two classes: the elite New Republicans and the 'great useless masses', 'the people of no account whatever, the classes of extinction, the People of the Abyss'.

Composed of the 'multiplying rejected of the white and yellow civiliza-tions' and 'a vast proportion of the black and brown races', the People of the Abyss were imagined in racist terms as humanity's dross, and Wells envisaged eugenic measures to extirpate them: 'the nation that most resolutely picks over, educates, sterilizes, exports, or poisons its People of the Abyss' will be dominant by the year 2000, he foretold.[5] These responses may have appealed to Jack. In the months immediately preced-ing his journey to London he was working on *The Kempton–Wace Letters* (1903), an epistolary novel co-authored with Anna Strunsky that charted a debate between an economist and a poet about marriage, love and repro-duction. London's half of the correspondence, written from the perspec-tive of the economist Herbert Wace, displays a Wellsian fervour for 'stirpiculture' (selective breeding) and the time when mankind will 'control and direct the operation of the reproductive force so that life will not only be perpetuated but developed and made higher and finer'.[6] This eugenic fantasy threatens to take a darker turn in *The People of the Abyss*. Contemplating the high mortality of casual paupers, Jack welcomes and rationalises their demise: 'These men of the spike, the peg, and the street, are encumbrances. They are of no good or use to any one, nor to themselves. They clutter the earth with their presence, and are better out of the way.'[7]

Jack's characterisation of the East End's 'nomads' as 'a new species', a description that rings with both racial and scientific connotations, mir-rored the perspective of many of his British contemporaries.[8] In *In Darkest London* (1889), for example, Margaret Harkness identified the loafer as a new human type that was ripe for scientific analysis: 'The loafer's mind is unknown as yet to psychologists', she wrote. 'It is the mind of a parasite, the creature who is content to exist on other people.'[9] These portrayals of the vagrant were enabled by the racialisation of the poor, an imaginative and quasi-scientific tradition that began in the mid-nineteenth century and served as a conduit for racial theories. Among these was extermination theory. Used to interpret 'primitive' nomads such as English Gypsies and indigenous Americans from the early 1800s, it was later applied to white beachcombers in the fin de siècle. Other racial theories included the theory of degeneration, which became inflected by social Darwinist and eugenic thought in the late Victorian period. This had a severe impact on the portrayal of loafers and the so-called residuum. The idea that the urban poor were biologically unfit, and an internal threat to the Anglo-Saxons – the 'imperial race' – allowed them to be characterised as a social excrescence that was malign and politically dangerous.

This resulted in dystopian speculations about human degeneration as well as a range of proposals that lobbied for their segregation and sterilisation.

However, although the discourse of vagrancy gained an increasingly scientific flavour during the nineteenth century, these ideas were seldomly applied with consistency. The racial theories discussed in this study were activated for rhetorical and representational purposes in the literature and journalism of the period, but they rarely betokened a firm understanding or zealous belief. George Borrow subscribed to the notion that English Gypsies might disappear due to miscegenation in *The Romany Rye* (1857), but he nonetheless depicted a flourishing Gypsy culture. Literary and cultural representations of vagrants were often ambiguous and refused to be solely governed by such theories, and in many instances scientific explanations were entirely absent. This is the case in several of the major canonical works analysed in this study: Charles Dickens's *The Chimes* (1844), Charles Kingsley's *Yeast* (1848), Luke Fildes's *Applicants for Admission to a Casual Ward* (1874) and Robert Louis Stevenson's *The Ebb-Tide* (1894). Furthermore, the portrayal of vagrants in the Victorian period was still reliant upon ancient prejudices and moral frameworks inherited from the medieval and early modern past. The most potent of these was the dichotomy of the deserving and undeserving poor. Circulating globally as well as locally, it influenced the portrayal of the casual queue in the British metropolis and was used to differentiate between the worthy immigrant in antebellum America and the anarchic vagabond who was drawn towards its frontiers. It was also integral to the representation of the American Indian, a figure that exemplifies the elasticity of the discourse of vagrancy, and how it could be deployed well beyond the parochial boundaries of Britain.

Understanding transatlantic and imperial conceptions of vagrancy is vital to our overall comprehension of vagrancy in nineteenth-century British culture, and this study has broached new ground by revealing how representations of vagrancy on the frontier interlocked with those of rural and urban Britain. This contributes to the recent work of Hidetaka Hirota and Kristin O'Brassill-Kulfan, who have discussed how legal and moral strategies for defining vagrants were exported from Britain to America; however, a considerable amount of scholarship remains to be done in this field, as the writings of Jack London suggest. His portrayal of the vagrant poor as a race apart, his subscription to eugenic and social Darwinist thought, and his mode of inquiry through cross-class dress demonstrates a strong correspondence between how the British and the

Americans approached, understood and imagined vagrants at the turn of the twentieth century. It is also clear that London assumed the same taxonomic thinking that structured British representations of vagrants throughout the Victorian period. In *The People of the Abyss* he differentiated the stranded American sailor 'on the beach', the 'American tramp royal' dedicated to life on the road, and the 'discouraged vagabond', the casual pauper who would work if he could but is too mentally, physically or morally unfit to do so.[10] Meanwhile, the beachcomber is a recurring figure in his Pacific tales. Stories such as 'The House of Pride' (1912) and 'The Seed of McCoy' (1911) open up questions about how vagrant types were translated from one literary culture to another, and to what extent they were understood in similar terms.

London's use of photographs to supplement the narrative of *The People of the Abyss* also alerts us to an emerging transatlantic tradition of representation. Lloyd Osbourne (also born in California) took photographs of beachcombers in the Pacific Islands, while Wells (as I argued in Chapter 4) adopted the photographic vision of the social explorer when describing the Morlock's lair in *The Time Machine* (1895). Flash photography became a popular tool of journalists and sociologists writing about vagrants in the late nineteenth century after Jacob Riis used it in his investigation of slum life in New York City, *How the Other Half Lives* (1890). As Tim Cresswell observes, the photographs that Riis produced were 'surveilling, voyeuristic and objectifying' and served to provide readers with '"scientific" evidence of tramp life'.[11] The pictures that London included in *The People of the Abyss* had the same purpose. Many of them were of anonymous homeless men and women in various stages of decrepitude and exhaustion. They were not designed to capture the individual lives and characters of the sitters, some of whom were photographed from afar or while asleep. Instead, they were supposed to inventory the life of the typical London vagrant and to confirm Jack's verdict that they 'live worse than the beasts, and have less to eat and wear and protect them from the elements than the savage Innuit'.[12]

However, not all of London's subjects could be conscripted into this narrative. 'Men Waiting Outside Whitechapel Workhouse' (1902) makes this evident (see Figure 7.1). The photograph depicts a file of men lined up against the wall of a utilitarian building that has 'casual ward' written above the door and a neat, well-groomed porter to guard it. This, of course, is the casual line for the workhouse, an image that was used to evoke the difficulty of sifting the deserving from the undeserving poor by Kingsley, Dickens and Fildes. For Jack, the scene was supposed to provide documentary evidence for his own stay in the same workhouse and to confirm

Figure 7.1.   Jack London, 'Men Waiting Outside Whitechapel Workhouse' (1902). JLP
466 Alb. 28, Jack London Papers, The Huntington Library, San Marino, California

the character of the men that he met there: 'poor, wretched beasts,
inarticulate and callous, but for all of that, in many ways very human'.[13]
But the men in the street refused to validate this assertion. Pinned outside
the casual ward by the promise of food and shelter, and unable to leave the
queue least they forfeit their night's respite, they were forced by circumstances to assume the position of casual paupers. Nonetheless, despite this
constraint, many near the front of the line, closest to the camera, chose to
cover their faces or turn to the wall, asserting their right to privacy. Their
actions put the cameraman to shame.

In one of his photograph albums, underneath another photograph of
the casual line, London wrote, 'casuals have a distinct objection to being
photographed, & turn their bodies directly they see the camera'.[14]
Unsurprisingly, neither this image nor 'Men Waiting Outside
Whitechapel Workhouse' was included in *The People of the Abyss*.
Instead, London chose an unpopulated picture of Poplar Workhouse,
taken from the outside, and an empty ward, two blank canvases onto

which the reader could project the casual paupers that he described. These did not baffle Jack's claim that he won the sympathy of working-class London, that 'when loungers and workmen . . . talked with me, they talked as one man to another, and they talked as natural men should'.[15] They did not articulate the gulf that existed between the social explorer and his subject of study. 'Men Waiting Outside Whitechapel Workhouse' provides an eloquent rebuttal to Jack's boast, and to many of the sources examined in this book, most of which were penned by middle-class observers with no real comprehension of the lived experience of vagrancy. It also helps to qualify what this study might lose sight of in its analysis of literary and cultural representation: that beyond the stereotypes of lawlessness, licentiousness, idleness and deceitfulness; beyond the dichotomy of the deserving and the undeserving poor; beyond the taxonomies dividing Gypsies from loafers and casuals from beachcombers; beyond the theories of race, society and environment; beyond all of these were individuals living complicated and precarious lives that could not be faithfully distilled into neat categories and easy definitions.

Notes

1 Jack London, *The People of the Abyss*, 2nd ed. (London: Hesperus Press, 2013), p. 8.

2 Ibid., p. 22; Henry Mayhew, *London Labour and the London Poor: A Cyclopaedia of the Condition and Earnings of Those That Will Work, Those That Cannot Work, and Those That Will Not Work*, 4 vols (London: Frank Cass, 1967), I, p. 1.

3 Mayhew, *London Labour and the London Poor*, I, p. 2.

4 It seems unlikely that London did not know that 'People of the Abyss' was a phrase coined by Wells. Not only does *The Time Machine* appear to have been London's inspiration for his investigation of the East End, as Bivona and Henkle claim, but Wells and London shared the same publisher: Macmillan. The firm published both *Anticipations* and *The People of the Abyss*. Dan Bivona and Roger B. Henkle, *The Imagination of Class: Masculinity and the Victorian Urban Poor* (Columbus: Ohio State University Press, 2006), p. 164. On the publication of *Anticipations*, see H. G. Wells, *An Experiment in Autobiography: Discoveries and Conclusions of a Very Ordinary Brain (since 1866)*, 2 vols (London: Faber and Faber, 2008), II, p. 646; on the publication of *The People of the Abyss*, see Earle Labor, *Jack London: An American Life* (New York: Farrar, Straus and Giroux, 2013), pp. 167–8.

5 H. G. Wells, *Anticipations of the Reaction of Mechanical and Scientific Progress upon Human Life and Thought*, 3rd ed. (London: Chapman & Hall, 1902), pp. 211–12, 227–8, 280.

6 Jack London and Anna Strunsky, *The Kempton–Wace Letters* (London: Mills & Boon, [1924]), p. 146. On the composition of *The Kempton–Wave Letters*, see Labor, *Jack London*, p. 146.

7 London, *The People of the Abyss*, p. 76.

8 Ibid., p. 200.

9 Margaret Harkness, *In Darkest London* (Cambridge: Black Apollo Press, 2003), p. 13.

10 London, *The People of the Abyss*, pp. 90–1, 139–40.

11 Tim Cresswell, *The Tramp in America* (London: Reaktion Books, 2001), pp. 178, 188.

12 London, *The People of the Abyss*, p. 223.

13 Ibid., p. 68.

14 'Girl Waiting before Whitechapel Workhouse', JLP 466 Alb. 28, Jack London Papers, Huntington Library, San Marino, CA.

15 London, *The People of the Abyss*, p. 13.

Bibliography

Primary Sources

Addleshaw, Percy, 'The Ebb-Tide', *Academy*, 13 October 1894, p. 272

Adolphus, John *Observations on the Vagrant Act, and Some Other Statutes, and on the Power and Duties of Justices of the Peace* (London: John Major, 1824)

[Advertisements], *Examiner*, 25 December 1841, pp. 630–2

'America and Her Slave States. No. III', *Sharpe's London Magazine*, 10 January 1846, pp. 163–5

The American Almanac and Repository of Useful Knowledge, for the Year 1838 (Boston: Charles Bowen, [1839])

[Anon.] A Barrister, *The Vagrant Act, in Relation to the Liberty of the Subject*, 2nd ed. (London: John Murray, 1824)

[Anon.] J.P.P.C., 'The Norwood Gypsies', *Literary Lounger*, February 1826, pp. 88–96

[Anon.] M.A., 'A Night in the Casual Ward of the Work-House, in Rhyme: Dedicated to the Million', in *Vicarious Vagrants: Incognito Social Explorers and the Homeless in England, 1860–1910*, ed. Mark Freeman and Gillian Nelson (Lambertville, NJ: True Bill Press, 2008) pp. 76–80

[Anon.] N.W., 'The Poacher', *New Sporting Magazine*, February 1841, pp. 127–30

[Anon.] N.W., 'The Poacher', *New Sporting Magazine*, April 1841, pp. 257–62

[Anon.] Y.Y., 'The Ebb-Tide', *Bookman*, October 1894, pp. 19–20

Arch, Joseph, *The Story of His Life: Told by Himself* (London: Hutchinson, 1898; repr. Garland, 1984)

Arnold, Matthew, 'Sohrab and Rustum', in *The Poems of Matthew Arnold*, ed. Miriam Allott, 2nd ed. (London: Longman, 1979), pp. 319–55

Banks, Elizabeth L., 'Sweeping a Crossing', in *Campaigns of Curiosity: Journalistic Adventures of an American Girl in Late Victorian London* (Madison: University of Wisconsin Press, 2003), pp. 129–38

Barlie, Ellen, *Our Homeless Poor: And What We Can Do to Help Them* (London: James Nisbet, 1860)

Barnett, Samuel, 'The Abodes of the Homeless', *Cornhill Magazine*, July 1899, pp. 58–64

'A Scheme for the Unemployed', *Nineteenth Century*, November 1888, pp. 753–63

Barrère, Albert, and Charles Leland, *A Dictionary of Slang, Jargon & Cant, Embracing English, American, and Anglo-Indian Slang, Pidgin English, Tinkers' Jargon and Other Irregular Phraseology*, 2 vols ([Edinburgh]: Ballantyne Press, 1889)

'Beach-Combers', *Standard*, 21 December 1883, p. 2

'Beachcombers', *Chambers's [Edinburgh] Journal*, 5 February 1881, pp. 81–3

'Beggars and Almsgivers', *New Monthly Magazine*, March 1849, pp. 301–6

Bellamy, Edward, *Looking Backward: 2000–1887*, ed. Matthew Beaumont (Oxford: Oxford University Press, 2007)

Bishop, Gilbert, *The Beachcombers; or, Slave Trading under the Union Jack* (London: Ward & Downey, 1889)

Bodkin, W. H., *The First Report of the Society Established in London for the Suppression of Mendicity* (London: J. W. Whitely, 1819)

The Fourth Report of the Society for the Suppression of Mendicity Established in London (London: F. Warr, 1822)

'Books of the Season', *Lloyd's Weekly*, 2 November 1890, p. 7

Booth, Charles, *Life and Labour of the People in London: First Series: Poverty*, revised ed., 5 vols (London: Macmillan, 1902; repr. Augustus M. Kelley, 1969)

Booth, William, *In Darkest England and the Way Out* (London: International Headquarters of the Salvation Army, 1890; repr. Cambridge: Cambridge University Press, 2014)

Borrow, George, *The Bible in Spain; or, The Journeys, Adventures, and Imprisonments of an Englishman in an Attempt to Circulate the Scriptures in the Peninsula*, ed. Ulick Ralph Burke (London: John Murray, 1905; repr. 1928)

George Borrow's Tour of Galloway and the Borders 1866, ed. Angus Fraser (Wallingford: Lavengro Press, 2015)

Lavengro (London: Heron Books, 1969)

Romano Lavo-Lil: Word-Book of the Romany (London: John Murray, 1874)

The Romany Rye (London: Heron Books, 1970)

Wild Wales: Its People, Language and Scenery (London: Collins, 1965)

The Zincali: An Account of the Gypsies of Spain, 9th ed. (London: John Murray, 1901; repr. 1907)

'Borrow and Lavengro', *New Monthly Magazine*, April 1851, pp. 455–61

'The Buccaneers of the Pacific', *Western Daily Press*, 8 November 1882, p. 7

Buller, Charles, 'Official Enforcement of the Distinction between Vagrancy and Destitution', *Spectator*, 4 November 1848, pp. 1059–60

Burleigh, Bennet, 'The Unemployed', *Contemporary Review*, July 1887, pp. 771–80

Cameron, V. L., 'How Jack Hawker Met His Bride', *Dundee Evening Telegraph*, 8 August 1891, p. 4

Carew, Charlton, *The Poacher's Wife: A Story of the Times*, 2 vols (London: Charles Ollier, 1847)

Carlyle, Thomas, *The French Revolution*, 3 vols (London: Folio Society, 1989)

Past and Present, ed. Chris R. Vanden Bossche (Berkeley: University of California Press, 2005)

'The Present Time', in *Carlyle's Latter-Day Pamphlets*, ed. M. K. Goldberg and J. P. Seigel (Ottawa: Canadian Federation for the Humanities, 1983), pp. 3–60

'Signs of the Times', in *Thomas Carlyle: Selected Writings*, ed. Alan Shelston (Harmondsworth: Penguin, 1971), pp. 59–85

'Carnival or Pandemonium', *Hampshire Advertiser*, 3 November 1900, p. 5

'The Casual Poor', *London City Press*, 9 November 1861, p. 4

'Casual Wards', *Pall Mall Gazette*, 16 January 1866, pp. 1–2

Catlin, George, *Letters and Notes on the Manners, Customs, and Conditions of the North American Indians*, 2 vols (London: George Catlin, 1841)

Chadwick, Edwin, *Report on the Sanitary Condition of the Labouring Population of Great Britain*, ed. David Gadstone (London: Routledge/Thoemmes, 1997)

'Cheap Jack', *Chambers's [Edinburgh] Journal*, 10 October 1846, pp. 236–8

'Christmas Books', *Saturday Review*, 6 December 1890, pp. 657–9

Clare, John, *John Clare by Himself*, ed. Eric Robinson and David Powell (Ashington: Carcanet Press, 1996)

'Cleveland – The Poacher's Wife', *Spectator*, 13 March 1847, pp. 256–7

Cobbett, William, *Rural Rides* (Harmondsworth: Penguin, 1985)

Conrad, Joseph, *Lord Jim: A Tale*, ed. Jacques Berthoud (Oxford: Oxford University Press, 2008)

Cooper, H. Stonehewer, *The Coral Lands of the Pacific: Their Peoples and Their Products*, 2nd ed. (London: Richard Bentley and Son, 1882)

Crabb, James, *The Gipsies' Advocate; or, Observations on the Origin, Character, Manner, and Habits of The English Gipsies*, 2nd ed. (London: Lindsay, 1831)

Dawson, William Harbutt, *The Vagrancy Problem: The Case for Measures of Restraint for Tramps, Loafers, and Unemployables, with a Study of Continental Detention Colonies and Labour Houses* (London: P. S. King, 1910)

A Descriptive Catalogue of Catlin's Indian Gallery: Containing Portraits, Landscapes, Costumes, &c. and Representations of the Manners and Customs of the North American Indians (London: C. Adlard, [1840])

Diapea, William, *Cannibal Jack: The True Autobiography of a White Man in the South Seas*, ed. James Hadfield (London: Faber & Gwyer, 1928)

Dickens, Charles, *American Notes for General Circulation*, ed. Patricia Ingham (London: Penguin, 2004)

Bleak House, ed. Nicola Bradbury (London: Penguin, 1996; repr. 2003)

The Chimes: A Goblin Story; or, Some Bells that Rang an Old Year Out and a New One In, in *Christmas Books*, intro. Eleanor Farjeon (Oxford: Oxford University Press, 1954; repr. 1997), pp. 77–154

The Cricket on the Hearth: A Fairy Tale of Home, in *Christmas Books*, intro. Eleanor Farjeon (Oxford: Oxford University Press, 1954; repr. 1997), pp. 156–234

Doctor Marigold's Prescriptions, ed. Melissa Valiska and Melisa Klimaszewski (London: Hesperus Press, 2007)

Great Expectations, ed. Charlotte Mitchell (London: Penguin, 2003)

The Mystery of Edwin Drood, ed. Matthew Pearl (London: Vintage, 2009)

'A Nightly Scene in London', *Household Words*, 26 January 1856, pp. 25–7

Oliver Twist, ed. Philip Horne (London: Penguin, 2003)

The Pilgrim Edition of the Letters of Charles Dickens, ed. Madeline House, Graham Storey and Kathleen Tillotson, 12 vols (Oxford: Oxford University Press, 1965–2002)

The Posthumous Papers of the Pickwick Club, intro. Peter Washington (London: Everyman, 1998)

'The Uncommercial Traveller', *All the Year Round*, 28 January 1860, pp. 321–6

'The Uncommercial Traveller', *All the Year Round*, 16 June 1860, pp. 230–4

Doyle, Arthur Conan, 'The Five Orange Pips', in *The Adventures of Sherlock Holmes*, ed. Richard Lancelyn Green (Oxford: Oxford University Press, 1993; repr. 2008), pp. 102–22

'The Ebb-Tide', *Saturday Review*, 22 September 1894, p. 330

Eliot, George, *Adam Bede*, ed. Margaret Reynolds (London: Penguin, 2008)

Middlemarch: A Study of Provincial Life, ed. Rosemary Ashton (London: Penguin, 1994; repr. 2003)

The Mill on the Floss, ed. A. S. Byatt (London: Penguin, 2003)

'The Natural History of German Life', in *Selected Essays, Poems and Other Writings*, ed. A. S. Byatt (London: Penguin, 1990), pp. 107–39

Ellis, Edward, *Lost in Samoa: A Tale of Adventure in the Navigator Islands* (London: Cassell, 1890)

'English Ballad-Singers', *New Monthly Magazine*, January 1822, pp. 212–17

'The English Gypsies', *Penny Magazine*, 20 January 1838, pp. 17–19

'An Experience on C. I. V. Day', *Outlook*, 3 November 1900, p. 429

Featherstonehaugh, G. W., *Excursion through the Slave States, from Washington on the Potomac to the Frontier of Mexico; with Sketches of Popular Manners and Geological Notices* (New York: Harper & Brothers, 1844)

Fenn, George Manville, *King o' the Beach: A Tropic Tale* (London: Ernest Nister, [1899])

Fenn, W. W., 'Our Living Artists', *Magazine of Art*, January 1880, pp. 49–52

'The Fens of England', *Chambers's [Edinburgh] Journal*, 18 November 1854, pp. 321–4

'Fiction', *The Speaker*, 29 September 1894, pp. 362–3

Fidler, Isaac, *Observations on Professions, Literature, Manners, and Emigration, in the United States and Canada, Made during a Residence There in 1832* (London: Whittaker, Treacher & Co., 1833)

'Five Nights in the Streets of London', *Pall Mall Gazette*, 9 September 1887, p. 5

Flynt, Josiah, *Tramping with Tramps: Studies and Sketches of Vagabond Life* (New York: Century Co., 1899)

Forbes, Litton, *Two Years in Fiji* (London: Longman, Green, 1875)

'Foreign Paupers', *Farmer's Gazette*, 10 April 1835, p. 3

'Foreign Paupers', *Portsmouth Journal of Literature and Politics*, 13 December 1834, p. 2

Fraser, John Foster, 'Vagabond Notes: Tramps, Hobbos, and Beachcombers', *Barnsley Chronicle*, 1 December 1900, p. 2

Garrett Fawcett, Millicent, 'The Vaccination Act of 1898', *Contemporary Review*, March 1899, pp. 328–42

'Gatherings about Gipsies', *Reynolds's Miscellany*, 17 June 1848, pp. 509–10

'Gift Books for the Young', *Daily News*, 11 November 1890, p. 7

'The Gipsies', *London Saturday Journal*, 12 June 1841, pp. 277–9

'Gipsies', *Sharpe's London Magazine*, July 1848, pp. 169–72

Gissing, George, *New Grub Street*, ed. John Goode (Oxford: Oxford University Press, 1993: repr. 2008)

Greenwood, James, 'A Night in a Workhouse', *Pall Mall Gazette*, 12 January 1866, pp. 9–10

  'A Night in a Workhouse', *Pall Mall Gazette*, 13 January 1866, p. 10

  'A Night in a Workhouse', *Pall Mall Gazette*, 15 January 1866, pp. 9–10

  The Seven Curses of London, ed. Jeffrey Richards (Oxford: Basil Blackwell, 1981)

Harkness, Margaret, *A City Girl*, ed. Deborah Mutch (Brighton: Victorian Secrets, 2015)

  In Darkest London (Cambridge: Black Apollo Press, 2003)

  'The Loafer: What Shall We Do with Him?', *Labour Elector*, 21 September 1889, p. 180

  A Manchester Shirtmaker: A Realistic Story of Today, intro. Trefor Thomas (Brighouse: Northern Herald, 2002)

  Out of Work, ed. John Lucas (London: Merlin Press, 1990)

  'A Year of My Life', *New Review*, October 1891, pp. 375–84

Harman, Thomas, *A Caveat or Warning for Common Cursetors, Vulgarly Called Vagabonds, Set fourth by Thomas Harman Esq. for the Utility and Profit of His Natural Country* (London: R. Triphook, 1814)

Hawker, James, *A Victorian Poacher: James Hawker's Journal*, ed. Garth Christian (Oxford: Oxford University Press, 1961; repr. 1978)

Hawthorne, Nathaniel, 'Consular Experiences', in *Our Old Home, and English Note-Books*, 2 vols (New York: Houghton, Mifflin and Company, 1887), I, pp. 19–55

'The Head-Hunters of the Solomon Islands', *All The Year Round*, 20 September 1890, pp. 279–84

Heath, Charles, 'The Arab of the City, Being the Autobiography of a London Thief', *The Ragged School Union Magazine*, February 1850, pp. 33–7

  'The Arab of the City, Being the Autobiography of a London Thief', *The Ragged School Union Magazine*, November 1850, pp. 273–80

Hewson, Edric, 'Larry Lee the Pedlar', *Sharpe's London Magazine*, January 1857, pp. 231–8

Higgs, Mary, *Glimpses into the Abyss* (London: P. S. King, 1906)

Hogan, J. F., 'A Secret of the Solomon Islands', *Chambers's [Edinburgh] Journal*, 23 September 1893, pp. 593–6

Hollingshead, John, *Ragged London in 1861*, ed. Anthony S. Wohl (London: J. M. Dent, 1986)

'The Homeless Poor', *Saturday Review*, 21 November 1863, pp. 664–5

Hood, Thomas, 'The Friend in Need', *New Monthly Magazine*, March 1841, pp. 389–99

Hooton, Charles, 'Texiana: Rides, Rambles, and Sketches in Texas', *Tait's Edinburgh Magazine*, March 1843, pp. 185–92
  'Texiana: Rides, Rambles, and Sketches in Texas', *Tait's Edinburgh Magazine*, May 1843, pp. 288–95

'Houseless and Hungry', *Graphic*, 4 December 1869, pp. 9–10

'The Houseless Poor', *South London Press*, 21 October 1865, p. 5

'The Houseless Poor Act', *Morning Post*, 1 January 1866, p. 3

'The Houseless Poor in Stepney', *The Times*, 27 January 1866, p. 12

Howitt, William, *The Rural Life of England*, 2 vols (London: Longman, Orme, Brown, Green & Longmans, 1838)

Hoyland, John, *A Historical Survey of the Customs, Habits, and Present State of the Gypsies* (York, 1816)

Hyndman, H. M., 'The English Workers as They Are', *Contemporary Review*, 1 July 1887, pp. 122–36

'Improved Treatment of the Poor', *Spectator*, 4 November 1848, p. 106

'The Increase in Vagrancy', *Morning Chronicle*, 9 August 1848, p. 2

'Isles of Eden', *Chambers's [Edinburgh] Journal*, 18 May 1872, pp. 315–18

Jefferies, Richard, *The Amateur Poacher*, in *The Gamekeeper at Home/The Amateur Poacher*, ed. Richard Fitter (Oxford: Oxford University Press 1948; repr. 1978), pp. 169–352
  The Gamekeeper at Home: Sketches of Natural History and Rural Life, in *The Gamekeeper at Home/The Amateur Poacher*, ed. Richard Fitter (Oxford: Oxford University Press, 1948; repr. 1978), pp. 1–168

'Joseph Rushbrook', *New Monthly Magazine*, August 1841, pp. 561–3

'Juvenile Literature', *St. James's Gazette*, 21 November 1889, p. 20

'The Kermadecs', *Chambers's [Edinburgh] Journal*, 2 April 1887, pp. 214–15

Kingsley, Charles, *Alton Locke, Tailor and Poet: An Autobiography* (London: Macmillan, 1885)
  Charles Kingsley: His Letters and Memories of His Life, 3rd ed., ed. Frances Kingsley, 2 vols (London: Henry S. King, 1877)
  Prose Idylls: New and Old, 2nd ed. (London: Macmillan, 1874)
  'The Value of Law', in *Sermons on National Subjects* (London: Richard Griffin, 1854), pp. 32–44
  Yeast: A Problem (London: John W. Parker, 1851)
  'Yeast; or, The Thoughts, Sayings, and Doings of Lancelot Smith, Gentleman', *Fraser's Magazine*, September 1848, pp. 284–300
  'Yeast No. IV', *Fraser's Magazine*, October 1848, pp. 447–60
  'Yeast No. V', *Fraser's Magazine*, November 1848, pp. 530–47

Kipling, Rudyard, *Kim*, ed. Harish Trivedi (London: Penguin, 2011)

Kirwan, Daniel Joseph, *Palace and Hovel; or, Phases of London Life*, ed. A. Allan (London: Abelard-Schuman, 1963)

Lamb, Charles, 'A Complaint of the Decay of Beggars in the Metropolis', *London Magazine,* June 1822, pp. 532–6

'The Old Benchers of the Inner Temple', *London Magazine,* September 1821, pp. 279–84

'The Lambeth Guardians and the Casual Poor', *Daily News,* 26 January 1866, p. 8

'The Lame Pedlar, A Story', *Chambers's [Edinburgh] Journal,* 20 January 1838, pp. 411–12

'Lavengro – "The Master of Words"', *Fraser's Magazine,* March 1851, pp. 272–83

'Lavengro: The Scholar – The Gypsy – The Priest', *Athenaeum,* 8 February 1851, pp. 159–60

Leland, Charles, *The Gypsies,* 4th ed. (Boston: Houghton, Mifflin, 1886)

The English Gypsies and Their Language (London: Trübner, 1873)

'Preface', in *The English Gipsies and Their Language* (London: Trübner, 1873), pp. v–xiii

'Life among the Vagabonds', *Leisure Hour,* 16 December 1858, pp. 787–90

'Literary "Packmen"', *Leisure Hour,* 5 April 1860, pp. 212–14

London, Jack, *The People of the Abyss,* 2nd ed. (London: Hesperus Press, 2013)

London, Jack, and Anna Strunsky, *The Kempton–Wace Letters* (London: Mills & Boon, [1924])

'London – Black and Blue', *Speaker,* 28 March 1891, pp. 365–6

'London Draymen', *London Saturday Journal,* 24 April 1841, pp. 193–4

Marryat, Frederick, *A Diary in America, with Remarks on Its Institutions* (Philadelphia: Carey & Hart, 1839)

Joseph Rushbrook; or, The Poacher, 3 vols (London: Longman, Orme, Brown, Green, 1841)

Narrative of the Travels and Adventures of Monsieur Violet, in California, Sonora, & Western Texas, 3 vols (London: Longman, Brown, Green & Longmans, 1843)

Martineau, Harriet, *Society in America,* 2 vols (London: Saunders and Otley, 1837)

'Marylebone Workhouse and the Casual Poor', *Daily News,* 25 October 1865, p. 4

Masterman, C. F. G., *From the Abyss: Of Its Inhabitants by One of Them* (London: R. Brimley Johnson, 1902)

'The Social Abyss', *Contemporary Review,* 1 January 1902, pp. 23–35

Mayhew, Henry, *London Labour and the London Poor: A Cyclopaedia of the Condition and Earnings of Those That Will Work, Those That Cannot Work, and Those That Will Not Work,* 4 vols (London: Frank Cass, 1967)

Mayhew, Henry, and John Binny, *The Criminal Prisons of London and Scenes of Prison Life* (London: Griffin, Bohn, 1862)

Mearns, Andrew, *The Bitter Cry of Outcast London,* in *The Metropolitan Poor: Semi-Factual Accounts, 1795–1910,* ed. John Marriott and Masaie Matsumura, 6 vols (London: Pickering & Chatto, 1999), VI, pp. 80–100

Melville, Herman, *Omoo: A Narrative of Adventures in the South Seas*, ed. Mary
K. Bercaw Edwards (London: Penguin, 2007)
Mitford, Mary Russell, 'The Old Gipsy', in *Our Village: Sketches of Rural
Character and Scenery*, 2 vols (London: George Bell, 1876), I, pp. 436–44
'The Young Gipsy', in *Our Village: Sketches of Rural Character and Scenery*,
2 vols (London: George Bell, 1876), I, pp. 449–58
More, Hannah, *Black Giles, the Poacher: With Some Account of a Family Who Had
Rather Live by Their Wits than Their Work* (London: C. J. G. &
F. Rivington, 1830)
Morrison, Arthur, *A Child of the Jago*, ed. Peter Miles (Oxford: Oxford University
Press, 2012)
'The Children of the Jago: Slum-Life at Close Quarters: A Talk with Mr Arthur
Morrison', in *A Child of the Jago*, ed. Peter Miles (Oxford: Oxford University
Press, 2012), pp. 171–2
Moss, Frederick J., *Through Atolls and Islands in the Great South Sea* (London:
Sampson Low, Marston, Searle, & Rivington, 1889)
Munby, A. J., *Munby, Man of Two Worlds: The Life and Diaries of Arthur
J. Munby, 1828–1910*, ed. Derek Hudson ([London]: John Murray, 1972)
Nicholson, John, 'The Poacher: A Tale from Real Life', in *Airedale in Ancient
Times* (London, 1825), pp. 63–92
'A Nineteenth-Century Pirate', *Chambers's [Edinburgh] Journal*, 27 November
1886, pp. 762–4
Noble, Leonard, 'Homeless at Night', *English Illustrated Magazine*, April 1892,
pp. 572–6
'Notes on America, No. I', *Monthly Magazine*, June 1832, pp. 640–6
'Notes on America, No. III', *Monthly Magazine*, August 1832, pp. 145–52
'On Loafers', *Gentleman's Magazine*, April 1890, pp. 398–408
Orwell, George, *Down and Out in Paris and London* (London: Penguin, 2001)
Owen, Hugh, 'Introduction', in *The Pauper Inmates Discharge and Regulations
Act, 1871: With Introduction and Notes by Hugh Owen*, ed. Hugh Owen
(London: Knight & Co., 1871)
'Packet Rats and Beachcombers', *Pall Mall Gazette*, 3 July 1879, pp. 11–12
'The Pauper Hotels of England', *Bell's New Weekly Messenger*, 24 September
1848, p. 4
Peek, Francis, 'The Workless, the Thriftless, and the Worthless', *Contemporary
Review*, 1 January 1888, pp. 39–52
[Phipps, Edmund], 'The Poacher's Progress', *New Monthly Magazine*, April 1841,
pp. 487–97
'The Plague of Beggars', *Fraser's Magazine*, April 1848, pp. 395–402
'The Poacher: A Tale from Real Life', *Mirror of Literature*, 18 January 1845,
pp. 56–8
'The Poacher's Wife', *Mirror of Literature*, 1 March 1847, pp. 206–10
'The Poacher's Wife', *Lloyd's Weekly*, 25 April 1847, p. 8
'The Poacher's Wife: A Story of the Times', *Critic*, 3 April 1847, p. 265
'Police Intelligence', *Standard*, 28 October 1887, p. 2

'Poor-Law Guardians in Rebellion', *Illustrated Times*, 28 October 1865, p. 262

Reade, Charles, 'Preface' [1868], in *Hard Cash: A Matter-of-Fact Romance* (London: Chatto & Windus, 1898)

'A Real Casual on Casual Wards: With an Introduction and Notes by J. C. Parkinson', *Temple Bar*, March 1866, pp. 497–517

'A Real Casual on Refuges: With Introduction and Notes by J. C. Parkinson', *Temple Bar*, April 1866, pp. 32–44

Report on the Departmental Committee on Vagrancy, 3 vols (London: Wyman & Sons, 1906)

Rice-Jones, D., 'In the Heart of London', *English Illustrated Magazine*, December 1886, pp. 208–33

In the Slums: Pages from the Note-Book of a London Diocesan Home Missionary (London: James Nisbet, 1884)

[Rolfe, Frederick], *I Walked by Night: Being the Life & History of the King of the Norfolk Poachers, Written by Himself*, ed. Lilias Rider Haggard (Woodbridge: Boydell Press, 1974)

Romilly, Hugh, 'A Tale of the South Seas', *Illustrated Sporting and Dramatic News*, 14 February 1891, pp. 767–70

'The Royal Academy', *Athenaeum*, 2 May 1874, pp. 599–602

'The Royal Academy', *Saturday Review*, 2 May 1874, pp. 561–2

Ruskin, John, *Sesame and Lilies*, ed. Deborah Epstein Nord (New Haven, CT: Yale University Press, 2002)

[Rutherford, John], *Indoor Paupers: By One of Them* (London: Chatto & Windus, 1885)

Sala, George Augustus, 'Houseless and Hungry', *Household Words*, 23 February 1856, pp. 121–6

'The Key of the Street', *Household Words*, 6 September 1851, pp. 565–72

My Diary in America in the Midst of War, 2 vols (London: Tinsley Brothers, 1865)

[Sargent, George], 'Frank Layton: An Australian Story', *Leisure Hour*, 2 March 1854, pp. 129–33

Scott, Walter, *Guy Mannering*, ed. P. D. Garside (London: Penguin, 2003)

Shakespeare, William, *King Henry IV, Part 1*, ed. David Scott Kastan (London: Arden, 2002; repr. 2004)

Sims, George R., *Horrible London*, in *How the Poor Live and Horrible London* (London: Garland Publishing, 1984), pp. 111–50

How the Poor Live, in *How the Poor Live and Horrible London* (London: Garland Publishing, 1984), pp. 1–110

'Sketches of the Mexican War', *Fraser's Magazine*, July 1848, pp. 91–102

'The Slum and the Cellar', *Saturday Review*, 27 October 1883, pp. 521–2

'A Slum Story Writer', *Evening News and Post*, 17 April 1890, p. 2

Smith, John Thomas, *Vagabondiana; or, Anecdotes of Mendicant Wanderers through the Streets of London: With Portraits of the Most Remarkable, Drawn from the Life by John Thomas Smith, Keeper of the Prints in the British Museum* (London, 1817)

Stallard, J. H., *The Female Casual and Her Lodging: With a Complete Scheme for the Regulation of Workhouse Infirmaries* (London: Saunders, Otley, 1866)

Pauperism, Charity, & Poor Laws: Being an Inquiry into the Present State of the Poorer Classes in the Metropolis, the Resources and Effects of Charity, and the Influence of the Poor-Law System of Relief: With Suggestions for an Improved Administration (London: Longmans, Green, Reader, and Dyer, 1868)

'Paupers and Pauperism', *Gentleman's Magazine*, July 1869, pp. 177–89

'The Scottish Poor Law, Examined in Its Relation to Vagrancy', in *Pauperism and the Poor Laws: The Lectures Delivered in Edinburgh under the Auspices of the Chalmers Association in 1869–70 with Kindred Papers*, ed. Thomas Ivory (Edinburgh: Seton & Mackenzie, 1870), pp. 1–22

Steel, Flora Annie, 'In the Permanent Way', in *In the Permanent Way and Other Stories* (London: Heinemann, 1898), pp. 27–42

Stevenson, Fanny Van de Grift, *The Cruise of the 'Janet Nichol' among the South Seas: A Diary by Mrs Robert Louis Stevenson* (New York: Charles Scribner's Sons, 1914)

'Preface', in *The Cruise of the 'Janet Nichol' among the South Seas: A Diary by Mrs Robert Louis Stevenson* (New York: Charles Scribner's Sons, 1914), pp. v–vii

Stevenson, Robert Louis, 'The Beach at Falesá', in *South Sea Tales*, ed. Roslyn Jolly (Oxford: Oxford University Press, 1996; repr. 2008), pp. 3–71

In the South Seas, in *In the South Seas and Island Nights' Entertainments* (London: J. M. Dent & Sons, 1925), pp. 5–230

The Isle of Voices, in *South Sea Tales*, ed. Roslyn Jolly (Oxford: Oxford University Press, 1996; repr. 2008), pp. 103–22

The Letters of Robert Louis Stevenson, ed. Bradford A. Booth and Ernest Mehew, 8 vols (New Haven, CT: Yale University Press, 1995)

Stevenson, Robert Louis, and Lloyd Osbourne, *The Ebb-Tide: A Trio and Quartette*, in *South Sea Tales*, ed. Roslyn Jolly (Oxford: Oxford University Press, 1996; repr. 2008), pp. 123–252

The Wrecker (London: Oxford University Press, 1950)

Thomas, Henry, *The Ancient Remains, Antiquities, and Recent Improvements, of the City of London*, 2 vols (London: Sears, 1830)

'The Tinkers of Scotland', *Penny Magazine*, 24 December 1836, pp. 502–3

'Told by a Tramp', *All the Year Round*, 28 April 1866, pp. 371–4

Trollope, Anthony, *North America*, 2 vols (London: Granville Publishing, 1986)

Trollope, Frances, *Domestic Manners of the Americans*, ed. Elsie B. Michie (Oxford: Oxford University Press, 2014)

'The Umbrella Pedler', *Chambers's [Edinburgh] Journal*, 16 August 1851, pp. 102–4

'Under the Black Flag', *Pall Mall Gazette*, 13 October 1887, p. 1

'The United States as an Emigration Field', *Chambers's Edinburgh Journal*, 16 June 1849, pp. 374–6

'Vagrancy', *Evening Mail*, 12 June 1848, p. 1

'The Vagrancy Question: Important Meeting of Union Clerks and Guardians at Stoke-on-Trent', *Staffordshire Advertiser*, 28 October 1848, p. 8

'The Vagrant Act', *London Magazine*, January 1825, pp. 7–15

'The Vagrants in Trafalgar Square', *Standard*, 26 October 1887, p. 2

'Vagrants and Vagrancy', *London Quarterly Review*, January 1888, pp. 321–42

Wakefield, Edward Gibbon, *A Letter from Sydney*, in *A Letter from Sydney and Other Writings on Colonisation*, ed. Ernest Rhys (London: J. M. Dent, 1929), pp. 1–106

Wakefield, Edward Jerningham, *Adventure in New Zealand, from 1839 to 1844; with Some Account of the Beginning of the British Colonization of the Islands*, 2 vols (London: John Murray, 1845)

Wells, H. G., *Anticipations; or, The Reaction of Mechanical and Scientific Progress upon Human Life and Thought* (London: Chapman & Hall, 1902 [1901])

  The Correspondence of H. G. Wells, ed. David C. Smith, 4 vols (London: Pickering & Chatto, 1998)

  An Experiment in Autobiography: Discoveries and Conclusions of a Very Ordinary Brain (since 1866), 2 vols (London: Faber and Faber, 2008)

  'A Slum Novel', *Saturday Review*, 28 November 1896, p. 573.

  A Story of the Days to Come, in *Tales of Time and Space* (London: Harper & Brothers, 1900), pp. 165–324

  The Time Machine: An Invention, ed. Roger Luckhurst (Oxford: Oxford University Press, 2017)

  When the Sleeper Wakes, ed. John Lawton (London: Everyman, 1994)

White, Arnold, 'The Cult of Infirmity', *National Review*, October 1899, pp. 236–45

  Efficiency and Empire (London: Methuen, 1901)

  'The Nomad Poor of London', *Contemporary Review*, 1 January 1885, pp. 714–26

Wilkinson, T. W., 'Vagrants in Winter', *Good Words*, December 1899, pp. 31–6

Woolf, Virginia, 'Street Haunting: A London Adventure', in *Selected Essays* (Oxford: Oxford University Press, 2008), pp. 177–87

Wordsworth, William, *The Major Works*, ed. Stephen Gill (Oxford: Oxford University Press, 2011)

'Yetholm, and the Scottish Gipsies', *Sharpe's London [Magazine]*, January 1851, pp. 321–5

Secondary Sources

Ager, A. W., *Crime and Poverty in 19th Century England: The Economy of Makeshifts* (London: Bloomsbury, 2014)

Archer, John E., *Social Unrest and Popular Protest in England, 1780–1840* (Cambridge: Cambridge University Press, 2000)

Arscott, Caroline, 'From Graphic to Academic', in *Art and the Academy in the Nineteenth Century*, ed. Raphael Cardoso Denis and Colin Trodd (Manchester: Manchester University Press, 2000), pp. 102–16

Arvin, Maile, *Possessing Polynesians: The Science of Settler Colonial Whiteness in Hawai'i and Oceania* (Durham, NC: Duke University Press, 2019)

Ashton, Rosemary, *George Eliot: A Life* (London: Hamish Hamilton, 1996)

Beaumont, Matthew, *Nightwalking: A Nocturnal History of London, Chaucer to Dickens* (London: Verso, 2015)

    The Spectre of Utopia: Utopian and Science Fictions at the Fin de Siècle (Bern: Peter Lang, 2012)

    Utopia Ltd.: Ideologies in Social Dreaming in England, 1870–1900 (Leiden: Brill, 2005)

Beer, Gillian, 'Island Bounds', in *Islands in History and Representation*, ed. Rod Edmond and Vanessa Smith (London: Routledge, 2003), pp. 32–42

Behlmer, George K., 'The Gypsy Problem in Victorian England', *Victorian Studies*, 28.2 (1985), 231–53

Beier, A. L., *Masterless Men: The Vagrancy Problem in England, 1560–1640* (London: Methuen, 1985)

Belchem, John, *Irish, Catholic and Scouse: The History of the Liverpool-Irish, 1800–1939* (Liverpool: Liverpool University Press, 2007)

Belich, James, *Replenishing the Earth: The Settler Revolution and the Rise of the Anglo-World, 1783–1939* (Oxford: Oxford University Press, 2009)

Bell, Duncan, *The Idea of Greater Britain: Empire and the Future of World Order, 1860–1900* (Princeton, NJ: Princeton University Press, 2007)

Bergonzi, Bernard, *The Early H. G. Wells: A Study of the Scientific Romances* (Manchester: Manchester University Press, 1961)

Bigelow, Gordon, *Fiction, Famine, and the Rise of Economics in Victorian Britain and Ireland* (Cambridge: Cambridge University Press, 2003)

Bivona, Dan, and Roger B. Henkle, *The Imagination of Class: Masculinity and the Victorian Urban Poor* (Columbus: Ohio State University Press, 2006)

Boddice, Rob, *The Science of Sympathy: Morality, Evolution, and Victorian Civilization* (Chicago: University of Illinois Press, 2016)

Brake, Laurel, 'Periodical Formats: The Changing Review', in *Journalism and the Periodical Press in Nineteenth-Century Britain*, ed. Joanne Shattock (Cambridge: Cambridge University Press, 2017), pp. 47–65

Brantlinger, Patrick, *Dark Vanishings: Discourse on the Extinction of Primitive Races, 1800–1930* (Ithaca, NY: Cornell University Press, 2003)

    Taming Cannibals: Race and the Victorians (Ithaca, NY: Cornell University Press, 2011)

Buckton, Oliver S., *Cruising with Robert Louis Stevenson: Travel, Narrative, and the Colonial Body* (Athens: Ohio University Press, 2007)

Burrows, Edwin G., and Mike Wallace, *Gotham: A History of New York to 1898* (Oxford: Oxford University Press, 1999)

Campbell, I. C., *Worlds Apart: A History of the Pacific Islands*, revised ed. (Christchurch: Canterbury University Press, 2003)

Campbell, Randolph B., *Gone to Texas: A History of the Lone Star State* (New York: Oxford University Press, 2003)

Charlesworth, Lorie, *Welfare's Forgotten Past: A Socio-Legal History of the Poor Law* (Abingdon: Routledge-Cavendish, 2009)

Chitty, Susan, *The Beast and the Monk: A Life of Charles Kingsley* (London: Hodder and Stoughton, 1974)

Cocks, H. G., *Nameless Offences: Homosexual Desire in the Nineteenth Century* (London: I. B. Tauris, 2003)

Cohn, Raymond L., *Mass Migration under Sail: European Immigration to the Antebellum United States* (Cambridge: Cambridge University Press, 2009)

Collie, Michael, *George Borrow: Eccentric* (Cambridge: Cambridge University Press, 1982)

Colloms, Brenda, *Charles Kingsley: The Lion of Eversley* (London: Constable, 1975)

Conn, Steven, *History's Shadow: Native Americans and Historical Consciousness in the Nineteenth Century* (Chicago: University of Chicago Press, 2004)

Cresswell, Tim, *On the Move: Mobility in the Modern Western World* (Abingdon: Routledge, 2006)

The Tramp in America (London: Reaktion Books, 2001)

Cressy, David, *Gypsies: An English History* (Oxford: Oxford University Press, 2018; repr. 2020)

Crowther, M. A., 'The Tramp', in *Myths of the English*, ed. Roy Porter (Cambridge: Polity Press, 1992), pp. 91–113

The Workhouse System, 1834–1929: The History of an English Social Institution (Athens: University of Georgia Press, 1982)

Curry, Kenneth, 'The Monthly Magazine', in *British Literary Magazines: The Romantic Age, 1789–1836*, ed. Alvin Sillivan, 4 vols (Westport, CT: Greenwood Press, 1983–86), II, pp. 314–19

Darby, H. C., *The Draining of the Fens* (Cambridge: Cambridge University Press, 1956; repr. 1968)

Dart, Gregory, *Metropolitan Art and Literature, 1810–1840: Cockney Adventures* (Cambridge: Cambridge University Press, 2012)

Darwin, John, *The Empire Project: The Rise and Fall of the British World System, 1830–1970* (Cambridge: Cambridge University Press, 2009; repr. 2015)

De Nie, Michael, *The Eternal Paddy: Irish Identity and the British Press, 1798–1882* (Madison: University of Wisconsin Press, 2004)

Dening, Greg, *Islands and Beaches: Discourse on a Silent Land, Marquesas 1774–1880* (Honolulu: University of Hawai'i Press, 1980)

Diamond, B. I., J. O. Baylen and J. P. Baylen, 'James Greenwood's London: A Precursor of Charles Booth', *Victorian Periodicals Review*, 17.1–2 (1984), 34–43

Duncan, Ian, 'Wild England: George Borrow's Nomadology', *Victorian Studies*, 41.3 (1998), 381–403

Eccles, Audrey, *Vagrancy in Law and Practice under the Old Poor Law* (Farnham: Ashgate, 2012)

Edmond, Rod, *Leprosy and Empire: A Medical and Cultural History* (Cambridge: Cambridge University Press, 2006)

Representing the South Pacific: Colonial Discourse from Cook to Gauguin (Cambridge: Cambridge University Press, 1997)

Eisler, Benita, *The Red Man's Bones: George Catlin, Artist and Showman* (New York: Norton, 2013)

Elledge, W. Paul, 'The New Monthly Magazine', in *British Literary Magazines: The Romantic Age, 1789–1836*, ed. Alvin Sullivan, 4 vols (Westport, CT: Greenwood Press, 1983–86), II, pp. 331–9

Ellis, Helen B., 'The London Magazine', in *British Literary Magazines: The Romantic Age, 1789–1836*, ed. Alvin Sullivan, 4 vols (Westport, CT: Greenwood Press, 1983–86), II, pp. 288–96

Erickson, Charlotte, *Leaving England: Essays on British Emigration in the Nineteenth Century* (Ithaca, NY: Cornell University Press, 1994)

Farrell, Joseph, *Robert Louis Stevenson in Samoa* (London: MacLehose Press, 2017)

Fildes, L. V., *Luke Fildes, R.A.: A Victorian Painter* (London: Michael Joseph, 1968)

Fischer, Steven Roger, *A History of the Pacific Islands*, 2nd ed. (Basingstoke: Palgrave, 2013)

Flint, Kate, 'Surround, Background, and the Overlooked', *Victorian Studies*, 57.3 (2015), 449–61

    The Transatlantic Indian, 1776–1930 (Princeton, NJ: Princeton University Press, 2009)

Ford, Charles Howard, *Hannah More: A Critical Biography* (New York: Peter Lang, 1996)

Foucault, Michel, *Discipline and Punish: The Birth of the Prison*, trans. Alan Sheridan (London: Penguin, 1977)

    'Right of Death and Power Over Life', in *Biopolitics: A Reader*, ed. Timothy Campbell and Adam Sitze (Durham, NC: Duke University Press, 2013), pp. 41–60

    '"Society Must Be Defended", Lecture at the *Collège de France*, March 17, 1976', in *Biopolitics: A Reader*, ed. Timothy Campbell and Adam Sitze (Durham, NC: Duke University Press, 2013), pp. 61–81

Fowler, Simon, *Workhouse: The People, the Place, the Life behind Doors* (Richmond: National Archives, 2007)

Freedgood, Elaine, *Victorian Writing about Risk: Imagining a Safe England in a Dangerous World* (Cambridge: Cambridge University Press, 2000)

Fuller, Jenn, *Dark Paradise: Pacific Islands in the Nineteenth-Century British Imagination* (Edinburgh: Edinburgh University Press, 2016)

Fyfe, Aileen, *Steam-Powered Knowledge: William Chambers and the Business of Publishing, 1820–1860* (Chicago: University of Chicago Press, 2012)

Grant, Robert D., *Representations of British Emigration, Colonisation and Settlement: Imagining Empire, 1800–1860* (Basingstoke: Palgrave Macmillan, 2005)

Greenslade, William, *Degeneration, Culture and the Novel, 1880–1940* (Cambridge: Cambridge University Press, 1994)

Griffin, Emma, *Blood Sport: Hunting in Britain since 1066* (New Haven, CT: Yale University Press, 2007; repr. 2008)

Harriman-Smith, James, 'Representing the Poor: Charles Lamb and the *Vagabondiana*', *Studies in Romanticism*, 54.4 (2015), 551–83

Hauʻofa, Epeli, *We Are the Ocean: Selected Works* (Honolulu: University of Hawaiʻi Press, 2008)

Heath, Deana, *Purifying Empire: Obscenity and the Politics of Moral Regulation in Britain, India and Australia* (Cambridge: Cambridge University Press, 2010; repr. 2013)

Hepburn, James, *A Book of Scattered Leaves: Poetry and Poverty in Broadside Ballads in Nineteenth-Century England: Study and Anthology*, 2 vols (Lewisburg, PA: Bucknell University Press, 2000–1)

Hilton, Boyd, *A Mad, Bad, & Dangerous People?: England, 1783–1843* (Oxford: Oxford University Press, 2008)

Hirota, Hidetaka, *Expelling the Poor: Atlantic Seaboard States and the Nineteenth-Century Origins of American Immigration Policy* (Oxford: Oxford University Press, 2017; repr. 2019)

Hitchcock, David, '"He Is the Vagabond That Hath No Habitation in the Lord": The Representation of Quakerism as Vagrancy in Interregnum England, c. 1650–1660', *Cultural and Social History*, 15.1 (2018), 21–37

 Vagrancy in English Culture and Society, 1650–1750 (London: Bloomsbury, 2016; repr. 2018)

Hitchcock, Tim, *Down and Out in Eighteenth-Century London* (London: Hambledon and London, 2004)

Hopkins, Harry, *The Long Affray: The Poaching Wars in Britain* (London: Secker & Warburg, 1985; repr. Faber and Faber, 2008)

Horn, Pamela, *Life and Labour in Rural England, 1760–1850* (Basingstoke: Macmillan, 1987)

Houghton-Walker, Sarah, *Representations of the Gypsy in the Romantic Period* (Oxford: Oxford University Press, 2014)

Hughes, Thomas, 'Prefatory Memoire', in *Alton Locke, Tailor and Poet: An Autobiography* (London: Macmillan, 1885), pp. ix–lxi

Hull, Simon P., *Charles Lamb, Elia and the London Magazine: Metropolitan Muse* (London: Pickering & Chatto, 2010)

Hume, Kathryn, 'Eat or Be Eaten: H. G. Wells's *Time Machine*', *Philological Quarterly*, 69.2 (1990), 233–51

Humphreys, Robert, *No Fixed Abode: A History of Responses to the Roofless and the Rootless in Britain* (London: Macmillan Press, 1999)

Hyde, George, 'Borrow and the Vanity of Dogmatising: "Lavengro" as Self-Portrait', *Cambridge Quarterly*, 32.2 (2003), 161–73

Jolly, Roslyn, 'Introduction', in *The Cruise of the 'Janet Nichol' among the South Seas: A Diary by Mrs Robert Louis Stevenson*, ed. Roslyn Jolly (Sydney: UNSW Press, 2004), pp. 13–43

 'Piracy, Slavery, and the Imagination of Empire in Stevenson's Pacific Fiction', *Victorian Literature and Culture*, 35 (2007), 157–73

Jones, David, *Crime, Protest, Community and Police in Nineteenth-Century Britain* (London: Routledge & Kegan Paul, 1982)

Kauanui, J. Kēhaulani, *Paradoxes of Hawaiian Sovereignty: Land, Sex, and the Colonial Politics of State Nationalism* (Durham, NC: Duke University Press, 2018)

Kent, Christopher, 'Introduction', in *British Literary Magazines: The Victorian and Edwardian Age, 1837–1913*, ed. Alvin Sullivan, 4 vols (Westport, CT: Greenwood Press, 1983–6), III, pp. xiii–xxvi

Korda, Andrea, *Printing and Painting the News in Victorian London: 'The Graphic' and Social Realism, 1869–1891* (Farnham: Ashgate, 2015)

Koven, Seth, *Slumming: Sexual and Social Politics in Victorian London* (Princeton, NJ: Princeton University Press, 2004)

Labor, Earle, *Jack London: An American Life* (New York: Farrar, Straus and Giroux, 2013)

Landry, Donna, *The Invention of the Countryside: Hunting, Walking and Ecology in English Literature, 1671–1831* (Basingstoke: Palgrave, 2001)

Langan, Celeste, *Romantic Vagrancy: Wordsworth and the Simulation of Freedom* (Cambridge: Cambridge University Press, 1995; repr. 2006)

Leary, Patrick, '*Fraser's Magazine* and the Literary Life, 1830–1847', *Victorian Periodicals Review*, 27.2 (1994), 105–26

Ledger, Sally, *Dickens and the Popular Radical Imagination* (Cambridge: Cambridge University Press, 2007)

Linnekin, Jocelyn, 'New Political Orders', in *The Cambridge History of the Pacific Islanders*, ed. Donald Denoon et al. (Cambridge: Cambridge University Press, 1997), pp. 185–217

Litvack, Leon, 'Dickens, Ireland and the Irish: Part I', *Dickensian*, 99.2 (2003), 34–59

Livesey, Ruth, *Writing the Stage Coach Nation: Locality on the Move in Nineteenth-Century British Literature* (Oxford: Oxford University Press, 2016)

Luckhurst, Roger, 'Introduction', in *The Time Machine: An Invention*, ed. Roger Luckhurst (Oxford: Oxford University Press, 2017), pp. vii–xxv

Maixner, Paul, ed., *Robert Louis Stevenson: The Critical Heritage* (London: Routledge & Kegan Paul, 1981)

Malik, Kenan, *The Meaning of Race: Race, History and Culture in Western Society* (Basingstoke: Macmillan, 1996)

Marriott, John, *The Other Empire: Metropolis, India and Progress in the Colonial Imagination* (Manchester: Manchester University Press, 2003)

Mathieson, Charlotte, '"A Still Ecstasy of Freedom and Enjoyment": Walking the City in Charlotte Brontë's *Villette*', *Journal of Victorian Culture*, 22.4 (2017), 521–35

Mayall, David, *Gypsy Identities, 1500–2000: From Egipcyans and Moon-Men to the Ethnic Romany* (London: Routledge, 2004)

Gypsy-Travellers in Nineteenth Century Society (Cambridge: Cambridge University Press, 1988)

Mazurek, Monika, 'George Borrow: The Scholar, the Gipsy, the Priest', in *Victorian Fiction beyond the Canon*, ed. Daragh Downes and Trish Ferguson (London: Palgrave Macmillan, 2016), pp. 71–86

McDonagh, Josephine, *Child Murder and British Culture, 1720–1900* (Cambridge: Cambridge University Press, 2003)

'Urban Migration and Mobility', in *Charles Dickens in Context*, ed. Sally Ledger and Holly Furneaux (Cambridge: Cambridge University Press, 2011), pp. 268–75

McLean, Steven, *The Early Fiction of H. G. Wells: Fantasies of Science* (Basingstoke: Palgrave Macmillan, 2009)

McPherson, James M., *Battle Cry of Freedom: The American Civil War* (Oxford: Oxford University Press, 1988; repr. London: Penguin, 1990)

Meckier, Jerome, *Innocent Abroad: Charles Dickens's American Engagements* (Lexington: University Press of Kentucky, 1990)

Mills, Catherine, *Biopolitics* (Abingdon: Routledge, 2018)

Mingay, G. E., *Rural Life in Victorian England* (London: Heinemann, 1977)

Moore, Grace, *Dickens and Empire: Discourses of Class, Race and Colonialism in the Works of Charles Dickens* (Aldershot: Ashgate, 2004),

Morrison, Kevin A., 'Foregrounding Nationalism: Mary Russell Mitford's *Our Village* and the Effects of Publication Context', *European Romantic Review*, 19.3 (2008), 275–87

Munsche, P. B., *Gentlemen and Poachers: The English Game Laws, 1671–1831* (Cambridge: Cambridge University Press, 1981)

Myers, Janet C., *Antipodal England: Emigration and Portable Domesticity in the Victorian Imagination* (Albany: State University of New York Press, 2009)

Nead, Lynda, *Myths of Sexuality: Representations of Women in Victorian Britain* (Oxford: Blackwell, 1988; repr. 1990)

Victorian Babylon: People, Streets and Images in Nineteenth-Century London (New Haven, CT: Yale University Press, 2000)

Newman, Rebecca Edwards, '"Prosecuting the Onus Criminus": Early Criticism of the Novel in *Fraser's Magazine*', *Victorian Periodicals Review*, 35.4 (2002), 401–19

Nord, Deborah Epstein, *Gypsies and the British Imagination, 1807–1930* (New York: Columbia University Press, 2006)

O'Brassill-Kulfan, Kristin, *Vagrants and Vagabonds: Poverty and Mobility in the Early American Republic* (New York: New York University Press, 2019)

Ocobock, Paul, 'Introduction: Vagrancy and Homelessness in Global and Historical Perspective', in *Cast Out: Vagrancy and Homelessness in Global and Historical Perspective*, ed. A. L. Beier and Paul Ocobock (Athens: Ohio University Press, 2008), pp. 1–34

Ogden, James, 'Nicholson, John (1790–1843)', in *Oxford Dictionary of National Biography*, www.oxforddnb.com (accessed 15 February 2018)

Okely, Judith, *The Traveller-Gypsies* (Cambridge: Cambridge University Press, 1983)

Osborne, Harvey, 'The Seasonality of Nineteenth-Century Poaching', *Agricultural History Review*, 48.1 (2000), 27–41

'"Unwomanly Practices": Poaching Crime, Gender and the Female Offender in Nineteenth-Century Britain', *Rural History*, 27.2 (2016), 149–68

Osborne, Harvey, and Michael Winstanley, 'Rural and Urban Poaching in Victorian England', *Rural History*, 17.2 (2006), 187–212

O'Toole, Sean, *The History of Australian Corrections* (Sydney: UNSW Press, 2006)

Pagetti, Carlo, 'Changes in the City: The Time Traveller's London and the "Baseless Fabric" of His Vision', in *H. G. Wells's Perennial Time Machine: Selected Essays from the Centenary Conference '"The Time Machine": Past, Present, and Future' Imperial College, London July 26–29, 1995* (Athens: University of Georgia Press, 2001), pp. 122–34

Palmer, Roy, 'Birmingham Broadsides and Oral Traditions', in *Street Ballads in Nineteenth-Century Britain, Ireland, and North America*, ed. David Atkinson and Steve Roud (Farnham: Ashgate, 2014), pp. 37–58

   The Painful Plough: A Portrait of the Agricultural Labourer in the Nineteenth Century from Folk Songs and Ballads and Contemporary Accounts (Cambridge: Cambridge University Press, 1973)

Parrinder, Patrick, *Shadows of the Future: H. G. Wells, Science Fiction and Prophecy* (Liverpool: Liverpool University Press, 1995)

Parry, Jonathan, *The Rise and Fall of Liberal Government in Victorian Britain* (New Haven, CT: Yale University Press, 1993)

Partington, John S., *Building Cosmopolis: The Political Thought of H. G. Wells* (Aldershot: Ashgate, 2003)

Peters, Laura, *Dickens and Race* (Manchester: Manchester University Press, 2013)

Piesse, Jude, *British Settler Emigration in Print, 1832–1877* (Oxford: Oxford University Press, 2016)

Pike, David L., *Subterranean Cities: The World beneath Paris and London, 1800–1945* (Ithaca, NY: Cornell University Press, 2005)

Porter, Roy, *London: A Social History* (1994; repr. London: Penguin, 2000)

Pratt, Mary Louise, *Imperial Eyes: Travel Writing and Transculturation* (London: Routledge, 1992)

Ralston, Caroline, *Grass Huts and Warehouses: Pacific Beach Communities of the Nineteenth Century* (Honolulu: University of Hawai'i Press, 1978; repr. St Lucia: UQ ePress, 2014)

Ransom, Teresa, *Fanny Trollope: A Remarkable Life* (Stroud: Sutton Publishing, 1995; repr. 1996)

Rappoport, Jill, *Giving Women: Alliance and Exchange in Victorian Culture* (Oxford: Oxford University Press, 2012)

Rennie, Neil, *Far-Fetched Facts: The Literature of Travel and the Idea of the South Seas* (Oxford: Clarendon Press, 1995)

Reynolds, David, *America, Empire of Liberty: A New History* (London: Allen Lane, 2009)

Richards, Jeffrey, 'Introduction', in *The Seven Curses of London*, ed. Jeffrey Richards (Oxford: Basil Blackwell, 1981), pp. v–xxi

Richardson, Angelique, 'The Eugenization of Love: Sarah Grand and the Morality of Genealogy', *Victorian Studies*, 42.2 (1999–2000), 227–55

   Love and Eugenics in the Late Nineteenth Century: Rational Reproduction and the New Woman (Oxford: Oxford University Press, 2003)

Ridler, Ann M., *George Borrow as a Linguist: Images and Contexts* (Wallingford: A. M. Ridler, 1996)

'George Eliot and George Borrow – A Note on Middlemarch', *George Eliot – George Henry Lewes Newsletter*, 5 (1984), 3–4

Roberts, M. J. D., 'Public and Private in Early Nineteenth-Century London: The Vagrant Act of 1822 and Its Enforcement', *Social History*, 13.3 (1988), 273–94

Robertson Scott, J. W., *The Story of the 'Pall Mall Gazette'* (London: Oxford University Press, 1950)

Robinson, Alan, *Imagining London, 1770–1900* (Basingstoke: Palgrave Macmillan, 2004)

Robinson, Alistair, 'Vagrant, Convict, Cannibal Chief: Abel Magwitch and the Culture of Cannibalism in *Great Expectations*', *Journal of Victorian Culture*, 22.4 (2017), 450–64

Rose, Lionel, *'Rogues and Vagabonds': Vagrant Underworld in Britain, 1815–1985* (London: Routledge, 1988)

Samuel, Raphael, 'Comers and Goers', in *The Victorian City: Images and Realities*, ed. H. J. Dyos and Michael Wolff, 2 vols (London: Routledge & Kegan Paul, 1973)

Sandall, Robert, *The History of the Salvation Army*, 7 vols (London: Thomas Nelson and Sons, 1947–86)

Seaber, Luke, *Incognito Social Investigation in British Literature: Certainties in Degradation* (Cham: Palgrave Macmillan, 2017)

Shakesheff, Timothy, *Rural Conflict, Crime and Protest: Herefordshire, 1800–1860* (Woodbridge: Boydell Press, 2003)

Shapira, Michal, 'Indecently Exposed: The Male Body and Vagrancy in Metropolitan London before the Fin de Siècle', *Gender & History*, 30.1 (2018), 52–69

Sheldon, Michael, '*The Chimes* and the Anti-Corn Law League', *Victorian Studies*, 25.3 (1982), 328–53

Sherborne, Michael, *H. G. Wells: Another Kind of Life* (London: Peter Owen, 2010; repr. 2012)

Slater, Michael, 'Carlyle and Jerrold into Dickens: A Study of *The Chimes*', *Nineteenth-Century Fiction*, 24.4 (1970), 506–26

Charles Dickens (New Haven, CT: Yale University Press, 2009)

Smith, Vanessa, *Literary Culture and the Pacific: Nineteenth-Century Textual Encounters* (Cambridge: Cambridge University Press, 1998)

Snyder, Katherine V., *Bachelors, Manhood, and the Novel, 1850–1925* (Cambridge: Cambridge University Press, 1999)

Stedman Jones, Gareth, *Outcast London: A Study in the Relationship between Classes in Victorian Society* (Oxford: Oxford University Press, 1971; repr. London: Verso, 2013)

Steer, Philip, 'Romances of Uneven Development: Spatiality, Trade, and Form in Robert Louis Stevenson's Pacific Novels', *Victorian Literature and Culture*, 43 (2015), 343–56

Sussman, Herbert L., *Victorians and the Machine: The Literary Response to Technology* (Cambridge, MA: Harvard University Press, 1968)

Swafford, Kevin R., 'Resounding the Abyss: The Politics of Narration in Jack London's *The People of the Abyss*', *Journal of Popular Culture*, 39.5 (2006), 838–60

Thoburn, Nicholas, 'Difference in Marx: The Lumpenproletariat and the Proletarian Unnamable', *Economy and Society*, 31.3 (2002), 434–60

Thomas, Julia, *Victorian Narrative Painting* (London: Tate Gallery, 2000)

Thompson, E. P., *Whigs and Hunters: The Origin of the Black Act* (London: Allen Lane, 1975)

Truettner, William H., 'Picturing the Murder of Jane McCrea: A Critical Moment in Transatlantic Romanticism', in *Transatlantic Romanticism: British and American Art and Literature, 1790–1860*, ed. Andrew Hemingway and Alan Wallach (Amherst: University of Massachusetts Press, 2015), pp. 229–58

Tuan, Yi-Fu, *Space and Place: The Perspective of Experience* (Minneapolis: University of Minnesota Press, 1977; repr. 2018)

Valiska, Melissa, and Melisa Klimaszewski, 'Introduction', in *Doctor Marigold's Prescriptions*, ed. Melissa Valiska and Melisa Klimaszewski (London: Hesperus Press, 2007), pp. xi–xvi

Van Vugt, William E., *Britain to America: Mid-Nineteenth-Century Immigrants to the United States* (Chicago: University of Illinois Press, 1999)

Vorspan, Rachel, 'Vagrancy and the New Poor Law in Late-Victorian and Edwardian England', *English Historical Review*, 92.362 (1977), 59–81

Walkowitz, Judith R., *City of Dreadful Delight: Narratives of Sexual Danger in Late Victorian London* (London: Virago Press, 1992)

    Prostitution and Victorian Society: Women, Class, and the State (Cambridge: Cambridge University Press, 1980; repr. 1982)

Ward, Stuart, 'Security: Defending Australia's Empire', in *Australia's Empire*, ed. Deryck M. Schreuder and Stuart Ward (Oxford: Oxford University Press, 2008), pp. 232–58

Waters, Catherine, 'Domesticity', in *Charles Dickens in Context*, ed. Sally Ledger and Holly Furneaux (Cambridge: Cambridge University Press, 2011), pp. 350–7

Webb, Sidney, and Beatrice Webb, *English Poor Law Policy* (London: Longmans, 1910)

Welshman, John, *Underclass: A History of the Excluded since 1880*, 2nd ed. (London: Bloomsbury, 2013)

White, Jerry, *London in the Eighteenth Century: A Great and Monstrous Thing* (London: Bodley Head, 2012)

    London in the Nineteenth Century: A Human Awful Wonder of God (London: Vintage, 2008)

Williams, David, *A World of His Own: The Double Life of George Borrow* (Oxford: Oxford University Press, 1982)

Williams, Raymond, *The Country and the City* (London: Chatto & Windus, 1973)

Woodbridge, Linda, *Vagrancy, Homelessness, and English Renaissance Literature* (Chicago: University of Illinois Press, 2001)

Woods, Robert, *The Population of Britain in the Nineteenth Century* (Cambridge: Cambridge University Press, 1995)

Woods Sayre, Robert, 'The Romantic Indian Commodified: Text and Image in George Catlin's Letters and Notes (1841)', in *Transatlantic Romanticism: British and American Art and Literature, 1790–1860*, ed. Andrew Hemingway and Alan Wallach (Amherst: University of Massachusetts Press, 2015), pp. 259–84

Yarbrough, Fay A., *Race and the Cherokee Nation: Sovereignty in the Nineteenth Century* (Philadelphia: University of Pennsylvania Press, 2008)

Index

A Real Casual (anonymous), 95, 104
Adams, John (beachcomber), 214
Alabama, 177–9, 187
All the Year Round, 27, 39
  'The Head-Hunters of the Solomon Islands',
    205
  'Told by a Tramp', 92
American Civil War (1861–5), 165, 170, 180
American Indians, 6, 38, 167, 174–81, 203,
    223–4
  displacement, 177, 181
  usage, 10
American tramps, 167, 225
American vagabonds, 167, 182–8
anarchism, 134, 152
Anglo-Saxonism, 172–3, 201, 203, 223
Arch, Joseph (union leader), 59
Arkansas, 182
Arnold, Matthew, 46
Australasian colonies (British), 200
Australia, 164, 186, 195, 199–200

ballads, 15–16, 66
Baltimore, 166, 169
Banks, Elizabeth (social investigator), 147, 222
Barlie, Ellen (reformer), 94
Barnett, Samuel, 131, 137
beachcombers, 4, 6, 195–216, 223, 225
  in adventure fiction, 204–6
  etymology, 215
  numbers of, 197
  occupations, 198, 214–15
  in periodicals, 199–200, 206
beggars and begging, 1–3, 12, 14, 47, 109, 147,
    169
  in America, 166, 170, 178
  children, 64
  women, 96, 153
Bellamy, Edward, 153
Bermondsey, 112
Bethnal Green, 144, 151

biopolitics, 11, 102–4, 139–41
Birmingham, 30
Bishop, Gilbert (novelist), 199, 205–6
Blackfriars Bridge, 100
Bloody Sunday (1887), 133–4
Boer War (1899–1902), 138, 149
Booth, Charles, 135, 147
Booth, William, 135, 150
Borrow, George, 10, 31, 41–52, 224
  The Bible in Spain, 43
  Lavengro, 43, 45–52
  Romano Lavo-lil, 42
  The Romany Rye, 43–5, 51
  Wild Wales, 42
  The Zincali, 41, 43, 51–2
Boston, 165–6, 170
Bright, John (politician), 68, 74, 131
Buller, Charles (civil servant), 105–9, 117
Bulwer-Lytton, Edward, 186
bummers, 130, 202
Burleigh, Bennet (journalist), 133, 137,
    149

Cain (biblical), 183
Cameron, V. L. (writer), 206
Canandaigua, 176–7
cannibalism, 150–2
Carew, Charlton, 74–7
Carlyle, Thomas, 5, 108, 111, 152–3
casual labour, 98–9
casual paupers, 93, 95–6, 103–23, 225
Casual Poor Act (1882), 102
casual ward queues, 93, 101, 105, 107–11,
    115–23, 224
casual wards, 93, 95–7, 100–5, 111–15
Catlin, George, 175–6
Chadwick, Edwin (civil servant), 97, 103
Chambers's Edinburgh Journal
  'Beachcombers', 202–3
  'The Fens of England', 47
  'The Kermadecs', 201

'The Umbrella Pedler', 40
'The United States as an Emigration Field',
  182
charity, 2, 92, 94, 109, 113, 118
Charity Organisation Society, 118
Cheap Jacks, 27, 39
Cheap Repository, 63
Cherokee, 177, 179
Chickasaw, 177
Choctaw, 177
Cincinnati, 168, 170, 172
Clare, John, 29
Clark, Aaron (politician), 166, 169
Clerkenwell, 94
Cobbett, William, 44, 174
Colvin, Sidney, 207, 210
common lodging-houses, 92, 96–7, 151
Condition-of-England novels, 73–81
Conrad, Joseph, 211
Contagious Diseases Acts, 19
Contemporary Review, 136
  'The English Workers as They Are', 138
  'The Nomad Poor of London', 138
  'The Unemployed', 137
  'The Workless, the Thriftless, and the
    Worthless', 136
Cooper, H. Stonehewer (travel writer), 201, 203,
  214
Cowper, Thomas, 37
Crabb, James, *The Gipsies' Advocate*, 33
Creek, 177–9, 181
crossing sweepers, 100, 147

Dawson, William Harbutt (civil servant), 139
Day, Tom (beachcomber), 207
de Gorostiza, Manuel Eduardo (diplomat),
  182
degeneration, 7, 135, 137–8, 141, 223
Dekker, Thomas, 4
deserving/undeserving dichotomy, 4–5, 8, 91,
  93, 106, 108, 111, 114, 133, 137, 164, 181,
  188, 224–7
Diapea, William (beachcomber), 197
Dickens, Charles, 10, 62, 134, 153, 167, 170,
  172, 175, 224
  American Notes, 171–2, 174, 183–6
  Bleak House, 100, 180
  The Chimes, 70–3
  The Cricket on the Hearth, 185
  Doctor Marigold's Prescriptions, 39
  Great Expectations, 151, 185
  Martin Chuzzlewit, 173
  The Mystery of Edwin Drood, 97, 118
  'A Nightly Scene in London', 109–11
  Oliver Twist, 185

The Pickwick Papers, 13, 96
The Uncommercial Traveller, 27
Doyle, Arthur Conan, 147

Egyptian Hall, Piccadilly, 168, 175
Eliot, George
  Adam Bede, 39, 76
  Middlemarch, 51
  The Mill on the Floss, 50
  'The Natural History of German Life', 50
Ellice Islands, 200
Ellis, Edward (novelist), 199, 204–5
Embankment, 100
enclosure, 29, 36, 39, 44–5
eugenics, 7–8, 135, 138–40, 188, 202, 223–4
extinction theory, 5, 36–9, 42, 51, 141, 174,
  179, 181, 188, 202–4, 223

fallen women, 76, 117
Fawcett, Millicent Garrett, 103
Featherstonehaugh, George William (travel
  writer), 177–80, 182
Fenn, George Manville (novelist), 214
Fidler, Isaac (travel writer), 169–71
Field Lane Refuge, 94–6
Fiji, 196–8, 200–2, 206, 210
Fildes, Luke, 10, 153, 224
  Applicants for Admission to a Casual Ward,
    118–23
  and Charles Dickens, 118, 122
  'Houseless and Hungry', 115–18
Flynt, Josiah (social investigator), 96–7, 105, 222
Forbes, Litton (travel writer), 196, 199, 202–3
Forster, John, 70, 122, 170
Foucault, Michel, 102–4, 139–40
Fraser, John Foster (travel writer), 211
Fraser's Magazine, 78, 107
Frith, William Powell, 120
frontiers, 9–10, 167, 181, 184–5, 224
  and gender, 185–8, 201
  and lawlessness, 182–3, 195–6, 198–9, 202–3

Galton, Francis, 138–9
game laws, 59, 68–9, 74
Gaskell, Elizabeth, 73, 134
Georgia, 177
Gilbert Islands, 200, 207
Gissing, George, 143
Graphic, 115, 120
Greene, Robert, 4
Greenwood, Frederick, 112, 114
Greenwood, James, 93, 104, 146, 222
  'A Night in a Workhouse', 112–13
Grellmann, Heinrich, 33–5, 38, 42
Gypsies, 6, 27, 31–40, 174, 203, 223

Gypsies (cont.)
  and America, 30–1
  in early modern England, 32
  extinction, 36–9, 42, 51
  miscegenation, 38, 51–2, 224
  and music, 28
  and poaching, 58–9, 64
  racialisation, 33–5, 38–9, 141
  usage, 10

Hares Act (1848), 74
Harkness, Margaret, 136, 143–5, 149, 151, 153, 223
Harman, Thomas, *A Caveat*, 4, 18, 33
Hawai'i, 195–8, 200, 206–7, 213
Hawker, James (poacher), 59, 61, 69
hawkers, 5, 15, 27, 39–41
Hawthorne, Nathaniel, 163–4
Hayes, Bully (pirate), 201, 211
Haymarket, 19
Herkomer, Hubert, 120
higglers, 30, 60
Higgs, Mary (social investigator), 97, 103, 105, 146
Highways Act (1835), 30, 60
Hogan, J. F. (politician), 205
Holborn, 104
Holl, Frank, 120
Hollingshead, John (journalist), 94
Hood, Thomas, 81
Hooton, Charles (travel writer), 182, 186
Howitt, William, 35
Hoyland, John, *A Historical Survey ... of the Gypsies*, 33
Hunt, Jesse (politician), 169
Hyndman, H. M., 138

imperialism, 197, 199–200, 215–16
incendiarism, 73–4, 77
indigenous Americans. *See* American Indians
Irish Famine, 105, 164
Irish migrants, 105, 164–7, 171–4
  anti-Irish prejudice, 171–4
Irish vagrants, 42–3, 105
Iroquois, 177
Islington, 104
itinerant occupations, 27–8, 45–8, 60, 98–9, 147

Jefferies, Richard, 58, 61, 81

Kingsley, Charles, 10, 62, 135, 224
  Alton Locke, 80, 97
  Politics for the People, 77, 107
  Prose Idylls, 78

Sermons on National Subjects, 78, 81
  Yeast, 79–81, 107–9
Kipling, Rudyard, 130
Kirwan, Daniel (travel writer), 92, 94, 96, 100, 147
Kosrae, 198

labour trade, 200, 205
Lamb, Charles, 1–3, 14
Lambeth, 104, 112, 114
Leeds, 30, 106
Leland, Charles (gypsiologist), 30, 130, 174
Leyton, 105
Limehouse, 94
Literary Lounger, 'The Norwood Gypsies', 35–7
Liverpool, 163–5, 169
loafers, 4, 130–53, 202–3, 209, 211, 223
  etymology, 130
Local Government Board, 101, 122
London, 170
  modernisation, 99–100
  police courts, 13
  size, 30, 95, 171
London, Jack, 105, 148, 222–7
London Bridge, 100
London Saturday Journal, 'The Gipsies', 35, 37

Maginn, William (editor), 78
magistrates, 13, 60
Manchester, 30, 106
Manihiki, 208
Marquesas, 198, 207, 209
Marryat, Frederick, 167
  A Diary in America, 171
  Joseph Rushbrook, 81
  Metropolitan Magazine, 78
  Narrative of the Travels and Adventures of Monsieur Violet, 183
Martineau, Harriet, 10, 167, 169–71, 176, 186
Marx, Eleanor, 134
Marx, Karl, 146, 152
Marylebone, 104, 112
Massachusetts, 165, 169, 187
Masterman, C. F. G. (politician), 149
Maurice, F. D., 107
Mayhew, Henry, 6, 91, 98, 117, 222
Mearns, Andrew, 131, 147
Melanesia, 195–6, 199–200, 206
melodrama, 72
Melville, Herman, 198
Metropolitan Houseless Poor Acts (1864, 1865), 101, 111, 117
Metropolitan Police Act (1829), 100
Metropolitan Police Act (1839), 15
Metropolitan Vagrancy, 93, 99

Micronesia, 195–6, 199, 207
migration, 16, 30, 105, 164–6, 172–3, 181–2, 186–7
Milwaukee, 186
Missouri, 182
Mitford, Mary Russell, 48–9, 58
Mohicans, 177
monogenesis, 172
Monthly Magazine
  'Notes on America', 167, 182, 187
  'The Old Gipsy', 58
More, Hannah, 62–7
Morrison, Arthur, 136, 143–4, 150–1
Moss, Frederick J. (travel writer), 202
mouchers, 4, 61, 72, 80–1
Munby, A. J. (diarist), 18

narrative painting, 120
New Caledonia, 195, 210
New Guinea, 195
New Monthly Magazine, 82
  'Beggars and Almsgivers', 109
  'Borrow and Lavengro', 44
  'English Ballad-Singers', 16
  'The Poacher's Progress', 67–8
New Poor Law, 69–70, 93, 95, 100
New Sporting Magazine, 'The Poacher', 68
New York (state), 165, 168–9
New York City, 165–6, 169–71, 225
New Zealand, 164, 195, 197, 200–1
Nicholson, John (poet), 62, 66–7
Nineteenth Century (periodical), 136
Norfolk Island, 195
Norwich, 106
Norwood, 35–6

O'Connell, James (beachcomber), 199, 209
Oceania, 4, 197, 200
Old Northwest, 165
Orwell, George, 103
Osbourne, Lloyd, 207–8, 210, 214, 225

Pacific Islanders, 196–8, 200–2, 205–6, 208–9
packmen. *See* hawkers
Pall Mall Gazette
  'A Night in a Workhouse', 112–14
  'Five Nights in the Streets of London', 133
  'Packet Rats and Beachcombers', 202
Parker, John (publisher), 78, 80, 107
Parkinson, J. C. (editor), 95
Pauper Inmates Discharge and Regulations Act (1871), 101–2
Pearson, Karl, 138
pedlars. *See* hawkers
Peek, Francis (journalist), 131, 134, 136

Peel, Robert, 70, 74, 100
Pennsylvania, 130, 175
Penny Magazine, 'The English Gypsies', 32–3, 37–8
Penrhyn, 207
Philadelphia, 165–6, 169, 185
Phipps, Edmund, 67–8
picturesque, 35, 37–41, 44–51, 174–8
Pitcairn, 214
Playhouse Yard, Cripplegate, 94–5
poachers and poaching, 58–82
  affrays, 69, 74
  and crime, 62, 64
  female poachers, 62–3
  gangs, 65
  in morality tales, 63–9
  motives for, 59–60
  in periodicals, 67–8
  in radical literature, 70–82
  and radicalism, 59, 62
  and vagrancy, 60–1, 107
poacher's progress, 63–8, 72
Pohnpei, 197–8
police, 14, 18–19, 30, 36–7, 39, 44, 97, 100, 106, 115–17, 121–2, 134
polygenesis, 172–3, 179, 181, 188
Polynesia, 195–6, 199
Poor Law Board, 103, 105, 112, 122
Poplar, 97, 104, 226
prostitutes and prostitution, 12–15, 18–19, 76, 96, 107, 222

Quakers, 5

racial theory, 5–8, 52, 137–41, 171–2, 179, 222–4
racism, 8, 140, 201, 206. *See also* racial theory
Reade, Charles, 205
refuges, 94–6
Rice-Jones, D. (Anglican priest), 99, 149
Riis, Jacob (social investigator), 148, 225
Ritchie, John, 120
Rolfe, Frederick (poacher), 63
Romantic Vagrancy, 3–4
Romilly, Hugh (writer), 206
Rotuma, 202
Rutherford, John (pauper), 96, 100, 114

Saffron Hill, 105
Sala, George Augustus, 93–4, 121, 167, 180–1
Samoa, 197, 204–7, 210
Sargent, George (novelist), 186
scientific racism. *See* racial theory
Scott, Walter, 49, 174
Seminole, 177

separate spheres ideology, 186–7
Seven Dials, 144, 172
Shakespeare, William, 81
Sharpe's London Magazine
    'America and Her Slave States', 182
    'Gipsies', 38
    'Larry Lee the Pedlar', 39
    'Yetholm, and the Scottish Gipsies', 28
Sheffield, 30
Sims, George, 132–3, 150
slum novels, 136, 143–5, 148, 150–1
slumdom, 132
slumming, 146–8
slums, 100, 105, 131–3, 137, 143, 150–1, 166, 172, 225
Smith, John Thomas (artist), 47
social Darwinism, 7, 137–8, 188, 202, 223–4
Society for the Suppression of Mendicity, 2–3
Solomon Islands, 200, 205–6, 210
South London Refuge, 94–6
sphinx, 111, 122, 152–3
squawmen, 202
St. Giles, 97, 99, 105
St. Louis, 182–3
Stallard, J. H. (reformer), 17, 94, 103, 114, 118
Steel, Flora Annie, 130
Stepney, 114
Stevenson, Fanny Van de Grift, 207, 209–10
Stevenson, Robert Louis, 10, 199, 212, 224
    'The Beach of Falesá', 212, 215–16
    The Beachcombers, 210
    The Ebb-Tide, 210–16
    In the South Seas, 207, 209
    'The Isle of Voices', 212
    The Pearl Fisher. See The Ebb-Tide
    The Wrecker, 209–10
Strunsky, Anna (writer), 223
Swing Riots, 66, 73

Tahiti, 197, 199, 206–7, 210
Texas, 181–3, 185–6, 196
Thavies Inn, 104
Tonga, 200–1
Town Police Clauses Act (1847), 15
Toynbee Hall, 131
Trafalgar Square, 100, 133–4
travel writing, 166–7, 174, 178
Trollope, Anthony, 167, 170–2, 181

Trollope, Frances, 10, 167–70, 176–7, 180–1, 183

urbanisation, 16, 30, 40, 99, 134–5

Vagrancy Act (1822), 13
Vagrancy Act (1824), 12–14, 29, 100, 107, 134, 164
vagrants and vagrancy
    children, 94, 108, 117, 120, 133
    and disease, 103, 107, 114
    in early modern England, 4–6
    and empire, 9–10, 174, 202, 224
    female vagrants, 17–19, 75–7, 95–6, 111, 117–18
    and homosexuality, 14
    nomenclature, 3–4, 18
    numbers of vagrants, 16–17, 93, 105, 118
    and obscenity, 15–16
    in periodicals, 32, 106
    and rebellion, 5, 73, 93, 111, 122–3, 133–4, 151–3
    and savagery, 179–80
Verne, Jules, 153

Wakefield, Edward Gibbon, 182
Wakefield, Edward Jerningham, 196
Wampanoag, 174
Webbs, Beatrice (Fabian), 100
Webbs, Sidney (Fabian), 100
Wells, H. G., 8, 10, 136, 141–3, 222, 225
    Anticipations, 138, 141, 222
    An Experiment in Autobiography, 142
    'A Slum Novel', 144
    A Story of the Days to Come, 153
    The Time Machine, 141, 145–53
    When the Sleeper Wakes, 145
West Ham, 105
Westminster, 94
White, Arnold (journalist), 7–8, 138
Whitechapel, 94, 96, 104–5, 109–11, 144, 225–7
Wilde, Oscar, 153
Woolf, Virginia, 185
Wordsworth, William
    'The Old Cumberland Beggar', 2–3
    'Resolution and Independence', 47
    'The Ruined Cottage', 41
Wyandot, 174

CAMBRIDGE STUDIES IN NINETEENTH-CENTURY LITERATURE AND CULTURE

GENERAL EDITORS:
Kate Flint, *University of Southern California*
Clare Pettitt, *King's College London*

Titles published

1. *The Sickroom in Victorian Fiction: The Art of Being Ill*
   MIRIAM BAILIN, *Washington University*
2. *Muscular Christianity: Embodying the Victorian Age* edited by
   DONALD E. HALL, *California State University, Northridge*
3. *Victorian Masculinities: Manhood and Masculine Poetics in Early Victorian Literature and Art*
   HERBERT SUSSMAN, *Northeastern University, Boston*
4. *Byron and the Victorians*
   ANDREW ELFENBEIN, *University of Minnesota*
5. *Literature in the Marketplace: Nineteenth-Century British Publishing and the Circulation of Books* edited by
   JOHN O. JORDAN, *University of California, Santa Cruz* and
   ROBERT L. Patten, *Rice University, Houston*
6. *Victorian Photography, Painting and Poetry*
   LINDSAY SMITH, *University of Sussex*
7. *Charlotte Brontë and Victorian Psychology*
   SALLY SHUTTLEWORTH, *University of Sheffield*
8. *The Gothic Body: Sexuality, Materialism and Degeneration at the Fin de Siècle*
   KELLY HURLEY, *University of Colorado at Boulder*
9. *Rereading Walter Pater*
   WILLIAM F. SHUTER, *Eastern Michigan University*
10. *Remaking Queen Victoria* edited by
    MARGARET HOMANS, *Yale University* and
    ADRIENNE MUNICH, *State University of New York, Stony Brook*
11. *Disease, Desire, and the Body in Victorian Women's Popular Novels*
    PAMELA K. GILBERT, *University of Florida*
12. *Realism, Representation, and the Arts in Nineteenth-Century Literature*
    ALISON BYERLY, *Middlebury College, Vermont*
13. *Literary Culture and the Pacific*
    VANESSA SMITH, *University of Sydney*

14. *Professional Domesticity in the Victorian Novel Women, Work and Home*
    MONICA F. COHEN

15. *Victorian Renovations of the Novel: Narrative Annexes and the Boundaries of Representation*
    SUZANNE KEEN, *Washington and Lee University, Virginia*

16. *Actresses on the Victorian Stage: Feminine Performance and the Galatea Myth*
    GAIL MARSHALL, *University of Leeds*

17. *Death and the Mother from Dickens to Freud: Victorian Fiction and the Anxiety of Origin*
    CAROLYN DEVER, *Vanderbilt University, Tennessee*

18. *Ancestry and Narrative in Nineteenth-Century British Literature: Blood Relations from Edgeworth to Hardy*
    SOPHIE GILMARTIN, *Royal Holloway, University of London*

19. *Dickens, Novel Reading, and the Victorian Popular Theatre*
    DEBORAH VLOCK

20. *After Dickens: Reading, Adaptation and Performance*
    JOHN GLAVIN, *Georgetown University, Washington D C*

21. *Victorian Women Writers and the Woman Question* edited by
    NICOLA DIANE THOMPSON, *Kingston University, London*

22. *Rhythm and Will in Victorian Poetry*
    MATTHEW CAMPBELL, *University of Sheffield*

23. *Gender, Race, and the Writing of Empire: Public Discourse and the Boer War*
    PAULA M. KREBS, *Wheaton College, Massachusetts*

24. *Ruskin's God*
    MICHAEL WHEELER, *University of Southampton*

25. *Dickens and the Daughter of the House*
    HILARY M. SCHOR, *University of Southern California*

26. *Detective Fiction and the Rise of Forensic Science*
    RONALD R. THOMAS, *Trinity College, Hartford, Connecticut*

27. *Testimony and Advocacy in Victorian Law, Literature, and Theology*
    JAN-MELISSA SCHRAMM, *Trinity Hall, Cambridge*

28. *Victorian Writing about Risk: Imagining a Safe England in a Dangerous World*
    ELAINE FREEDGOOD, *University of Pennsylvania*

29. *Physiognomy and the Meaning of Expression in Nineteenth-Century Culture*
    LUCY HARTLEY, *University of Southampton*

30. *The Victorian Parlour: A Cultural Study*
    THAD LOGAN, *Rice University, Houston*

31. *Aestheticism and Sexual Parody 1840-1940*
    DENNIS DENISOFF, *Ryerson University, Toronto*

32. *Literature, Technology and Magical Thinking, 1880-1920*
    PAMELA THURSCHWELL, *University College London*
33. *Fairies in Nineteenth-Century Art and Literature*
    NICOLA BOWN, *Birkbeck, University of London*
34. *George Eliot and the British Empire*
    NANCY HENRY *The State University of New York, Binghamton*
35. *Women's Poetry and Religion in Victorian England: Jewish
    Identity and Christian Culture*
    CYNTHIA SCHEINBERG, *Mills College, California*
36. *Victorian Literature and the Anorexic Body*
    ANNA KRUGOVOY SILVER, *Mercer University, Georgia*
37. *Eavesdropping in the Novel from Austen to Proust*
    ANN GAYLIN, *Yale University*
38. *Missionary Writing and Empire, 1800–1860*
    ANNA JOHNSTON, *University of Tasmania*
39. *London and the Culture of Homosexuality, 1885–1914*
    MATT COOK, *Keele University*
40. *Fiction, Famine, and the Rise of Economics in Victorian Britain and Ireland*
    GORDON BIGELOW, *Rhodes College, Tennessee*
41. *Gender and the Victorian Periodical*
    HILARY FRASER, *Birkbeck, University of London*
    JUDITH JOHNSTON and STEPHANIE GREEN, *University of Western Australia*
42. *The Victorian Supernatural* edited by
    NICOLA BOWN, *Birkbeck College, London*
    CAROLYN BURDETT, *London Metropolitan University* and
    PAMELA THURSCHWELL, *University College London*
43. *The Indian Mutiny and the British Imagination*
    GAUTAM CHAKRAVARTY, *University of Delhi*
44. *The Revolution in Popular Literature: Print, Politics and the People*
    IAN HAYWOOD, *Roehampton University of Surrey*
45. *Science in the Nineteenth-Century Periodical: Reading the Magazine of Nature*
    GEOFFREY CANTOR, *University of Leeds*
    GOWAN DAWSON, *University of Leicester*
    GRAEME GOODAY, *University of Leeds*
    RICHARD NOAKES, *University of Cambridge*
    SALLY SHUTTLEWORTH, *University of Sheffield* and
    JONATHAN R. TOPHAM, *University of Leeds*
46. *Literature and Medicine in Nineteenth-Century Britain from Mary
    Shelley to George Eliot*
    JANIS MCLARREN CALDWELL, *Wake Forest University*

47. *The Child Writer from Austen to Woolf* edited by
CHRISTINE ALEXANDER, *University of New South Wales* and
Juliet McMaster, *University of Alberta*

48. *From Dickens to Dracula: Gothic, Economics, and Victorian Fiction*
GAIL TURLEY HOUSTON, University of New Mexico

49. *Voice and the Victorian Storyteller*
IVAN KREILKAMP, *University of Indiana*

50. *Charles Darwin and Victorian Visual Culture*
JONATHAN SMITH, *University of Michigan-Dearborn*

51. *Catholicism, Sexual Deviance, and Victorian Gothic Culture*
PATRICK R. O'MALLEY, *Georgetown University*

52. *Epic and Empire in Nineteenth-Century Britain*
SIMON DENTITH, *University of Gloucestershire*

53. *Victorian Honeymoons: Journeys to the Conjugal*
HELENA MICHIE, *Rice University*

54. *The Jewess in Nineteenth-Century British Literary Culture*
NADIA VALMAN, *University of Southampton*

55. *Ireland, India and Nationalism in Nineteenth-Century Literature*
JULIA WRIGHT, *Dalhousie University*

56. *Dickens and the Popular Radical Imagination*
SALLY LEDGER, *Birkbeck, University of London*

57. *Darwin, Literature and Victorian Respectability*
GOWAN DAWSON, *University of Leicester*

58. *'Michael Field': Poetry, Aestheticism and the Fin de Siècle*
MARION THAIN, *University of Birmingham*

59. *Colonies, Cults and Evolution: Literature, Science and Culture
in Nineteenth-Century Writing*
DAVID AMIGONI, *Keele University*

60. *Realism, Photography and Nineteenth-Century Fiction*
DANIEL A. NOVAK, *Lousiana State University*

61. *Caribbean Culture and British Fiction in the Atlantic World, 1780–1870*
TIM WATSON, *University of Miami*

62. *The Poetry of Chartism: Aesthetics, Politics, History*
MICHAEL SANDERS, *University of Manchester*

63. *Literature and Dance in Nineteenth-Century Britain: Jane Austen
to the New Woman*
CHERYL WILSON, *Indiana University*

64. *Shakespeare and Victorian Women*
GAIL MARSHALL, *Oxford Brookes University*

65. *The Tragi-Comedy of Victorian Fatherhood*
   VALERIE SANDERS, *University of Hull*

66. *Darwin and the Memory of the Human: Evolution, Savages, and South America*
   CANNON SCHMITT, *University of Toronto*

67. *From Sketch to Novel: The Development of Victorian Fiction*
   AMANPAL GARCHA, *Ohio State University*

68. *The Crimean War and the British Imagination*
   STEFANIE MARKOVITS, *Yale University*

69. *Shock, Memory and the Unconscious in Victorian Fiction*
   JILL L. MATUS, *University of Toronto*

70. *Sensation and Modernity in the 1860s*
   NICHOLAS DALY, *University College Dublin*

71. *Ghost-Seers, Detectives, and Spiritualists: Theories of Vision in Victorian Literature and Science*
   SRDJAN SMAJIĆ, *Furman University*

72. *Satire in an Age of Realism*
   AARON MATZ, *Scripps College, California*

73. *Thinking About Other People in Nineteenth-Century British Writing*
   ADELA PINCH, *University of Michigan*

74. *Tuberculosis and the Victorian Literary Imagination*
   KATHERINE BYRNE, *University of Ulster, Coleraine*

75. *Urban Realism and the Cosmopolitan Imagination in the Nineteenth Century: Visible City, Invisible World*
   TANYA AGATHOCLEOUS, *Hunter College, City University of New York*

76. *Women, Literature, and the Domesticated Landscape: England's Disciples of Flora, 1780-1870*
   JUDITH W. PAGE, *University of Florida*
   ELISE L. SMITH, *Millsaps College, Mississippi*

77. *Time and the Moment in Victorian Literature and Society*
   SUE ZEMKA, *University of Colorado*

78. *Popular Fiction and Brain Science in the Late Nineteenth Century*
   ANNE STILES, *Washington State University*

79. *Picturing Reform in Victorian Britain*
   JANICE CARLISLE, *Yale University*

80. *Atonement and Self-Sacrifice in Nineteenth-Century Narrative*
   JAN-MELISSA SCHRAMM, *University of Cambridge*

81. *The Silver Fork Novel: Fashionable Fiction in the Age of Reform*
   EDWARD COPELAND, *Pomona College, California*

82. *Oscar Wilde and Ancient Greece*
IAIN ROSS, *Colchester Royal Grammar School*

83. *The Poetry of Victorian Scientists: Style, Science and Nonsense*
DANIEL BROWN, *University of Southampton*

84. *Moral Authority, Men of Science, and the Victorian Novel*
ANNE DEWITT, *Princeton Writing Program*

85. *China and the Victorian Imagination: Empires Entwined*
ROSS G. FORMAN, *University of Warwick*

86. *Dickens's Style* edited by
DANIEL TYLER, *University of Oxford*

87. *The Formation of the Victorian Literary Profession*
RICHARD SALMON, *University of Leeds*

88. *Before George Eliot: Marian Evans and the Periodical Press*
FIONNUALA DILLANE, *University College Dublin*

89. *The Victorian Novel and the Space of Art: Fictional Form on Display*
DEHN GILMORE, *California Institute of Technology*

90. *George Eliot and Money: Economics, Ethics and Literature*
DERMOT COLEMAN, *Independent Scholar*

91. *Masculinity and the New Imperialism: Rewriting Manhood in British Popular Literature, 1870–1914*
BRADLEY DEANE, *University of Minnesota*

92. *Evolution and Victorian Culture* edited by
BERNARD LIGHTMAN, *York University, Toronto* and
BENNETT ZON, *University of Durham*

93. *Victorian Literature, Energy, and the Ecological Imagination*
ALLEN MACDUFFIE, *University of Texas, Austin*

94. *Popular Literature, Authorship and the Occult in Late Victorian Britain*
ANDREW MCCANN, *Dartmouth College, New Hampshire*

95. *Women Writing Art History in the Nineteenth Century: Looking Like a Woman*
HILARY FRASER *Birkbeck, University of London*

96. *Relics of Death in Victorian Literature and Culture*
DEBORAH LUTZ, *Long Island University, C. W. Post Campus*

97. *The Demographic Imagination and the Nineteenth-Century City: Paris, London, New York*
NICHOLAS DALY, *University College Dublin*

98. *Dickens and the Business of Death*
CLAIRE WOOD, *University of York*

99. *Translation as Transformation in Victorian Poetry*
ANNMARIE DRURY, *Queens College, City University of New York*

100. *The Bigamy Plot: Sensation and Convention in the Victorian Novel*
MAIA MCALEAVEY, *Boston College, Massachusetts*

101. *English Fiction and the Evolution of Language, 1850–1914*
WILL ABBERLEY, *University of Oxford*

102. *The Racial Hand in the Victorian Imagination*
AVIVA BRIEFEL, *Bowdoin College, Maine*

103. *Evolution and Imagination in Victorian Children's Literature*
JESSICA STRALEY, *University of Utah*

104. *Writing Arctic Disaster: Authorship and Exploration*
ADRIANA CRACIUN, *University of California, Riverside*

105. *Science, Fiction, and the Fin-de-Siècle Periodical Press*
WILL TATTERSDILL, *University of Birmingham*

106. *Democratising Beauty in Nineteenth-Century Britain: Art
and the Politics of Public Life*
LUCY HARTLEY, *University of Michigan*

107. *Everyday Words and the Character of Prose in Nineteenth-Century Britain*
JONATHAN FARINA, *Seton Hall University, New Jersey*

108. *Gerard Manley Hopkins and the Poetry of Religious Experience*
MARTIN DUBOIS, *Newcastle University*

109. *Blindness and Writing: From Wordsworth to Gissing*
HEATHER TILLEY, *Birkbeck College, University of London*

110. *An Underground History of Early Victorian Fiction: Chartism,
Radical Print Culture, and the Social Problem Novel*
GREGORY VARGO, *New York University*

111. *Automatism and Creative Acts in the Age of New Psychology*
LINDA M. AUSTIN, *Oklahoma State University*

112. *Idleness and Aesthetic Consciousness, 1815–1900*
RICHARD ADELMAN, *University of Sussex*

113. *Poetry, Media, and the Material Body: Autopoetics
in Nineteenth-Century Britain*
ASHLEY MILLER, *Albion College, Michigan*

114. *Malaria and Victorian Fictions of Empire*
JESSICA HOWELL, *Texas A&M University*

115. *The Brontës and the Idea of the Human: Science, Ethics,
and the Victorian Imagination* edited by
ALEXANDRA LEWIS, *University of Aberdeen*

116. *The Political Lives of Victorian Animals: Liberal Creatures
in Literature and Culture*
ANNA FEUERSTEIN, *University of Hawai'i-Manoa*

117. *The Divine in the Commonplace: Recent Natural Histories and the Novel in Britain*
AMY KING, *St John's University, New York*

118. *Plagiarizing the Victorian Novel: Imitation, Parody, Aftertext*
ADAM ABRAHAM, *Virginia Commonwealth University*

119. *Literature, Print Culture, and Media Technologies, 1880-1900: Many Inventions*
RICHARD MENKE, *University of Georgia*

120. *Aging, Duration, and the English Novel: Growing Old from Dickens to Woolf*
JACOB JEWUSIAK, *Newcastle University*

121. *Autobiography, Sensation, and the Commodification of Identity in Victorian Narrative: Life upon the Exchange*
SEAN GRASS, *Rochester Institute of Technology*

122. *Settler Colonialism in Victorian Literature: Economics and Political Identity in the Networks of Empire*
PHILLIP STEER, *Massey University, Auckland*

123. *Mimicry and Display in Victorian Literary Culture: Nature, Science and the Nineteenth-Century Imagination*
WILL ABBERLEY, *University of Sussex*

124. *Victorian Women and Wayward Reading: Crises of Identification*
MARISA PALACIOS KNOX, *University of Texas Rio Grande Valley*

125. *The Victorian Cult of Shakespeare: Bardology in the Nineteenth Century*
CHARLES LAPORTE, *University of Washington*

126. *Children's Literature and the Rise of 'Mind Cure': Positive Thinking and Pseudo-Science at the Fin de Siècle*
ANNE STILES, *Saint Louis University, Missouri*

127. *Virtual Play and the Victorian Novel: The Ethics and Aesthetics of Fictional Experience*
TIMOTHY GAO, *Nanyang Technological University*

128. *Colonial Law in India and the Victorian Imagination*
LEILA NETI, *Occidental College, Los Angeles*

129. *Convalescence in the Nineteenth-Century Novel: The Afterlife of Victorian Illness*
HOSANNA KRIENKE, *University of Wyoming*

130. *Stylistic Virtue and Victorian Fiction: Form, Ethics and the Novel*
MATTHEW SUSSMAN, *The University of Sydney*

131. *Scottish Women's Writing in the Long Nineteenth Century: The Romance of Everyday Life*
JULIET SHIELDS, *University of Washington*

132. *Reimagining Dinosaurs in Late Victorian and Edwardian Literature: How the 'Terrible Lizard' Became a Transatlantic Cultural Icon*
RICHARD FALLON, *The University of Birmingham*

133. *Decadent Ecology in British Literature and Art, 1860–1910: Decay, Desire, and the Pagan Revival*
DENNIS DENISOFF, *University of Tulsa*

For EU product safety concerns, contact us at Calle de José Abascal, 56–1°, 28003 Madrid, Spain or eugpsr@cambridge.org.

www.ingramcontent.com/pod-product-compliance
Ingram Content Group UK Ltd.
Pitfield, Milton Keynes, MK11 3LW, UK
UKHW020355140625
459647UK00020B/2485